THE
ANCIENT CONSTITUTION AND
THE FEUDAL LAW

THE
ANCIENT CONSTITUTION
AND
THE FEUDAL LAW

A STUDY OF
ENGLISH HISTORICAL THOUGHT
IN THE
SEVENTEENTH CENTURY

A Reissue with a Retrospect

J. G. A. POCOCK
Johns Hopkins University

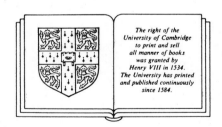

The right of the
University of Cambridge
to print and sell
all manner of books
was granted by
Henry VIII in 1534.
The University has printed
and published continuously
since 1584.

CAMBRIDGE UNIVERSITY PRESS
Cambridge
London   New York   New Rochelle
Melbourne   Sydney

Published by the Press Syndicate of the University of Cambridge.
The Pitt Building, Trumpington Street, Cambridge CB2 1RP
32 East 57th Street, New York NY 10022, USA
10 Stamford Road, Oakleigh, Melbourne 3166, Australia

First published 1987

Printed in the United States of America

Library of Congress Cataloging-in-Publication Data
Pocock, J. G. A. (John Greville Agard), 1924–
    Ancient constitution and the feudal law.
        Includes index.
    1. Great Britain—Constitutional history.
2. Political science—Great Britain—History—17th
            century. I. Title.
JN191. P6   1986   941.06   86–21583
        ISBN 0-521-30352-4 hard covers
        ISBN 0-521-31643-X paperback

Contents

v

Contents

Part Two
The Ancient Constitution Revisited:
a Retrospect from 1986

vi

Preface

This book is now thirty years old. Published in 1957, it was as the original preface shows completed in Dunedin during 1954 and 1955,[1] and the doctoral dissertation of which it is an outgrowth was written between 1948 and 1951, and accepted in 1952. A great deal has happened since then to enlarge our understanding of the history which it contains or implies, but the book has continued to enjoy readers and a certain standing. The present reissue has seemed worth while, both as a means of keeping the original before the public, and as an occasion of presenting it for inspection in the context of research and interpretation carried out since it was first published.[2] In this preface, therefore, I have attempted to place it in the context of work being done at the time when it was written, and in the retrospective essay which follows to consider it in the context of work published since that time. Some of the latter calls, more or less pressingly, for modification of the premises and conclusions which the book originally contained, and I have attempted to consider some of the questions thus raised and at the same time to review the present state of the relevant historical knowledge.

The research which led to *The Ancient Constitution and the Feudal Law* was in some ways connected with that of the late Sir Herbert Butterfield, director of my doctoral dissertation; in

[1] My former colleague Gordon Parsonson retired from the University of Otago at the end of 1984, and I take this opportunity of thanking him for his moral support at a time in those distant days when I badly needed it.

[2] From 1967 to 1983, *The Ancient Constitution and the Feudal Law* was published in the United States by W. W. Norton & Company of New York. I am indebted to Mr Donald S. Lamm, president of that company, for his suggestion that the Cambridge University Press might be interested in resuming publication, and to Mr Frank Smith, of the Press's New York office, for the alacrity with which he acted on it.

vii

particular with his *The Englishman and His History*, published in 1944 by the Cambridge University Press. This little book was a work of the Second World War years, and its neo-Burkean tone may have been produced by the mood of that period. It was Butterfield who suggested that I should modify my intention of studying the anti-Normanism of the Interregnum radicals (the 'Norman Yoke'[3]) and investigate the monarchist historiography of Robert Brady and his associates; and though their thinking was somewhat far removed from that of Edmund Burke, an interest in connecting the prescriptivism of the ancient constitution with that expressed by Burke a century and a half later[4] may have originated with *The Englishman and His History*. However, I do not recall that Butterfield especially urged me to the study of Burke. He was at that time engaged on the history and historiography of George III's reign,[5] and though this part of his work contains interesting information on the ancient-constitutionalism of the Yorkshire petitioners in 1780, my own did not intersect with it for a number of years. In retrospect the main link between Butterfield's work and mine seems to connect this book, through *The Englishman and His History*, with the problem of how one should relate the complacent progressivism which he criticized in *The Whig Interpretation of History* (1931) to the

---

[3] The term was popularized by Christopher Hill (see p. 54 below, and comment on anti-Normanism at pp. 126–7). I endeavour in the retrospective essay to make it clear that 'the ancient constitution' and 'the Norman yoke' are antithetically related.

[4] See Pocock, 'Burke and the Ancient Constitution: A Problem in the History of Ideas', *Historical Journal*, vol. III, no. 2 (1960), reprinted in *Politics, Language and Time* (New York: Atheneum, 1971); also 'The Origins of Study of the Past: A Comparative Approach', *Comparative Studies in Society and History*, vol. IV, no. 2 (1962), reprinted in P.B.M. Blaas (ed.), *Geschiedenis als Wetenschap* (The Hague: Martinus Nijhoff, 1980), and 'Time, Institutions and Action: An Essay on Traditions and Their Understanding', in Preston King and B. C. Parekh (eds.), *Politics and Experience: Essays Presented to Michael Oakeshott* (Cambridge University Press, 1968), reprinted in *Politics, Language and Time*.

[5] See his *George III, Lord North and the People* (London: G. Bell and Sons, 1949), and *George III and the Historians* (London: Collins, 1957). Related articles and letters are listed in the bibliography forming part of J. H. Elliott and H. G. Koenigsberger (eds.), *The Diversity of History: Essays in Honour of Sir Herbert Butterfield* (London: Routledge & Kegan Paul, 1970).

equally complacent traditionalism which he rather admired in writing the later book (1944). It has taken many years to show how it was possible for both attitudes to co-exist and be equally 'Whig';[6] Duncan Forbes's first essay on 'scientific Whiggism', which had already appeared when this book was published,[7] did much to point the way.

Research for this book[8] early intersected, and continued to do so as long as he remained active in the history of political thought, with that of Peter Laslett. His edition of the works of Filmer appeared in 1949[9] and greatly illuminated the discovery, to which I was then being led, that William Petyt and William Atwood (and Robert Brady writing against them) were responding fairly directly to the re-publication of *The Freeholders Grand Inquest* as part of the works of Filmer in 1679.[10] A link between their activities and those of John Locke in reply to *Patriarcha* is provided by the correspondence and publications of James Tyrrell, Locke's close friend and author of *Patriarcha Non Monarcha* (1681) and *Bibliotheca Politica* (1694).[11] By 1957, Laslett was far advanced on the research which led to the completion in 1960 of his pathbreaking discovery that Locke's *Treatises of*

---

[6] See especially John Burrow, *A Liberal Descent: Victorian Historians and the English Past* (Cambridge University Press, 1981), and in addition Pocock, 'The Varieties of Whiggism: A History of Ideology and Discourse', in *Virtue, Commerce, and History: Essays on Political Thought and History, chiefly in the Eighteenth Century* (Cambridge University Press, 1985).

[7] 'Scientific Whiggism: Adam Smith and John Millar', *Cambridge Journal*, vol. VIII, no. 11 (1954).

[8] For one year, during Butterfield's absence from Cambridge, my doctoral research was supervised by Dr J. H. Plumb (as he then was).

[9] Peter Laslett (ed.), *Patriarcha and Other Political Works by Sir Robert Filmer* (Oxford: Basil Blackwell, 1949).

[10] See below, pp. 187–8, and in greater detail (though in language I might now consider immature) pp. 101–120 of Pocock, 'The Controversy over the Origins of the Commons, 1675–88; A Chapter in the History of English Political and Historical Thought,' Ph.D. dissertation, Emmanuel College, Cambridge, 1952.

[11] A full-length study of Tyrrell's life and writings remains highly desirable. At present we have only the last work (I believe) of J. W. Gough, 'James Tyrrell, Whig Historian and Friend of John Locke', *Historical Journal*, vol. XIX, no. 3 (1976), pp. 581–610.

Government are work of the early 1680s, situated in contexts formed by the re-publication of Filmer and the Exclusionist predicament of 1679–83.[12] *The Ancient Constitution and the Feudal Law* may be said to have played some part in making this discovery and in bringing out the complexity and diversity of the Filmerian controversy, of which what is termed the 'Brady controversy' was part. It has also helped to make clear that the relatively conservative justification of the Revolution of 1688–9 as an act carried out within the undissolved framework of the ancient constitution, which came to prevail among ruling Whigs and Revolution Tories, was one which Locke did not endorse and may have opposed. Like Laslett's redating of the *Treatises*, my work tends to reinforce the modern interpretation of Locke as a political thinker more Exclusionist radical than Revolution Whig. At the same time, it emphasizes and makes central the strength of a conservative language in which he took no part; and both here and elsewhere, I have been concerned in isolating and exploring modes of argument which were of great importance to Locke's contemporaries and friends, but apparently did not interest him at all. In consequence, I have put forward the claim[13] that the character, rather than the degree, of his importance needs to be re-defined: a claim displeasing to those scholars who wish to present a Locke both radical and universal, a figure at once in advance of his age and furnishing essential clues to the thought of the eighteenth century. There must be reassessment of that thought, as well as of Locke's, if we are to understand his place in it, and in the retrospect which closes this volume I return to the attempt to provide such a reassessment.

There is another respect in which this book may be said to have intersected with work begun and carried on by Peter

[12] Peter Laslett (ed.), *John Locke: Two Treatises on Government* (Cambridge University Press, 1960).

[13] A deliberately challenging statement of this position may be found in 'The Myth of John Locke and the Obsession with Liberalism', printed as part of J. G. A. Pocock and Richard Ashcraft, *John Locke: Papers Read at a Clark Library Seminar* (Los Angeles: William Andrews Clark Memorial Library, 1980). It has less to do with Locke's indifference to ancient-constitutionalism than with his indifference to neo-Harringtonian classical republicanism.

Laslett. In 1956, the year before its publication, he was editor of the first volume of *Philosophy, Politics and Society*,[14] and there is a real, if indirect, connection[15] between the linguistic analysis of political utterances which the contributors to that volume propounded, and the historical resolution of political discourse into the idioms and 'languages' in which it has been conducted that has transformed the historiography of political thought over the last thirty years. I believe it can be claimed on behalf of *The Ancient Constitution and the Feudal Law* that—indebted as it was to *The Englishman and His History* and other works—it established the existence and extent of a 'language' of precedent, common law and ancient custom, in which a significant part of English political argument was, for long periods and with important consequences, carried on. Both in 1957 and when writing a foreword to the Norton edition in 1966, it seemed to me that this language or idiom carried significant information among, and subsequently from, the inhabitants of seventeenth-century England, regarding the supposed mode and manner of their society's existence in time and history.[16] Since 1957, however, several other such languages—anti-Norman and apocalyptic, humanist and republican, civilian and commercial— have been brought to light in the history of English political discourse and shown to have exerted comparable effects; and the historical field has been enlarged to include both Scottish and American political thought in the eighteenth century. *The Ancient Constitution and the Feudal Law* must be considered as one of a number of books published in recent decades which have

[14] *Philosophy, Politics and Society: A Collection Edited by Peter Laslett* (Oxford: Basil Blackwell, 1956).

[15] I explored this connection in 'The History of Political Thought: A Methodological Enquiry', in Peter Laslett and W. G. Runciman (eds.), *Philosophy, Politics and Society: Second Series* (Oxford: Basil Blackwell, 1962); 'Languages and Their Implications: The Transformation of the Study of Political Thought', ch. 1 of *Politics, Language and Time* (*op. cit.*); and 'Introduction: The State of the Art', ch. 1 of *Virtue, Commerce, and History* (*op. cit.*).

[16] 'Foreword', p. xi of *The Ancient Constitution and the Feudal Law* (New York: Norton Library, 1967). See also 'Modes of Political and Historical Time in Early Eighteenth-Century England', ch. 3 of *Virtue, Commerce, and History*.

contributed to building up a history of past political thought in its discursive complexity, and in the retrospective chapters which follow at the end of this book an attempt will be made to present it in the context furnished by this literature.

Yet the book deals with only one of the languages constituting English political discourse, and to consider this as co-existing and interacting with others is to raise questions about its genesis, use and development. There have been criticisms which suggest that the two chapters on 'The Common-law Mind' present it in over-simplified terms, and as isolated from the operations of other languages to a greater degree than the evidence justifies; it seems possible that some of these criticisms are justified. There has been a great deal of research and discovery regarding the political debates of the Civil War and Interregnum periods; and above all, we now possess studies of English, Scottish and American political thought after 1685—when this book effectively concludes—which show the theme of the ancient constitution persisting, among others, far into the eighteenth and nineteenth centuries, yet undergoing challenges and transformations that leave parts of the concluding chapter published in 1957 altogether inadequate. These have been allowed to stand, but in reviewing research and interpretation since that year an attempt will be made to inspect the premises and conclusions on which I proceeded when writing of 'The Common-law Mind', and to inquire whether these need modification or replacement; and a further attempt will be made to enlarge the field in directions which it has become possible to explore only since the book was published. Such will be the programme of 'The Ancient Constitution Revisited', a postface or retrospect which has been left to the end of this edition so that the reader may consult it after perusing the original text.

J. G. A. Pocock
Johns Hopkins University

Preface to the First Edition

I have tried in this book to present a theory of the fundamental nature and problems of constitutional historiography in the seventeenth century. I have not attempted to analyse exhaustively the character of English thought about the past, or to study the way in which constitutional history and theory were used as a source of arguments in contemporary political debate. It has seemed more illuminating instead to oppose to one another what appear to have been the two most important schools of thought: the common lawyers with their belief that the constitution was immemorial, and the few dissentients who sought to upset this theory by pointing out that it had once been informed with the principles of feudal tenure; to show how these interpretations arose; and to consider how they were related to some of the essential ideas in contemporary political theory and how these connexions encouraged or hampered their development. From the whole, it is hoped that there will emerge a picture of one of the most typical and necessary, but by historians one of the most neglected, strands in the thought of the seventeenth-century English: the attempt to understand themselves by understanding their past and their relation to it. This may partly excuse my failure to deal with Elsynge, Selden, Twysden, Somner, and many other good historians of that age, as fully as they deserve.

In trying to carry out this purpose, I have been led to put forward a certain generalization about the history of historiography. This is, in brief, that during the sixteenth and seventeenth centuries one of the most important modes of studying the past was the study of the law; that many European nations obtained knowledge of their history by reflecting, largely under the stimulus of contemporary political developments and theories, upon the character of their law; that the

xiii

historical outlook which arose in each nation was in part the product of its law, and therefore, in turn, of its history; and that the importance of this aspect of the subject has been too little observed by historians of historiography. I have endeavoured to show, by contrasting English historical thought at one point with French and at another with Scottish thought, that the former's fundamental limitations in this age arose from its having been compelled to contemplate the national past through one system of law alone. The full working-out of the theory would necessitate a history of English historiography far more exhaustive than anything attempted here, and probably also a comparative study designed to show how its character diverged from that of historiography in other western nations, in obedience to the determining forces suggested above. (I may be allowed to express my sense of indebtedness to Sig. Rosario Romeo's study of the development of Sicilian historical thought in his *Il Risorgimento in Sicilia*, from which I have received far more illumination than appears on the surface.) The history of historiography is a branch of study still in process of establishing itself, and it has been said that in England its main problems are not yet even defined; as a contribution to the studies of the future, this work may be allowed some place.

It grows out of a thesis submitted in 1952 for the Ph.D. degree, entitled 'The Controversy over the Origin of the Commons, 1675–88', which was in essence a study of Robert Brady and of the polemic in which he took part. I must express my gratitude to Professor H. Butterfield and Dr J. H. Plumb for their help and encouragement, and it would be improper not to mention two studies of seventeenth-century historiography without which this study would certainly never have been written: Professor Butterfield's *The Englishmann and His History* and Professor D. C. Douglas's *English Scholars*. The work has been completed under the auspices of the University of Otago, and it is a pleasure to mention those sources in New Zealand from which I have received help in procuring the books necessary to this investigation: first, the University of New Zealand for two research grants used in making purchases;

second, the librarian, head of accessions and staff of the Otago University Library; and the Alexander Turnbull Library and General Assembly Library, Wellington, and the Supreme Court Law Library, Dunedin. And both in Cambridge and New Zealand, the friends whose aid and criticism I have enjoyed are too numerous to mention.

J. G. A. Pocock
Dunedin, 1955

Note: In quotations from printed books I have followed as far as possible the punctuation, capitalization and italicization of the original; but where contemporary manuscripts are quoted I have expanded the contractions and taken little account of practices differing from modern usage. In translating Latin and French passages quoted I have not attempted to give complete and exact versions; the translations are intended as guides to the sense rather than exact renderings of the often recherché Latin of the scholars of a past time.

THE
ANCIENT CONSTITUTION AND
THE FEUDAL LAW

CHAPTER I

Introductory: the French Prelude to Modern Historiography

I

THIS book has been written in an attempt to throw light upon one aspect of the rise of modern historiography, a movement whose beginnings in general may with some assurance be dated from the sixteenth century. For it was then that the historian's art took on the characteristic, which has ever since distinguished it, of reconstructing the institutions of society in the past and using them as a context in which, and by means of which, to interpret the actions, words and thoughts of the men who lived at that time. That this is the kernel of what we know as historical method needs no demonstration; that it distinguishes modern from ancient historiography may be seen by means of a comparison with the historical methods of the Greeks and Romans. The ancient historians discovered and brilliantly developed the art of constructing an intelligible narrative of human affairs; they described contemporary societies alien to their own and noted the varieties of human conduct and belief that arose in the context of different climates and traditions; but they did not quite reach the point of postulating that there existed, in the past of their own civilization, tracts of time in which the thoughts and actions of men had been so remote in character from those of the present as to be intelligible only if the entire world in which they had occurred were resurrected, described in detail and used to interpret them. Nor did Greco-Roman historians assert that there existed a distinct and satisfactory method of doing this. The histories that they wrote, therefore, consisted of narratives of military and political affairs, or of comparative political analysis; they did not consist of researches into the past, conducted on the assumption that the past was a special field of study, to be understood only by the discovery of its own laws and the develop-

I

ment of an appropriate technique of investigation.[1] Yet this is so much the dominant characteristic of modern historiography as to have taken precedence over the older art of constructing narratives; when (but only when) the historian has completed his researches into a past stage of society, he faces the problem of incorporating his conclusions into a narrative, the theme of which will be not only the actions of men and governments, but the never-ceasing changes in the structure of society—and the interactions between these two aspects of his subject. To discover how the notion of reconstructing the past began to dominate the minds of historians and compete for their attention with the older claims of history conceived as a narrative art is, then, of prime importance to the historian of historiography.

The Greco-Roman historians did not develop a special technique for the exploration of the past because—paradoxical though it may seem in the pioneers of historiography—the past as such was not surpassingly important to them. This is not the place to discuss the problem of *spatium historicum*, of the boundaries of the historical and the mythical in their vision of the past,[2] but one point can be made which is essential to the present argument. The Greeks and Romans were not conscious, as medieval and modern Europeans have alike been conscious, of an organized civilization existing in their immediate past and affecting the whole range of their life through the survival of its institutions, its ideas, its material remains and its documents. There was no past world which they felt the need, or possessed the evidence, to explore; and their historical sense was

---

[1] The peculiar shrewdness of Thucydides' comments on the past history of Hellas (Book I, ch. I) underline rather than modify the point made here. There is no past civilization for him to reconstruct from its documents; and if, in the absence of written material (other than recorded tradition), he shows a keen sense of the importance of such things as the size and site of towns, the date of their construction, the development of sea power and the fertility of the soil, neither he nor the other Greek historians founded a science of handling this sort of evidence. Modern historiography depends on the survival of a great many documents from a past state of society, and on a deep sense that these are important in the governance of the present.

[2] Some comments on this question are made in an article, 'Spatium Historicum', by W. von Leyden, in the *Durham University Journal*, XLII, no. 3 (n.s. XI, no. 3), June 1950, p. 89.

developed in the exploration of their own world and its comparison with contemporary alien societies. But the sense that Rome is a past world ever present to us, and the need to understand it and define our own relation to it, have been cardinal facts in the thoughts of Europeans both medieval and modern; and if the desire to conduct researches into the past is a distinguishing mark of modern European historiography, it is surely in Europe's sense of indebtedness to the ancient world that we should look for its rise and origins.

An obvious field in which to make our inquiries is that subtle change in the techniques of classical scholarship—in, that is to say, the method of approach to the ancient world—which we denote by the name of humanism. It has long been a commonplace that phrases like 'the revival of classical antiquity' are meaningless as applied to humanism, unless modified in the light of the fact that medieval thought was fully as obsessed with the importance of classical antiquity as was the thought of the Renaissance, and that the two differed only, if profoundly, in the methods which they adopted in order to understand it better. Medieval and Renaissance men alike sought to model themselves upon antiquity, to accept its teachings and its canons as authoritative so far as they could: but the methods adopted by the synthesizing and allegorizing mind of the Middle Ages were such on the whole as to lead to an imaginative conflation of the life of antiquity with the life of the contemporary world. Hector and Alexander were knights; Christ's trial before Pilate was imagined as taking place according to the forms of feudal law; and, on a more serious and practical level of scholarship, the terminology of Roman law was unhesitatingly applied to the governance of medieval Europe. It lies beyond the present writer's competence to determine how far, if at all, medieval men were conscious of what they were doing in this respect; some sense that Rome was not Christendom there obviously was; but it seems sufficiently clear that no need was felt to distinguish, to point out in what respects the life of the past differed from that of the present, or to found a systematic science of doing so. This came about, however, as a result of the new approach to the past initiated by the humanists; but it came about accidentally, indirectly and paradoxically.

3

Introductory: the French Prelude to Modern Historiography

Humanist thought insisted, even more strongly than medieval, on the need to take the ancient world as a model, but it expressed vehement dissatisfaction with the presentation of antiquity by medieval learning. It pointed out that the supposedly authoritative ancient texts had been overlaid with many layers of commentary, allegory and interpretation, and that often it was the commentary and not the text which was being studied. It called for a return to the pure text—such a cry had been raised before—and it claimed continually to understand the text better than the commentators had—a claim which increased source-material and improved techniques often enabled it to make good. At this point, however, we encounter what is at once the paradox and the true importance of the humanist movement, viewed from the standpoint of the history of historiography; for it is not too much to say that in making these claims and demands the humanists were calling for a return to the ancient world 'as it really was'—and we cannot express their programme in these words without realizing that we stand on the threshold of the modern historical consciousness. And the paradox which was to complete the transition was this: the humanists aimed at resurrecting the ancient world in order to copy and imitate it, but the more thoroughly and accurately the process of resurrection was carried out, the more evident it became that copying and imitation were impossible—or could never be anything more than copying and imitation. That which was ancient belonged to the ancient world, was bound up with and dependent upon innumerable things which could not be brought back to life, and consequently it could not be simply incorporated with contemporary society. A recent study[1] has traced anew the way in which the humanist endeavour to return to the language and grammar of classical Latin ended with Latin a dead language, one which could no longer be freely and naturally used as part of every-day European life. It became, says the author, something of merely historical or even antiquarian interest, part of a vanished world important only to those who cared to study it for its own sake. But he also shows how this process was accompanied by the growth of new branches of study aimed at describing the world

[1] R. R. Bolgar, *The Classical Heritage and its Beneficiaries* (Cambridge, 1954).

in which Latin authors had lived, sometimes even at seeing it through their own eyes, and at interpreting their writings as part of that world.[1] In short, the humanists, going far beyond their original purpose, relegated Greco-Roman wisdom inescapably to the past and robbed it, in the end, of all claim to be applied immediately and directly to modern life; but at the same time they called attention to the problem of the past as an independent field of study and began vigorously to perfect techniques for its exploration. If research into the past conceived as a distinct science is the mark of the modern historian, it was the humanists who laid its foundations.[2] Nor was this all. They showed that Greco-Roman civilization formed an independent world, a world of the past, but they did not, indeed could not, rob the European mind of its sense of being deeply and vitally affected by the fact that the past, in some way, still survived. Thus their work raised the whole question of the relation between past and present. Was the past relevant to the present? was there any point in studying it? what was the status of its survivals in the present? and, perhaps above all, how had it become the present? The problem of historical change, conceived as more complex and universal than ever before as new researches into the character of ancient civilization were undertaken, was affecting European thought well before the end of the sixteenth century. It is, then, to the paradox of humanism that we should look for the beginnings of modern historiography.

The humanist contribution was to institute a historical outlook and the rudiments of a historical technique in many branches of European scholarship. But the importance of this movement does not seem to have received the attention it deserves in our histories of

[1] Bolgar, *op. cit.* pp. 376–7. The auxiliary studies he mentions are geography, botany, literary criticism, archaeology and chronology, all in application to classical antiquity.

[2] A similar process is described by some students of the revolutionary changes that have come about in Confucian scholarship in China during the last half-century—see e.g. Ku Chieh-kang, *The Autobiography of a Chinese Historian* (Leiden, 1931), translator's preface by A. W. Hummel. It would be interesting to have some comparative studies of the effects which the transmission and scrutiny of authoritative texts have produced upon historical thought in different civilizations.

historiography. Many causes may be assigned for this apparent neglect. The movement was extremely slow—its full effects were not felt before the early eighteenth century—and it was often helped on its way by scholars unaware of the full import of what they were doing, who continued to believe that the past should be studied for the sake of moral instruction, as a storehouse of examples to be imitated or avoided. This cardinal principle of humanism, as is often pointed out, hindered, or at least did not favour, the development of historical thought; yet it is not the whole story about the history of historiography in the sixteenth and seventeenth centuries, and the mistake should not be made of writing as if it were. The development of historical thought can be shown to have continued, in a multitude of diverse ways, in spite of the humanist bent for moralizing. But the neglect of historians can be further accounted for by the fact that this development was so various and diffuse. Its history is not a simple question of one or two distinct and easily recognizable sciences evolving rapidly and carrying others along with them—as mathematics, physics and astronomy provide the central theme in the history of the scientific revolution—but of a historical approach developing accidentally and perhaps marginally upon the fringes of innumerable departments of scholarship, and evolving in each case a historical technique appropriate to that branch of study. The history of historiography cannot therefore be written as the study of a single evolution; all that can be done, at least for the present, is to trace the growth of the historical outlook in some of the fields where it most plainly manifests itself.

But it is one of the great facts about the history of historiography that the critical techniques evolved during the sixteenth and seventeenth centuries were only very slowly and very late combined with the writing of history as a form of literary narrative; that there was a great divorce between the scholars and antiquarians on the one hand, and the literary historians on the other; that history as a literary form went serenely on its way, neither taking account of the critical techniques evolved by the scholars nor evolving similar techniques of its own, until there was a kind of pyrrhonist revolt, a widespread movement of scepticism as to whether the story of the past could be reliably told at all. The character of this revolt has been studied by Paul Hazard;[1] the eyes of its leaders were plainly fixed upon history in the sense of literary narrative, to the exclusion of the critical methods of determining the reliability of facts about the past which were being rapidly developed by scholars such as Mabillon. If they had paid closer attention to such men, the intensity of their pyrrhonist despair might have been less.[2] But a rather similar error seems to have been made by modern historians. The history of historiography has been studied as if it could be identified with the history of those literary works which bear the title of histories, and in consequence a one-sided view has arisen which ascribes not nearly enough importance to the work of scholars who did not write narrative histories. The late Johan Huizinga, for example, wrote on one occasion that of all the modern sciences history owed least to the medieval university.[3] With this one exception, he said, the modern sciences had evolved by a process of budding-off from one or other of the three great faculties of theology, medicine or law, or from one of the lesser arts of the trivium or quadrivium; but if history figured in the medieval curriculum at all, it was as a sub-department of rhetoric, as a mere form of declamation without critical purpose or method, and consequently its evolution into a critical science had occurred outside the university altogether.

Now this is a judgment which can be maintained only if we are resolved to identify history with the literary form bearing that name. Once we are rid of that obsession, we shall remember the fact—perfectly well known from a variety of standard works[4]—that non-

[1] In ch. 2 of *La Crise de la conscience européenne* (Paris, 1935), 'De l'ancien au moderne'. See also A. Momigliano, *Contributo alla storia degli studi classici* (Rome, 1955), pp. 79–94.

[2] Marc Bloch's *Métier d'historien* brings out most clearly the contrast between Mabillon's critical method and any sort of pyrrhonism.

[3] In *Sobre el estado actual de la ciencia histórica* (Madrid, 1934), pp. 12 ff.; quoted in F. Rosenthal's *A History of Muslim Historiography* (Leiden, 1952), p. 29 n.

[4] E.g. F. W. Maitland's *English Law and the Renaissance*; Holdsworth's *History of English Law*, vol. IV; H. D. Hazeltine, 'The Renaissance', in *Cambridge Legal Essays* (1926); W. F. Church, *Constitutional Thought in Sixteenth-century France* (Cambridge, Mass., 1941); M. P. Gilmore, *Argument from Roman Law* (Cambridge, Mass., 1941); J. Declareuil, *Histoire générale du droit français* (Paris, 1925); R. Dareste, *Essai sur François Hotman* (Paris, 1850).

narrative historical work of the highest originality and complexity was being carried on in the French universities of the sixteenth century—a time when their organization and curriculum were certainly still medieval—and that this historical thought had developed in the faculty of law. The historical school of Renaissance jurists furnishes the subject of the remainder of this chapter, but one further point remains to be made. Text-book accounts of the history of historiography tend to produce the impression that, when the contribution of the sixteenth- and seventeenth-century scholars came to be reunited with narrative history to produce major historical writings recognizably like those of the present day, it amounted to little more than a vast accumulation of more or less verified facts, of which giants like Robertson or Gibbon could make use. This is not altogether so, as will be seen. The earlier scholars were more or less consciously engaged in returning facts to their historical context and interpreting them there, and it has already been suggested that this was bound to present complex problems for historical reflexion; problems concerning the relation of the past to the present, and its survival in the present. With the lawyers this was peculiarly the case, because the data they were assigning to a past context were simultaneously the principles on which present society was endeavouring to govern itself. The historical problems with which a sixteenth-century scholar found himself concerned could therefore be adult, practical to the point of urgency, and even philosophically profound. His thought about them might be of great importance to himself and his generation, and might permanently affect the historical understanding of his civilization. Thought of this kind therefore forms a real and significant part of the history of historiography.

II

The historical approach to the study of Roman law was a product of humanism and shared in the characteristics, already traced, of that movement. It arose, primarily in French universities but under some Italian influence, in the form of a reaction against the methods of legal study associated with the name of Bartolus. The principal humanist criticism of the Bartolist school was that they had overlaid the original Justinianean text with an unmanageable wealth of glosses and commentaries, and that a return should be made to the purity of the original. But it had also been Bartolus's constant endeavour to adapt the Roman text to the world he himself lived in by applying Roman principles and definitions to contemporary phenomena—the degree of his historical awareness does not form part of the present inquiry—and this lent a peculiar importance to the legal humanists' endeavour to return, not only to the pure text of the Roman original, but to the meaning which these laws had possessed in the minds of the Romans who penned them. In the first place, it may be imagined, many of the humanists set about their task in the belief that the true principles of Roman jurisprudence, when found, would prove of such surpassing wisdom that they need only be directly imitated and applied in the present day; but they ended by achieving something much more than even a complete undoing of the work of Bartolus. They set out to establish the exact meaning of the Roman texts, and this, as they rightly saw, involved a detailed exegesis of the exact meaning of all technical or doubtful words which the texts contained. Therefore they set about comparing and establishing the various meanings which all such words bore, first in the separate legal texts which employed them, and secondly, in any other works of ancient provenance in which they might be found; and thus it was that detailed and conscious historical criticism made its appearance in the schools of jurisprudence under the name of 'grammar', the science of the meaning and use of words.[1] It is the peculiar characteristic of a comprehensive system of law like the Roman that it provides a close and extensive description of the principal institutions and many of the ideas of the society for which it was formed; and the historical school—as the humanist lawyers soon became—could not translate the language of Roman law back into its original meanings without reconstructing just such a picture of the society of imperial

[1] The best study of a jurist of this school at work seems to be P. E. Viard's *André Alciat* (Paris, 1926, for the University of Nancy). See also L. Delaruelle, *Guillaume Budé (1468–1540): les origines, les débuts, les idées maîtresses* (Bibliothèque de l'Ecole des Hautes Etudes; Sciences Historiques et Philologiques, 162e fascicule, Paris, 1907).

Rome. They gathered much of their evidence for this picture from the text of the law itself, but much more important was the fact that they sought to interpret the law according to the context of a reconstructed society. Inadequate, piecemeal and *ad hoc* their work may have been, but the essentials of the historical method were there and were known to be there. In this way the legal humanists came to be historians, and the full impact of their work on European thought has never yet been measured.

They had begun to study the past on principles which assumed its unlikeness to the present, and this soon brought them into contact with profound educational and practical problems. The society they were reconstructing was one which differed in all its structure from their own, and one, furthermore, which no longer existed. The law which they were studying belonged to that past world, and all its language and all its thoughts had reference to social institutions which were no longer anywhere to be found. Yet this same law was still in force over a wide, indeed an increasing area of Europe, and the world stood deeply committed to an endeavour to rule itself according to Roman principles. Were not the historical school making nonsense of that endeavour, for how should a law be obeyed which had been framed for utterly different conditions and no longer bore its original meaning? And if this question were satisfactorily answered, why then should young men spend years of their lives reducing the law to its original meanings? What was the status of ancient law in a changed world; why should it any longer be studied? The lawyers here touched unexpectedly on the problem of time, encountering it in a new and urgently practical form. There are signs of mounting discontent with the historians soon after 1560; for as France moved into an era of administrative breakdown and devastating civil war, it became more than ever necessary for her intellectuals to lay down clear principles of right and obligation, which might guide her back to order and peace. The whole medieval attitude to questions of legal and secular wisdom, the whole tradition of French governmental and political thought, predisposed her to seek such principles in Roman law. But the very possibility of this the professors of Bourges and Toulouse seemed to deny. Cujas (the story may be apocryphal), when asked to apply his learning to contemporary problems, would reply merely: 'Quid hoc ad edictum praetoris?' It was a heroic answer, for in the name of pure scholarship he was in effect denying European civilization the use of one of the principal canons by which she was accustomed to guide herself. That civilization had been shaped, in large measure, by the traditional interpretation of certain authoritative documents. In the name of a more accurate interpretation, a historical interpretation had been formulated; and in the name of historical interpretation, the relevance of the past to the present was apparently being denied. The moment was revolutionary and the tension could not be allowed to endure. A remedy was indeed found, but one which took account of the new learning. Though the attempt to draw fundamental political principles from Roman law continued, it had suffered a radical criticism which could not but modify its character.[1]

In the first decade of the French religious wars three books at least were written—each of them addressed, in whole or in part, to the Chancellor, Michel de l'Hôpital—in the endeavour to solve the problem, bring history and jurisprudence back into concord, and restore the past to some sort of relevance to the present. These were François Baudouin's *De institutione historiae universae et ejus cum jurisprudentia conjunctione* (1561), Jean Bodin's *Methodus ad facilem historiarum cognitionem* (1566), and François Hotman's *Anti-Tribonian* (1567). Of the three, Hotman's book is probably not the greatest; that title must be granted to the strange semi-ruinous mass of Bodin's *Methodus*; but *Anti-Tribonian* tells us much about the directions in which historical thought in the field of law was moving, and reveals to what lengths the new method of criticism might be carried by an impudent and restless mind. With the promptness of the *enfant terrible* (admittedly he was forty-three and about to take up Cujas's chair at Bourges) Hotman announces that the Roman law is the most useless of all studies to the modern Frenchman, be he practising lawyer or cultivated amateur. He bases this declaration on the ground that Roman law is the law of a past society, radically differ-

---

[1] Gilmore's *Argument from Roman Law*, just cited, traces the successive interpretations of the Roman concept of *merum imperium* and shows how they were affected by the methods of Cujas and by the reaction against them.

ent in structure from that of contemporary France, so that when he reproaches the 'grammarians' like Cujas with devoting themselves to useless antiquarianism, it is actually their own discovery that he is using to make them ridiculous. In all that he wrote, Hotman was standing on the shoulders of the historical school and endeavouring to carry their method beyond anything they had envisaged and indeed to reduce it to absurdity. They had shown that Justinian's code was the law of a past society; he would show that it was not even that. His two-edged criticism of Roman law as a subject worth studying is expressed in the heading of his third chapter: 'Que l'estat de la Republique Romaine est fort different de celuy de France, & neantmoins ne se peut apprendre par les liures de Iustinian.'[1]

The Codes and Digests are useless to the lawyer because they bear no relation to modern society; they are useless to the historian because they are not the law that was practised at Rome at any time in its history. Justinian's codifiers preserved no connected body of earlier law; they altered much and what they did not alter they scattered and rearranged; what they did not retain they destroyed; and, in short, there is nothing in their work which gives us any picture worth having of Roman law under either the republic or the empire—as is clear from the work of those scholars who have attempted to reconstruct Roman methods of government and have been compelled to do so from sources outside the law.[2] Nor are the Codes of much assistance even to the historian of Byzantium:

> Quant au Constantinopolitain (qui fut blasonné le nouueau Romain) ie confesse que l'on en void à la trauerse quelques traces & enseignes, principalement aux trois derniers liures du Code, mais si petites & si escartees par-cy par-là, que par le iugement d'vn chacun il en faut deuiner les deux tiers: & qui plus est, tant s'en faut que des trois liures du Code on cognoisse l'estat du dernier Empire Romain, qu'au contraire il est impossible d'entendre lesdits liures sans preallablement auoir acquis la cognoissance dudit estat par la lecture des historiens: comme (apres les sus-nommez) d'vn Iulius Capitolinus, d'vn Vopiscus, d'vn Ammianus, Procopius, Zonaras et

[1] All quotations are from the 1603 edition of *Anti-Tribonian*, published at Paris.
[2] *Anti-Tribonian*, pp. 13–15, 18, 35–6, 86–7.

Introductory: the French Prelude to Modern Historiography

leurs semblables: tellement que c'est vne pure mocquerie de dire qu'il faille lire les liures de Iustinian pour cognoitre l'histoire. Car tout à rebours il est force de sçauoir l'histoire pour les entendre, & encores auec fort grande difficulté; & mesmes vsant souuentesfois plutost de coniecture que de fondement certain & asseuré.[1]

The criticism is in some respects shallow, in others profound. In its virtues and its vices, it is dominated by the idea of carrying historical criticism to the point where it destroys itself. The school of Cujas had shown that it was possible to describe law in terms of the society from which it came; but Hotman believed he could prove that the law of Justinian was not the law of Roman society at any time before Justinian's own. This in his eyes robbed it of nearly all its value. Law must be appropriate to the state it was designed to govern—Cujas's researches had underlined that truth—but the fact that Roman law could not be used as a guide to the historical interpretation of republic or empire showed that it was appropriate to none, and was therefore hardly a law at all. In *Anti-Tribonian*, Hotman would not even allow that it was appropriate to the conditions of Justinian's own time, although in a later work[2] he admitted that the Byzantine lawyers, 'qui non Rempub. ad Leges, sed has ad illam accommodandas esse intelligebant', did right to alter most of the Roman law in favour of 'nouas suas leges ad suae Graeciae rationem accommodatas'. But in the earlier book Justinian's law is nothing but a mass of 'inconstances et mutabilitez', neither a clear statement of Rome's traditional law nor an exposition

[1] 'As for the law of Constantinople (which proclaimed itself that of new Rome) I confess that we can dimly perceive a few hints and traces of it, mostly in the last three books of the Code, but so small and so scattered are those that by common consent we must attempt to divine two thirds of it; and what is more, so far from true is it that from these three books of the Code we can understand the condition of the late Roman Empire, that on the contrary it is impossible to understand these books of law without having previously acquired some knowledge of that state by reading the historians: such as (in addition to those mentioned earlier) Julius Capitolinus, Vopiscus, Ammianus, Procopius, Zonaras and their fellows; so that it is complete nonsense to say that we must read the books of Justinian in order to understand history. Quite the reverse; we are compelled to learn history in order to understand them, and even then it is extremely difficult, and we must often rely on conjecture rather than certain and assured knowledge.' *Anti-Tribonian*, pp. 20–1.   [2] *De feudis commentatio tripertita* (Lyons, 1573), dedication.

of the principles of jurisprudence. Of the controversy between Bartolists and humanists Hotman observes that it is not the method of either which is at fault.

> Nous parlons du vice naturel & du deffaut interieur qui est en la matiere et substance de la discipline: lequel est bien plus difficile à corriger que les corruptions qui y sont arriuées par accidens exterieurs.[1]

In order to emphasize further the unreality and unsatisfactoriness of Roman law, Hotman contrasts it with the customary and feudal law prevailing in other parts of France; and it is here that the argument of *Anti-Tribonian* leads us into a new field, of wide significance. The writer rolls out the gnarled terminology of customary law, and points out with relish that if a man came into a French court knowing only the Roman code, though he knew it 'aussi parfaittement...comme fait vn Caton, vn Sceuola, ou vn Manlius', he might as well be among American savages.

> Car là il n'orra jergonner que d'heritages cottiers ou surcottiers, des droits seigneuriaux, de iustice directe, censiue, recognoissance, de retraits lignagers ou feodaux, de rente fonciere ou volage, vest, deuest, saisine, dessaisine, droit de quart ou de requart, quint ou requint, droit d'afeurage ou chambellage, droit de champart, de frarenseté ou escleiches, de douaire coustumier ou prefix, de communauté de biens, & autres semblables propos qui lui šeront aussi nouueaux & estranges, comme s'il n'auoit en iour de sa vie ouy parler ny de loy ny de police.[2]

Now it is clear that these uncouth vocables, 'barbarous' according to all humanist standards, are being contrasted favourably with the classical clarity of Roman law, and that this is being done on the ground that they are custom and therefore appropriate to the state of France in a way that the written law of Constantinople can never be. Hotman's appeal from written to customary law is part of a fairly widespread reaction that was going on in sixteenth-century juristic thought; and one of the attractions of custom was precisely that it offered a means of escape from the divorce of past and present threatened by the criticisms of the historical school. Because Roman

---

[1] 'We are talking of the vices and faults which are inherent in the substance of this discipline, and are much harder to correct than the corruptions which have arrived by accident from outside.' *Anti-Tribonian*, p. 130.

[2] *Anti-Tribonian*, pp. 36–7.

law was written and unchangeable, it could be subjected to grammatical analysis and proved to belong to a past state of society, but because custom was by its nature unwritten law, the usages of the folk interpreted through the mouths of judges, it could be argued with some plausibility that it could never become obsolete. If this custom no longer suited the needs of the people, it was said, they would by now have thrown it away; that they have not done so proves that, however ancient it may be, it cannot be out of date. Conversely, the essence of custom was that it was immemorial, and the argument could with equal facility be used that, since the people had retained a given custom through many centuries, it had proved itself apt to meet all the emergencies which had arisen during that period. Custom was *tam antiqua et tam nova*, always immemorial and always perfectly up-to-date. We shall see both arguments developed, and the idealization of custom carried to an extraordinary height, by the English common lawyers of James I's reign. Hotman does not adopt such extreme views, but there can be little doubt that it is as custom that he is praising French native law in the passage quoted. He emphasizes that France is à feudal society of non-Roman origin; that the purity of Frankish custom was preserved for five hundred years untrammelled by Roman influences;[1] and that it is legal dogma that the authority of Roman law is never so great as that of use and custom.[2] There were good reasons, as we shall see, why Hotman's juristic theory could never be founded exclusively on custom, but we are safe in seeing in *Anti-Tribonian* one sign of that reaction towards the customary, the native, the feudal and the barbarous, which was discernible in contemporary thought and may have furnished one of the roots of European romanticism:[3] for it constantly opposed the folk to the legislator, the primitive, the inarticulate and the mutable to the rigidities of ordered reason.[4]

But with the reaction in favour of customary and native codes of

---

[1] *Anti-Tribonian*, pp. 137–8.   [2] *Anti-Tribonian*, pp. 101–2.
[3] H. D. Hazeltine, *loc. cit.*, termed this reaction that of the 'national jurists'.
[4] 'We were having a little Renaissance of our own; or a Gothic revival, if you please'; Maitland (in *English Law and the Renaissance*) on the renewal of common-law studies, which took the form of an idealization of custom.

law we enter the field of contemporary political thought. If it is no longer as certain as it once was that the extension of monarchical authority and the reception of Roman law went everywhere hand in hand, the fact remains that the sixteenth and seventeenth centuries were throughout western Europe a time of collision between the authority of kings and local or national privileges, liberties and constitutions. Many of these latter were rooted in feudal custom, some could even be dimly traced back to the customs of the Germanic invaders of the empire, and all were more or less permeated by the essential medieval idea of law as a thing ancient, immanent and unmade, proof against invasion by human wills because no will had made it. Since there was an increasing tendency to claim sovereignty in the full sense for the king, it was natural that those who sought to defend threatened privileges or liberties should emphasize in return that their rights were rooted in a law which no king could invade. Theologians and philosophers might try to equate these rights with reason and nature, which should be above all wills; but another and no less telling argument was to demonstrate that they partook of the nature of immemorial, sacred custom. In this way there grew up—or rather, there was intensified and renewed—a habit in many countries of appealing to 'the ancient constitution', of seeking to prove that the rights it was desired to defend were immemorial and therefore beyond the king's power to alter or annul. Hotman in *Francogallia* asserted the antiquity of the assembly of the nation; Coke in England that of parliament and the common law; Pietro de Gregorio in Sicily that of baronial privilege and the *parlamento*; François Vranck in the Netherlands that of the sovereign and independent Dutch towns; Erik Sparre in Sweden that of the nobles in their *riksrad*.[1] By 1600 or there-

---

[1] *Francogallia* was first printed in 1573. Coke began to publish his *Reports* in 1600. De Gregorio's chief works were published in 1596; there is a full study of the evolution of Sicilian historical opinion down to 1848 in R. Romeo, *Il Risorgimento in Sicilia* (Bari, 1950), *passim*. Vranck's *Corte Vertooninghe* appeared in 1587; see G. N. Clark, 'The Rise of the Dutch Republic', *Proc. Brit. Acad.* (1946), pp. 196–7. Sparre was executed at Linköping in 1600; Michael Roberts in *Gustavus Adolphus: a History of Sweden, 1611–32*, vol. 1 (London, 1953), pp. 16–17, says his 'legal antiquarianism, his appeal to the *landslag*, recall Coke's brandishing of Magna Carta'.

Introductory: the French Prelude to Modern Historiography

abouts there was hardly any constitutional movement without its accompanying historical myth. No man granted us this liberty, it was said; it has been ours from beyond the memory of man; and consequently none can take it from us. In reply, the kings and their partisans tried to show that, in the words of James VI (and I), 'kings were the authors and makers of the laws and not the laws of the kings'.[1] If the constitutionalists could show that the laws were as old as, or older than, the kings, they might go on to assert a contractual or elective basis for kingship; but if the laws had come into being at a time when there was already a king, then nothing but the king's authority could have sanctioned them or made them law, and the king might assert a sovereign right to revoke what his predecessors had granted. The constitutionalists were therefore always being driven to argue that the laws were of a practically infinite antiquity, immemorial in the sense of earlier than the earliest king known. It could happen in this way that historical criticism became one of the sharpest weapons of monarchy, while the constitutionalists were forced into a kind of historical obscurantism—compelled to attribute their liberties to more and more remote and mythical periods in the effort to prove them independent of the will of the king. There were thus great dangers to the clarity of historical thought in the multiplication of these constitutional myths; but their importance in the history of historiography is nevertheless great.

There existed, therefore, in a number of European nations a kind of political thought which cannot satisfactorily be termed 'constitutionalism', since it involved a more intensive use of historical and antiquarian thinking than the use of that term normally implies. It may be provisionally defined as the attempt to settle fundamental political questions, notably those involving law, right and sovereignty, by appeal not directly to abstract political concepts, but to the existing 'municipal' laws of the country concerned and to the concepts of custom, prescription and authority that underlay them, as well as to the reverence which they enjoyed by reason of their antiquity—an attempt which necessarily involved the study, critical or otherwise, of their origins and history. One may reasonably

[1] *Political Works of James I*, ed. C. H. McIlwain (Cambridge, Mass., 1918), p. 62.

claim that the history of European political thinking, at any rate in the sixteenth to eighteenth centuries, will be incomplete until we know more about this branch of thought than we now do; but relatively little work has been done upon it and we still lack a compendious term with which to describe it. To call it 'constitutional antiquarianism' would perhaps do less than justice to the quality of the historical thought which its practitioners sometimes displayed; and the South Italian scholars, who appear to be the only historians who have studied its evolution as naturally forming part of the history of their states, use such terms as 'cultura storicogiuridica' and 'tradizione giuridica', which do not go well into English.[1] This form of thought is found in many countries besides Italy and, until Cartesian and Lockean techniques of political argument in part overcame it about 1700, it placed no small part in the history of political thinking. It is a thread which leads to Montesquieu, and to Burke. But its importance is not less in the history of historiography. It was largely through these attempts to determine the antiquity of their institutions that the nations of Europe embarked on the study of their medieval past and barbaric origins; and just as the Roman law had provided a highway to the historical study of Roman society, so now antiquarian-minded lawyers began to study the medieval past through the interpretation and analysis of those medieval systems of law which concerned them by surviving in their midst. But these forms of law differed so greatly, in their character and basic ideas, from the law of Justinian that it was inevitable that the historical thought engendered in their study should differ as greatly from that of Alciati and Cujas; and it is easy to see that in this way the idea of custom exerted a wide influence upon European historiography. Roman law, for instance, laid stress upon the concepts of will, command and the legislator, and tended therefore to encourage the already existing idea that each institution had originated at a particular time in the will of a particular individual who had established it in substantially its present form. This was the period in which Polydore Vergil wrote his *De inventoribus rerum* on the assumption that every invention

[1] Both terms are employed by Romeo, *op. cit.*; e.g. pp. 49, 81. See also L. Marini, *Pietro Giannone e il Giannonismo a Napoli nel Settecento* (Bari, 1950).

could be traced to an individual discoverer;[1] and in the field of legal history, Machiavelli could write with what seems singular naïveté of the man 'chi ordinó' so complex a creation of history as the monarchy of France.[2] To thought of this kind the idea of custom offered a salutary corrective; all its emphasis was on gradual process, imperceptible change, the origin and slow growth of institutions in usage, tacit consent, prescription and adaptation. We may never know how much of our sense of history is due to the presence in Europe of systems of customary law, and to the idealization of the concept of custom which took place towards the end of the sixteenth century. To it our awareness of process in history is largely owing.

But this freedom was bought at a great price, and the concept of custom undoubtedly did much to impede the growth of a critical approach to medieval and barbarian history. As we have seen, it was because Roman law was written that it could be reduced to the context of a past society and its relevance to the present day questioned; and custom owed much of its popularity to its unwritten character, which enabled it to elude such drastic criticism and present the dangerously attractive spectacle of a form of law which was ever-changing yet ever the same, immemorial yet perfectly adapted to present needs. Custom therefore escaped the fate of being relegated to form part of a vanished society, while conversely medieval society was not reconstructed around the framework of a reinterpreted custom; and a critical spirit in medieval historiography was consequently slow to develop. The concept of the immemorial encouraged the fabrication of myths about immensely remote times, and the fact that the appeal to early national history took the form of partisan controversy between sovereign and constitution enhanced this tendency in the way already outlined. In minds preoccupied with the idea of custom there arose a species of sixteenth-century romanticism: their myths derived the national laws not only from legendary and heroic times, but also from the primitive and inarticulate wisdom of the folk, expressed in age-old custom which

[1] See Denys Hay, *Polydore Vergil* (Oxford, 1952), ch. III.
[2] *Discorsi*, I, xvi; discussed by Pierre Mesnard, *L'Essor de la philosophie politique au XVIme siècle* (Paris, 1951), p. 83, who quotes de Maistre's comment, 'Je voudrais bien le connaître.'

was often contrasted favourably with the mere conscious ratio-cination of individual legislators. Since their pursuit of ancient laws and liberties often led them to seek these things in the customs of the barbarian invaders, whom they identified with the Germans described by Caesar and Tacitus, they made many contributions to the legend of primitive Teutonic freedom and virtue, which was growing up so rapidly in the sixteenth century and can expect so little sympathy in the twentieth. There was a constant temptation to deny that the law's history could be known, to wrap its origins in mystery and assert that it had always, since time out of mind, been as it was now. The study of the past through the medium of customary law was a dangerous business, and the enthusiast for custom too often ended by alleging that his people had changed their laws not at all since their heroic German ancestors had brought their free institutions, already ancient, out of the forest to overthrow a Roman Empire corrupted by tyranny.

Hotman's *Francogallia* may seem a book of this kind. The original freedom of the Gauls, it says, virtually destroyed by the Romans, was restored by the life-giving incursions of the Franks, and for centuries thereafter, until the successful usurpations of Louis XI, the assembly of the nation was supreme if not sovereign. By writing in this way, Maitland thought, Hotman 'made himself in some sort the ancestor of the Germanists',[1] and his pursuit of liberty into barbaric times does indeed suggest that he idealized both ancient custom and primitive Teutonic liberty. But the truth, it appears, is less simple. To André Lemaire, the publication of *Francogallia* in 1572 marked precisely the moment at which French publicists ceased to represent their liberties as founded in ancient custom and derived them instead from an original act of the sovereign people—a very different idea, scholastic and civilian in its origin and not rooted in the study of customary law. The medieval belief in custom, according to this interpretation, was decaying in French thought, assailed by partisans of royal absolutism on one hand and popular sovereignty on the other.[2] There is the further difficulty that any

[1] *English Law and the Renaissance*, n. 28.
[2] Lemaire, *Les Lois fondamentales de la monarchie française d'après les théoriciens de l'ancien régime* (Paris, 1907), pp. 92–102.

theory of sovereignty, rigorously interpreted, renders the appeal to the past unnecessary or of only emotional weight. If Hotman thought the people were sovereign, he added little to his argument by declaring that they had been so always; and J. W. Allen characteristically concluded that Hotman could not have given a satisfactory explanation of why he wrote in the form of an interpretation of history at all.[1] But on Lemaire's own showing, the older idea that French fundamental law derives its force from ancient custom is never far below the surface of Hotman's thought and he is prepared to revert to it at need. We should not think, therefore, that his political ideas were uninfluenced by his preference for customary over Roman law. But, as we shall see, it is not certain that he was in the habit of exalting the primitive liberty of the Germans. Neither idealization of custom nor idealization of German freedom appears to account satisfactorily for the thought of *Francogallia*, and it seems necessary to modify the account of constitutional antiquarianism so far given. If we now make a fresh approach to the question which Allen thought unanswerable, it may not solve the riddle of *Francogallia*, but it may further the objects of the present inquiry.

III

It has been assumed so far that the purpose of alleging an 'ancient constitution' was always to prove that the existing constitution, or some part of it, was immemorial custom and derived legally binding force in the present from that alone. But this is not altogether true: the sanctity of immemorial custom was only one reason why a law proved to be ancient should be immune from the sovereign's interference at the present day. It might instead be argued that the people were originally (and had remained) free and sovereign, and could be discerned in the deeps of time arranging their constitution to suit their convenience; or it might merely be held that the ancient constitution had kept the people happy for centuries and should accordingly be retained, or restored, as the case might be. There were a great many reasons why the ancient

[1] *Political Thought in the Sixteenth Century* (London, 3rd ed. 1951), pp. 309–10.

should be authoritative, and a great many influences at work to determine which of those reasons a polemicist would adopt. One of the most important of these determining factors must have been the character of the system of law prevailing in the country where the appeal to antiquity was being made. The various concepts of what is essential to law—custom, command, reason—were differently blended in different structures of legal thought, and as the blend varied so would the reasons for appealing to the past and thinking it authoritative in the present. A people accustomed to thinking in terms of customary law would naturally emphasize the idea that what was ancient and unmade was binding for that reason alone; a people accustomed to Roman law and the *lex regia* would go to the past in search of the original transfer of sovereignty and the character of that transaction. In countries where both systems of law obtained, thinking of this kind would be more complicated still. If a country was governed wholly by customary law, then it would be easy and natural to believe that everything in the constitution was rooted in immemorial usage and binding even on kings for that reason alone. But if the country was divided between a system of customary law and a system of law deriving its authority from the commands of named emperors living at stated times, then the appeal to the merely immemorial could not be made with at all the same degree of confidence; we should expect to find that if there was an appeal to antiquity, it was being made for much more complex and perhaps indeterminate reasons, and that the concept of custom itself was being subjected to criticism by those whose profession disposed them to think of law in terms of command. In this so far hypothetical comparison it would be possible to see that where there were different systems of law, the appeal to antiquity would be made for different reasons, and radically different attitudes to the history of institutions might arise.

France was a country of this kind, with Roman law in some of her provinces and various systems of customary law in others; and if we now return to the argument of *Anti-Tribonian*, we shall find that, though Hotman uses the naturalness and flexibility of custom as a stick with which to beat Roman law, his programme of legal reform by no means involved the wholesale abandonment of *droit écrit* in favour of *coutume*. Instead he proposes a plan of legal training in which the pupils undertake a comparative study of all known and valuable systems of law with the aim of distilling the essential principles of juristic reason which are common to all, until at the end all systems are swallowed up in the developed thought of the perfect judge, who (like St Louis under the oak at Vincennes) can dispense pure equity with no need of a law-book.[1] Hotman thus enunciates the principle known as neo-Bartolism, which came to dominate French juristic thought towards the end of the century, its central concept being that of discovering the fundamental principles of all systems of law. Since neo-Bartolism arose as a reaction against the rigidly historical approach of Cujas, its place in the history of historiography ought to be considered. Its primary aim was to restore the unity of past and present and deliver Roman law from the reproach of being irrelevant to the present day. The means it adopted strongly recall the humanist doctrine that the utility of history in general was that it could provide moral and practical examples to be imitated or avoided in the present; yet neo-Bartolist thought is somewhat more subtle than that. In the first place, like the destructive criticism of *Anti-Tribonian*, it virtually admits the validity of the theory it intends to displace. It tacitly agrees that Roman law belongs to the vanished world of Rome and cannot uncritically be taken over and used today; what is asserted is that Roman law contains certain principles of universal value, which may be isolated and universally applied. But this process must logically follow the process of historical criticism, and to that extent the validity of Cujacian procedure is not denied. 'I regret none of the time I have spent in expounding the law,' said Baudouin, 'but something more is needed.'[2] In the second place it ought to be noted that the neo-Bartolist, like any other lawyer, was not regarding the past as something dead and finished and merely to be imitated—a reproach which may sometimes be justly brought against the literary humanist. He started from the incontestable

---

[1] *Anti-Tribonian*, p. 140.

[2] Quoted in R. Dareste, *Essai sur F. Hotman*, p. 20. Baudouin's words were 'in jure docendo', and he appears to have meant the Cujacian technique of establishing the text and its meaning.

fact that laws belonging to a vanished past survived in the present and were playing an active part in shaping his own world, and he wanted to know how this was possible. If the explanations he put forward were sometimes unhistorical, this could not altogether change the fact that to the lawyer the past is alive in the present and history is contemporary history. There again is the peculiar importance of law in the history of historiography.

But Hotman's version of neo-Bartolism is not simply a means of bringing the study of Roman law back into relevance to the present —indeed, his criticisms had carried him past the point where he could admit that Roman law would be of much use in his scheme of legal education. It also affects the relations, within France, of written law and custom. Hotman does not make it perfectly clear in *Anti-Tribonian* whether the student will also study the *coutumes* and distil essential principles from them, though qualified judges have thought it safe to assume that this was his meaning.[1] But it seems just possible that custom was to be immune from this process of digestion. The end of Hotman's plan was to fill the pupil's mind with unwritten principles of equity, which he could apply to all circumstances and cases without need of a law-book—as St Louis did at Vincennes. But the law dispensed by St Louis might very well be termed the custom of his people, and it would not be impossible to claim that the collective wisdom of the folk achieved in custom an unwritten law applicable to all cases and capable of being identified with the unwritten equity to be evolved in Hotman's scheme of training. Custom might be idealized and described as perfect equity; the English common lawyers virtually reached this point. However, it is true that Hotman alludes to the possibility of codifying the customs,[2] and French historians have not found it possible to think of his proposals without relating them to the great labours of codification carried out in and after his time. In this process custom was subjected to the neo-Bartolist techniques of criticism, conflation and digestion; Du Moulin, the master of codi-

[1] E.g. Dareste.

[2] *Anti-Tribonian*, pp. 154–5; however, the reference here is to a plan of Louis XI's, who appears in *Francogallia* as the subverter of the ancient constitution.

fication, rather than Hotman, Bodin or Baudouin, is the great figure of the neo-Bartolist tradition. Let us take it, then, that the thought of *Anti-Tribonian* leads to the digestion of custom into more developed systems of law or equity.

But in this process custom lost much of its essential character. It has been shown at length in an American study[1] how in sixteenth-century France custom ceased to be regarded as something almost aboriginal, law merely in virtue of its antiquity, and was increasingly interpreted as subject to the authority of the king, until it was denied any legitimacy unless formally recognized and registered by a royal court. Now this did not come about merely because the king drew upon Roman ideas which found the origin of all law in *quod principi placuit*; it could only occur because the French king was ruler alike over *pays de droit écrit* and over *pays de coutumes*, and therefore imposed his authority alike upon both forms of law. Codification was an act of sovereignty, an assertion that the ruler's will and reason were superior even to ancient custom, and consequently it gave rise to the historical claim that custom had never had force but by the king's permission. And when replies were attempted, French constitutionalists could not very well assert that the laws of all the land at large were immemorial custom, because those of the *pays de droit écrit* manifestly were not. Some more universal reason must be found for the sanctity of ancient law. The reply usually made to the claim that custom was subject to the king, therefore, was, as the century went on, less and less that custom was simply immemorial usage, and more and more that it was derived from the people's right to provide for their own needs; and so a doctrine of popular sovereignty—itself perhaps of Roman origin—came to replace the older, purely medieval appeal to ancient unmade law.[2] Where custom co-existed with Roman law, thinkers could not simply allege that the laws of the land were immemorial; nor could the very doctrine that custom was immemorial escape

[1] W. F. Church, *Constitutional Thought in Sixteenth-century France*, pp. 100–20.

[2] Church, pp. 86–7, associates this doctrine with the name of Simon Marion (1570); it 'had rarely been expressed in France earlier in the century'. Of course the doctrine of popular sovereignty was itself medieval; the difference is that the doctrine of pure custom did not survive the transition to modern times.

criticism in the light of the competing idea that law originated in command. There would be a tendency for historians—whether party men or impartial scholars—to search for the act of will that had set up custom, and this would, in the first place, help to correct the obscurantist tendencies latent in the idea of custom; but in the second place, it would tend to dissolve the concept altogether and replace it by some doctrine of sovereignty, whether popular or royal. The simultaneous existence of systems of law that could be compared had a complex but stimulating effect upon both historical and political thought.

We are now perhaps better placed to understand the nature of the thought in *Francogallia*. Hotman is putting forward a doctrine of ancient liberty; yet its antiquity is not that of pure custom. Perhaps those scholars are right who take him to mean that popular sovereignty originally lay with the Gauls, was restored by the Franks and remained binding until his own day;[1] perhaps Allen had the truth of the matter, and Hotman fell between two stools and did not know what he meant. What is more, he is still writing as a neo-Bartolist who would like to see a conflation of all laws into some form of enlightened equity—a programme which could hardly be carried out without the assertion of some species of sovereignty; but though we hear once more of St Louis and the ideal unwritten justice which he dispensed at Vincennes, the saint's judgments, as quoted in *Francogallia*,[2] prove to have been commands that disputes between himself and his vassals should be heard in courts of vassals, and not in assemblages of learned lawyers such as the *parlements*, so that St Louis's justice would seem to have been essentially an injunction to observe feudal custom. It is not necessary to the present argument to determine exactly what Hotman meant in *Francogallia*; all that is necessary is to show why his appeal to ancient liberty cannot be reduced to the simple statement that the existing constitution of France is rooted in immemorial custom. It cannot be so, because there is no single system of customary law in France; because only parts of the constitution can be attributed to immemorial custom; and because the existence of laws with a

[1] Church, *op. cit.* p. 87, following Lemaire, *op. cit.* pp. 101–2.
[2] See pp. 143–5 of Robert Molesworth's translation (2nd ed., London, 1721).

known origin in command makes it harder than it would otherwise be to think of custom itself as immemorial. The thought of *Franco-gallia* is (it seems possible) incoherent, but if we turn to a work which its author published in the same year we can observe that, on the whole, these conditions stimulated rather than hampered a critical approach to the history of non-Roman systems of law, and that Hotman, for all his appeals to the *francsgaulois*, was far from idealizing Teutonic law as such.

De feudis commentatio tripertita, a study of the history of the feudal law, was written before the St Bartholomew massacres drove Hotman to flee from his chair at Bourges and was published in 1573; it is dedicated to Caspar Seydlitz, one of the German students who had urged him to lecture on the feudal law at Bourges.[1] Here if anywhere Hotman might have given rein to the 'Germanizing' tendencies so often attributed to him, and expressed the view, not uncommon in his day, that freedom was ancient Germany's gift to Europe. But after summarizing the attacks first made in *Anti-Tri-bonian* on the study of Roman law, he turns in his epistle dedicatory to the laws of the conquering barbarians.[2] 'Dici vix potest, quam absurdae atque inconditae leges'; the early Germans excelled beyond doubt as men of war, but as legislators they can only be compared to men teaching the Cimmerians to distinguish colours in the dark, while those who solemnly study and annotate their attempts to draw up codes are like the philosophers in Lucian, of whom some milked the he-goat while others held the sieve. In 'Francogallia nostra' there are as many laws and customs as there are cities and provinces, and a man might think there was no one form of justice or equity. Very little can be said about the written *coutumes* which was not said by the sophists who collected them. The Neapolitan Constitutions are a joke even to their editors; the law of England, as Polydore Vergil has shown, is dangerous, in-comprehensible and written in a barbarous dialect; the authors of

[1] E. Blocaille, *Etude sur François Hotman* (Dijon, 1902), p. 40. Seydlitz seems to have been a Silesian; 'hic apud nos esses, de magno Germanorum adolescentum numero'.

[2] The rest of this paragraph is from the epistle dedicatory to Seydlitz, which is not paginated in the edition of 1573.

the *Sachsenspiegel* were probably fine fighting men. As for the feudal law, to which the sizable volume prefaced by this diatribe is entirely devoted, Hotman seems to regard it as worth studying principally for the light it sheds on the history of titles, honours and posts of government throughout all the states of Europe.

In the rather heavy facetiousness of this dedication, it may be felt that we have the humanist at his petulant worst; but that is in a sense its importance. Hotman remained a humanist, trained in the school of Bourges, and his attitude to all systems of law remained that of a historian, modified in the direction of neo-Bartolism. Because he thought it necessary to study all systems of law for the essential principles that were in them, he regarded none of them as more than relatively important or valuable. He regarded neither custom nor Germanic law as containing anything essential, original or fundamental that any other system of law might not contain. Each must be studied critically, which implied a readiness to reduce it to the context of the society from which it had sprung. We shall meet him in a later chapter performing this operation in a search for the origins of feudal custom, and there too it will be apparent that he was less disposed to emphasize the Germanic element in European law than is sometimes suggested. But the point of immediate importance is that Hotman's historical thought, even in its confusions, reflects the duality of custom and written law that marked the French legal structure. It was reaction against the Cujacian school that made him a neo-Bartolist in his attitude to Roman law, and gave him some traces of a tendency to idealize custom; but in the last analysis it would appear that he extended the neo-Bartolist critical approach to custom as well. Because custom in France existed side by side with Roman law it was possible to envisage the two growing up together in a single historical process, and this powerfully checked any tendency to exaggerate the purity and antiquity of custom. There were myths of constitutional antiquity in French thought, but they were formed in other ways.[1]

[1] See Jacques Barzun, *The French Race* (Columbia, New York, 1932); and Franklin L. Ford, *Robe and Sword* (Cambridge, Mass., 1953), ch. 12, 'The Restatement of the *Thèse Nobiliaire*'. But see also Lemaire, *op. cit.*, for a fuller study of the concepts of an 'ancient constitution' prevailing in France.

Introductory: the French Prelude to Modern Historiography

It could not be maintained that the whole of French law was custom, and it was hard to maintain that custom was immemorial in any too literal sense of the word. But where nothing but custom existed, there might be no such checks on the development of its myths.

It is suggested therefore that law did much to determine the character of sixteenth-century historical thought in the various countries of Europe: that the historical thinking encouraged by the study of Roman law, for instance, was of a different character from that bred in the study of customary law, and that each nation's thought about its past—it might be said, each nation's relationship with its past—was deeply affected by the character of its law and the ideas underlying it. That is the case for the importance of jurists and constitutional antiquarians and controversialists in the history of historiography.[1] The remainder of this book is concerned with the legal historiography of England—with the sort of historical thought that developed in a country where only one system of law, and that essentially customary, seemed ever to have prevailed.

[1] Readers of Professor Momigliano's paper 'Ancient History and the Antiquarian' (in his book cited above, pp. 67-106) may like to consider whether the legal historians of this epoch did not occupy a place midway between the historian and the antiquarian as defined by him. They were not narrative historians, but neither were they collectors of facts about the past like the antiquarians. The nature of their subject forced them to consider questions of the relevance of past to present and even (if in a rudimentary form) of historical development. Nevertheless, the present writer suspects that Professor Momigliano exaggerates a little (pp. 77-8) the extent of the rapprochement between historians and antiquarians in the field of post-classical history, with which, of course, the lawyers and constitutionalists were mostly concerned. His book, it must be added, is of the greatest value to the history of historiography.

CHAPTER II

The Common-law Mind: Custom and the Immemorial

I

AS a key to their past the English knew of one law alone. It was possible for them to believe that, as far back as their history extended, the common law of the king's courts was the only system of law which had grown up and been of force within the realm; for the records and histories of England did not reveal that any other law had been of comparable importance. The common law was and had been the only law by which land was held and criminals deprived of life by their country, and by which consequently the greater part of men's secular rights and obligations were determined. Civil and canon law and law merchant could be regarded, especially after the Reformation, as systems borrowed from abroad and confined within limits by the common law; and, most significant of all, there were no *pays de droit écrit* in which civil law governed the main fabric of social life. Except in Ireland, Celtic law was forgotten, and local customs, like those of Kent, survived only because the king's courts recognized them. The English need not think, as the French must, that a different system of law existed alongside their ancient native custom, one which had a different origin, had been introduced into the land at a different time and had grown up along different lines. Once the French began to think historically of their written law, they were bound to make some extension of this way of thinking to their customary law as well, and this acted as a check to any tendency they may have had to represent the whole of their law as immemorial custom. But in England it was precisely this tendency which ran riot. The English supposed that the common law was the only law their land had ever known, and this by itself encouraged them to interpret the past as if it had been governed by the law of their own day; but in addition the fact that the common law was a customary law, and that lawyers defined custom in a way which heavily emphasized its immemorial character, made even more radical the English tendency to read existing law into the remote past. An inclination to do this, to interpret the past according to the ideas and institutions of the present, is probably common to all societies aware of their history; it can never be absolutely expunged from historical thought, and there have been times in the history of historiography when it has been altogether dominant. But the historical thought of seventeenth-century England is not merely an example of a universal tendency; it acquired much of its special character and its power over the English mind from the presence and nature of that uniquely English institution, the common law.

The interpretation which the English of this period made of their legal, constitutional and, consequently, national history was accordingly one which arose within the schools of the common law, spreading from them to become the general belief of the gentry they did so much to educate. As we shall see, some of its assumptions are also the basic assumptions of the common law, and there is a sense in which it is as old as that law or older. But deeply rooted though it was in medieval thought, for its formulation in the version which was to dominate the seventeenth century we should no doubt look to that recrudescence of inns-of-court and parliamentary activity, intellectual as well as practical, which marks the later Tudor period. It received its classic formulation soon after 1600 from Sir Edward Coke, who was born in 1552; but a common lawyer who was a mature man at the time of Coke's birth would not have thought quite as Coke was to do half a century later. He would have been far more aware of the civil law as a part of the English fabric, and far more open to the medieval concept of law as a thing universal, more important in its universal characteristics than in its local and municipal manifestations. His mind would probably have been less insular than Coke's, less massively convinced that English law was purely English and that the only purely English law was the common law; and his interpretation of English history would have differed accordingly. Between 1550 and 1600 there occurred a great hardening and consolidation of common-law thought, whether this arose as the common law sought to defend itself against aggressive conciliar rivals, or whether the effect of Tudor centralization was to deliver it from more rivals than it created and actually make it easier for it to regard itself as the sole and supreme system of law in England. Coke's thought does not read like that of a man on the defensive; he does not insist or argue that the common law is the only system that has ever prevailed in England, but takes it as much for granted as the air he breathes; and the assumption seems to be made no less instinctively by the other lawyers of his generation and by most of the royalists and parliamentarians of the mid-century. It is hard to believe that the common-law interpretation of history was consciously and polemically constructed; it is much easier to see it as the result of deep-seated and unconscious habits of mind; but a detailed study of Tudor common-law thought would be necessary to show how and when it came into being. All that will be attempted here is an analysis of the assumptions on which it was founded and built up in the reign of James I.

In the first decade of the new century, then, English lawyers were prepared to define common law as custom and to defend custom against written law in language which recalls certain French ideas of an earlier generation. Whether this was done as a direct reaction to the humanist and civilian criticisms described by Maitland, neither he nor Holdsworth has perhaps made absolutely clear;[1] but whatever the cause, Sir John Davies, then Attorney-General for Ireland, in dedicating his *Irish Reports* to Lord Chancellor Ellesmere in the year 1612, stated the case for common law and custom in prose of admirable clarity, which reveals some degree of unconscious kinship with the ideas of *Anti-Tribonian*.[2]

For the *Common Law* of *England* is nothing else but the *Common Custome* of the Realm: and a Custome which hath obtained the force of a Law is always said to be *Jus non scriptum*: for it cannot be made or created either by

[1] Maitland, *English Law and the Renaissance*; Holdsworth, *History of English Law*, vol. IV, pp. 252–93.

[2] All quotations from Davies in this chapter are from the unpaginated preface dedicatory to *Irish Reports* (*Les Reports des Cases & Matters en Ley, Resolves & Adjudges en les Courts del Roy en Ireland. Collect & digest per Sir John Davis Chivaler, Atturney Generall del Roy en cest Realm*), London edition of 1674. 'Davies' is the spelling favoured by *D.N.B.*

Charter, or by Parliament, which are Acts reduced to writing, and are alwaies matter of Record; but being onely matter of fact, and consisting in use and practice, it can be recorded and registered no-where but in the memory of the people.

For a Custome taketh beginning and groweth to perfection in this manner: When a reasonable act once done is found to be good and beneficiall to the people, and agreeable to their nature and disposition, then do they use it and practise it again and again, and so by often iteration and multiplication of the act it becometh a *Custome*; and being continued without interruption time out of mind, it obtaineth the force of a *Law*.

And this *Customary Law* is the most perfect and most excellent, and without comparison the best, to make and preserve a Commonwealth. For the *written Laws* which are made either by the Edicts of Princes, or by Councils of Estates, are imposed upon the Subject before any Triall or Probation made, whether the same be fit and agreeable to the nature and disposition of the people, or whether they will breed any inconvenience or no. But a *Custome* doth never become a Law to bind the people, untill it hath been tried and approved time out of mind, during all which time there did thereby arise no inconvenience: for if it had been found inconvenient at any time, it had been used no longer, but had been interrupted, and consequently it had lost the virtue and force of a Law.

Fortescue had long ago written that the laws of England must be the best in the world, because they were certainly the most ancient— older than those of Rome or Venice—and from the Romans to the Normans the rulers of the land had had ample opportunity to change them if they had not seen that they were good.[1] But his words, important as they are in the English cult of the law's antiquity, do not of themselves imply Davies's elaborate argument from the nature of custom, which has much in common with the sixteenth-century revolt against written law. Hotman had laid it down that law must be appropriate to the nature and circumstances of the people, and had hinted that the essential character of custom was such that it must satisfy this requirement. Davies made this explicit and proceeded to praise English customary law:

so framed and fitted to the nature and disposition of this people, as we may properly say it is connatural to the Nation, so as it cannot possibly be ruled by any other Law. This Law therefore doth demonstrate the strength of wit and reason and self-sufficiency which hath been always in the People

[1] *De laudibus legum Angliae*, ch. XVII.

33

of this Land, which have made their own Laws out of their wisedome and experience, (like a silk-worm that formeth all her web out of her self onely) not begging or borrowing a form of a Commonweal, either from *Rome* or from *Greece*, as all other Nations of *Europe* have done; but having sufficient provision of law & justice within the Land, have no need *Justitiam & judicium ab alienigenis emendicare*, as King *John* wrote most nobly to Pope *Innocent* the Third....

And—just as Hotman had revealed his pleasure in the unclassical terminology of French customary law—Davies wrote a defence of law French, admitting that it was a wholly artificial language which had never been spoken outside the English courts, but arguing that centuries of use had invested its words with meanings so exactly appropriate to the legal terms and ideas they were expected to convey that it could not possibly be replaced by any other language without serious loss to the law's intelligibility. The implication was that usage had made it more perfect than any mode of expression which the individual intelligence could devise. An idealization of custom was developing which would exalt its wisdom above that of the individual. The laws enacted by prince or parliament may grow obsolete, but custom must always be perfectly up-to-date, since if it had proved inadequate to the problems of the present age the people would simply have abandoned it. On the other hand, the fact that they have retained it shows that it has confronted and solved more problems over the centuries than the present age can hope to imagine. Written laws contain no more than the wisdom of one man or one generation, whereas custom in its infinite complexity contains the wisdom of many generations, who have tested it by experience, submitting it to a multitude of demands, and by retaining it have shown that it has proved equal to them all. Custom therefore embodies a wisdom greater even than the wisdom of parliament, for, says Davies, it has often happened that a statute has altered some fundamental rule of the common law and bred thereby such a multitude of inconveniences that it has had to be repealed. Last of all, custom is purely native: that the people are ruled by customary law is proof that they have evolved their own law 'out of their wisedome and experience' and disdained foreign borrowings, which—as well as being open to the reproaches which may be directed against any merely enacted law—would be derogatory to the people's glory and self-sufficiency.

All these arguments, including the defence of law French, are to be met with in Coke; the preface to his *Fourth Reports*, for instance, lists many statutes which have injudiciously altered the common law and been repealed in consequence. Coke's emphasis is less upon custom, in the pure sense in which Davies uses the word, than upon the activity of the judges in constantly refining the law, declaring its principles with even greater precision and renewing it by application to the matter in hand. But the idea of judge-made law is only a sophistication and extension of the idea of custom. The law which the judges declare is unwritten and immemorial, and Coke praises it for precisely the same reasons as Davies. It embodies the wisdom of generations, as a result not of philosophical reflexion but of the accumulations and refinements of experience. This is Coke's famous concept of 'artificial reason'; what speaks through the judge is the distilled knowledge of many generations of men, each decision based on the experience of those before and tested by the experience of those after, and it is wiser than any individual—even James I—can possibly be. In his much quoted burst of eloquence upon *Calvin's Case*, Coke declared:

we are but of yesterday, (and therefore had need of the wisdom of those that were before us) and had been ignorant (if we had not received light and knowledge from our forefathers) and our days upon the earth are but as a shadow in respect of the old ancient days and times past, wherein the laws have been by the wisdom of the most excellent men, in many successions of ages, by long and continual experience, (the trial of light and truth) fined and refined, which no one man, (being of so short a time) albeit he had in his head the wisdom of all the men in the world, in any one age could ever have effected or attained unto. And therefore it is *optima regula, qua nulla est verior aut firmior in jure, neminem oportet esse sapientiorem legibus*: no man ought to take it on himself to be wiser than the laws.[1]

As will appear further when we study the thought of Sir Matthew Hale, this concept of law is essentially Burkean.[2] There is a process by which society constantly adapts its institutions to the dictates of

---

[1] Coke, *Seventh Reports, Calvin's Case*; here from the edition of the *Reports* by Thomas and Fraser (London, 1826), vol. IV, p. 6. Subsequent references to the *Reports* (T.F.) are all to this edition.　　[2] Ch. VII, section III, below.

new situations. Institutions which have survived this process for a long time must be presumed to have solved innumerably more problems than the men of the present age can imagine, and experience indeed shows that the efforts of the living, even mustering their best wisdom for the purpose, to alter such institutions in the way that seems best to their own intelligence, have usually done more harm than good. The wisdom which they embody has accumulated to such a degree that no reflecting individual can in his lifetime come to the end of it, no matter how he calls philosophy and theoretical reason to his aid. These propositions may all be found in the writings of Coke, Davies and Hale, as well as in those of Burke. In the three former they depend unmistakably on the notion of custom, and if Burke owed any debt at all to preceding generations, the foundations of his thought were laid at the end of the sixteenth century, when the common lawyers learned to define their law as custom in opposition to written law.

But in saying this we come upon a paradox. If the idea that law is custom implies anything, it is that law is in constant change and adaptation, altered to meet each new experience in the life of the people; and it might seem that there was no theory more likely to lead to a historical conception of the nature of law. Yet the fact is that the common lawyers, holding that law was custom, came to believe that the common law, and with it the constitution, had always been exactly what they were now, that they were immemorial: not merely that they were very old, or that they were the work of remote and mythical legislators, but that they were immemorial in the precise legal sense of dating from time beyond memory—beyond, in this case, the earliest historical record that could be found. This is the doctrine or myth of the ancient constitution, which bulked so large in the political thought of the seventeenth century and furnishes this book with half its title. The present chapter and the next are devoted to studying the assumptions and the limitations of thought on which it was based.

The clue to the paradox lies in the fact that the concept of custom is ambiguous; Selden was never more suggestive than when he called the common law the English Janus. We may regard it as that which is in constant adaptation, and to do so will give rise to ideas that are unmistakably historical. But it is equally possible to regard it as that which has been retained throughout the centuries and derives its authority from its having survived unchanged all changes of circumstances; and once we begin to think of custom as unchanging, we must remember that it is also immemorial, for if it were known to be the work of some founder it would be written or statute law and not custom at all. The political thought of the age underlined this point heavily. The Middle Ages, often seeing no essential difference between written law and custom, had spoken quite happily of kings who ordained new customs and of the two or three lifetimes which qualified a law to be considered immemorial.[1] But by Coke's time the increasing activity of a nearly sovereign monarchy had made it seem to most common lawyers that if a right was to be rooted in custom and rendered independent of the sovereign's interference it must be shown to be immemorial in the full sense of 'traceable to no original act of foundation'. The idea of the immemorial therefore took on an absolute colouring, which is one of the key facts in Stuart historico-political thought. It ceased to be a convenient fiction and was heatedly asserted as literal historical truth; and the more that came to be known about remote ages, the more vigorously it was insisted that the law was before Abraham.

The common law was by definition immemorial custom. For hundreds of years before Coke and Davies it had been accepted, by an assumption common in medieval thought, that English law was *jus non scriptum* and that the function of the courts was to declare the ancient custom of the realm. Even statutes could be so interpreted, and Coke eagerly takes at least the earliest of them to be declaratory judgments. Innumerable decisions were consequently on record as declaring that everything which they contained, down to the most minute and complex technicality, had formed part of the custom of England from time out of mind; or at least so the common lawyers read them to mean, and this fact is at the root of their interpretation of history. They took everything in the records of the common law to be immemorial, and they treated every piece of evidence in those records as a declaration of what was already

[1] The classic discussion of the medieval ideas of custom and ancient law is in Kern, *Kingship and Law in the Middle Ages* (ed. Chrimes), Cambridge, 1939.

immemorial; so that the beginning of the records of the king's courts in the twelfth century was proof, not that those courts began at that time, but of their great antiquity, and it was usual and— given the presumptions—logical to add that if the earlier records had not been lost or stolen, they would prove the existence of the courts in times earlier still. But at however remote a date the series of records had begun, the common-law mind would still have taken their beginning as proof that at that time the laws were already immemorial; since *jus non scriptum* must by definition be older than the oldest written records.

The belief in the ancient constitution therefore rested on assumptions which were fundamental to the practice of the common law, and it had very great influence in a society whose political and social thinking were so largely dominated by this one law. It cannot therefore be regarded as the creation of any single mind. But Coke did more than any other man to summarize it and make it authoritative; at the same time he reveals the patterns of thought on which it was based with the clarity of truly representative genius. His historical thought could be described as founded on the presumption that any legal judgment declaring a right immemorial is perfectly valid as a statement of history. Thus in the preface to the *Third Reports*—his first published exposition of the view that the law was immemorial and the *locus classicus* of his methods of historical reconstruction—he selects a case from the books of assize of 26 Edw. III:

it appeareth that in a writ of assise the Abbot of B[ury] claimed to have conusance of pleas and writs of assise, and other original writs out of the King's courts by prescription, time out of mind of man, in the times of St Edmund, and St Edward the Confessor, Kings of this realm before the Conquest, and shewed divers allowances thereof, and that King H.I. confirmed their usages, and that they should have conusance of pleas, so that the Justices of the one bench, or the other should not intermeddle; out of which record (being now above three hundred years past) it appeareth that the predecessors of that Abbot had time out of mind of man in those Kings' reigns, (that is whereof no man knew the contrary either out of his own memory, or by any record or other proof,) writs of assise, and other original writs out of the King's Courts.[1]

[1] Preface to *Third Reports* (T.F. vol. II), pp. ix–x. Cf. *First Institutes* (8th ed. 1670), fol. 71 b, and *Second Institutes* (4th ed. 1671), pp. 22–5.

The Common-law Mind: Custom and the Immemorial

The fact—often paralleled—that a fourteenth-century abbot had alleged that he had precedents from pre-Conquest times, should remind us of the extreme antiquity and universality of this way of pleading and thinking in English society. Coke and his contemporaries were indeed only continuing and developing a habit of mind as old as the common law itself; but now he goes on,[1] in a way too full of antiquarian learning to be simply a continuation of medieval thought, to argue that since writs of assize have been proved immemorial and older than the Conquest, so too must be sheriffs, because the writs are directed to them; trials by the oaths of twelve men, since the writs instruct the sheriff to conduct them; the king's courts, since the writs are returnable into them; the court of chancery, since it issues the writs; and the entire science and practice of the common law, since, as Fitzherbert points out, the procedure to be followed when writs are issued provides the fundamental rules about which it is built up. Thus a judgment that one part of the law is immemorial is first taken with historical literalness that might have surprised some of the judges, and then made the basis of an argument that the whole of the law must be of equal antiquity. Coke uses a similar technique in the preface to the *Ninth Reports*, when, having proved to his satisfaction that there were parliaments before the Conquest, he proceeds to argue that there were representatives of the commons in them.

It is evident that there were tenants in ancient demesne before the Conquest; and for a certainty therein, and to know of what manors such tenants did hold, it appears by the book of Domesday, that all the tenants that did hold of any of those manors that were in the hands of King Edward, the son of King Ethelred, or of King William the Conqueror, were tenants in ancient demesne. And these tenants then had, and yet have these privileges amongst others, for that they were bound by their tenure to plow and husband, etc. the King's demesnes before and in the Conqueror's time, and therefore they were not to be returned Burgesses to serve in Parliament, to the end they might attend the King's husbandry the better.

2. They were not to be contributory to the fees to the Knights of Shires that served in Parliament: which privileges (though the cause ceaseth,)

---

[1] *Third Reports* (T.F. vol. II), pp. x–xii.

continue to this day: therefore there were Parliaments unto which the Knights and Burgesses were summoned both before and in the reign of the Conqueror.[1]

Here it is matter of record, rather than an actual judgment, on which the case is built up; but the procedure is exactly the same. The presence of tenants in ancient demesne in Domesday Book is taken to mean that they existed before the Conquest (and therefore from time out of mind); and their exemption from parliamentary attendance at a later date still is taken to prove the existence of a parliament with commons, both at the time of Domesday and before. The fact that Coke allows the unwary reader to assume that the parliamentary exemption is in Domesday is probably not proof of disingenuousness; he would simply take it for granted that what was mentioned at a later date must have been present at an earlier.

In the preface to the *Third Reports* Coke follows up the passage already cited with further proof of the law's antiquity, drawn from early British history as it was then understood.[2] Brutus of Troy, he said, the first king of Britain, was reputed to have drawn up a book of laws; so had King Dunwallo Molmutius, Mercia the queen of King Gwintelin, Sigebert of East Anglia, Alfred, Edward the Elder and reputedly many others, so that there had been at least seven books of the law (two of them Dunwallo's) before the Conquest. It is of importance to the understanding of this subject to note that it was not Coke's belief in fabulous kings out of Geoffrey of Monmouth which was primarily responsible for his belief in the antiquity of the law. He had his doubts about Brutus— 'I will not examine these things in a quo warranto; the ground thereof I think was best known to the authors and writers of them' —and his interpretation of the past was soon to survive unscathed the disappearance of the legendary Trojan and British kings from the stage of serious history. His references to Brutus and Dunwallo occupy second place after the proof of the law's antiquity founded on legal, not historical sources. Coke not only accepts a legal judgment dating a law from time out of mind as historically valid,

[1] Preface to *Ninth Reports* (T.F. vol. v), pp. xxi–xxiii.
[2] Preface to *Third Reports* (T.F. vol. II), pp. xiv–xx.

but he regards such statements as better historical evidence than those made by chroniclers. Where the courts have adjudged an institution immemorial and a historian alleges that it was set up in such a king's reign, Coke leaves little doubt that we are to think the historian wrong, and he urges the historiographers of his own day to consult a lawyer before making any statement about the history of the law.[1] He was not relying upon legendary histories, but using them to illustrate a proof that the law was immemorial which he drew from the thought of the law courts; and conversely, he was not seeking to derive the law from any mythical founder. When, with the aid of the *Mirror of Justices*, he had traced parliament back to the reign of King Arthur, he added: 'Not that this court and the rest were instituted then, but that the reach of his [Horn's] treatise extendeth no higher than to write of the laws and usages of this realm continued since the reign of that king.'[2] In the same way Davies had written:

> Neither could any one man ever vaunt, that, like *Minos*, *Solon*, or *Lycurgus*, he was the first *Lawgiver* to our Nation: for neither did the King make his own *Prerogative*, nor the Judges make the *Rules* or *Maximes* of the Law, nor the common subject prescribe and limit the *Liberties* which he injoyeth by the Law. But, as it is said of every Art or Science which is brought to perfection, *Per varios usus Artem experientia fecit*; so may it properly be said of our Law, *Per varios usus Legem experientia fecit*. Long experience, and many trials of what was best for the common good, did make the *Common Law*.[3]

The law was immemorial and there had been no legislator. In this respect at least common-law thought was independent of fashionable classical models. Its eyes were turned inward, upon the past of its own nation which it saw as making its own laws, untouched by foreign influences, in a process without a beginning.

---

[1] Preface to *Third Reports* (T.F. vol. II), p. xxiii; *Second Institutes*, p. 499. See Sir Roger Twysden, *Certain Considerations upon the Government of England* (Camden Society Publications, XLV, 1849, p. 23).

[2] Preface to *Ninth Reports* (T.F. vol. v), p. xi.

[3] Davies, preface to *Irish Reports*.

II

But if neither a putative Trojan nor a putative Arthurian origin was of much importance in this interpretation of legal history, there was one event in the English past over which the common lawyers expended floods of ink and burned much midnight oil. This was the Norman Conquest, the one great apparent breach in the continuity of the nation's history. The motives which spurred them to their unending denials that this event had caused any change in the essential character of the law were various: sheer patriotism furnished one, and Polydore Vergil, that gadfly of the older English historiography, another with his gibes at a law derived from the semibarbarous Normans and still uttered in their jargon; while, as we shall see, once the interpretation of history became involved in the struggle of king and parliament, a powerful political motive was added to the others. But from whatever point of view it was regarded, the idea that William I had carried out a systematic importation of new law cut right across the belief in custom and the immemorial that was coming to be an integral part of English political thought, and the common lawyers set out to deny it with all the resources of their learning and ingenuity. With Coke the argument that the courts, parliament or the law are immemorial often seems to be identical with the argument that they are pre-Conquest. Once over that stumbling-block, the rest may be taken for granted; and all the subtleties of the common-law technique of reading history backwards are called into play.

But Coke's endeavours were powerfully abetted by the conduct of the Normans themselves. While the main features of common-law historiography must be deduced from habits of mind peculiar to that profession, it remains true that the feeling that all rule must be by ancient law was one of the deepest-seated preconceptions of the medieval mind. It had seemed of scarcely less importance to the Normans than it did to Coke himself to maintain that they governed England according to the *laga Eadwardi*, and throughout the twelfth and thirteenth centuries a succession of political programmes had been expressed, by claimants to the throne or dissident barons, in the form of promises or demands to restore the good old law of Edward the Confessor. The story that among the Conqueror's first acts had been to codify and confirm the Confessor's law had found its way into most of the chroniclers; and not only this, but several ingenious and quite possibly sincere men had in and after the twelfth century sat down to supply the absence of any text of this law or the Conqueror's by composing the apocryphal *leges Edwardi Confessoris, Willielmi, Henrici Primi,* the chronicle of 'Ingulf of Croyland' (supposed to be an eye-witness of the confirmation), and so on. The edifice had been completed by the insertion in the coronation oath—where it remained until 1688—of a promise to observe the laws of St Edward. When the common lawyers began to write their histories, therefore, the belief that the laws of the last Anglo-Saxon king had been confirmed by the Conqueror and his Norman and Angevin successors had long been orthodox history, though the reprehensible Polydore had as usual expressed some doubts. Furthermore, William Lambarde had in his *Archaionomia* (1568)— one of the key books of the common-law interpretation—published the apocryphal *leges* in unbroken series with such genuine texts of Anglo-Saxon law as he had been able to collect. Coke, and nearly all other historians, accepted them at their own valuation; and as the authors of the *leges Confessoris* and the *leges Willielmi* (which were supposed to represent the Anglo-Saxon laws as amended by the Conqueror) had not unnaturally attributed to pre-Conquest times the feudal institutions, described in the Norman terminology of their own day and age, there was no sign in these apparently authoritative texts of any radical breach with the past at the Conquest. Coke indeed was able to make very extensive use of Lambarde's book to prove that institutions which had in fact been introduced by the Normans formed part of the immemorial law; and he employed with no less faith and frequency two other medieval apocrypha, the fourteenth-century *Modus Tenendi Parliamentum* and (with far less excuse) the lavishly fantastic *Mirror of Justices,* to attribute to the times of Alfred and Arthur the characteristic machinery of Angevin and Plantagenet monarchy. There are few pages of his *First* or *Second Institutes* on which one of these works is not cited.

The picture thus constructed of the early history of the law

43

is summarized by Coke—speaking in this for nearly every English-man of the seventeenth century—in the preface to the *Eighth Reports*.[1] Explaining that he has been asked whether the chroniclers agree with him that the law is immemorial, and first carefully re-minding us that the proofs drawn from the law itself stand in no need of their corroboration, Coke proceeds to narrate that William I swore to observe the ancient laws, ordered twelve men in each shire to state what they were, and summarized them, with a few emendations of his own, into a Magna Carta, the first of its kind, under the name of the 'laws of King Edward'. Henry I, promising at his accession to take away all evil customs, restored King Edward's laws in a purer form, and thereafter both Stephen and Henry II confirmed them anew in coronation charters. Matthew Paris says that John's charters contain little that is not in Henry II's charter or in those laws which are called King Edward's, not because the latter enacted them but because he reduced them to writing. All this, as Coke proudly points out, is extracted from medieval chroniclers; but to get its seventeenth-century flavour we have to read it in the belief that the whole apparatus of common law was immemorial. But the apocryphal *leges* and Lambarde's Anglo-Saxon dooms are not of course the common law; Coke describes them as statutes, but succeeds in some peculiar way in regarding their existence as proof of the antiquity of the unwritten law which they do not contain:

> ...by all which it is manifest, that in effect, the very body of the common laws before the Conquest are omitted out of the fragments of such acts and ordinances as are published under the title of the Laws of King Alfred, Edward the First, Edward the Second, Ethelstane, Edward, Edgar, Etheldred, Canutus, Edward the Confessor, or of other Kings of England before the Conquest. And those few chapters of laws yet remaining, are for the most part certain acts and ordinances established by the said several Kings by assent of the Common Council of their kingdom.[2]

The myth of the confirmations, as it may be called, culminates with Magna Carta (which Coke liked to say had been confirmed by more than thirty parliaments), and his treatment of it, both in the posthumously printed *Second Institutes* (1641) and in the Commons

[1] T.F. vol. IV, pp. iii–xi.
[2] *Ibid.* p. xi.

The Common-law Mind: Custom and the Immemorial

debates leading up to the Petition of Right, has received most attention of all his historical interpretations.[1] It has two aspects. In the first place he links the Charter, through Stephen Langton and Henry II, with the successive confirmations of the Confessor's law; and in the second he studies it clause by clause to prove that it enacts the main principles of common law and parliamentary liberty in his own day, so that the men of 1628 could believe that they were not only repeating the solemn act of 1215, but taking part in a recurrent drama of English history at least as old as the Conquest. This second process, by which Coke discovers the rights of parliament and property in a feudal document of the thirteenth century, was at bottom one with the greatest work of his life, the revitalization of the common law so that precedents and principles laid down by the king's courts in the attempt to govern a feudal society could be used and found apt in the freeholding and mercantile England of James I. Coke, as we shall see further in the next chapter, had no conception that in the early common law he was dealing with the law of a society organized upon feudal principles. Therefore—still on the presumption that the law declared what had been law always —he was able to identify the law of his own day with the law of the earliest records, just as he had established the doctrine that the latter contained what had been law since time out of mind before the Conquest. At this point the identification of past and present was complete, and the possibility that the idea of custom might give rise to ideas of law being in continuous development was altogether suppressed.

Such then—assuming that Coke, whose vast influence was after all partly posthumous,[2] may be taken as a safe guide to the thought

---

[1] *First Institutes*, fols. 80b–81b; *Second Institutes*, pp. 1–78; Faith Thompson, *Magna Carta: its Role in the Making of the English Constitution, 1300–1629* (Minnesota, 1948), part III in general and ch. XII in particular; H. Butterfield, *The Englishman and his History* (Cambridge, 1944), pp. 54–68.

[2] The first eleven books of the *Reports* were published between 1600 and 1615; the *First Institutes* in 1628 and revised in 1629. Coke died in 1634. The *Second Institutes* were published in 1642, the *Third* and *Fourth* in 1644 and the *Twelfth* and *Thirteenth Reports* in 1655 and 1658. But of those writings which reveal most of his historical mind only the *Second Institutes* are posthumous, and the writer's views on Magna Carta, which form perhaps their most

of his profession—seem to have been the main features of what may be termed the common-law interpretation of English history, the predecessor and to a large extent the parent of the more famous 'Whig interpretation'. It arose essentially from latent assumptions governing historical thinking, which had been planted deep in the English mind by centuries of practice of a particular form of law; but it possessed also a political aspect, the need to make a case for an 'ancient constitution' against the king; and though this book is designed primarily as a study, not of the uses which were made of it in political argument, but of the historiographical conditions which made its existence possible, the former question is an inseparable part of the latter. Only a very detailed study of seventeenth-century thought could fully reveal the variety of uses to which it was put, or enable us to estimate accurately its importance as compared with other forms of political discussion. But the greatness of that importance cannot be denied. Put very briefly, what occurred was that belief in the antiquity of the common law encouraged belief in the existence of an ancient constitution, reference to which was constantly made, precedents, maxims and principles from which were constantly alleged, and which was constantly asserted to be in some way immune from the king's prerogative action; and discussion in these terms formed one of the century's chief modes of political argument. Parliamentary debates and pamphlet controversies involving the law or the constitution were almost invariably carried on either wholly or partially in terms of an appeal to the past made in this way; famous antiquaries were treated as authorities of recognized political wisdom; and nearly every thinker noted for his contribution to political theory in its usual sense—Hunton, Milton, Lilburne, Hobbes, Harrington, Filmer, Nevile, Sidney: only Locke appears to be an exception among notable writers—devoted part of his pages to discussing the antiquity of the constitution. It would be possible to construct both a history of the

prominent feature, would already be well known from the parliamentary debates culminating in 1628. (See Thompson, *Magna Carta, passim.*) These facts would suggest that all Coke's historical opinions could have been well known while he lived, even if we do not suppose that he was giving voice to ideas already widely accepted.

ways in which historical thought was used in political argument, and a study of the ways in which historical and political theory were related in the minds of the men who wrote and thought in both modes. To the typical educated Englishman of this age, it seems certain, a vitally important characteristic of the constitution was its antiquity, and to trace it in a very remote past was essential in order to establish it securely in the present. We may therefore maintain that the historical thought which lay behind this belief helped to shape the mind of the century and will consequently help us to understand it.

It must be evident in the first place that historical thinking of the kind we have seen in Coke would make it possible to claim, with sincere and entire conviction, that many of the privileges or rights which parliament, or the courts of common law under a vigorous chief justice, desired to possess in the present had been theirs in the remote past. Thought of this kind encouraged the production, from legal or chronicle sources, of evidence of action taken in very distant times, which could then be identified with contemporary conditions and claimed as a precedent. This must very largely explain the intense interest taken in the production of remote precedents during every controversy of the period before the Civil War—as for instance during the *Ship-money Case*, when evidence from the reign of Egbert was produced and examined with perfect seriousness by both sides. But it would be insufficient to explain the seventeenth-century's habit of recourse to the past merely as a search for precedents, as an eager legal antiquarianism; it was plainly much more. To claim that a precedent exists is to claim that a system of law as old as that precedent is still in force, and the arguments used in the *Ship-money Case* implied Coke's principle that the law of England was of pre-Conquest antiquity. When it was claimed that a remote precedent existed for such a right, it might very well be claimed in addition that the right was of immemorial antiquity. When Elizabeth I's parliaments began to claim rights that were in fact new, they indeed produced precedents, but they did much more. They made their claim in the form that what they desired was theirs by already existing law—the content of English law being undefined and unwritten—and it could always be claimed, in the way that we have seen, that anything which was in the existing law was immemorial. The common lawyers began to rewrite English history on parliamentary lines in the Elizabethan House of Commons—Sir John Neale comments on the process[1]—and by the time of the Apology of 1604 the Commons were already insisting that the whole body of their privileges should be recognized as theirs by right of time immemorial. The search for precedents resulted in the building-up of a body of alleged rights and privileges that were supposed to be immemorial, and this, coupled with the general and vigorous belief that England was ruled by law and that this law was itself immemorial, resulted in turn in that most important and elusive of seventeenth-century concepts, the fundamental law. Much has been written about fundamental law by modern scholars in the light of the contrary theories of judicial review and parliamentary sovereignty,[2] but it does not seem to have been stated in so many words that if you had asked the representative seventeenth-century Englishman the question 'What is it that makes the fundamental law fundamental?' he might indeed have been embarrassed for an answer,[3] but would probably in the

[1] *Elizabeth I and her Parliaments, 1558–81* (London, 1953), pp. 155–6, 305–6, 407–10, 420. The case of Arthur Hall is the best-known example of controversy on this question; see H. G. Wright, *Life and Writings of Arthur Hall of Grantham* (Manchester University Press, 1919).

[2] The latest study is that of J. W. Gough, *Fundamental Law in English Constitutional History* (Oxford, 1955). It does not appear that the seventeenth-century habit of appealing to the past gives us much help in deciding how far it was believed that parliament declared law, or how far that it made new law. Plainly, the whole weight of the appeal to ancient custom would tend to make parliament think it was declaring law; but that does not mean that parliament was incapable of knowing when it was making new law, only that it could believe itself to be declaring old whenever it chose to do so. The preamble to the Act in Restraint of Appeals reminds us that there were no limits to its power to believe this, and that in fact the distinction is often meaningless.

[3] An interesting instance is that of 1641, when Edmund Waller asked what the fundamental laws might be, and was told by Maynard that if he did not know, he had no business to sit in the house. This incident reads as if Waller had succeeded in exploding the whole concept, but we should remember that Maynard probably identified the fundamental law with no single set of enactments, but with the entire body of unwritten customary law; to him, therefore, Waller's question would practically amount to a demand to be told what the laws of England were, and his retort may have been more of a

end have replied: 'Its antiquity, its character as the immemorial custom of England.' The adjective 'ancient' was used little less often than 'fundamental', was frequently coupled with it and (it may be suggested) could in the majority of cases have been substituted for it without serious loss of meaning. The fundamental law or constitution was an ancient law or constitution; the concept had been built up by the search for precedents coupled with the common-law habit of mind that made it fatally easy to presume that anything which was in the common law, and which it was desired to emphasize, was immemorial.

The content of the concept differed from time to time (as also from man to man): as parliament laid claim to new powers these were represented as immemorial and included in the fundamental law, and close study would probably also reveal that as later controversies, particularly those of the mid-century, gave rise to new political ideas and principles, these also were included. It would certainly reveal that as the century progressed assertions that the law was immemorial tended to be replaced by assertions that parliament, and especially a house of commons representing the property-owners, was immemorial. One of the underlying themes in the history of seventeenth-century political thought is the trend from the claim that there is a fundamental law, with parliament as its guardian, to the claim that parliament is sovereign. Books are still being written in the attempt to decide how far this transition was carried and at what times; but it seems to be fairly well agreed that it was both incomplete and largely unrealized. Parliament claimed its increasing powers in virtue of the fundamental law; when in 1642 its claims reached such a height as to become a claim to arbitrary sovereignty, it still alleged that these were substantiated by fundamental law. The lower house's claim to be sole sovereign often took the form of a claim that it was immemorial and therefore subject to no checks. The attempt at single-chamber despotism failed, and both the Restoration and the Revolution of 1688 could be represented as efforts to restore the fundamental law, rather than to

sincere explosion and less of a debater's trick than one at first supposes. But the occasion was the attainder of Strafford, and what was said is not to be scrutinized too closely. Gardiner, *History of England, 1603–1642*, vol. IX, p. 336.

establish the sovereignty of king in parliament. The concept of fundamental law therefore did much both to cloak and to delay the transition to a full assertion of parliamentary sovereignty. Granted the importance of fundamental law, and granted also that the concept rested on Coke's concept of ancient law, we have here perhaps the true importance of common-law historical thought in the seventeenth century.

To what ultimate political principle were men appealing when they made the claim that their rights formed part of a pre-Conquest constitution? Why did they think a law's antiquity made it binding in the present? Taking Coke as representative, we have analysed the assumptions and arguments on which that claim was based, and they have been shown to rest on the basic assumption that the law declared the immemorial custom of England. It was the idea of custom which convinced men that the law was ancient; the conclusion is a tempting one that it was as custom that they thought it was still binding. Coke and still more Davies do indeed seem to have thought at bottom in just this fashion; but does it follow that the average parliament man, barrister or pamphleteer, who made his appeal to 'our ancient and fundamental laws, our ancient constitution', was knowingly and deliberately appealing to the binding force of immemorial custom, and was clear in his mind what those words meant? It seems unlikely, yet it is hard to imagine what other ultimate basis his appeal could have had. No doubt for many it was enough to declare that the laws were ancient and fundamental, without troubling to inquire why that should make them binding. Some research, it seems, might profitably be done on the place which the concept of custom occupied in seventeenth-century thought. It appears to have been far less prominent and familiar in the scholastic and academic tradition of political discourse—the political theory of the text-books—even in the schools of natural law, than it was among common lawyers. If this impression is upheld, what are we to make of it? Was there some unifying body of assumptions, or were there more ways than one to approach political problems, arising in different intellectual milieux and stressing different basic concepts? and if this was so, which was the more representative and effective in seventeenth-century England?

The Common-law Mind: Custom and the Immemorial

To ask such questions, or suggest that they might be asked, is to raise in a new form the problem of the relations between historical thought of Coke's kind and academic political theory. Was the chief justice a political thinker and, if so, in what sense? But, however such a line of inquiry might turn out, it could probably be agreed that, even if a clearly thought-out concept of custom were proved to be not specially prevalent in the seventeenth-century mind, still the concept of an ancient constitution, very prevalent indeed, rested ultimately upon the idea of custom; and that, in this sense, common-law historical thought represented a most vigorous survival of the medieval concept of custom in English political thinking. As for the men who said 'this is the ancient law' without troubling to inquire on what juridical principle that law rested, they too were carrying on the tradition of many medieval minds, who lived so much surrounded by the notion of 'law' that they did not find it necessary to say very clearly from what authority—other than God or nature—the law in question derived.[1] In the common-law interpretation of history, it seems, we have a powerful stream of medieval thought flowing into the seventeenth and eighteenth centuries, its strength surviving at least until the coming of philosophical radicalism.

But the attraction which the concept of the ancient constitution possessed for lawyers and parliamentarians probably resided less in whatever ultimate principle provided its base, than in its value as a purely negative argument. For a truly immemorial constitution could not be subject to a sovereign: since a king could not be known to have founded it originally, the king now reigning could not claim to revoke rights rooted in some ancestor's will. In an age when people's minds were becoming deeply, if dimly, imbued with the fear of some sort of sovereignty or absolutism, it must have satisfied many men's minds to be able to argue that the laws of the land were so ancient as to be the product of no one's will, and to appeal to the almost universally respected doctrine that law should be above will. A later generation, we shall see, having witnessed

[1] This observation does not of course apply to most of the systematic political thinkers of the Middle Ages, but there must have been many who thought in the way here described.

with alarm the spectacle of a revolutionary sovereignty styling itself that of the people, and by no means anxious in consequence to derive the laws from the act of some original popular assembly, found in the ancient constitution the perfect argument for pre-Lockean Whigs; as when the Lords were told in 1688 that 'the original contract between king and people' consisted in the king's undertaking to maintain laws which he certainly had not made.[1] Once more we see how the concept of antiquity satisfied the need, still widely felt, for a rule of law which, like Magna Carta, 'would have no sovereign'. But it was an argument which fell far short of logical perfection. By the very vehemence with which they insisted that the laws were immemorial and not of the king's making, its champions tacitly conceded that if the laws were not immemorial they were of the king's making—since few were prepared to go to the quasi-republican length of asserting that the laws had preceded the kingly office and brought it into being[2]—and that if they were of the king's making the reigning king was sovereign over them. These conditional propositions appear to have been accepted more or less on all sides; some few tried to find a way round them but hardly any succeeded. The notion of historical relativity—the suggestion that the law still in force might indeed have been made by a king in some high and far-off time, but in conditions so remote that neither 'king' nor 'law' meant what they meant at the present day, and that consequently no conclusions could be drawn as to current rights and liberties—was after all still virtually unknown. Consequently, to prove that the laws of England had originated at a time within the memory of man was to suggest the existence at that time of some human sovereign possessing the right to make law; and the heirs of that sovereign could not be denied the right to unmake all that he had made. Once men had appealed to the immemorial, the laws must be either absolutely immemorial or subject to an absolute sovereign—there seems to have been no idea of a middle way. A polemical situation could therefore arise, in which to put forward any theory as to the origin of English law at a time

[1] See ch. IX, below.
[2] For the most part this argument belongs to the Civil War period and after.

within recorded human history could be interpreted, and even intended, as an argument in favour of absolute monarchy. We shall see this happening in 1681.[1] For their part, those who saw in the immemorial constitution a good argument for limiting the prerogative would sooner or later be compelled by the same logic to attribute to it an altogether fabulous antiquity, insisting that it could be traced in and before the remotest events known to contemporary historical thought, and denying, in essence, that its origins could ever be discovered by the historian.

The doctrine of antiquity was therefore most vulnerable to criticism, and some awareness of this must explain why those who believed in it were so tirelessly and monotonously insistent that the establishment of the Normans in England did not constitute a conquest. In theory, one can easily see why this should have been so. If the monarchy of England had ever been sovereign, it had been at that moment; and if Duke William, even for a single instant, had been an absolute ruler—if he had been king by *jus conquestus*—then it did not matter if he had maintained English law instead of introducing French, and it did not matter what charters and grants of liberties he had subsequently made to his new subjects; all that had been done—even to increase the sphere of freedom and law—had been done by virtue of his unfettered will, on which his grants depended and on which (transmitted to his descendants) the laws and liberties of England for ever afterwards must depend likewise. To admit a conquest was to admit an indelible stain of sovereignty upon the English constitution. A conquest was therefore not admitted in the age of Blackstone any more than in the age of Coke. William was no conqueror, said the lawyers and the antiquaries and the parliamentarians in chorus; he was a claimant to the crown under ancient law who had vindicated his claim by trial of battle with Harold, a victory which brought him no title whatever to change the laws of England. If he had done so, it was a lawless act without validity, put right within a few generations of his death by the coronation charters of his successors and by Magna Carta, which had restored and confirmed the immemorial law of the Confessor's time.

[1] Ch. VIII, below.

The Common-law Mind: Custom and the Immemorial

But the remarkable fact is that the contrary argument was very seldom put forward—certainly with insufficient frequency to justify the incessant refutations which appeared. A writer of 1680, William Petyt, casting about for names with which to substantiate his allegation that a conspiracy existed to establish absolute monarchy on the theoretical basis of a conqueror's right, was able to name none who had argued in this sense except 'one Blackwood, a Scotchman'—and, he might have added, a good deal of a Frenchman as well[1]—and Mr Christopher Hill, who believes that the conquest theory was a staple argument of pre-Civil War monarchism, can add to the mention of Blackwood only some half-hearted remarks by James I[2] and a few sentences of Laud's which appear to bear a rather different meaning.[3] The fact seems to be that the conquest theory was no more an essential part of pro-Stuart reasoning before the Civil Wars (or indeed after them) than was absolute sovereignty.[4] Those who supported what the Stuart kings were doing did not normally regard their ruler as a sovereign maker of law—however vigorously they might assert his prerogative—and consequently did not argue that the laws flowed from his will or that he ruled above the law as a conqueror—the two doctrines to which a theory based on historical criticism would have led. This conclusion makes it hard to explain why the opposition constantly thought it necessary to refute an argument which nobody was putting forward; but it reminds us that the belief in an immemorial law was not a party argument put forward by some clever lawyer as a means of limiting the king's prerogative: it was the nearly universal belief of Englishmen. The case for the crown was not that the king ruled as a

[1] W. Petyt, *Miscellanea Parliamentaria* (1680) and *The Antient Right of the Commons of England Asserted* (1680).

[2] Mr Hill's essay 'The Norman Yoke' is to be found in a volume entitled *Democracy and the Labour Movement* (Lawrence and Wishart, 1954). The relevant passage is on pp. 19–20.

[3] What Laud says, as quoted by Hill (*ibid.*), is that the Conqueror's following insisted on being governed by his will and would not accept the laws of St Edward; but in a generation or two 'they became English' and appealed to the ancient law to protect them against King John. This is hardly a claim to *jus conquestus* on behalf of the king.

[4] It will be argued later (chs. VII and VIII) that there is no serious attempt to derive the royal power from William's conquest until 1680–8.

sovereign and that there was no fundamental law, but that there was a fundamental law and that the king's prerogative formed part of it. The antiquity of the law and the denial of the Conquest are arguments scarcely less frequently or vigorously employed by crown lawyers, or at a later date by royalist pamphleteers, than by their opponents. It is too easily forgotten that there was a common-law case for the crown as well as against it, and the former case was expressed in the same language and based on the same assumptions as the latter. Consequently, the king's side was late, slow and half-hearted in developing any historical criticism of the doctrine of immemorial law. Later chapters of this book attempt to explain how they came to do so in the end; but the conclusion seems inescapable that English historical ideas—those, that is, on the constitution and its antiquity—were not created primarily by party polemics. They were, before all else, the result of assumptions latent in the common-law mind, themselves the result of centuries of practice and experience of a purely insular form of law: the product, in short, of English history itself, reflected in the character of the country's legal structure and shaping and limiting the way in which her lawyers thought. Those who wished to change them must do more than put forward a theory of sovereignty, founded on a doctrine of conquest or on the idea that kings were older than laws; they must destroy the limitations under which English historical thinking was carried on. What these limitations were is further explored in the following chapter.

CHAPTER III

The Common-law Mind: the Absence of a Basis of Comparison

COKE'S mind, it is clear, was as nearly insular as a human being's could be. He saw the law he idolized as the immemorial custom of England, and he imagined it as being immemorial purely within the island. For this reason his doctrine of ancient law should be sharply distinguished from another contemporary belief, at this time spreading in popularity: that the liberties of western Europe, including the English law and parliament, were derived from the 'Goths', as the early Germans were then termed. An American scholar, S. L. Kliger, has lately shown[1] that this belief was held in England, and in common-law circles, from a time as early as 1567, when Rastell seems to have adopted it; but it is not to be found in Coke. When the latter quotes from Tacitus' *Germania*, ever a favourite work with believers in early Teutonic liberty, it is 'concerning the Antiquity of descents which the Germanes had agreeable with the ancient Laws of the Britons, continued in England to this day'.[2] The purely insular character of his ideas could hardly appear more clearly; the law is immemorial in Britain and ancient Continental law merely happens to agree with it. Moreover, as we have seen, when he has traced a law back to the time of some ancient king, whether Alfred or Arthur, he never fails to add that this king was merely confirming what was already immemorial, a habit scarcely reconcilable with the theory that the law was imported by Hengist. Contemporary Saxon scholarship, the work of Nowell, Verstegan and Camden, with its tendency to idealize the Saxons as beneficent conquerors and derive many things from them, seems to have made little impact on Coke; he shows no special interest in the Saxons as a people, and if they

---

[1] *The Goths in England* (Cambridge, Mass., 1952); for Rastell see pp. 24–5.
[2] Coke, *Second Institutes*, p. 7.

figure prominently in his writings this is because the need to prove the law older than the Conquest renders it important to show that every feature of later law can be discovered in their time. But Coke would never have been content to stop with the Saxons; for him the law was immemorial and the Saxons only one stage on the journey into its ever-receding past. He plunged into British and Trojan antiquities, in which probably even he only half believed, rather than admit that the law had a beginning. Contemporary Saxonists could criticize him for this; we shall see how Spelman used the similarities between Anglo-Saxon and early Germanic law to argue that the laws of England were less ancient and less native than sometimes supposed.[1] To be a Teutonist was to think differently from Coke, to derive English law from a Continental instead of a purely insular source. His thought owed little or nothing to the Gothic school, and was built entirely on the single assumption that the common law was the immemorial custom of England.

Mr Kliger is constrained to remark in a footnote that though Coke was 'strong for the common law', he does not figure importantly as a 'Gothicist'.[2] This is certainly true; but if so overpowering a figure as the chief justice was no 'Gothicist', that fact alone would seem sufficient ground for supposing that common-law and 'Gothic' thought were two different, if intermingled, lines of intellectual development. But Mr Kliger sometimes appears to be treating every seventeenth-century reference to the existence of law and parliament among the Anglo-Saxons as evidence of 'Gothicism'; and the agreed fact that Coke stressed Anglo-Saxon possession of these things without being a 'Gothicist' should show that the distinction exists and ought to be maintained. To work it out fully would be difficult, because it would involve deciding and proving whether insular 'Cokean' thought or 'Gothic' thought was more important and characteristic in seventeenth-century England, as well as keeping track of what were doubtless many occasions on which the two were blithely combined and confused by persons unaware of the different foundations on which each rested. But the distinction exists: there can be no reconciling a view which insisted on the antiquity of the law within the island and which

[1] Below, pp. 96-7.   [2] *The Goths in England*, p. 122 n. 19.

could not have survived in minds aware of the similarities between early English and early Continental law, with one which based itself on these similarities to argue that English law had once formed part of a body of barbarian institutions common to all western Europe. Contemporaries intent only on asserting the antiquity of the law might combine the two; the historian of ideas must keep them, initially at least, distinct.

This book is concerned with a series of writers who followed and argued with one another throughout the century, in a continual debate which appears to possess a fair degree of logical unity; but it so happens that in their writings the Gothic idea does not figure at all prominently.[1] All can be explained on the assumption that the common-law writers took their law to represent the immemorial custom of their country and did not derive it from any source outside their own coasts. Without, therefore, any necessary implication that 'Gothic' thought was unimportant in seventeenth-century England, it is henceforth neglected; and a pattern of ideas—asserted to have been at least of no less importance and to have existed on a basis relatively untouched by 'Gothicism'—is worked out as a contribution to some larger history of English thought.

Maitland, on more than one occasion,[2] observed that the principal defect of the common lawyers' historical and legal thought was their ignorance of any law but their own, and added that some degree of comparative knowledge was an essential prerequisite of historical understanding where the law was concerned. Like many of Maitland's remarks in this field, this is a highly compressed judgment in which several meanings are hidden. It will help the progress of this study to distinguish some of them and place them in order.

In the first place, it must already be evident that the presumption that the law declared what was already immemorial would have been quite impossible if more than one system of law had obtained in England in the way in which they did in France. If it had been known that two laws had existed side by side and that they had

---

[1] Harrington is an exception (see ch. VI), but he is not engaged in the controversy for or against the ancient constitution.

[2] *Constitutional History of England*, pp. 142–3; *Collected Works*, I, p. 489.

competed and conflicted with, and borrowed from, one another, it would have been an inescapable conclusion that each law had reached its present state as a result of a complicated process whose stages could be dated and character known. If, for example, the civil law had been more than an importation and had taken territorial hold and competed with the common law as an alternative means of judging the same range of matters, it might have been evident three centuries before Maitland that civilian principles were embedded in the common law and had been used to build it up in its early stages. As it was, neither Fulbecke nor Cowell succeeded in bringing out this truth—perhaps because the *mos Italicus* prevailed among English civilians and they seem to have known little of the historical method of the Frenchmen—and Selden and the whole common-law school expressly denied it. No system of law was so constantly before the eyes of the English as to compel the realization that its principles had played a part in the creation of their own law.

But for the seventeenth-century mind, to be compelled to study the history of two laws in contact gave rise to historical ideas more far-ranging than this; and that stimulus too the English were denied. A partial exception which nevertheless illustrates this rule is to be found in the works of that Sir John Davies whose eulogy of custom we have already studied. In 1612, two years before the *Irish Reports*, he published *A Discoverie of the True Causes why Ireland was never entirely Subdued, nor brought under Obedience of the Crowne of England, untill the Beginning of His Maiesties happie Raigne,*[1] and in it he analysed the shortcomings of English policy since Henry II under two principal heads. The first is the failure to achieve a complete military conquest, and this Davies explores in some detail: though he knows little about medieval military organization, he utilizes the Tower, Westminster and Dublin Castle records in an attempt to estimate the number of soldiers on various expeditions from the arrangements made for their pay.[2] But the second aspect of his theme is the failure to bring Ireland at an early time under the rule of English law. Davies quotes Bodin for the view that a prince

[1] All quotations are from Davies, *Discoverie etc.* (London, 1747); reprinted from the edition of 1612.
[2] *Discoverie*, pp. 12, 23–6, 39, 45, 70.

is not sovereign where others (in this case the Irish chiefs) give law without reference to him;[1] but he carries the consequences of failure to impose the common law much further. He recognizes that the Irish are a historical paradox: they are far from an uncivilized people, yet their social life is barbarous.

> For, though the Irishry be a Nation of great Antiquity, and wanted neither wit nor valour; and though they had received the Christian Faith, above 1200 yeares since; and were Lovers of Musicke, Poetry and all kinde of learning; and possessed a Land abounding with all thinges necessary for the Ciuill life of man; yet (which is strange to bee related) they did never builde any houses of Bricke or stone (some few poor Religious Houses excepted) before the raigne of King *Henrie* the second, though they wer Lords of this Island for many hundred yeares before and since the Conquest attempted by the English.... Neither did any of them in all this time, plant any Gardens or Orchards, Inclose or improve their Lands, live together in setled Villages or Townes, nor made any provision for posterity....[2]

Davies finds the explanation of this in the 'unreasonable' inheritance customs which prevail under Irish brehon law, particularly in that of tanistry and the division of the inheritance among the heirs, legitimate and illegitimate, which he calls by the Kentish name of gavelkind. These have given rise to constant civil war over the succession to chiefdoms, and a state of things in which no man's inheritance is safe and no material progress possible. Now that Ireland is conquered and the king's writ runs everywhere, the brehon law of tenure and inheritance must be replaced by common-law tenures which the royal courts will protect and which will guarantee a sensible system of primogeniture (for gavelkind 'must needs in the end make a poore Gentility'[3]); and the Irish will learn husbandry and swiftly become as peaceable and prosperous as the Welsh have done in similar circumstances.[4]

In Ireland Davies had before his eyes two laws and two incompatible social systems. He was therefore able to observe, first, that each law consisted essentially of a particular way of holding, inheriting and doing service for land; and second, that from

[1] *Discoverie*, pp. 17–18. [2] *Discoverie*, pp. 170–1 *et seq.*
[3] *Discoverie*, p. 172.
[4] *Discoverie*, pp. 120–2, 131–3. Davies himself was of Welsh descent.

observance of one or other system of law there followed consequences in every department of economic and social life. He can be seen applying these two ideas to the history of the Anglo-Irish, whom (rather than the 'mere' Irish) he rightly saw to be the key to the medieval story of Ireland; and it is in his treatment of them that his historical thought is most highly developed. Because the medieval kings failed to keep sufficient forces in Ireland, it fell to the Anglo-Irish lords to raise and maintain men. Unable to pay or equip them out of their own resources, they had recourse to the Irish custom of 'coign and livery' and simply quartered them on their tenants. English yeomen settlers refused to endure this and returned to England in large numbers, but the Irish expected nothing better, and it became to the lords' interest to stock their lands with Irish tenants whose tenure and services were those prescribed by brehon law. The lords thus came to stand in exactly the same relation to their tenants as an Irish chief, and by natural consequence they adopted Irish customs, dress and language.[1] Even if they did not join the ranks of the *Hibernis ipsis Hiberniores*, they became a class neither enemies to nor servants of the crown. The conquest of the island, originally held up because the king had not sent forces sufficient to carry it out, was now much further delayed. The lords discovered an interest in excluding the Irish from the benefits of English law[2] and keeping up a constant state of border warfare, because these conditions brought them franchises and delegations of royal authority from a king whose power they had ceased to advance; but they were equally interested in discouraging further royal conquests, because if all Ireland were brought under the king's writ the courts of common law would give their tenants justice even against themselves.[3] If their power were threatened by royal activity they did not hesitate to rebel and even to Hibernicize.[4] Thus the mere Irish, the Hibernicized English and the Anglo-Irish maintained a semi-chaotic balance of forces from which the chief sufferers were the populace and the royal power. It was for these reasons that no solution existed short of the systematic conquest of

[1] *Discoverie*, pp. 29–32, 56.   [2] *Discoverie*, pp. 99–120, 133–4.
[3] *Discoverie*, pp. 144–6.
[4] *Discoverie*, pp. 147–55 *et seq.*, 183–227.

the whole country, carried out by forces organized, maintained and commanded from England and aimed at making the king's writ run everywhere and ultimately at replacing brehon land law with common-law tenures which the king's courts would recognize and protect. The glory of Mountjoy and James I was to have achieved the former and prepared the way for the latter—work in which Davies was himself engaged.

Specialists in Irish history will no doubt find faults in Davies's analysis—though it may still be read with profit—but it remains perhaps the most outstanding piece of historical writing achieved by an Englishman in James I's reign. Davies describes men's actions in terms of the social system of which they form part, and shows how the Anglo-Irish were caught between two such systems and reacted by creating a border world of their own, which possessed the strength of neither but kept an uneasy balance between them. They were compelled to do this by the military weakness of the English government, and when this deficiency was remedied their world was at an end. Davies writes like this only because he views Ireland, in his own day and for long past, as the battleground of two laws, and is aware that each law can be reduced to a particular manner of holding land and doing military service for it, but on the other hand has the widest consequences in every department of life —so wide that the whole history of the Anglo-Irish, of their agriculture, speech and habits as well as of their political conduct, can be written in terms of their adherence to one or other law. Such were the effects which contemplation of a nation's history as comprising more than one system of law could have on historical thought.[1]

But Irish history was remote and alien, and brehon law had come into contact with common law only when the latter was already well developed. It presented no striking points of resemblance, no principles of its own which might be found embedded in the com-

---

[1] It might be observed here that Davies's ideas represent a definite tradition among English officials (and especially lawyers) in Ireland; many of his points are taken from a manuscript treatise on the 'Decay of Ireland' written by Baron Finglas in Henry VIII's reign, and he seems to have used other similar works. (For Finglas, see *D.N.B.*; his treatise was published in 1770.)

mon law and suggest new ideas as to how the latter had been built up; for in that process brehon law had of course played no part. Davies's Irish researches therefore had no effect whatever upon his thought about English legal history; as we have seen, two years after the *Discoverie* he was able to repeat unhesitatingly the theory of immemorial law and give almost classical expression to its underlying assumptions. His English and his Irish writings compared, therefore, underline the point that was made at the beginning of this chapter: there was nowhere within the dominions of the English crown or within the four seas of Britain a rival system of law which might be seen to have radically influenced the growth of the common law and thus compel Englishmen to think that their law had grown up under varying influences and at varying times. Until they were thus brought to think of the law as a product of history they would go on accepting its assumption that every record, judgment and statute was a declaration of immemorial custom. But no such basis of comparison was to be found within the British Isles. Civil law was an exotic; Scots law too little unified and articulate for the purpose;[1] Irish law the product of a wild and uncomprehended society. None had played a discernible part in English legal history, which, since the records began, revealed nothing but the self-perpetuation of the common law of the king's courts.

It was the kernel of Maitland's contention, therefore, that a basis of comparison must be found outside Britain. Until English law was viewed as part of the law of western Europe, none of the influences which had shaped its development could be discerned, and consequently no historical analysis of its growth was thinkable. The root of Coke's thought was his firm belief that the law was a purely insular product, and as far back as the records extended he was right; during all that period English law had received no important access of ideas from outside. The first comparative attack on common-law history, consequently, was unlikely to be made by the common lawyers themselves, engrossed in the study of their own records; and it must be made at a point in time belonging to the prehistory of the common law, when England could be shown

[1] However, the works of Sir John Skene were useful to Spelman; see ch. v, below.

to have received from Europe some at least of those institutions and ideas out of which the common law was afterwards built up. The most recent obvious example of such an occasion—and the most important of all—was the Norman Conquest. The common law was above all a law regulating the tenure of land, and the rules of tenure it contained in fact presupposed the existence of those military and feudal tenures which had been imported by the Normans; but this fact had been forgotten and could only be rediscovered by comparing English law with those continental laws which were avowedly feudal—since even the meaning of the word had been largely forgotten in England. When this was done, it became evident that a large part of English law could be identified as based upon a form of tenure no older than the Conquest and distinguished from those elements in the law which were older; and by a secondary operation, that since many of the obligations and ideas which had once flowed from feudal tenure no longer obtained in England, some kind of distinction must be drawn between the law of the twelfth century and the law of the seventeenth. These consequences were far greater in importance than those of the near-contemporary discovery that Anglo-Saxon law was so like that of the continental barbarians that it could be no older in England than the fifth century A.D. This discovery abolished Brutus and Arthur as lawgivers for all time, but the Anglo-Saxons remained a people of the dawn about whom legends clustered; and by a blending of the myth of immemorial law with that of Gothic liberty, it was possible as it were to transfer 'time beyond memory' to the primitive German forest. On the whole, therefore, the discovery of a Germanic element in early English history encouraged the spread of myths rather than checking them. But with the introduction of Norman feudalism, brought in when highly developed and imposed on an already articulate society by a single catastrophic act of conquest, no such devices were possible; and English historiography has oriented itself about that conquest ever since. The rediscovery of feudalism—which Maitland has permanently associated with the name of Sir Henry Spelman[1]—had other consequences, which must be considered in their place; but the next few chapters are concerned

[1] *Constitutional History, loc. cit.*

with the conditions under which it was made. First, then, we must examine the thought of the common lawyers on the subject.

Coke had administered one of his more resounding rebukes to the memory of Hotman, who had in his *De feudis commentatio tripertita* spoken disrespectfully of Littleton's *Tenures*; and Maitland pointed out that this was probably connected with Littleton's definition of what Hotman saw to be the *feudum*:

> Feodum idem est quod haereditas, et simplex idem est quod legitimum vel purum, et sic feodum simplex idem est quod haereditas legitima vel haereditas pura.[1]

As late, then, as the opening years of the seventeenth century no alternative to this definition was accepted by the chiefs of the common law. Sir Thomas Smith had indeed attempted to suggest that the word was current in continental law-schools in a very different sense, to which English jurists ought to pay some attention; but the rejoinder had instantly been made that Littleton's definition was the only one valid in English law.[2] This as far as it went was perfectly correct, but to accept it unquestioningly was the sign of a radical deficiency in the historical knowledge of English lawyers; one, however, which was a natural product of English history. Over the centuries, the courts of common law had operated to rob English custom and its language of any meaning except that which they themselves recognized, so that *feudum*, in the present case, had come to mean nothing more than a piece of land held in a tenure which the courts recognized as heritable according to certain fixed rules—the subject of most of Littleton's *Tenures*. It was no longer thought of as a piece of land given and received in a special way between lord and vassal, a consequence of the relationship expressed in homage, involving the vassal in the performance of certain express or implied services and radically affecting the way in which justice was done between the two men. Yet tenure *in capite*, homage,

---

[1] Hotman, *Opera*, ed. 1599, vol. II, p. 913; Coke, *First Institutes*, lib. I, cap. I, sect. I, and preface to *Tenth Reports*; Maitland, *English Law and the Renaissance*, pp. 12–14 and n. 29.

[2] See L. Alston's edition of Smith's *De republica Anglorum* (Cambridge, 1906), pp. xlvi, li, 133–7.

knight service, a multitude of usages incidental to the *feudum*, survived in England to a greater or lesser extent and were known to the common law and commented on by its learned men, even while the meaning of the relationship upon which all had been founded was now quite forgotten. Coke and Littleton, therefore, treated these things not as consequences of the vassal's homage and the lord's grant, but simply as part of the immemorial custom of England, known to be such because recognized by the courts. It is usual, and quite correct, to say that Coke knew nothing of feudal law; but he knew that doing homage was distinct from taking an oath of allegiance, though the two commonly went together.[1] He knew that it was legal dogma that all the land in England was held of some lord by some service, and ultimately of the crown, so that the tenant might have a hierarchy of lords above him.[2] He knew that the tenant could not alienate parcel of his fee to the prejudice of the lord's right to distrain in any part of it for the services due him.[3] He knew that knight-service was a thing common to many nations, and that in every language but English the word for knight reflected the fact that he was bound to serve on horseback.[4] He knew all these things and a great deal besides; in fact, it could well be maintained that he knew all there was to know about feudal law in England, except the single fact that it was feudal. Since his definition of the *feudum* was also Littleton's, he could not deduce all these things from its nature, and therefore saw very little connexion between them. He knew that they were all linked in a general way with lordship and tenure, but did not know that the characteristics of the *feudum* explained them all and that they formed a distinct class of legal phenomena, to which some such adjective as 'feudal' could properly be applied. To him their only essential characteristic was that the courts of England recognized them as custom; they were in no way distinguished from any other part of the law so recognized.

He could not therefore think historically of this element in the common law. It is true that when he writes of the law that we

---

[1] *First Institutes*, 8th ed., fol. 65.
[2] *Ibid.*
[3] *Ibid.* fols. 43a–43b.
[4] *Ibid.* fol. 74b.

should call feudal he shows some signs of knowing that he is dealing
with a state of things now past. He is aware that lords no longer
exact homage from their tenants—though he deplores this and
thinks that they could still do so if they chose[1]—or lead them to
battle in the king's wars.[2] He recognizes that tenure *in capite* was
once an indispensable adjunct to territorial titles and baronies, but
now is so no longer;[3] and he knows that the legislation of Edward I
brought about important departures from the law of tenure described by Bracton.[4] But this awareness of change rests upon general
impressions and is quite unsystematized. Coke never comes near
to saying that these things were based on the *feudum* and that with
the *feudum* they declined. What is more serious, since he does not
regard these institutions as feudal, but merely as part of immemorial
custom, he takes them too to be immemorial and dilates upon
their antiquity. On the authority of the *Mirror of Justices* he states
that the first kings of the realm, notably King Alfred, enfeoffed the
barons with their lands and gave them the right to hold courts
baron;[5] and as we have already seen, with the aid of the apocryphal
leges printed by Lambarde, there is something like a wholesale
attribution of Norman feudal usages to the times before the Conquest.[6] It is likely that no other shortcoming in their historical
knowledge did more to make the common lawyers' interpretation
of history possible than their ignorance of the *feudum* and feudalism,
and here a word should perhaps be spoken about Coke's alleged
credulity. Certainly he was a credulous man, in the sense that he
had always far too passionate and extreme a conviction of the
truth of the case he was pleading,[7] and beyond doubt that affected
his treatment of history; he ought, for example, to have smelt one

[1] *Ibid.* fol. 68 a.

[2] *Ibid.* fol. 71 a. Note that Coke is here talking of the indenture system.

[3] *Ibid.* fol. 83 b; *Second Institutes*, 4th ed., pp. 5–6.

[4] See the treatment of these statutes in *Second Institutes* generally.

[5] *First Institutes*, fols. 58a–58 b.

[6] See both *First* and *Second Institutes, passim*. A partial exception is to be
found in *Fourth Institutes, sub* 'Court of Wards and Liveries' (ed. London,
1889, pp. 190–3), where Coke admits that wardship and marriage were imposed by the Conqueror, though knight service was already ancient.

[7] His conduct in the *causes célèbres* of Raleigh and Overbury would seem to
bear this out.

or two of the horde of rats which populate the pages of the *Mirror*. But if the interpretation of his historical thought put forward in this chapter and the last is correct, it must follow that he was largely the prisoner of intellectual conditions imposed upon his age by the whole course of English law and history. There was an enormous weight of tradition and evidence supporting the view that the law was immemorial; while as long as Littleton's definition of the *feudum* was accepted, the feudal element in English law could not be identified, much less treated historically. The whole power of the 'Edward the Confessor' myth supported the belief that there was nothing in Anglo-Norman law which had not been in Anglo-Saxon, and until a new definition of the *feudum* was adopted, and its implications pressed home in defiance of all orthodoxy, this belief must remain. Such a new definition would never be found by study of the common law alone. Littleton's authority was too great and 'idem quod haereditas' appeared a perfectly satisfactory account of *feudum* as the common law had always used the term. The stimulus to new thought must come from outside.

We have now almost arrived at the full inner meaning of Maitland's remarks on this question. English lawyers would never attain to a historical view of their own law by study of its records alone, since these revealed no important changes in the course of their history and nothing interfered with the presumption that the record declared the immemorial custom. But, as Maitland pointed out in the *Constitutional History*, comparison of English with continental law would reveal that the former contained certain principles, institutions and usages common to nearly every law of western Europe, and that many of them were those known outside England as 'feudal' and related to a definition of *feudum* very unlike Littleton's. This discovery must lead to the realization that the myth of the immemorial must be abandoned, since an important element of English law was of foreign origin and had been brought in by some European people among whom it had grown up. Moreover, said Maitland in another context,[1] what was needed was 'a theory of feudalism': as the common law's definition of *feudum* could not be employed as a basis on which to explain the whole range of

[1] *Collected Works*, vol. I, p. 489.

feudal phenomena, another definition, drawn from continental law, must be put in its place, so that an entire sector of the common law would be interpreted by a principle which it did not itself contain. When English law was compared with continental law, the thought of English lawyers would be stimulated by a graft from abroad. Of the resistance which this process would meet in England Maitland said nothing; but we must now investigate the way in which it was set going.

CHAPTER IV

The Discovery of Feudalism: French and
Scottish Historians

IT is one of the paradoxes of European historiography that the
most recent authority on the character of feudalism, Professor
F. L. Ganshof, should have laid it down that the feudalism of
Lombardy can no longer be regarded as typical of that form of
society as we see it in European life as a whole.[1] A paradox because
it was through the study of Lombard feudal law that the Renaissance historians first became aware of the existence of feudalism—
though so abstract a term lay beyond their vocabularies[2]—as a
complex and variable set of institutions, whose place in the general
pattern of European law (and, therefore, in history) required to be
explained. The historians of law in western Europe, as we have seen,
were students of written law before they turned to the unwritten
customs and the archival deposits of particular regions; and
Lombard feudalism possessed, in the *Libri Feudorum*, the only
written systematization of feudal law which had become part of
the general legal heritage of Europe. To the original Milanese
studies of the law of the *feudum*, compiled in the twelfth century,
had been added a number of imperial constitutions, chiefly
Salian and Hohenstaufen, bearing upon the feudal law of descent
and forfeiture; and the *Libri Feudorum* had thus a peculiar authority for any European lawyer concerned with the interpretation
of these matters. Though they were hardly working or enforce-

---

[1] F. L. Ganshof, *Feudalism* (*Qu'est-ce que la féodalité?*), Eng. trans. by
P. Grierson (London, 1952), p. 60.

[2] Terms such as 'feudalism', 'féodalité', seem not to occur in any of the
writers discussed in the present volume. They speak only of 'the feudal law',
'jus feudale', which is thought of as a single set of institutions arising in
Lombardy and disseminated throughout the West. The word 'feudalism'
has, however, been used on occasion in the following attempt to convey their
thought to the modern reader.

able law anywhere, they had doctrinal authority in most lands where there was feudalism; it was recognized that the *feudum* was a universal institution, and that the Lombard books, in virtue both of the clarity of the original expositions and of the authority of the imperial decrees which they contained, possessed the status of universal law. They were, in effect if not formally, part of the *Corpus Juris Civilis*, and as such were glossed by Bulgarus in the thirteenth century and were the subject of *Summae* by Hugolinus and Odofredus and *Commentarii* by Baldus, Jason and others.[1]

In the southern and south-eastern provinces of the kingdom of France they were cited and studied with particular attention—less because these lands were strongly feudal in their law and character than because, formerly associated with the empire, these were *pays du droit écrit*. When therefore the French humanist school of legal scholars in the sixteenth century set about their work of textual criticism and historical interpretation, the *Libri Feudorum* received their attention. Both Cujas and Hotman produced critical editions —Cujas adding new texts to the compilation in 1567—and Hotman was able to quote the opinions (with which he disagreed) of a formidable array of European scholars, including Budé, Zasi, Connan, Torelli and Du Moulin. It is characteristic of both Hotman and his age that the context in which he quoted them was a debate on the origins of the *feudum*, and this contention arose at a most fruitful time. Legal scholarship, as we have seen, was willing and able as never before to turn aside from the history of the Roman texts to explore the customary and barbaric elements in European law, and the legal foundations of French society and monarchy were being investigated, alike by civil and by customary lawyers, with close attention to the diverse and multiracial origins of the rights of monarch and people. The study of the *Libri Feudorum*, therefore, swiftly passed the limits of merely textual clarification. It was recognized as presenting the problems of explaining exhaustively the social arrangements which arose when a fee was given and received, and of ascertaining the place occupied by this phenomenon in the tangled Roman and Germanic history of Europe. The

[1] Declareuil, *Histoire du droit français à 1789* (Paris, 1925), pp. 858–9.

systematic thoroughness of the medieval Lombard lawyers made it possible to arrive at a definition of the *feudum* whereby it could be recognized in any part of Europe, and the new interest in Germanic philology made it possible to open the question of the fee's barbaric origins. Both discoveries were to be of the utmost importance in the belated development of English historiography; but first it will be necessary to study that phase of continental scholarship in which it seemed uncertain whether feudalism and the fee were to be thought of as Roman or Germanic in origin, and to see how this problem and the definition of the fee were treated in the works of Cujas and of Hotman.

Cujas's edition of the *Libri Feudorum* was dedicated from Bourges in June 1566.[1] Earlier humanist commentators—Budé, Torelli, Zasi—had not unnaturally tended to seek for an explanation of feudal law in the Roman world.[2] They had followed medieval etymologists (among whom one of the original Milanese compilers, Obertus de Orto, must be counted) in deriving *feudum* from *foedus* or *fides*; and out of their encyclopaedic knowledge of Roman law and classical historical sources, they remembered a wide variety of patron-client relationships and of land-tenancies of a precarious or conditional kind, involving various degrees of dependence, clientage, service or actual loss of rights or liberty. Among all these it was natural that a large number of 'Roman' theories of feudal origins should be put forward, and in the third quarter of the century an alternative 'Germanic' interpretation was only beginning to gain ground, chiefly among the students or the partisans of French customary law, whose paths (in the nature of their work) lay largely among the Frankish and Teutonic materials for early French history. Cujas, a man of the south, might be pardoned for leaning to the Roman side, but in actual fact he displays a respectable knowledge of the possible German derivations of several characteristic terms in feudal law. Saying that the derivation of *feudum* from *fides* is to be preferred to that from *foedus*, he points out that the recipient of benefices among the Franks were known as *leudes*, the French *loyaux*: 'unde puto Germanos feudum appellare Leudum, sive

---

[1] In Cujas (*Iacobi Cuiacii operum quae de iure fecit*, t. 2, Paris, 1637).
[2] Cf. R. Dareste, *Essai sur François Hotman* (Paris, 1850), pp. 27–8.

Lehnen'.[1] Whatever may be thought of his etymology in these instances, Cujas was at least not unconscious of the need to explore barbaric and Germanic sources (though it will be observed that his argument would support the idea that the Franks and Goths translated a pre-existing term *fideles* by *leudes*); a number of lines lower he observes:

> Sed et Vassi, et Vassali nomen, quod eisdem competit, servitium significat, sive comitatum, cum deducatur non ex eo quod sint quasi in vasario nobilium, et vasa eorum instrumentaque censeantur, sed a Germanica, et veteri Gallica voce *Gessel*, qua significatur comes, qui nobis servit mercede certa....[2]

Throughout his lengthy preface, however, Cujas is concerned rather to define the *feudum* and its accompanying relationships than to seek for its origins, and it is on these grounds that he repudiates the identification of *vassus/vassalus* with *cliens*. The clients owed no military service, which was the essence of vassalage; they 'praedia sua pleno iure possident', while the vassals had only the temporary or perpetual usufruct; the clients received *sportulae* or dined at the patron's table, whereas the vassal abandoned property in his own land to receive a grant from his lord. 'Clienti respondet patronus.... Vassalo autem respondet dominus, qui et senior dicitur....'[3] But having gone thus far on the road towards describing the feudal relationship as one in which a man gives himself to a lord while remaining free, performing military service in return for a usufruct in a piece of land, Cujas turns back to the question of origins. Gerardus, he says—Gerardus Niger, traditionally supposed the author of the first of the *Libri Feudorum*—describes feudal law as 'antiquissimum'; and since Gerardus was himself a Lombard:

---

[1] Cujas, p. 791.

[2] 'But the term "vassus" (or "vassalus", which is applied to the same people) implies service or companionship, for it is derived not from the fact that the vassals are as it were part of the nobleman's equipage (*vasarium*) or are regarded as his utensils (*vasa*) or tools, but from the old German and Gaulish word "gessel", which means a companion serving for a fixed reward.' Cujas, p. 791.

[3] 'The client has a patron.... But the vassal has a lord, also known as a seigneur....'

inepte id repetieris ex Langobardis ipsis sive Gothis, quorum leges nihil de feudis habent palam, nec antiquissimum esse nobis unquam persuaseris, nisi id liquido deduxeris ex moribus P. Romani, quod siet ita commodissime.[1]

The argument is very much less dogmatic than it seems. Not the least of Gerardus's services to posterity—and in it he displayed a historical sense not too common at the beginning of the twelfth century—was his clear statement that the *feudum* had within human memory passed through an evolution of several distinct stages, from tenure at will or for a limited period, through tenure for one life, to tenure which was perpetual and heritable with few or no limitations.[2]

Antiquissimo tempore sic erat in dominorum potestate connexum, ut quando vellent possent auferre rem in feudum a se datam. Postea vero

[1] 'It would be a mistake to seek its origin among the Lombards themselves or the Goths, whose laws contain no clear reference to "feuda"; nor are we to be persuaded that it was "antiquissimum", unless it can be convincingly derived from the institutions of the Roman people, which would be very suitable.'

[2] 'In the very earliest times the benefice was so far subject to the lord's authority that he might take away at will what he had granted in fee. But afterwards it came about that the vassal had security of tenure for a year only; and then it was ordained that this should be extended to the length of his life. But still his sons had no right of succession; so the next stage was that the benefice should pass to the sons, that is to whichever of them the lord chose to grant it, which today is agreed to mean that it belongs to all of them equally. When, however, Conrad journeyed to Rome, the vassals in his service petitioned him to enact a law extending the succession to the sons of a son, and granting that the brother of a man who died without legitimate heirs would succeed him in their father's benefice. But if one of a number of brothers accepted a fief from a lord and died without legitimate heirs, his brother should not succeed him; if, on the other hand, the brothers received the fief jointly, one should not succeed the other unless this were expressly provided: with the condition, that if one died without legitimate heirs his brother should succeed him, but that the survival of an heir removed the brother from the succession. It should also be noticed that though daughters as well as sons may succeed their father, they are by law excluded from succeeding to a fief; and so are their sons likewise, unless it is specially stated that the daughters may succeed. It must in addition be observed that a benefice does not descend to collaterals, other than the sons of a father's brother, in the usage established by the lawyers of antiquity; but in the modern epoch the succession has been extended even to the seventh degree. So that in contemporary law a benefice passes to the male descendants *ad infinitum*.' Cujas, *Libri Feudorum*, lib. I, tit. I. Spelman's transcript of the passage (*Archaeologus*, 1626, p. 257) contains one or two interpolations and transpositions. The page is wrongly numbered 158.

74

eo ventum est ut per annum tantum firmitatem haberent: deinde statutum est ut usque ad vitam fidelis produceretur. Sed cum hoc iure successionis ad filios non pertineret: sic progressum est ut ad filios deveniret, in quem scilicet, dominus hoc vellet beneficium confirmare, quod hodie ita stabilitum est, ut ad omnes aequaliter filios pertineat. Cum vero Conradus Romam proficisceretur petitum est a fidelibus qui in eius erant servitio, ut lege ab eo promulgata, hoc etiam ad nepotes ex filio producere dignaretur, et ut frater fratri sine legitimo herede defuncto, in beneficio quod eorum patris fuit succedat. Sin autem unus ex fratribus a domino feudum acceperit, eo defuncto sine legitimo herede, frater eius in feudum non succedit: quod etsi communiter acceperint, unus alteri non succedit, nisi hoc nominatim dictum sit: scilicet, ut uno defuncto sine legitimo herede, alter succedat: herede vero relicto alter frater removebitur. Hoc autem notandum est, quod licet filiae et masculi patribus succedant: legibus tamen a successione feudi removentur: similiter et earum filii, nisi specialiter dictum fuerit ut ad eas pertineat. Hoc quoque sciendum est quod beneficium ad venientes ex latere, ultra fratres patrueles, non progreditur successione, secundum usum ab antiquis sapientibus constitutum: licet moderno tempore usque ad septimum geniculum sit usurpatum. Quod in masculis descendentibus novo iure usque in infinitum extenditur.

Round this invaluable statement all legist thought on the history of feudalism was to organize itself. What Cujas is saying above is that feudal law cannot as a whole be *antiquissimum*, because its significant characteristics were formed in a process of development after the intrusion of the Lombards into the Roman empire. He declares that he finds nothing feudal in the first written laws of the Lombards or the Goths, and leans to the opinion that the essential features of feudal tenure (i.e. all that is truly *antiquissimum*) were drawn by the invaders from late Roman law. Nor can he be accused of uncritical Romanism even in this judgment. He thinks he detects in the feudal tenant the lineaments of various types of usufructuary and temporary tenant whom he knows from the Roman law, and suggests that under the Lombards these became hereditary and at the same time militarized, assuming the character and the nomenclature of members of the barbarian *comitatus*. The whole passage should perhaps be quoted:

Fit saepe in libris nostris hominum mentio, qua appellatione frequentius servi significantur. Sed et liberi, puta actores, procuratores, custodes praediorum insularii, conductores emphiteuctarii [*sic*], chartularii, precarii possessores. His possessio conceditur ad tempus. Quae actori, feudum est gastaldiae. Quae custodi, feudum gardiae. Iisdem postea coepit concedi in perpetuum, quod est verum et proprium feudum, atque ita...paulatim qui erant actores, custodesque praediorum nostrorum temporarii, perpetui esse coeperunt. Latinumque Hominum nomen retinuerunt, novum et exterum Vasallorum sive Leodum et Feudatariorum acceperunt a principibus et nobilioribus, qui eis sua praedia in perpetuum concedere maluerunt, si militiae oneribus se obligarent, invecta in Italiam nomina a principibus Germanis, quibus fuere semper multi Comites (sic Cor. Tacitus vasallos vocat. Glossae συστρατιωτάς interpretantur) et principum aemulatio magna, cui plurimi et accerrimi.[1]

He proceeds to give further Tacitean characteristics of the *comites*, and without interruption to quote Constantine Porphyrogenitus for the existence of lands held 'eadem fere hominum conditione', and under the obligation of military service, in the Eastern Empire.

Cujas, it is plain, must not be accused of a 'Roman' bias in his account of the history of the *feudum* without one all-important qualification: he knew that it was a problem of the development of barbarian institutions within the Roman world. Subject to that statement of the question, he thought the *feudum* could be explained by a conflation of the Roman law regarding the tenure of land with the *mores* and vocabulary of the barbarian war-band; but he knew, as all students of the *Libri Feudorum* knew, that he was not merely looking for the origin of the *feudum*, but tracing its evolution towards

---

[1] 'Our books make frequent mention of "homines", a term generally employed to designate slaves. But it can also refer to free tenants, such as "actores", "procuratores", "custodes praediorum insularii", "conductores emphiteuticarii", "chartularii", and "precarii possessores". Possession was granted to such tenants for a time only. The grant to an "actor" corresponds to "feudum gastaldiae", that to a "custos" to "feudum gardiae". At a later time these grants began to be perpetual, which constitutes the true *feudum*, and so... by degrees those who had been temporary "actores" and "custodes" of estates began to be so in perpetuity. They kept the Latin name of "homines", but adopted also the new foreign names "vassals", "leudes", "feudataries" from their chieftains and nobles, who preferred to grant them perpetual estates if they would bind themselves to do military service. These names were brought into Italy by the German chieftains, who always had many "comites" (so Tacitus designates the vassals; the glosses call them συστρατιωταί) and competed keenly to see who could acquire the largest and most daring following.' For this and the preceding passage, Cujas, p. 793. See also pp. 799–800.

76

the full heritability guaranteed by the constitutions of Conrad II. Within the idea that feudalism is at once Roman and Germanic, there was and is room for an infinite variation of emphasis and definition, and subsequent developments of thought have taken us away from Lombardy altogether; but the fact that Cujas struck a balance, recognized that he faced a complex evolution, and gave no crude or one-sided interpretation of the problem, is very largely due to the historical perspective of the medieval Milanese whom he knew as Gerardus Niger.

As for François Hotman, though it is true that he stressed the Germanic aspects of the *feudum*, very much the same must be said of his treatment of the problem. In the 'Disputatio de feudis', which forms part of his *De feudis commentatio tripertita* (published in 1573), he begins by emphasizing the essentially military character of the *feudum*. The word is old Lombard, he says, and concerns the horse-soldier—'atque ad praedia equitibus alendis assignata pertinet'.[1] The fact that the *feudum* is a military grant did more than any other consideration to convince Hotman that the word is to be derived, not from *foedus* or *fides*, 'sed a Germanica voce Feed', which the barbarian laws use in the sense of 'blood-feud' or private, as well as public, war. He emphasized that the *Libri Feudorum* are predominantly concerned with fees granted by lords to their followers in their private contentions. Lastly, he challenges the world to show him any mention 'aut verbi huius, aut iuris, hoc est clientelae feudalis,' before the Gothic and Germanic invasions.[2]

It will be observed that Hotman's argument for the Germanic character of the *feudum* is based rather on a conviction of its military purpose than on any subtleties of philological science. In all that follows, he seems to be concerned much more to distinguish the military vassal-relationship from other forms of subordinate tenure than to argue for its 'Germanism'; and he is scarcely whole-hearted, much less dogmatic, in the attempt to ascribe the *feudum* to German prehistory. Thus, he remarks that it does seem reasonable ('mihi non inconcinnum videtur') to seek for the origins of vassalage ('Vasallicarum clientelarum') among the ancient Germans, and

[1] Hotman, *op. cit.* 'Disputatio de feudis', p. 6.
[2] Hotman, p. 7.

proceeds to quote, *in extenso*, Tacitus' account of the *comitatus*.[1] But he adds instantly that in the *Germania* 'nulla prorsus beneficiorum, aut feudorum, aut militarium praediorum mentio fit'. Moreover, two pages later[2] we find him controverting François Connan's attempt to derive vassalage from the Gallic *comitatus* described by Caesar, and urging in the forefront of his argument that the express obligation of the *comites* to die with their fallen chief is unknown among feudal vassals—and he can hardly have failed to recall that the selfsame custom occurs in the passage of Tacitus quoted, two pages earlier, by himself. Hotman's case against the claim of all forms of *comitatus* to figure as the prototype of feudal vassalage is the same: 'non certos et proprios agros ei rei attributos fuisse: qua tamen in re magnam feudorum partem constare, deinceps pro locis intelligetur.'[3] Was it in his mind that some point in time must be found at which the *comites* began to acquire grants of land held in virtue of their military service? Cujas had attempted, as we have seen, to provide just such a theory; but Hotman—without naming Cujas—dissents expressly from the view that the origin of the *feudum* may be found in the precarious tenures of the *actores*, *custodes*, and the rest, grown perpetual. We know what became of these tenants, he says: they became *coloni* and lost their freedom; their tenure became perpetual only in the sense that they were bound to the soil; and they were expressly debarred from the practice of arms. Nothing less like the feudal vassal—'conditio ...non modo liberalis, atque ingenua, verum etiam plane militaris' —could very well be imagined.[4] But Hotman's conclusions are ultimately no more than negative; he has singled out the *comitatus* for special emphasis, urged against it that its members were not feudally endowed with land, refuted Cujas's attempt to show how this came about and offered no alternative explanation.

[1] Hotman, pp. 7–8.

[2] Hotman, p. 9. This is part of the chapter: 'Variae doctorum hominum sententiae de Feudorum origine et instituto' (ch. II).

[3] 'that there was no assignation of definite and individual grants of land in connexion with it; but that the great majority of *feuda* rested on this basis will be constantly evident from the sources.'

[4] 'a condition not only free and freeborn, but actually military.' Hotman, pp. 10–11.

Discovery of Feudalism: French and Scottish Historians

It would appear that Hotman's real purpose was not to argue for either a 'Roman' or a 'Germanic' origin for the feudal relationship, but, by refuting all theories of its origin which he thought obscured its true nature, to keep its full complex character clearly before the minds of his readers. Thus he repudiates Budé and Zasi, who would identify it with Roman clientage, because this obscures the fact that it was military in character; Connan, who would identify it with the *comitatus*, because it was founded on grants of land; Torelli, who wanted to connect it with the Roman *limitanei*, because the vassal is not a veteran being rewarded for his services to the republic, but a warrior endowed by a lord out of the lord's own land. The multitude of arguments in the opening chapters of the 'Disputatio' describe exhaustively what the giving and receiving of *feuda* was like, and what it was unlike. From the whole emerges the picture of a unique and many-sided relationship, which must be regarded as having been born at or after the irruption of the Germans (notably the Lombards) into the empire, and matured at the time when the fee became fully inheritable under Conrad II.[1] That this work of definition, presenting as it did a picture of the fee universally recognizable and easily related to a single process of development, was what European historiography chiefly needed, is demonstrated by the subsequent work of English and Scottish historians, and first of all the Scot Sir Thomas Craig.

Craig was born in 1538 and studied law in Paris from 1555 to 1561. It is stated that his master in the civil law was François Baudouin.[2] He was therefore in direct contact with French thought at a time which antedates by some years the work of Cujas and Hotman on the feudal law; but the historical chapters of his *Jus Feudale* (published in 1603 and dedicated to King James) reveal the influence of Hotman at every turn, notably in the chapter designed to refute the theory that feudal tenures derive from the Roman law, and the work must certainly be taken as displaying the effects of French thought concerning feudal history on the mind of a highly intelligent foreigner who carried on his studies throughout the second half of the century. The peculiar significance which his book derives from its Scottish authorship must be considered later.

[1] See Hotman, ch. II, *passim*.   [2] *D.N.B.*, *sub* 'Craig, Thomas'.

For Craig, feudal law is a European fact of the first importance; it is a universal law and the law of his own country:

> in eo subjecto circa quod versatur, juris sibi principatum in potentissimis totius Europae regnis occupav[it], et adhuc retin[et]. Hoc jus Feudale, hujus nostri regni proprium et peculiare jus esse, et ad quod in rebus dubiis decidendis sit recurrendum, quoties de rebus immobilibus, id est, de hereditatis acquisitione vel amissione agitur, contendo....[1]

and its history therefore needs to be traced from the beginning. In carrying this out he has no documents more authoritative than those contained in the *Libri Feudorum*, and these in the view he has received from his teachers prove the *feudum* to be primarily a Lombard institution. He is aware of the necessity to pursue its origins at least as far back as the Germanic invasions; but it soon becomes apparent that no more than Hotman can he document the gap between the *comitatus* and the *feudum*. He begins, therefore, by explaining that, for reasons of climatic influence which recall Bodin, servitude among the northern peoples was more just and clement than among the southern, and took in fact the form of the voluntary devotion displayed by the Tacitean *comites*. We next behold the war-bands invading and partitioning the Roman empire, and here the origin of the *feudum* is explained by a subtle and remarkable piece of reconstruction. The Germanic chief, keeping the better land for himself, left the worse to be cultivated by *coloni*, exacting from them various rents, principally in kind since the use of money was then nearly unknown. But 'robustiores in comites assumebat, eis, unde alerentur, praestabat';[2] he maintained his retainers out of the dues paid him. In time, however, the *comites* preferred to settle in person upon the estates out of which they

---

[1] 'in that branch of jurisprudence with which it is concerned, it has occupied and holds to this day the chief place among forms of law in all the greatest realms of Europe. That this feudal law is the true and unique law of this kingdom of ours and should be referred to in the deciding of all doubtful matters, whenever it is a question of immovable property, that is, of the acquisition or loss of an inheritance: such is my contention.' Craig (*D. Thomae Craigii de Riccarton, equitis...Jus Feudale tribus libris comprehensum*, Edinburgh, 1732: 3rd edition, ed. James Baillie), p. 24.

[2] 'he took the strongest for his companions and provided them with a source of upkeep.'

had formerly been maintained, the lord caring little whether his men occupied the land or merely consumed its yield ('utrum res ipsas, an fructus omnes ac utilitates assignar[et]'[1]), so long as he retained the actual *potestas*. (So that, despite the choice of words in the phrases just quoted, in assigning the *res ipsas* he would grant no more than a usufruct.) He therefore at first insisted on making all grants, whether of lands or pensions, precarious and at will; but in time came about that gradual development, known to us from the *Libri Feudorum*, towards the full heritability of fees, ending in the paradoxical climax that a mere usufruct has become perpetual, hereditary and forfeit only under strict codified rules.[2]

What we have here—whether it issues from Craig's mind or another's—can only be highly intelligent and indeed brilliant conjecture, designed to fill the gap which Hotman had noted and left between *comites* and vassals. Acknowledging that the feudal and barbarian laws do not provide a sufficient answer, some thinker has turned from the strictly legal analysis made by Cujas and Hotman, and has succeeded in linking three well-known facts rather of an economic order—that the *comites* fed at the board of their lord, that colonial tenures paying rents largely in kind increased under Germanic domination, and that the vassal or feudatory enjoyed the usufruct of the land granted him. This learned and plausible account of a social development can scarcely have been based on more evidence than that, and the modern reader is left with an acute sense of the adventurous vigour of the historical thought bred in the French law schools. At the same time, it emerges with clarity that study of the feudal law was peculiarly calculated to cause men's minds to pass from reflexions on the forms of the law to inquiry into the social and economic realities which underlay them.

Craig distinguishes three phases in the progress of the *feudum*: its infancy, in which it was entirely precarious or granted for one life, its adolescence, in which it became heritable by the son only, and its maturity, in which it became fully heritable, as did duchies, counties and baronies.[3] In a digression at the outset of this part of his argument, he makes the remarkable suggestion that the first

---

[1] 'whether he assigned them the land itself or the fruits and the use thereof.'
[2] Craig, pp. 26–7.   [3] Craig, pp. 27–30.

age may justly be compared to the *timar* system of contemporary Turkey. The Sultan ('Imperator Turcicus') grants out the frontier provinces of his empire in estates to be held 'sub ea lege ut ad omnes expeditiones certum numerum equitum paratum habeant pro quantitate et bonitate *Timarriae*'.[1] Since the historiography of our own age still holds debate with itself how far the term 'feudalism' may be applied to similar institutions which cannot be derived from western Europe in the tenth century, it is interesting to notice how early in the history of feudal studies the Ottoman empire began to furnish European scholars with illuminating comparisons. Thirty years before Craig's book was published, Hotman had suggested that 'quos Turcae Bassas appellant' might not unjustly be compared with the *vassi* and considered 'eodem ex fonte nomen sumpsisse'. Craig's comparison is notably better informed and he is aware of dissimilarities. On the death of the timariot, he observes, the holding reverts to the Sultan who regrants it to whom he will and for life only, and it is for this reason that the *timar* system can be compared only to the *feudorum infantiae*.[2]

It is out of this comparison, however, that the greatest difference between Craig's view of feudalism and ours emerges. He seems to think of the Germanic invaders, as of the Turks, as settling their conquered provinces with a strong centralized military class, instantly obedient to the prince's call; Hotman's emphasis on the origin of vassalage in the private blood-feud finds little place in his account of the matter, and the almost 'manorial' account of the rise of the *feudum*, given by Craig a page or two earlier, does not recur. The explanation of this must be seen in the fact that his notion of feudal society was drawn from the relatively ordered world revealed in the *Libri Feudorum*. The lords and vassals of Lombardy lived in a society which had been brought under a single rule at least to the point where a single code of feudal law could be drawn up and prove of some use, and, as we shall see, Craig looked upon feudal law as the law of a well-ordered and strongly monarchical society. He would be criticized by a modern student, also, for

---

[1] 'with the legal obligation to have ready for every military operation a certain number of cavalry, related to the size and value of the *timar*.'
[2] Craig, p. 30; Hotman, p. 13.

thinking of feudalism, at least in the first place, not as a disinte-
gration of the heart of Carolingian society, but as a law which one
people possessed and another could copy—an attitude more typical
of what is usually attributed to Renaissance historiography than
is much else in his writings. Because the feudal law he has is
Lombard law, he assumes that it had been the law of the Lombards,
at least in its essentials, for centuries before it was written down.
Therefore Charlemagne must have discovered it in operation when
he conquered the Lombard kingdom, and it must have been from
this source that it spread to the rest of the Frankish empire. However,
any tendency Craig may have had to give a naïve account of mere
imitation and communication was checked by his awareness that
the *feudum* had developed from a precarious to a hereditary tenure,
and that the story of this growth was to be read in the constitutions
of various emperors of whom Charlemagne was only the first.
Conrad II, Hugh Capet and Barbarossa had brought the process to
its culmination, and Craig's summary account of the matter is
anything but unhistorical.

Sed nihil certius quam ex Caroli Magni, et Imperatorum qui eum
sequuti sunt, constitutionibus primum in Gallia Cisalpina, quae nobis
Transalpina est, quam hodie Longobardiam dicimus, coepisse; mox ad
Transalpinam penetrasse: non ut unum universale jus de feudis a principio
constitueretur, sed tantum ut peccata, quae ex diversa feudorum observa-
tione eo tempore admittebantur, corrigerentur....Nec dubito quin toto
illo tempore, quod inter Carolum Magnum et Fridericum primum interces-
serat, multae aliae constitutiones Imperatorum promulgatae sint de feudis,
saepe inter se diversae, aliquando contrariae, prioribus posteriores, tamen
quae jus illud vagum et varium certis limitibus coercerent.[1]

[1] 'But there is nothing more certain than that the custom originated with
the constitutions of Charlemagne and the Emperors who followed him, first
in Cisalpine Gaul (Transalpine to us), today called Lombardy, and then made
its way across the Alps; not that a single universal feudal law was set up from
the beginning, but rather that the faults which were committed through the
variations of feudal custom in that age were corrected....Nor can it be
doubted that, in the long period between Charlemagne and Frederick I, many
other Imperial constitutions were promulgated on the subject of *feuda*, and
that these often differed among themselves, the later sometimes contradicting
the earlier, but were calculated to bring this uncertain and varying custom
within definite limits.' Craig, p. 34.

And the *Libri Feudorum*, he stresses—that is, the works of Gerardus Niger and Obertus de Orto—consist of a conflation of diverse Lombard customs made at the very end of this complex process. In an age when Machiavelli's praise of the legislator who had instituted the law and kingship of France was still widely read and admired, Craig can certainly not be accused of lacking a sense of the gradual development of institutions or of being blind to the partial and often contradictory actions of particular men through which that development pursues its course.

Having defined the *feudum* by a picture of its rise and progress in history, Craig turned to demonstrate the feudal character of Scots law. So convinced was he that his country's existing land law was essentially feudal and European that he taught that, where written and customary law failed them, Scots judges and jurisconsults might safely have recourse to the books of the continental feudists.[1] In the *Libri Feudorum*, as taught at Paris and edited by Cujas and Hotman, he saw a systematic exposition of the principles of tenure, forfeiture and inheritance which sufficed to render intelligible the laws of Scotland. This he was prepared to explain—first historically, by an account of how feudal law had arisen and come into Scotland; and next juridically, by a detailed analysis of Scots law based on the principles of the *Libri Feudorum*. But Craig was, in addition, aware that the history of his own country could only with the utmost care be separated from that of the neighbour kingdom—he was after all addressing himself to the king of both; and the peculiar importance of his book to the present study is that, publishing in the first year of the union of the crowns, he set out to show that the land law of England, no less than of Scotland, was feudal in character, and that the history of each country formed part of the history of law in Europe.

There is not much detailed analysis of English common law and reduction of it to feudal principles. Craig was not an authority on English law and he was but writing an introductory chapter to a book for Scotsmen. We may take it for granted that he was aware that, on Littleton's own showing, the basis of the common law of real property was the *feudum* and that, in the light of continental

[1] Craig, p. 52.

84

scholarship, it could hardly be denied what the *feudum* was; but he does not trouble to make this point. His arguments are really two. In the first place he remarks that nearly all the essential terms of French feudal law are in use in the English courts. From Rastell's book in exposition of the terms of English law and from the language employed in both common and statute law, it is safe to deduce the Norman and therefore French origin of all the land law in use among the English, 'et praecipue de wardis et maritatione heredum'.[1] Secondly, in a different place Craig gives a long list of the common law's better-known maxims and says that their Norman and feudal character is plain.[2] This seems to have sufficed, in his view, to demonstrate that feudal principles were an essential part of English law; he now devoted himself to the historical question of their introduction.

This he uncompromisingly ascribed to the Normans. For his authorities, Craig—true to his continental training—preferred to rely on recent European historians, rather than wrestle with the interpretation of medieval chroniclers; and he made considerable use of Polydore Vergil. Like another intelligent Italian, the author of a *Relation of England* penned about 1500, Vergil had been able, without (as far as is known) any special training in feudal law, to discern that the Norman settlement of England must have been based on some sort of feudal relationship, and to provide an account of it in those terms.[3] But Craig knew far more than Vergil of pre-Conquest society; in particular he had before him the Saxon and pseudo-Saxon laws collected by Lambarde; and his argument required him to show that the *feudum* had not existed among the Saxons. The proof he somewhat sketchily employs is drawn from his broad view of the history of feudalism. In Norman England we find a fully matured form of the *feudum*, in which the process of development from precarious to perpetual has reached its culmination. This corresponds exactly with the feudal law of Normandy in the earliest form in which we have it; whereas, if we test the social

[1] Craig, p. 39. [2] Craig, pp. 43–4.
[3] Cf. the passage from Vergil's *Historia Anglica*, book 9, quoted by Craig, p. 39; and *An Italian Relation of England about the year 1500*, Camden Society, No. 37 (1847), pp. 38–9.

relationships of Anglo-Saxon England by the characteristics of the fully developed *feudum*, we find that they fall so far short of requirements as not to deserve the name. Craig's arguments are not very full or uniformly happy—he quotes a charter of Athelstan against one of William I to Hugh Earl of Chester and then has to confess that neither corresponds to the typical form of a feudal grant—but he regarded them with sufficient confidence to ignore the numerous assertions, ancient and modern, of the Conqueror's confirming the laws of King Edward, and to insist that the law had become wholly Norman and feudal at William's entry and had remained substantially so ever since.[1]

He allowed one important exception, which alone does no small credit to his historical insight. Although nearly all Anglo-Saxon law perished at the Conquest,

illud tamen *de pace domini Regis fracta*, licet ex Anglosaxonum Regum statutis descenderet, tenacissime Conquaestor retinuit, omnesque ab eo descendentes, quod maxime rationibus fisci conveniret.[2]

It is very doubtful if any other historian of 1603 had detected that the concept of the king's peace was the most noteworthy element of old English law to survive conquest, or that the reasons for this were largely fiscal. Though Craig allows for certain elements of pre-Conquest custom having survived or crept back into the Norman law, he will admit nothing of the story that later kings restored the Confessor's law to placate the English. The people, he says, did indeed beseech Henry I to do so, but the king cunningly eluded their requests by giving them a parliament instead, in which the ancient law may be amended and new law introduced, but nothing can be done but by petitioning the prince, who gives or withholds his assent as he pleases. This account of parliamentary origins—which owes something to Polydore Vergil—may be worthless, but it too gives some measure of Craig's energy and resource as a historian.[3]

[1] Craig, pp. 39–40.
[2] 'only the "breach of the King's peace", although derived from the laws of the Anglo-Saxon Kings, was resolutely retained by the Conqueror and all his successors, which was very convenient for fiscal purposes.' Craig, p. 42.
[3] *Ibid.*

Discovery of Feudalism: French and Scottish Historians

Feudal learning did much for Craig, but it did not wholly free him from bondage to national myths. When he turned to consider the introduction of feudal law into Scotland, he made use of the apocryphal early laws, prefixed to certain editions of the *Regiam Majestatem*, to show that Scottish feudal custom, so far from finding its origin in conquest (like that of England) or in the activities of Norman barons from England, was already established in the reigns of Malcolm II, of Macbeth and even of Kenneth III (*c.* 970), and was 'ex contracta cum Gallis amicitia', the product of a tenth-century Auld Alliance.[1] Craig was perhaps influenced by the thought which almost obsessed his English brethren, that it was disgraceful for a country to derive its laws from conquest; more probably still, uppermost in his mind—as it was throughout his scholarly life— was the need to prove that the kingdom of Scotland was not held by homage to the English crown. If he could prove that for half a century or more the Scots had known of homage when the English had not, the original independence of Scotland would be unassailable. In the same way, he emphasizes that the feudal law of Scotland is purer and closer to its Frankish origins than that of England; nevertheless, English law can be regarded only as feudal and Norman, 'licet illi dissimulent, nullumque jus nisi suum agnoscere profiteantur'.[2] In both lands the law is feudal and he exhorts James VI and I to make full use of feudal principles in his government of each. It is a defect, as we have seen, of Craig's historical thought that he regards feudalism not as a dissolution of the state, but as a connected and unified body of law. It is another and consequent defect that he treats it as a system of royal and hierarchical authority binding all men to personal dependence on the king. Nothing, he says, could conduce more to the tranquillity of the king and his realms,

quam ut hujus Feudalis juris praecepta et consuetudines quam arctissime observentur: nam si tota Britannia in partes vel minutissimas secetur, nulla

[1] Craig, pp. 46–9. The words quoted are from the summary prefixed to ch. VIII.

[2] 'although they deny it and profess to acknowledge no law save their own.' Craig, p. 44.

erit quae non in feudo de M[ajestate] T[ua] teneatur, (ut in foro loqui solemus,) nulla quae non fidem debeat.[1]

Possessed of little more than a reasonable acquaintance with the *Libri Feudorum* and the French commentaries upon them, Craig had been able to construct an impressively broad historical synthesis, explaining the general history of European law since the barbarian invasions and fitting both Scotland and England into their place in this pattern. If we are to think of him as a product of what is called the Reception in Scotland, it is plain that in him at least reception of civil-law principles produced no contempt for or desire to displace native customs; rather, a new understanding and respect, produced by his new-found ability to see them in their historical context as part of the universal law of the western world. Only if the Scottish crown had been able to enforce feudal tenure as a universal dependence on the sovereign's will might Craig's admittedly over-centralized view of feudalism have become a source of danger to the traditional law of his country; as it is, we are told, 'to this day the land law of Scotland is the most feudal of all the systems of land law which exist',[2] and Craig would certainly not have lamented the fact.

The evident paradox is that Scotland's poverty in law had much to do with the breadth and clarity of Craig's historical thought, while England's unique possession of an organically evolved system of native law was a positive bar to the progress of historical self-knowledge. It would be merely cruel to compare Craig's history with Coke's; what is much more striking is that *Jus Feudale* anticipates by twenty-three years most of the main conclusions in Sir Henry Spelman's *Archaeologus* (1626), the first book in which an Englishman recognized and analysed in something like fullness the feudal element in his country's history. Englishmen, it is plain, felt little need to study the *Libri Feudorum* and apply their lessons to

---

[1] 'than that the rules and customs of feudal law should be observed with the utmost rigour; for were all Britain divided into the minutest fragments of land, there would still be none which was not held in fee of your Majesty (as we say in the Courts) or did not owe you fealty.' Craig, p. vii (dedication).

[2] Lord Cooper, *The Dark Age of Scottish Legal History* (David Murray Foundation Lecture), Glasgow University Press, 1952.

their own law; and they had not in fact the Scots lawyers' motives for doing so. Scotland in Craig's day stood in a position somewhat analogous to that of England in the twelfth century: that is, she was still borrowing from the civil law the principles around which to organize the diversity of customs pleadable in her courts. The Scot, therefore, went abroad as he had always done, to see his own law the better. From the mid-sixteenth century on, he came in the French universities under the influence of the new historical approach to jurisprudence. In the civil law he studied not merely the law of the late Roman empire, but the books of feudal law which had been added during the Middle Ages and were now receiving new and instructive emphasis. He returned armed with general ideas which enabled him not only to systematize his native customs but to understand their historical origins; with a legal and historical definition of the *feudum* which made him see that his own law was feudal and write its history, however sketchily, into the history of Europe. The failure of his country to achieve a common law of her own compelled him to be a European and view his law in a wider context and therefore historically.

But there was no need for the English common lawyer to look abroad, for there was no feature of English law which the presumption of immemorial custom did not explain to his satisfaction. It was several hundred years since he had been compelled to borrow ideas abroad if he was to have a law at all, and as learned a man as Selden could not imagine that there had ever been such a time. The recurrent theme of his *Dissertatio ad Fletam* is that civil-law influences have never been more than incidental to the unbroken development of English custom. The common lawyer was confident that the history of English law could be explained entirely by reference to the English past; and the more he developed the myths to which this inevitably gave birth, the greater his repugnance grew to any suggestion that his law might have sprung from an alien stock. To the end of his days Spelman was to complain of the common lawyer's refusal to look abroad and view his law from a European standpoint; but where the Scot was compelled by the needs of his practice to do so, the Englishman's professional outlook actively discouraged him. If an ultimate origin was sought, it must be in the custom of England, as interpreted by the judges; and there were enough records here to keep a man happily drowning all his lifetime in the search for precedent before precedent. There was no reason why a common lawyer should compare his law with that of Europe, except an intellectual curiosity arising and operating outside the everyday needs of his profession. The discovery of England's place in the legal history of Europe was therefore made by antiquarians, not by lawyers; it was made—if we date it from Spelman's *Archaeologus*—almost a quarter of a century after Craig's publication of his conclusions; and it faced a long and hard struggle for acceptance. It must therefore be admitted that the whole effect of the common law upon the Englishman as historian was to keep him isolated, a provincial, on the edge of European learning.

CHAPTER V

The Discovery of Feudalism: Sir Henry Spelman

I

THE English were to discover feudalism in the way fore-shadowed by Craig: in the form, that is, of a single code of law which, it was believed, had been observed, or borrowed from in, every nation of the west; they were to borrow definitions from the Lombard books and their French commentators and apply these to their common law. But they were to do this very late. The common lawyers resisted the discovery, and it was not made by English civilians. It may be that the influence of Gentili and the *mos Italicus* distracted the latter's attention from the work that had been done at Bourges. Civilians were certainly not encouraged to undertake independent investigations of the common law, but in neither Fulbecke nor Cowell, the two doctors of James I's reign who did attempt comparison of the two laws, do we find historical work comparable to Craig's.[1] There are the beginnings of it in Cowell's *Interpreter*: he took definitions of feudal terms (including *feudum* itself) from the *Libri Feudorum*, Hotman and other Continental feudists and pointed out that they were applicable and useful in the study of English law, and suggested that the close similarity of the Norman *Grand Custumier* to feudal law on one hand and common law on the other provided an obvious clue to the manner in which such law had come into England.[2] But Cowell continued to

---

[1] Cowell, *Institutiones juris anglicani ad methodum et seriem institutionum imperialium compositae et digestae* (1605 and 1630); *Interpreter or Booke containing the Signification of Words* (1607, 1637 and many subsequent editions). Fulbecke, *Parallele or Conference of the Civil Law, the Canon Law and the Common Law of this Realme of England* (1601 and 1618).

[2] *Interpreter*, ed. 1637 (not paginated), articles on 'Ayde', 'Baron', 'Bayliffe', 'Fealtie', 'Fee', 'Maner', 'Parlament' and elsewhere. Note also 'Custom' for Cowell's purely technical and conventional treatment of 'time out of mind'.

believe in the *Mirror of Justices*;[1] and more generally, he did not attempt the reinterpretation outlined by Craig, which would suggest that there had been a period in the past when English law was explicable only on the assumption that the principles of feudal law belonged to it also. The first English civilian to say dogmatically that the common law presupposed the *feudum* in the continental sense of the word, and that this had been imported with the military tenures of the Normans, seems to have been Richard Zouche, and he wrote after Spelman and acknowledged his debt to him.[2] Cowell made useful suggestions and supplied useful material to Spelman, but he did not anticipate his conclusions to the extent that Craig had done.

Nevertheless the English set to work in a fashion very different from Craig's or any lawyer's. If neither civilians nor inns-of-court men made the discovery of feudalism in the English past, it was the work of a different if closely connected group of men: the antiquarians, and particularly some of the members of the Society of Antiquaries that flourished about 1614. It seems fairly clear that a diffused and piecemeal knowledge of the *Libri Feudorum*, of Cujas and Hotman and of their importance to English learning was making steady progress about this time, but we do not yet know by just what stages this happened or to what extent the giants of Jacobean scholarship—Camden, Cotton, Ussher, Selden, Spelman—assisted one another in this branch of their all but universal erudition. This chapter is devoted to Spelman, not because it is desired to suggest that he and he alone made the rediscovery of feudalism, or even because he was probably the greatest of those who made it; but because he reveals in great detail the way in which the antiquarians set to work, and because, more than any other scholar of his age, he showed to what uses it might be put. In his writings we see, more fully than elsewhere, the revolution which it wrought in traditional English historiography.

---

[1] *Interpreter, sub* 'Approvour', 'Maner'.

[2] In *Elementa iurisprudentiae...quibus accessit Descriptio iuris et iudicii temporalis secundum consuetudines feudales et normannicas...* (Oxford, 1636); see prefatory letter *Iuventuti iurisprudentiae studiosae*. Cf. Holdsworth, vol. IV, pp. 17–20, 24–5 (for the slightly later work of Arthur Duck).

The Discovery of Feudalism: Sir Henry Spelman

These writings, however, are scattered. Spelman's work divides itself into four parts. First, there is *Archaeologus*, the glossary of obsolete and barbaric words in the ecclesiastical and legal vocabularies, of which one volume was published in 1626 and another lay in manuscript until, long after its author's death in 1641, William Dugdale sent the whole work to the printers in 1664. Spelman's enormous labours in writing and editing the *Concilia* occupy a second place. Next, there is a series of works of a high-church character, vindicating the sanctity of tithes and deploring lay ownership of sacred property.[1] The *History of Sacrilege*, most interesting and most startling of these, was not published until 1698. Last, there is a group of tracts and treatises, mainly legal and antiquarian in character, which Spelman left in manuscript at his death; almost all were published, also in 1698, by Edmund Gibson in his *Reliquiae Spelmannianae*, but one—the *Codex Legum Veterum*—had to wait until David Wilkins brought out his edition of the Anglo-Saxon laws in 1721. The matter relevant to our present purposes is to be found in both parts of the *Archaeologus*, the *Reliquiae*, the *Codex* and the *History of Sacrilege*. Spelman's writings on feudal and legal history are consequently scattered and unsystematized, and many of them could have no effect on the public mind until long after his death.

Like Cotton, Twysden, Dugdale and many others of the great antiquaries—perhaps most of them, if we except the churchmen— Spelman was a man deeply imbued with the spirit of the common law, yet not fully committed to the outlook of the practising lawyer.[2] After a brief stay at Cambridge he entered Lincoln's Inn, from which he was withdrawn at the age of twenty, and for thirty years led the life of a prominent Norfolk gentleman, much employed both in county office and on commissions for the crown, one of which took him into Ireland. At the age of fifty—this would be about 1614—he removed to London and was so fortunate as to spend twenty-seven years more in intensive and productive scholarship.

[1] They include *De non temerandis ecclesiis* (1613); and the *Larger work of tithes*, published posthumously in 1646.

[2] The main authorities for Spelman's life are: his preface to the 1626 *Archaeologus*; Gibson's life, prefixed to *Reliquiae Spelmannianae*; Sir Maurice Powicke, 'Sir Henry Spelman and the *Concilia*', Raleigh Lecture on History, *Proc. Brit. Acad.* (1930); *D.N.B.*

In his writings he laments his early withdrawal from common-law studies;[1] but had he remained in the atmosphere of readings and year-books, it is easy to imagine him developing an intellect as powerful and (historically speaking) as misdirected as Coke's, for he was not by nature free from the common beliefs and prejudices of his age. As it was, however, his county activities ensured that he was well acquainted with the common law, while his decision to devote himself to general erudition left him free to regard it from a more detached point of view than that of the professional lawyer. The law never filled his intellectual horizon. When he returned to London at fifty, he was fully as much interested in ecclesiastical studies as in legal, and he continued all his life to conduct them side by side. Indeed, there have been those who have thought that the latter were too much sacrificed to the former.[2] Be that as it may, a turning-point in Spelman's life as a scholar was reached when he realized that the problem of obsolete and barbaric words was common to both branches of his studies, and determined that he must himself provide some sort of glossary to these before his work, and that of his friends and correspondents, could make further progress. *Archaeologus* was the fruit of this resolution, and it is a book devoted as much to ecclesiastical as to legal terminology. Nevertheless, it was in this glossary[3] that Spelman began systematically to study the common law from the point of view of the scholar, not the lawyer, and to treat it as material from which to extract answers to his own questions. The difference between Coke's approach and Spelman's is profound: for one the history of the law consists of precedents and justifications for present-day rights and actions, for the other it is a question of words no longer used and of meanings that words have now lost. Spelman was an antiquarian and his attitude to the common law was, to this extent at least, scholarly and critical from the start.

Archaeologus, then, is a study of words; but Spelman's interest in

[1] In the preface to the 1626 *Archaeologus*.

[2] Powicke, *loc. cit.* p. 34, quotes a letter of Ussher, dated 6 November 1638, to this effect.

[3] In a note to the 1626 edition, headed 'Clavis', Spelman described the book as less a glossary, although having that form, than a collection of general commentaries.

philology remained that of an ecclesiastical and legal scholar, and the words he chose to study were all the names of usages, offices, ranks, ceremonies and rules in the medieval church and law. In studying the name he studied the thing, and this historical dictionary of several thousand words is designedly a historical inquiry into the past of an organized society. Furthermore, it was of the very greatest importance that Spelman did not confine himself to elucidating words from English historical sources, but sought to understand them better by comparing them with

peregrini labii vocabula; Gothici, Vandalici, Saxonici, Germannici, Langobardici, Normannici, etc.—ignotae functionis ministeria, Officia, dignitates, Magistratus, et infinita huiusmodi.[1]

His correspondence with French, German and Netherlandish scholars—who outnumber the English and Scots in the list of his acknowledgments by twelve to seven[2]—helped him acquire an enormously varied knowledge of European laws, customs, cartularies, decrees, chronicles and documents of all kinds, and consequently of the legal and ecclesiastical aspects of medieval society in the west. Yet the range of his erudition is not so important as the comparative use he made of it. All this material he studied minutely for the words it employed and the usages it revealed, and he took note of a multitude of resemblances to the laws and terminology of his own country. Studying language for the sake of law, he approached the English past as part of the history of Europe; he did more than any English scholar before him to initiate the comparative investigation of the English and continental Middle Ages, and the gratitude of Peiresc, Bignon and other Frenchmen was energetically expressed.[3]

[1] 'words of foreign origin—Gothic, Vandal, Saxon, German, Lombard, Norman etc.—services, offices, dignities, magistracies of unknown function; and an infinity of things of this kind.' *Archaeologus*, 1626, 'Praefatio'.

[2] Peiresc, Bignon, Maussac, Gaulmin, Rigault, Salmasius, Meursius, Lindenbrog, the Pithou brothers, Goldast, Lydius; Camden, Ussher, Lord Keeper Williams, Cotton, Selden, Cowell and Skene.

[3] Some of Spelman's correspondence with foreign scholars may be found in British Museum Additional MSS. 34599, ff. 51, 60, 74, 81, 84; 34601, f. 14; 25384, f. 13. See also L. Van Norden, 'Peiresc and the English Scholars', *Huntington Library Quarterly*, vol. XII, no. 4 (1948–9), pp. 369–89.

The Discovery of Feudalism: Sir Henry Spelman

Spelman went to work as he did because he fully accepted the fact—established by Nowell, Camden and Verstegan—that Anglo-Saxon and Old English formed part of a family of early Germanic tongues; nor was it news in his time that Anglo-Saxon law showed marked similarities with the *leges barbaricae*. He noticed also that when medieval English institutions resembled those of Carolingian France or Norman Sicily, the relationship could often be traced back to something recorded of the barbarian invaders. Spelman therefore decided that English law was largely Germanic in its origins, but this conclusion did not lead him to adopt any romantic or primitivist cult of the rude Gothic forbears. On the contrary, its value to him was that it placed a definite check on the exaggerations of those who sought to trace the law back into times more remote still—to assert with Fortescue that it was older than the Romans, or to engage in the not yet extinct fantasies of Geoffrey of Monmouth. In a paper originally composed for the Society of Antiquaries in 1614, but later enlarged and rewritten, he attacked those who derived the law from 'Brutus, Mulmutius, or the Druids'; the context points to Fortescue, but could equally well be aimed at Coke's *Third Reports*.[1] In Spelman's mind as he viewed the thought of his age, to prove that English law could be traced to a Germanic origin and to the time of the Anglo-Saxon settlements was to limit its antiquity, to prove it neither mythical nor immemorial, and to compel the reader to think of it in relation to the

[1] 'The Original of the Four Terms of the Year', especially foreword 'The Occasion of this Discourse'. Dr L. Van Norden, 'Sir Henry Spelman on the Chronology of the Elizabethan College of Antiquaries', *Huntington Library Quarterly*, vol. XIII, no. 2 (1949–50), pp. 131–60, uses this foreword in an attempt to revise the hitherto accepted dating both of its composition, and of the period at which the Society was most active; her arguments appear most convincing. The passage referred to runs (*Reliquiae*, p. 103): 'They therefore that fetch our Laws from *Brutus, Mulmutius*, the *Druides*, or any other *Brutish* or *British* Inhabitants here of old, affirming that in all the times of these several Nations, (viz. *Britains, Romans, Saxons, Danes* and *Normans*) and of their Kings, this Realm was still ruled with the self same customes that it is now (*viz.* in the time of King *Henry* VI.) govern'd withal; do like them that make the *Arcadians* to be elder than the Moon, and the God *Terminus* to be so fixed on the *Capitoline-hill*, as neither Mattocks nor Spades, nor all the power of men nor of the other Gods, could remove him from the place he stood in.' The reference to the time of Henry VI points plainly to Fortescue.

96

history of other peoples instead of indulging in the manufacture of purely insular legends.[1]

Spelman did not think that German custom had retained its pristine purity, because he too owed his debt to Gerardus Niger and knew that the laws of the barbarians had undergone important developments after their entry into the empire. He had read the *Libri Feudorum*—we do not know when or on whose suggestion—in the editions of Cujas and Hotman; he was acquainted with the work of Loyseau and Pasquier; and, though he does not seem to have read Craig, he was familiar with Scottish feudal law through the writings of Sir John Skene, who held views very like Craig's on the date of its introduction into Scotland. Spelman amicably dissents.[2] He therefore held, as all these writers did, that an important process had taken place in the structure of barbarian law, namely the rise and diffusion of the *feudum* and its evolution from a precarious grant to a perpetual and hereditary tenure. Like Craig, but in far greater detail, he saw that this general concept could be employed in the effort to understand the history of his own country. The stages by which he reached this understanding have to be collected and pieced together from many scattered paragraphs and references, but in all they amount to what is probably his most important single contribution to historiography.

Under the heading 'Feudum', Spelman gives us his account of general feudal history. He shares with Craig the apparently universal delusion that 'feudal law' was an hierarchical system imposed from above as a matter of state policy; thus land was granted to the great nobles not for their own enjoyment, but so that they might provide soldiers for the defence of the realm and particularly of its frontier provinces.[3] (There is, however, no Turkish analogy in his writings.) He is most like Hotman in his cautious acceptance of a Germanic origin for the *feudum*: its terminology is predominantly German, it has arisen only among Germanic peoples, and under careful inspection (*oculatius*) the *comites* described by Tacitus

[1] See the article 'Lex' in the 1626 *Archaeologus*, p. 435: 'Iactent igitur, etc.'
[2] *Reliquiae*, pp. 27–8.
[3] 1626 *Archaeologus*, p. 256 (misnumbered p. 254), cols. 1–2. ('Feudum' begins on p. 255, continues to p. 262.)

certainly appear the most likely ancestors of the vassals. It is noteworthy, however, that the characteristic of the *comites* on which
Spelman bases this opinion is not their military union with the
chieftain, but their obligation 'principibus pagorum *consilium ad-
fuisse et authoritatem*';[1] in the light of his later writings it is probable
that he was already preparing the way for a treatment of the lord
and his vassals as constituting not only a war-band, but a feudal
court. On these grounds, then, Spelman holds that the origin of
the *feudum* is German, but not that it existed fully grown among
the primitive Germans. In the first written Lombard laws we find
mention of the *feudum* never and of the *beneficium* hardly at all;
yet it was among the Lombards, much later, that the feudal law
was first reduced to writing. What we do find in the earliest Lombard, Frankish, Anglo-Saxon and barbaric laws generally is 'plurima
quae apprime huc conducunt'.[2] The *feudum* evolved slowly, taking
rise from a multitude of Germanic customs, and the decisive
point at which it assumed its full classical form in medieval
Europe was the visit of Conrad the Salian to Italy and his decree
extending the right to inherit from the son to the grandson or
nephew. Later emperors added further legislation, Spelman says,
but the essential history is that set down by Gerardus Niger—whom
he proceeds to quote *in extenso*, if not with perfect accuracy—
tracing the successive stages through which the *feudum* passed on its
way from precarious to perpetual.[3] He adds that Hugh Capet,
acquiring the French throne a generation before Conrad went to
Italy, made not only *feuda*, but duchies, counties and baronies
hereditary and perpetual, from which time the nobles began to call
themselves by the territorial names of their several fees.[4]

[1] '...to provide the district chieftains with advice and authority for their
doings.' P. 257 (misnumbered 158), col. 1. This seems to be Spelman's
adaptation of the last words of Tacitus, *Germania*, 12.
  [2] 'many things which come very close to it.' Same page, col. 2.
  [3] Same page, cols. 1–2. Gerardus had not identified his Conrad, but
Spelman rightly calls him Conradus Salicus. In the *Treatise of Feuds and
Tenures*, however, he confuses him with Conrad I, and dates his journey to
Rome in 915—an error by a great scholar which, though it does not affect
his essential argument, should serve as a warning to all (*Reliquiae*, p. 4).
  [4] Same page, col. 2.

Spelman now proceeds to use the stages through which Gerardus describes the *feudum* as passing to account for a wide variety of customs, found among different peoples, which he evidently regards as survivals of the barbarians' evolution towards the true feudal law. Thus the phase in which the *beneficium* was divided equally among the sons is the explanation of Kentish gavelkind[1] and of the similar custom among the Irish (a people 'veterum Germaniae morum tenacissimos').[2] The period in which the feudal aids were not fixed, but imposed by the lord according to his needs, accounts for such Irish exactions as the 'cutting'.[3] The earliest stage of all, that in which tenure was merely precarious, survives in English copyhold, where the tenure is *ad voluntatem domini*.[4] Little as may be the permanent value of such a classification, it is important in Spelman's thought; it shows that he was systematically employing the categories of the *Libri Feudorum* to arrange and account for the phenomena that were occupying his mind, and it enabled him to distinguish sharply between usages such as the above, which to him were approximations to true feudalism, and the *feudum* proper, which must possess all the characteristics which Gerardus attributes to the last stage of its growth—above all that of being fully and perpetually heritable. He next applies this test to distinguish the tenures of the Anglo-Saxons from those which prevailed under the Normans.

The Saxons possessed many customs dating from earlier stages in Gerardus' scheme, and in this sense Spelman would allow that the origin of feuds was to be found among them. But if they had the origins, they had not the thing itself.

Feodorum servitutes in Britanniam nostram primus invexit Gulielmus senior, Conquestor nuncupatus: qui lege ea e Normannia traducta, Angliam totam suis divisit commilitibus. Innuit hoc ipsum (ut Authores taceam) codex eius agrarius qui Domesdei appellatur....Deinceps vero resonarunt omnia *Feodorum* gravaminibus; Saxonum aevo ne auditis quidem.[5]

[1] Same page, col. 1.
[2] 1626 *Archaeologus*, p. 312, *sub* 'Gavelkind'.
[3] 1626 *Archaeologus*, p. 63, col. 1, *sub* 'Auxilium'.
[4] 1626 *Archaeologus*, p. 257 (misnumbered 158), col. 2; see also p. 253.
[5] 'Feudal burdens were first introduced into Britain by William I, known as the Conqueror; who, bringing this law with him from Normandy, divided

The Discovery of Feudalism: Sir Henry Spelman

Spelman became involved in controversy over these words and once at least modified his doctrine by saying that it was not *feuda* that were new with the Conquest, but only their burdens such as wardship, marriage and relief;[1] but at the same time he argued that these services revealed the existence of a fully developed *feudum*, because they could only be charged on a hereditary tenure. For this passage from *Archaeologus* was challenged, years later, in a court of law, and Spelman wrote a classic treatise in order to defend it. In the important *Case of Defective Titles*, the Irish judges were asked to consider whether a grant of land by letters patent, admittedly void in what it said about tenure, was therefore invalid altogether. For the grantees it was argued that while the tenure concerned was feudal and therefore—on Spelman's authority—no older than the Conquest, grants were part of the common law and therefore immemorial, so that they could not be invalidated merely because they were void in respect of the tenure. In condemning the grant, the judges denied Spelman's historical opinion and invoked the rival authority of Selden to support the view that feudal knight-service, with all its incidents, existed among the Anglo-Saxons. Spelman replied in 1639 with the *Treatise of Feuds and Tenures by Knight-service in England* (not printed until 1698) in which his version of feudal history was set forth in detail.[2]

He expanded his earlier argument:[3] the test of knight-service is not merely military service done in respect of tenure, but the subjection of the tenant to wardship, marriage and relief; the tenure must therefore be hereditary. Now feudal tenure is the product of an

up all England among his companions. This is indicated (to say nothing of the chroniclers) by his agrarian survey which is called Domesday Book....From that time we hear constantly of all the obligations of feudal tenure, which are unknown in the Saxon epoch.' 1626 *Archaeologus*, p. 258, col. 2.

[1] *Reliquiae*, p. 46.

[2] The whole controversy, with the relevant passages from the Irish judgment, is set forth in Gibson's preface to *Reliquiae*. The official report of the case was printed at Wentworth's command and appears as an appendix to the 1725 edition of Molyneux's *The Case of Ireland Truly Stated* (1st ed. 1698), whose arguments it is intended to support.

[3] What follows is a summary of an argument so rich that it is almost an impertinence to compress it, and there seems no necessity to assign every statement to the page which authorizes it.

evolution common to all the Germanic nations, and the roots from which it grew can no doubt be found among the Anglo-Saxons as elsewhere; but on the Continent it followed a well-marked evolution towards heritability, whose stages are known and which culminated in the actions of Hugh Capet in 988 and Conrad II in 1026. The Normans can be shown to have reached the final stage shortly before the Conquest, by comparing their usages in England with those they followed in Sicily, where they were established by 1031. It is in the first place improbable that English law, which we know to have undergone no French or imperial influence before the Conquest, should have anticipated this continental evolution on its own account. But we need not rely on this argument. We possess, in the *Libri Feudorum* and from French and other sources, many details of the hereditary *feudum* and the burdens it imposed, and it is perfectly possible to ascertain whether this relationship existed among the Anglo-Saxons.

Spelman proceeded to demonstrate that the military service performed by English thanes neither arose from homage nor was imposed together with a grant of land by a lord; and that since no such relationship existed there was nothing that could properly be called a *feudum*, still less a hereditary *feudum*, and consequently no rights of wardship, marriage or relief. Moreover, none of the words in which these things were described in the language of all other nations could be found in English documents before 1066; whereas all the relevant words and all the customs characteristic of the *feudum* could be found in plenty once the Normans were established. He had achieved his end in two ways: he had learnt the set of characteristics by which the *feudum* could be identified anywhere and distinguished from those social relationships which more or less resembled it, and he possessed a theory of its growth which satisfactorily explained why it should have appeared in England at a particular time and no earlier. In this way he had proved that the mature *feudum* had been imported into England by the Normans and had played an important part there. For, he added—both in *Archaeologus* and in the *Treatise*—it was now possible to see why Littleton had defined the *feodum* as 'idem quod haereditas'. That was no more than the culminating step in the age-old evolution of the *feudum* towards heritability. Sir Thomas Smith had been wrong in suggesting that Littleton's definition was unsound; the common-law *feodum* was a true *feudum*, even when treated 'pro haereditate et perpetuo rei immobilis dominio, licet ex more feudali, dominum agnosceret superiorem'.[1] For every piece of land in England did in fact (said Spelman) recognize a superior lord, namely the king, and it was therefore clear, both that common-law tenure naturally formed part of the feudal evolution, and that all the land of England had once been held feudally, in the *Libri Feudorum* sense of the word. The Conqueror must therefore—as the best chroniclers declared—have divided the whole country among his followers to hold in *feuda* of the Lombard and Norman pattern.

Spelman had thus established that the basic tenure of English law had at a time past involved the whole complex of lord-vassal relationships described by Gerardus, Obertus and a great company of continental writers on feudal and customary law. It could now be seen that a large number of these relationships were in fact mentioned or implied in the books of the common law and could be explained by reference to a common origin. It was this which constituted the seventeenth-century revolution in English historiography. By comparative study it had been discovered that English law had a great deal in common with the laws of other western nations, and that most of these common characteristics could be explained by using the academic definitions of feudalism to be found in the *Libri Feudorum* and their French editors. The feudal relationship as thus defined—a thing existing only in the past as far as England was concerned—could now be employed to bring about a radical reinterpretation of the whole body of English law as it had existed in the Middle Ages, simply by explaining every feature susceptible of that treatment as one of its consequences. This was the beginning of the genuinely historical study of English institutions and the only possible alternative to the pseudo-historical thought of Coke and the common lawyers. Because the latter lived in a closed

---

[1] 'as the inheritance and perpetual lordship of a piece of real property, although by feudal custom it should acknowledge a superior lord.' 1626 *Archaeologus*, p. 262, col. 2: 'Cum autem eo perventum esset, etc.'; cf. *Reliquiae*, p. 6.

intellectual world, the new technique possessed a highly abstract and even *a priori* character. 'Let us then see', Spelman once wrote, 'how the practice of those ancient ages agreed with this Theoreme',[1] and the words fairly describe his historical method. It was necessary to adopt a new definition of the basic English tenure from foreign sources, quite outside those of the common law, and to use this academic account of the *feudum* to redefine the whole body of the law as it had existed in times past. There is something reminiscent of contemporary advances in the natural sciences about this procedure; Bacon would surely have approved of this rearrangement of the evidence in the light of a single fundamental hypothesis independently arrived at. If, as Maitland intimated, Spelman's 'introduction of the feudal system' is too systematic and too abstract,[2] the fault lies mainly in the insularity of English thought.

II

It remains to see how far Spelman carried the remodelling of English history which he had made possible. The history of historiography contains far fewer examples of systematic revisions of entire fields of study, carried out in the clear light of day, than of the gradual emergence of a new standpoint from a mass of traditional preconceptions, and Spelman's thought is no exception to this rule. He recognized, however, that it was now theoretically possible to construct a completely new historical analysis of the law by distinguishing the elements of various origin which it contained. In the paper, already cited, which he first wrote in 1614, he pointed out that English law could be shown to consist, first, of primeval custom Germanic in its origins, heavily influenced by subsequent borrowings from the civil and canon law; and second,

in matters touching Inheritance, Fees, Tenure by Knights-service, Rents, Services, Wards, Marriage of Wards, Reliefs, Treason, Pleas of the Crown, Escheats, dower of the third part, aids, fines, Felony, Forfeiture, Tryal by battel, Essoine, Warrantie, etc. from the Feudal Law chiefly; as those that read the books of those Laws collected by *Obertus* and *Gerardus* may see apparently. Tho' we and divers other Nations (according as befitteth every

---

[1] *Reliquiae*, p. 61.   [2] *Constitutional History*, pp. 142-3.

one in their particular respects) do in many things vary from them, which *Obertus* confesseth to be requisite, and to happen often among the *Longobards* themselves. I do marvel many times that my Lord *Cooke*, adorning our Law with so many flowers of Antiquity and foreign Learning; hath not (as I suppose) turned aside into this field, from whence so many roots of our Law, have of old been taken and transplanted. I wish some worthy Lawyer would read them diligently, and shew the several heads from whence these of ours are taken. They beyond the seas are not only diligent but very curious in this kind; but we are all for profit and *Lucrando pane*, taking what we find at Market, without enquiring whence it came.[1]

This is impressive; and Spelman more than once shows himself capable of distinguishing between the Germanic, civil, canon and feudal elements in common law and studying particular aspects of legal and juridical history in terms of their successive influences. An instance is the discourse, dated 1633, *Of the Original of Wills and Testaments and of their Probate*, in which he shows the Anglo-Saxons first as primitive Germans knowing nothing of the testament, then as moved to adopt it by Roman influence felt through ecclesiastical channels, and increasingly transferring the probate to priestly hands. Next he depicts the joint sitting of earl and bishop in the shire courts, which brought pre-Gratian canonical ideas to bear on testamentary and many other types of case. The Normans put an end to this phase by excluding ecclesiastics from the shire courts and by introducing feudal tenures which virtually withdrew the land from testamentary disposition. With a few remarks on the probate in Norman times, Spelman concludes: 'I am now come to the lists of the modern Common Law, and I dare venture no further';[2] an interesting remark, if it means that he still looked on the law, as revealed in its records, as being the professional mystery of the lawyers, and did not presume to apply himself to its historical development once the records had begun.

There was nothing in the common law which Spelman need regard as immemorial, and he had dissolved the notion of custom into a series of influences of diverse origins. Thus there seems no reason in theory why he should not have analysed it into its component elements and written its history at least to the time of the

---

[1] *Reliquiae*, pp. 98–9.   [2] *Reliquiae*, pp. 127–32.

first records. Even if every statement it contained had required subsequent correction, this work by an English Cujas would have been one of the most important books in the national historiography. But it remained unwritten. Spelman neither completed the writing of *Archaeologus* nor printed all that he had written. About 1630 he seems definitely to have turned away from legal and towards ecclesiastical studies,[1] and though he wrote some short papers on legal history during the 1630's, he was hardly likely to embark on a general history of the law before he had finished his study of the legal vocabulary. The truth is that no one man could finish all that Spelman had begun, and it would have been in keeping with his age if he had felt that the history of the common law were better left to 'some worthy Lawyer', despite the improbability that any member of the profession would undertake a task so destructive of cherished convictions.

But the *Codex Legum Veterum*, which he completed in 1627, the year after printing the first volume of *Archaeologus*, and designed to publish in 1640, but which was not printed until 1721,[2] shows that traditional ideas of the law's antiquity had not yet lost their hold on him. The *Codex* combines an account of how the Normans introduced feudal tenure into England with the older doctrine—to which Spelman had already given some countenance in *Archaeologus*—that they confirmed the law of Edward the Confessor. The Conqueror, in the first place, was no conqueror:

conquestus enim in antiquis chartis illud notat quod jure haereditario non habemus a parentibus, sed quod labore comparatum est vel parsimonia.[3]

None the less, he brought in feudal tenures. Spelman explains how the *feudum* had become established in Europe and had grown to be hereditary among the Normans, while remaining unknown in its true sense among the Saxons, and considers the evidence for holding that William brought all English land under French feudal tenures

[1] See Sir Maurice Powicke's lecture, cited above.

[2] In Wilkins, *Leges Anglo-Saxonicae*, pp. 284 ff. All references to the *Codex* are to this edition.

[3] 'for "conquestus" in the old records means that which we do not inherit from our parents, but acquire by our labour or thrift.' Wilkins, p. 285, cols. 1–2.

and converted earldoms into hereditary titles involving tenure in chief of the crown. But 'distributis praediis, de *Legibus* cogitat innovandis';[1] he meditated introducing the Danish law, under which he had been brought up, but was deterred by the prayers of the *proceres* and instead restored, with much solemnity and after verification by twelve men of each shire, the laws of Edward the Confessor. This, however, he did not do, as contemporaries tell us, without amending them heavily by the introduction of Norman customs. Spelman repeats the assertion, already made in *Archaeologus,* that the *leges Confessoris,* whether we take them from Hoveden or from 'Ingulf of Croyland'—in whose authenticity he believed—cannot be the law exactly as it was in the Confessor's time; they contain far too many French words and feudal customs which can only be Norman in origin.[2] While it is known that William inserted Norman customs in the Confessor's law, these have never been collected and are not easy to distinguish from those of the preceding age; Spelman identifies them, however, by discussing the difference between Saxon usages and Lombard feudal tenures and noting the presence of the latter in William's so-called *leges Confessoris.*[3] Nevertheless, he does not deny that a text of the Confessor's law existed and was confirmed, though amended, by the Conqueror. William Rufus and Henry I built up their credit with the English by promising them their ancient law, and Henry issued his charter confirming the *leges Confessoris*; this example was followed by Stephen and Henry II; and so the story runs until Magna Carta, of which Spelman's interpretation—even though he singles out and emphasizes every feudal element in the document—is as 'Confessorial' as the most ardent common lawyer could desire. He does not carry his narrative beyond the early years of Henry III.

In the *Codex,* evidently, Spelman was trying to pour his new wine into old bottles. He described at length the feudal tenures introduced by the Normans and lost no opportunity of showing how much they had influenced English law and government thereafter; yet he attempted to reconcile this newly discovered

---

[1] 'having distributed estates among his men, he thought of making new laws.' Wilkins, pp. 287–8.

[2] Wilkins, p. 291, col. 2.   [3] Wilkins, pp. 288 ff.

The Discovery of Feudalism: Sir Henry Spelman

pattern in our early history with the common-law 'myth of the confirmations'. We must not forget the weight of evidence and authority, both medieval and modern, which had made this legend an ingrained part of the English tradition. But we shall see in a later chapter that Robert Brady, the first true disciple of Spelman's feudal interpretation, while accepting the chronicle stories of William's confirming the ancient law, so far emphasized the feudal content of Anglo-Norman law as to rob the idea of confirmation of virtually all its meaning. Brady would never have written 'distributis praediis, de *Legibus* cogitat innovandis', because he saw that the distribution of the land in feudal tenures was the fundamental fact which determined the character of the law: once this was accomplished, the law could not be other than feudal and attempts, then or now, to pretend that it was the old English law could be dismissed as hollow.[1] Brady, in short, followed the consequences of Spelman's discovery further and more ruthlessly than Spelman himself. The latter's conservatism may be accounted for by sheer caution, or—like his insistence that William was no conqueror—by the obstinate survival of inherited ideas; and it may not be irrelevant that the *Codex* was written in the year before the Petition of Right, and that Spelman is thought to have supported the view that the demands of that document amounted to a claim for the ancient liberties. But the author of the *Codex* was not likely to rewrite the whole history of the law in the way that the author of *Archaeologus* had made possible. Spelman instead turned his attention to the history of parliament, and in this no less important field achieved his most revolutionary conclusions.

What he did was to find means of reinterpreting the history of parliament in the light of the *feudum*. He had always been interested by what may be termed the curial aspect of the feudal relationship; we have seen how he selected words of Tacitus which implied that the *comites* were obliged to furnish their lord with counsel. In the article 'Felo, felonia', which forms part of *Archaeologus*, he carried this idea further. Felony, he pointed out, was a word used by both Hostiensis and the *Libri Feudorum* in the purely feudal sense of that dereliction of duty for which the vassal forfeits his fee. In England

[1] See ch. VIII, below, section II.

it had been applied especially to the relations between the king and his subjects and had come to mean the offence for which the king exacted the *pretium feodi*; and this term the common law had expanded to include the forfeit 'totius haereditatis, fortunarum omnium, ipsiusque vitae'. It was like Spelman to see that the central concept of English criminal justice was developed from the feudal relationship; and in working out the history of *felonia* he traced, parallel to the evolution of the *feudum* from precarious to perpetual, the evolution from a state of things in which the vassal could be dispossessed at the mere will of the lord to one in which dispossession was controlled by law and legal only in the case of certain specified felonies. The stages in this development he took from the imperial constitutions included in the *Libri Feudorum*, and he thought that it had culminated in a constitution of Conrad's which declared that tenants were to be dispossessed only 'convicta culpa, et approbata iudicio parium curiae'. Just as—he went on— the vassal's one-time liability to dispossession at will was reflected in the English copyholder's tenure *ad voluntatem domini*, so too the judgment of the *pares curiae* corresponded to that verdict of the tenants of the manor by which alone the copyholder could be forfeited in the English court baron. Obertus had remarked that definitions of felony differed as widely as the usages of the various types of *curia*.[1] Spelman was clearly impressed with the versatility and wide distribution of the *curia* and its *pares*, and in the article 'Baro' he took the decisive step of applying these concepts to the history of parliament.

He knew—as did every educated Englishman; it was a matter of everyday knowledge of the law—that one of the essential marks of baronage was the right to a personal summons to parliament, and that there were three grounds on which this right could be claimed: tenure *in capite* of the crown, the hereditary receipt of a writ of summons and the possession of letters patent creating one or one's ancestor a baron with right to sit in parliament. But because he had already shown that *baro* was a feudal term common to most western nations and that in England it had formerly borne the purely feudal connotations by which it was recognized elsewhere,[2]

[1] 1626 *Archaeologus*, pp. 252–3.   [2] 1626 *Archaeologus*, pp. 77–9.

Spelman concluded that of these three claims that based on tenure of the crown was the original and fundamental one; and, more important still, that the right by which the baron attended his king in parliament was the same as that which determined the composition of his own court baron.

Illud certissimum est; eos olim maiores Barones habitos esse, qui de Rege tenentes in Capite, iudiciis praefuere Aulae Regiae; nuperius qui in Parlamentariis Comitiis Regi assident et suffragia ferunt, *Parlamentarii* inde *Barones* nuncupati Anglice *Lords of Parlament*....Quemadmodum itaque neque *Barones* ipsi *maiores*, neque *minores*, quempiam in Curiis suis ad iudicia consiliave ferenda de rebus sui dominii admittunt, nisi vassallos suos, qui de ipsis immediate tenent, hoc est, Milites suos et Tenentes libere: ita in summa Curia totius regni, nulli olim ad iudicia et consilia administranda personaliter accersendi erant, nisi qui proximi essent a Rege, ipsique arctioris fidei, et homagii vinculo coniuncti, hoc est, immediati vassalli sui, *Barones* nempe cuiuscunque generis qui de ipso tenuere in Capite, ut partim videas in *Brevi summonitionis*, partim in Charta libertatum Regis Iohannis inferius citatis.[1]

There had been a time when all barons had attended the king merely by reason of their tenure, and when parliament, so far as their attendance determined its character, had been simply a feudal *curia* in which the barons met their king, as vassals their lord, to discuss the affairs of his lordship. It had next to be shown how this state of things had come to an end. Like his great contemporary John Selden, Spelman attached much importance to the clause of Magna Carta in which it is said 'summoneri faciemus' the greater

---

[1] 'This much is certain: that those were once considered greater barons who held of the king in chief and presided over the judgments of his court; and more recently, those who sit with the king and vote in his parliamentary assemblies, deriving thence the name of *barones parlamentarii*, or in English "lords of parliament"....In the same way as neither greater nor lesser barons admitted anyone to their *curiae* to give judgment or counsel on the affairs of their lordships, except their vassals who held of them direct, that is their knights and free tenants; so in the supreme *curia* of the whole kingdom, none was formerly summoned in person to give judgment and counsel except those who were nearest to the king and bound to him by the strictest ties of fealty and homage: that is his immediate vassals, the barons of whatever degree who held of him in chief, as you may see in the writ of summons and in King John's charter of liberties, both of which are cited below.' 1626 *Archaeologus*, pp. 79–80.

tenants in chief by individual letters, and 'omnes alios qui de nobis tenent in capite . . . in generali per vicecomites et ballivos nostros'.[1] He assumed that the assembly which this described was a parliament, and he thought that these provisions had been included in the Charter because it was desired to safeguard every tenant in chief's right to that summons to parliament which was an essential mark of baronage. As early as 1215, he suggested, the king was using his prerogative of issuing writs of summons to omit from parliament some who were tenants *in capite* and to summon others who were not; these discriminations tended to become permanent and those summoned to be known as barons whatever their tenure. 'Aegre hoc ferentes Proceres', they compelled John to guarantee every tenant his summons, while perpetuating the distinction between *barones maiores* and *minores* by means of the personal summons as opposed to the general. But the attempt failed; the use of the writ continued, under Henry III and Edward I, to act as a solvent on the purely tenurial nature of baronage; and

sic antiqua illa Baronum dignitas secessit sensim in titularem et arbitrariam, regioque tandem diplomate idcirco dispensata est.[2]

The creation of barons by patent completed the process, and in Spelman's own day those who claimed their baronies *ratione tenurae* did so by prescription or descent from the ancient baronial families, rather than because they now held in chief of the crown.[3]

Selden's interpretation of *summoneri faciemus* is discussed elsewhere;[4] it is broadly similar, and both men were prepared to envisage that baronage had once been a purely tenurial status and the whole kingdom a single feudal estate. But Spelman went further than Selden and applied this concept to the history of parliament as a whole. Believing as he did that the *summoneri faciemus* clause described the regular form of holding a parliament in the thirteenth

---

[1] Clause 14 in the 1215 Charter. Spelman took his text from Matthew Paris and the Red Book of the Exchequer.

[2] 'so that ancient dignity of baronage became by degrees a mere arbitrary title, and at length came to be granted by royal patent.' 1626 *Archaeologus*, p. 80, col. 1.

[3] *Loc. cit.* cols. 1–2.

[4] In ch. VI, below, pp. 137–8.

century, he could not but notice that parliament at that time had consisted exclusively of tenants *in capite*, great and small, all of whom attended in right of their tenure and all of whom were performing the vassal's duty to counsel the lord in his *curia*. It must therefore follow that the knights and burgesses of his own day, men who appeared in answer to the writ of summons because they had been chosen to represent their fellows and not because they owed the king personal service as his immediate tenants, had come into existence at a time subsequent to 1215. The historian's task now became to trace and explain the emergence of the Commons from a feudal background.

The practice of interpreting medieval law as the consequence of relationships based on the *feudum* had now resulted in a denial that parliament was immemorial, and in a very strong argument that the kingdom had once been a feudal estate, in which all relationships had been determined by tenure of the crown, and in which consequently the only kind of parliament that could be imagined as existing was a feudal council on the exact analogy of the *curia*. This is very probably the most important single discovery that has ever been made in the historiography of the medieval constitution, and the fact that Spelman made it dwarfs into insignificance the outmoded postulates which it contains and on which it is partly based. He believed that *summoneri faciemus* described a parliament which had met regularly, and it seems almost certain—this point will be further discussed when we compare his thought with that of his successor Brady—that he regarded the *omnes alios qui tenent in capite* as a class of knights who held direct of the crown and out of whom the knights of the shire had in some way developed. These are ideas which no one now accepts, but they enabled Spelman to approach the next great task of his historiography, that of ascertaining how the purely tenurial council had given place to the parliament of freeholders' representatives—which, with all the modifications which have subsequently been found necessary, is still recognizably the form in which we conceive the problem of parliamentary history.

The article entitled 'Parlamentum' which Spelman wrote for inclusion in *Archaeologus* was not printed in the 1626 volume, which extends only to the letter L, and consequently it was not published until Dugdale's complete edition appeared in 1664; and though it was through this essay that his interpretation of parliamentary history made its impact on the thought of the century, there is almost no sign of this before 1675. Spelman presented a theory of the origins of parliament and the rise of the House of Commons founded throughout on the conception that vassalage was the organizing principle of medieval society. The first step was to establish that though William I 'acquisivit, non conquisivit Angliam', he nevertheless caused every foot of land to be held of him by some tenant in chief 'per servitium plerumque baroniae'. Spelman next reiterated the identity of the medieval king's *concilium* with the feudal *curia*, and stressed that as the king was feudal lord of all the land, there were none but his barons whom he would admit to give him counsel:

rex perinde, qui totius regni dominus est supremus, regnumque universum, tam in personis baronum suorum, quam e subditorum ligeantia, ex jure coronae suae subjectum habet, consilio et assensu baronum suorum leges olim imposuit universo regno.[1]

Since there was no land that was not feudalized, there could have been no proprietors in the realm who were not either tenants *in capite* or their sub-tenants—the *allodium* being unknown in English law[2]—and Spelman believed it to be a universal feudal principle that the sub-tenant's assent was taken to be included in that which his lord gave in the king's court in matters touching his fee.[3] So long as feudal tenure endured unmodified, therefore, none but the king's tenants *in capite* could possibly appear to give him counsel in his court, and the advent there of persons who were not tenants must be a sign of the ending of the feudal world. As late as 1215, the Charter provided what Spelman evidently regarded as a classic

[1] 'the king likewise, who is supreme lord of the whole land and holds all the kingdom subject by right of his crown, whether by his immediate authority over his barons or by the allegiance which their sub-tenants owe him, once gave the whole kingdom laws by the counsel and assent of his barons.' *Glossarium Archaiologium* (1664; this is Dugdale's title for his complete edition of *Archaeologus*), p. 451, col. 1.

[2] See article 'Allodium' in 1626 *Archaeologus*.

[3] Further discussed in ch. VIII, section II, below.

picture of the feudal council in its maturity: the greater tenants summoned personally, the lesser generally through the sheriffs, but all attending out of the ancient obligations of the vassals.

When and how had this state of things come to an end? Spelman considered the evidence for the first summoning to parliament of the *plebs*—by which he clearly meant the commons who did not attend *ratione tenurae*—and, after rejecting various more or less remote dates, decided that there was no sign of their presence 'ab ingressu Gulielmi I ad excessum Henrici III'. He offered no single date at which they had first appeared, because the theory he was about to put forward was such as to preclude anything of the kind.[1] Though he is not perfectly explicit on this point, Spelman clearly thinks that the elected knights of the shire are in some way descended from the lesser tenants in chief of Magna Carta: that the latter, on receiving their general summons through the sheriff, elected some of their number to represent them, and that in time electors and elected ceased to be confined to the immediate tenants of the crown. In an unfinished paper, 'Of Parliaments', composed near the end of his life, he suggested that the fact that there were only two knights for each shire might be explained by supposing that the number of lesser tenants in chief had never been very great.[2] But he is noticeably vague on the manner in which the transition was accomplished. Here his thought might be held to suffer from a failure to make full use of the shire court. He knew that from an early time this body had included

omnis *Baronum* feodalium species, in uno quovis Comitatu degentium: Proceres nempe et Maneriorum domini, nec non libere quique Tenentes, hoc est, fundorum proprietarii. Anglice, *freeholders*,[3]

and it would have been easy to depict the shire court acting upon the general summons as the royal writ had acted upon the personal, altering the basis of parliamentary attendance until it was no longer tenurial. He preferred, however, to depict the change to free-holders' representatives merely as part of the general decline of

---

[1] *Glossarium* (1664), p. 451, col. 2.
[2] *Reliquiae*, p. 64.
[3] 1626 *Archaeologus*, p. 84, col. 2, *sub* 'Barones comitatus'.

feudal relationships. In 'Of Parliaments' he wrote that the *libere tenentes* of mesne lords,

> because they could not always be certainly distinguish'd from them that held *in capite*, (which encreased daily) grew by little and little to have voices in election of the Knights of the Shire, and at last to be confirm'd therein by the Stat. 7. *Henr.* IV and 8. *Henr.* VI.[1]

Here the shire court is the theatre in which the vital development takes place, but it is scarcely an actor therein. The nature of the process by which the lesser tenants *in capite* became indistinguishable from the other *libere tenentes* is not made clear, but, in his earlier-quoted discussion of the shire court, Spelman remarked that the county freeholders were formerly not so inconsiderable as they had later become, 'nam villas et Dominia in minutas haereditates nondum distrahebant'; and he may have thought that subdivision of land held of the crown had played a part in that blurring of distinctions between the crown's and other men's military tenants on which his whole theory of the rise of the commons depended.[2] But when all is said and done, Spelman's account of the social processes which brought feudal society to an end is never specific; he knows only that such processes must have occurred and that they must have been very gradual—so much so that he will fix no date for the origin of the commons, since no date can be fixed for the moment at which the lesser tenants in chief became finally indistinguishable from the freeholders. This is both a strength and a weakness in his historical thought: on the one hand it prevented him from giving too much importance to individuals and isolated actions and directed seventeenth-century attention to the gradual processes it was inclined to ignore; on the other the fact that Spelman knew that feudalism must have declined, but was unable to particularize the process or go into its causes, contained dangers for lesser minds. We shall see that James Harrington, possessing no better knowledge, imagined that feudal society had remained more or less intact until the legislation of the first Tudors.

[1] *Reliquiae*, p. 64.

[2] See ch. VIII, section II, below, for a.discussion of the way in which his view of the knight's fee may have influenced his beliefs at this point.

The Discovery of Feudalism: Sir Henry Spelman

The idea of a gradual decay of feudal ties completes the account of parliamentary history given in 'Parlamentum'.

> Post susceptionem plebis in comitia parlamentaria sensim decerpitur fastigiosa illa magnatum potestas, coercito alias eorum in tenentes imperio, et laxata alias plebis in eo servitute. Fit hoc statutis plurimis, adeoque labefactata est superbia procerum, ut adversus Regem nemo suscitare ausus est novorum quidpiam, si de regno non ageretur. Sed ecce novus iam Leviathan grassari coepit. Liberata iam ab imperio dominorum, offensa ex quavis causa, plebs quae ad arma hactenus absque voluntate dominorum nunquam convolant; iam non habentes quibus audiant in gravissimas insurgunt rebelliones, quod ne semel unquam factum est anterius.[1]

Whose were the statutes that relaxed the feudal ties—whether Edward I's or, as Harrington thought, Henry VII's or VIII's—Spelman does not tell us; but it is of far more interest to ask who precisely made up the 'new Leviathan' which waxed fat on its liberation from feudal authority until it became a grave danger to ordered society. Whoever they were, they menaced the crown when they swelled the power of the magnates; the king in parliament took steps to emancipate them, but thus raised up a new power which he could not altogether control. This statement occurs in the course of an essay on parliamentary history and the context makes it very tempting to assume that the *plebs*, the new Leviathan, is the parliamentary freeholders. If this is Spelman's meaning, we have passed at one stride into the world of James Harrington, and the rebellious conduct of the House of Commons is being explained as

---

[1] 'After the admission of the commons to parliament, the exalted power of the magnates was by degrees pared away, both because their authority over their tenants was restricted and because the services which these owed them were relaxed. This was brought about by many acts of parliament, and so far was the pride of the magnates brought low, that none dared to raise any new movement against the king unless it were a question of the crown. But now a new Leviathan began to prowl. The people, freed from the dominion of their lords, took offence at the slightest cause; and though they had never before resorted to arms unless by the will of their lords, there were no longer any for them to obey, and they broke out in rebellions of the utmost gravity, a thing which had never happened in previous centuries.' *Glossarium* (1664), p. 452. In the corrected manuscript of this paragraph (Bodleian Library MS. e Mus. 48, f. 471) the first sentence runs, '...potestas coercita, alias...'. The emendation seems clear. It will be seen that Spelman's Latin is shaky.

the consequence of the creation of a new class as feudalism decays. But Spelman died in October 1641, when civil war was not yet universally foreseen; and we have no means of knowing whether this paragraph was written in the last years of his life. If the *plebs* are the parliamentary Commons, in what *gravissimae rebelliones* had they engaged of which Spelman might have been thinking? It is possible to gain some rather uncertain light on this problem by referring to his *History of Sacrilege*.

This book forms one of a number which Spelman wrote against lay possession of sacred things, in this case church lands and impropriated rectories, his ownership of some of the latter having involved him in a vexatious lawsuit. He became convinced that the whole process of dissolution had been sacrilegious, and wrote largely to exhibit the effects of the divine displeasure under which England lay as a consequence; and he gave so many often scandalous instances of the decay of families who had acquired abbey lands that, in an age when country-house opinion was peculiarly strong and the possessors of church land decidedly touchy about their titles, none could be found to publish it until 1698, when White Kennett brought out an edition to forestall its appearance under impious auspices.[1] No class in the kingdom, said Spelman, had benefited by the dissolution, and certainly not Henry VIII.

> I speak not of his prodigal Hand in the Blood of his Subjects, which no doubt much alienated the Hearts of them from him. But God in these eleven Years space visited him with 5 or 6 Rebellions. In *Lincolnshire*, Anno 28, and 3 one after another in *Yorkshire*, Anno 33; one in *Somersetshire*, Anno 29, and again in *Yorkshire*, Anno 33. And though Rebellions and Insurrections are not to be defended, yet they discover unto us what the displeasure and dislike was of the common People for Spoiling the Revenues of the Church; whereby they were great losers, the Clergy being mercifull Landlords, and bountifull Benefactors to all Men by their great Hospitality and Works of Charity.[2]

In the formidable agrarian outbreaks of the sixteenth century, which Spelman might see reflected in the not inconsiderable fen-land disorders of his own Norfolk generation, we have a possible alternative explanation of the new Leviathan and its *gravissimae*

[1] See his preface to the 1698 edition.   [2] *History of Sacrilege*, pp. 190-1.

rebelliones. But it remains true that logically the passage from 'Parlamentum' should refer to the freeholders. What of the gentry since the dissolution? Having described the many personal disasters which befell Henry VIII's peers, Spelman proceeds:

> Now I labour in observing the Particulars, seeing the whole body of the Baronage is since that fallen so much from their ancient lustre, magnitude and estimation. I that about 50 Years ago did behold with what great respect, observance, and distance, principal Men of Countries apply'd themselves to some of the meanest Barons, and so with what familiarity inferiour Gentlemen often do accost many of these of our times, cannot but wonder either at the Declination of the one, or at the Arrogance of the other.... To say what I observe herein, as the Nobility spoiled God of his Honour by putting those things from him, and communicating them to lazy and vulgar persons; so God to requite them hath taken the ancient Honours of Nobility, and communicat[ed][1] them to the meanest of the People, to Shopkeepers, Taverners, Taylors, Tradesmen, Burghers, Brewers, Grasiers; and it may be supposed, that as *Constantine the Great* seeing the inconvenience of the multitude of *Comites* of his time distinguished them, as *Eusebius* reporteth, into three degrees making the latter far inferior to the former; so may it one day come to pass among these of our times; and it shall not want some precedent of our own to the like purpose.[2]

Here we seem very close to Harrington and to a 'rise of the gentry, 1540–1640'. But whatever Spelman's estimate of the numbers of social upstarts, he does not present the whole class of the gentry as a people waxing rich and unmanageable. Certainly the king had to sell the church lands as fast as they came in to him, and his ancient crown lands as well, and all these passed into the hands of private proprietors;[3] but all Spelman's emphasis falls upon the fact that the purchasers received the new land subject to the reservation of a tenure *in capite*, which rendered them liable to the intolerable burdens of wardship. Among the Goths and Lombards, where blood-feuds abounded, there was an obvious case for seeing that the tenant did not marry among the lord's enemies, but there can be no justification for its extension to so many English landowners since the dissolution.[4] A sense of anachronism, of the revival

---

[1] The text has 'communicating'.   [2] *Hist. Sacr.* pp. 224–5.
[3] *Hist. Sacr.* pp. 225–7.   [4] *Hist. Sacr.* pp. 229–35.

and perversion of ancient laws, of what we should call 'bastard feudalism', pervades all that Spelman writes on this topic. The gentry have not been delivered from feudal controls and left to grow omnipotent; they have been thrust back under a feudal service that was extinct (says Spelman) except among a few peers and owners of great estates. There is no hint that their dominance as a class is imminent.

It appears, on the whole, unsafe to suppose that Spelman was a Harringtonian before Harrington, or that the rebellious *plebs* of 'Parlamentum' can with any certainty be identified with the parliamentary freeholders or with what moderns call 'the gentry'. Nevertheless, the paragraph whose meaning we have been disputing reveals that Spelman had realized an historical truth which underlies the thought of Harrington and many other writers of the age. In the past the mass of people had been sub-tenants of the great lords and this had constituted a menace to the power of the crown. Now they were free of feudal services, and there was a growing impression that action on the crown's part had been largely responsible for this; but it had left the crown exposed to the attacks of people who were neither great lords nor bound to it by any sort of tenure. The crown had thus, by a kind of dialectic, raised up forces which it could not control. This generalization, which has remained potent in our historical thought to this day, appeared in the seventeenth century as soon as the existence of a feudal state of society in the past was at all widely realized. It owes much of its power and some of its unsatisfactoriness to the fact that it has always been easier for the English historian to anatomize in detail the workings of the feudal world than to particularize the processes of its decline; it is probably true that the average graduate of today knows the eleventh to thirteenth centuries far better than the fourteenth and fifteenth. This in its turn, in the obscure processes of the history of thought, can almost certainly be traced to Spelman's possession of a quasi-theoretical formula of the nature of feudalism which he could apply to medieval law and parliament with the most brilliant and astonishing results, but which left him with little more to say about the decline of the state of things founded on the *feudum* than that it must have occurred. The great value of his contribution, in being among the first to draw attention to this enormously important subject, must be offset by his inability to make any very useful contribution to its study. The feudal interpretation raised, but did not solve, the problem of the place occupied in English history by a monarchy which had once rested on a foundation of feudal relationships, had later contributed in some way to their decline and now survived them.

III

The main achievement of the feudal revolution in English historiography—of which Spelman was not the sole, but the principal architect—was to impose upon English history the division into pre-feudal, feudal and post-feudal periods which has ever since characterized it. The Conquest transformed Anglo-Saxon society by the systematic importation of Continental feudal tenures; the relationship of the barons to the crown from the eleventh to thirteenth centuries is to be understood in terms of vassalage and its obligations; the appearance of the county freeholders in parliament, where they were not obliged to attend by their tenures, could come about only in a society where feudal relationships were beginning to lose their exclusive importance. We may find much to criticize in this statement of the case, but it may be doubted whether we have found any more satisfactory set of generalizations to put in its place, or whether we have added anything which is more than a modification—except indeed the idea that the growth of the common law, centralized in the royal courts, had a unique and radical effect upon English feudalism and differentiated it from that of any other country. This we shall not find in Spelman, or apparently any other writer of the seventeenth century, because they were not yet capable of thinking independently and historically about the common law once its records had begun. But he and his peers created the only conditions of thought in which it could have been recognized that the common law had been the crown's means of acting within and upon feudal society and ultimately transforming its nature together with its own.

To the seventeenth century the feudal interpretation made another contribution of no less importance. It provided the only means of escape from the thought of the common lawyers and a powerful battery of critical weapons which could be used against them. Nothing would prevent Englishmen believing that their law and constitution were immemorial, unless it could be shown that at a time in the past both law and parliament, though they contained much that still existed today, had in fact been radically different and intelligible only on the basis of principles that were not those of the present age. This proof the feudal interpretation provided, and it did so the more effectively because of the abstract and systematic element which we have noted it contained. The revolution occurred because scholars had reduced the feudal relationship to a small number of simple general ideas and were willing to apply these, almost in the manner of scientific formulae, to the reconstruction of medieval society. They could now lay down a single hypothesis—that Anglo-Norman law and society were feudal law and society—and proceed to outline the whole past condition of England by pitting that hypothesis against the masses of evidence. In Spelman's hands this became a demonstration that England had once been a feudal lordship and the king's council a feudal *curia*, and that neither the Lords nor the Commons of the contemporary parliament could consequently be immemorial. Nor would any of the arguments in the armoury of the school of Coke suffice to prove that the common-law *feodum* was not the *feudum* of the feudal law, and without such a proof the whole theory of the ancient constitution lay open to devastating attack.

Here the feudal interpretation entered the sphere of practical politics. As the tides were running in England, the antiquity of parliament was soon to be a cry of greater political and intellectual importance than the antiquity of the law in general, and Spelman seems to have recognized this. The unfinished treatise 'Of Parliaments', which has already been quoted, opens with these words:

When States are departed from their original Constitution, and that original by tract of time worn out of memory; the succeeding Ages viewing what is past by the present, conceive the former to have been like to that they live in, and framing thereupon erroneous propositions, do likewise make thereon erroneous inferences and Conclusions. I would not pry too boldly into this ark of secrets: but having seen more Parliaments miscarry, yea suffer shipwrack, within these sixteen years past, than in many hundred heretofore, I desire for my understanding's sake to take a view of the beginning and nature of Parliaments; not meddling with them of our time, (which may displease both Court and Country,) but with those of old; which now are like the siege of *Troy*, matters only of story and discourse.

It has been suggested that this treatise belongs to the very last phase of Spelman's life and that 'these sixteen years' began in 1624 or 1625.[1] The evidence may seem flimsy; the sixteen years from 1614 to 1630 contain almost as many troublesome parliaments, and Spelman's ideas of parliamentary history were probably well formed by the last date. However, it is noteworthy that in July 1640 he obtained Chief Justice Bramston's *imprimatur* to the publication (which did not then take place) of the *Codex Legum Veterum*, much of whose contents would have supported the argument in 'Of Parliaments'.[2] It may even be relevant that an attempt to secure Spelman's election (despite his age and poor eyesight) as one of the burgesses for the University of Cambridge miscarried about this time.[3] But whatever the date of this treatise, Spelman was by then convinced that historical error—and the error characteristic of Englishmen in his time—was politically dangerous, but seems to have thought that correction of the error could be undertaken disinterestedly and without giving offence. How wrong he was he might have learned had he completed 'Of Parliaments' and seen it published; for the immemorial nature of parliament had become an article of militant faith with not a few. But he began to set out, in English instead of Latin, his feudal interpretation of parliamentary history, with the intention—it seems fairly certain—of persuading the House of Commons to see itself in historical perspective and abate its more extreme claims.

Parliaments, he proceeds, are younger than kings, as is shown by

[1] *Reliquiae*, p. 57. Cf. L. Van Norden, *Huntington Library Quarterly*, vol. XII (1948–9), p. 371 n. 17: 'can be dated by internal evidence, pp. 57, 58, between the Short and Long Parliaments.' The passage quoted seems to be the only piece of evidence of the kind.

[2] Thus an autograph note on the MS. itself, reported by Gibson in his preface to *Reliquiae*.

[3] Spelman to Abraham Wheelock, 9 Nov. 1640, in Ellis (ed.), *Letters of Eminent Literary Men*, Camden Society (1842), pp. 163–4.

the fact that kings summon them. Moreover, it was the kings who originally granted every man his land, in return for which he owed them loyalty and services, 'not *ex pacto vel condicto* (for that was but *cautela superabundans*) but of common right and by the Law of Nations (for so I may term the Feodal-law then to be in our Western Orb)...tho' no word were spoken of them'.[1] There follows the portrait of a feudal society: in such a world only the king's own tenants could be admitted to give him counsel, all others having their consent included in that of their lord and owing him besides a variety of vexatious services. The Commons, we feel, are to realize not only that their appearance in the councils of the realm is of comparatively late date, but that the very class of freeholders which they represent could not exist in a strictly feudal society. About the time of Henry II

there hapn'd...a notable alteration in the Commonwealth. For the great Lords and owners of towns which before manur'd their lands by Tenants at Will, began now generally to grant them Estates in Fee, and thereby to make a great multitude of Freeholders more than had been. Who by reason of their several interests, and being not so absolutely ty'd unto their Lords as in former times, began now to be a more eminent part in the Commonwealth, and more to be respected therefore in making Laws, to bind them and their Inheritance.[2]

The exact grounds for this statement that the character of sub-tenancy changed in the late twelfth century are not clear, but Spelman's purpose in making it is plain. For these are the freeholders—*libere tenentes*—who were later to blend with the lesser tenants *in capite* to elect knights of the shire and form the modern freeholder class; but since 'Of Parliaments' breaks off in the early years of Henry III we learn no more of how they came to do so.

The feudal interpretation of parliamentary history was to be used many times in the future to check the claims of the lower house. There were two lines along which it could point to royalist and even to absolutist conclusions: one was the argument that since the Commons were manifestly not immemorial, they owed their being to the king whose will had instituted them as a house; the other, that in virtue of his position as feudal suzerain the king stood

[1] *Reliquiae*, p. 57.   [2] *Reliquiae*, p. 62.

in a seigneurial relation to the whole of society and was entitled to homage and loyalty from the proprietor of every piece of land— much as Craig had pointed out to James VI and I. Both these arguments are hinted at by Spelman, but he develops neither of them and his thought on the whole question was on a much grander scale; he depicts the Commons as coming into being as the result of a historical process, far too complex to be the mere product of the king's will, at the end of which the king's position as head of a feudal hierarchy was a thing of the past. Thought which reached so far was fundamentally more akin to that of Harrington. But the feudal interpretation was to be used in both the ways just described, and was to meet the stubborn, angry and usually uncomprehending opposition of common lawyers, political pamphleteers and parliamentary theorists until the end of the century. The remarkable fact, however, as we shall see, is the extreme slowness with which the royalists took it up; not until the time of the Exclusionist crisis, forty years after Spelman's death, was it put into action. The reason must be found primarily in the extraordinary persistence of the common-law tradition, which—it seems desirable to repeat—was the natural way for all Englishmen, of whatever party, to think of their history until they had been brought to perform the complex and unfamiliar intellectual operations which we have studied in Spelman; or until something had happened to jolt them out of the medieval reverence for ancient law which was natural even to royalists, and accustom them to think of the law as the product of the king's will and therefore, in a sense, of history. A subsidiary reason is Spelman's failure to collect his scattered writings on the feudal law into a single reasoned argument, or to arrange for the publication at his death of all that he had written. All the writers studied in the present volume worked without benefit of the *Treatise of Feuds and Tenures* or 'Of Parliaments', and even the article 'Parlamentum', which was to have so marked an effect in stimulating the growth of new ideas, was not published till 1664 or noticed till 1675. Spelman's impact upon his countrymen's conceptions of parliamentary history was to be very long delayed and it was to be felt by a generation living in an England very unlike that which he had known.

CHAPTER VI

Interregnum: the 'Oceana' of James Harrington

THE next part of this book must be in the nature of an interlude. Viewed as a whole, the work of Spelman shows that it was in his lifetime theoretically possible to subject the common-law interpretation of English history to destructive criticism and build up a new version on radically different lines; but it has already been pointed out that his work could not be viewed as a whole until 1721, eighty years after his death, and the line of advance he had indicated was not taken up until 1675 or 1680.[1] The probability that Spelman was far ahead of the scholars of his generation is supported by the fact that not until some of his literary remains had been published, and not until—some years later still—their true meaning began to be understood, was the feudal reinterpretation of constitutional history resumed in detail. In addition, the years after his death were revolutionary in their effect on the English use of history, as in so much else, and his work was reread in a new setting. It will be best to treat the mid-century as a period during which the minds of scholars and polemicists were prepared to make full use of Spelman's ideas when the meaning of these was at last made plain to them.

By 1649, the fundamental problem of the Interregnum had emerged: a truncated single chamber was ruling, and claiming powers to which there seemed no clear limit, in the name of the ancient constitution. Since the concept of an ancient constitution was embodied in the historical myth of the common lawyers, their version of history was still incessantly repeated; but so unparalleled a situation could not be without its effect even upon the myth. In the name of ancient law, the parliament had arrogated to itself what was constantly discovered, and as constantly denied, to be sovereignty, and it was bound to happen that elements of parliamentary and popular sovereignty should make their way into the mythical

[1] See ch. VIII, below.

124

accounts of early history.[1] Rather less began to be heard of the antiquity of the law, rather more of the antiquity of parliament. What must have been fairly common form by the end of the Civil War is recorded for us with admirable simplicity by a Russian, Gerasimus Dokhturov, who, arriving as ambassador to Charles I in 1645, was dismayed to find that the Muscovy merchants who greeted him at Gravesend were at war with their king.

> The king wished—said the merchants—to govern the kingdom according to his own will, as do the sovereigns of other states. But here, from time immemorial, the country has been free; the early kings could settle nothing; it was parliament, the men who were elected, that governed. The king began to rule after his own will, but the parliament would not allow that, and many archbishops and Jesuits were executed. The king, seeing that the parliament intended to act according to its own wishes, as it had done from all time, and not according to the royal will, left London with the queen, without being expelled by anyone, saying that they were going away into other towns.[2]

Except in the matter of archbishops, Dokhturov would seem to have given an accurate enough account of what was said to him. But if the later Long Parliament and the Rump modified history to suit their new situation, those who attacked single-chamber government did so in the name of English history also. Some of these attacks were conservative, some revolutionary, and their treatment of antiquity varied accordingly; it is with a selection of them that this chapter and the next are concerned.

Something must be said first of the Leveller reinterpretation of the Norman Conquest, if only because it is usually misunderstood. The Levellers denounced Norman usurpation and looked backwards to Anglo-Saxon liberty; and on the assumption that, when Coke discovered law and parliament among the pre-Conquest English, he was indulging in fantasies of a golden age and primitive Germanic freedom, it is often maintained that the Leveller doctrine

---

[1] E.g. in Nathaniel Bacon's *Historical Discourse of the Uniformity of the Government of England* (1647–51), sometimes falsely attributed to Selden.

[2] The writer is indebted to his friend Liliana Archibald for this translation and for the reference, which is С. Н. Кологривов, 'Материалы для истории сношений России с иностранными державами в XVII веке' (St Petersburg, 1911).

was at bottom one with that of the common lawyers and made the same appeal to antiquity.[1] But, in reality, no two attitudes of mind could have been more deeply opposed. Coke's essential belief was that the common law had been proved good because it had lasted from time immemorial: there had been no Conquest and the law rested on the foundation of its antiquity and not of William's arbitrary will. What Walwyn, Lilburne and Winstanley said was the very reverse of this. Being engaged in a revolt against the whole existing structure of the common law, they declared that there had indeed been a Conquest; the existing law derived from the tyranny of the Conqueror and partook of the illegitimacy that had characterized his entire rule. Their historicism was not conservative. It was a radical criticism of existing society; the common-law myth stood on its head, as Marx said he had stood Hegel. Both parties indeed looked to the past and laid emphasis on the rights of Englishmen in the past, but what the common lawyers described was the unbroken continuity between past and present, which alone gave justification to the present; while the radicals were talking of a golden age, a lost paradise in which Englishmen had enjoyed liberties that had been taken from them and must be restored. If asked by what right Englishmen could claim the liberties they had lost, they could not appeal to the law, but to natural right and reason; and it is at this point that we notice they were talking the language of political rationalism.

[1] E.g. in D. B. Robertson, *The Religious Foundations of Leveller Democracy* (Columbia, 1951), pp. 112–13. There is a much more accurate interpretation in A. S. P. Woodhouse, *Puritanism and Liberty* (London, 1950), pp. 95–7 of the introduction, and Kliger, *The Goths in England*, pp. 263–7. Much may also be learnt on the difference between true anti-Normanism and the appeal to a past constitution, both among the Levellers and among radicals after 1780 and down to the Chartist movement, from Christopher Hill's 'The Norman Yoke' (see p. 54 n. 2 above). Mr Hill's Marxist analysis is not specially illuminating on conservative thinkers, but his eye for different shades of radicalism is most informative. He is particularly interesting on the tendency of some Leveller and near-Leveller writers to find ancient precedents for the subordination of parliament to outside assemblies exercising a direct popular sovereignty; he finds this marked in Nathaniel Bacon. J. Frank, *The Levellers* (Cambridge, Mass., 1955), brings out the ambiguities of an anti-historical doctrine expressed in historical language.

Interregnum: the 'Oceana' of James Harrington

Ye were chosen [wrote Richard Overton to parliament] to work our deliverance, and to estate us in natural and just liberty agreeable to reason and common equity, for whatever our forefathers were, or whatever they did or suffered, or were enforced to yield unto, we are the men of the present age, and ought to be absolutely free from all kinds of exorbitancies, molestations or arbitrary power.[1]

The Leveller attitude to history is a strange hybrid. Their anti-Normanism, as it is sometimes called, amounts in the end to a rejection of history and existing law; there has been a fatal breach in the continuity of law, six centuries of usurpation during which we have had only fragments of our natural liberties, and now we are free either to reconstruct our society according to reason and equity, or to await the next operation of the Spirit that works in us all. But so inescapable by this time was the clutch of history on English political thought, that this fundamentally anti-historical theory could only be expressed in historical language; the past could only be rejected through a reinterpretation of the past. Here, it may be conjectured, we have a possible explanation of the strange fact, which has puzzled historians of thought, that the anti-Norman ideas of the Levellers reappear in the democrats of 1780 and after, between whom and the men of 1648 there can hardly be any direct continuity.[2] If history was the natural language even of political rationalists, it is intelligible enough that the next time there arose a radical criticism of existing institutions, it too should have seized upon the same weak point in conservative historiography and reinterpreted 1066 as a means to the rejection of the historic constitution.

But the revolt of the lower ranks of the army was only the first of a long series of attempts to reduce the power of the Interregnum parliament within bounds, and anti-Normanism was only one of many attempts to do so by a reinterpretation of English history. The problem proved insoluble by either commonwealth or protectorate, and the rewriting of history to this end went on steadily, and not altogether vainly, until the Restoration. The most remark-

[1] *A Remonstrance of Many Thousand Citizens* (1646), in Haller (ed.), *Tracts on Liberty in the Puritan Revolution* (New York, 1933), vol. III, pp. 354–5.
[2] For a study of the historical ideas of the Yorkshire Association in 1780, see H. Butterfield, *George III, Lord North and the People* (London, 1949), pp. 344 ff.

able, the most systematic and the most ambitious of these attempts was *Oceana* (1656), in which James Harrington was moved to put forward a new account not merely of English, but of European history and a new theory of political power. He is included in the present study because it is evident that the feudal scholars had a profound effect on his work.

Harrington owes his prominence in nearly all text-books on the history of political thought to two interpretations which are normally made of his fundamental doctrine that property is the basis of political power. In the first place, it is usually taken for granted that, in saying this, Harrington imported into political theory some consideration of the economic foundation on which any political society must ultimately rest. The statement that he did so may well be true, but needs to be precisely interpreted. It is a commonplace that Harrington overrated the political importance of land and neglected that of trade; but it is usually pointed out that, according to modern economic historians, the economic society of the day was such that Harrington may be excused—in the light of such facts as the investment of commercial profits in land—for thinking that the distribution of real property provided a sufficient explanation of the distribution of political power.[1] But it needs to be further emphasized that Harrington is not looking, even in the most primitive manner, at the economic society of his day and arriving at the conclusion that land is the most important factor in the economic determination of power. He is not doing this, because he has no conception whatever that there exists a complex web of economic relationships between men which can be studied in itself and which determines the distribution of power among them. Compared to the best Tudor writers on social reform he is not so much ignorant of as uninterested in the realities of an agrarian political economy, and it has not occurred to him that the exchange of goods and services on an agrarian basis either can be studied in order to determine its own laws, or ought to be studied in its relation to political power. There were men in the sixteenth century far ahead of him in this regard; Harrington is thinking

[1] R. H. Tawney, 'Harrington's Interpretation of his Age', *Proc. Brit. Acad.* vol. XXVII (1941), pp. 221–2.

about something else. His sole comment on the economic relations between men—and the sole foundation of all that he has to say about property as the basis of power—is, 'an army is a beast that hath a great belly and must be fed'; he that has the land can feed the soldiers. Harrington, we must keep in mind, was a Machiavellian, and the starting-point of his thought was Machiavelli's perception that in a republic the soldiers must be citizens and the citizens soldiers; if the soldiers follow private men for reward, then the republic cannot survive. To this Harrington's historical studies had added the further reflexion that the soldier normally lives on the land; if the land is in the hands of one man, or of a few, then the soldier will be the tenant of a lord and pledged by his tenure to fight for him. Only when the land is distributed among a class of freeholders, therefore, can the soldiers be citizens (or freemen) and the citizens soldiers.

That is the sum total of reflexion on the relation between property and power which will be found from one end to the other of Harrington's collected works. Economic it certainly is, in the sense that it points out the connexion between that which keeps a man alive and the direction his political action will probably take; but it considers the man solely in his capacity of soldier, and never comes near to asking how the relations which he enters into as producer and consumer will determine his action as a citizen. It is important—in view of what eminent authorities have said—to realize that Harrington had no concept of economic society as an aspect of human life possessing laws of its own, and therefore none of economic history as the evolution of economic relationships according to a logic of their own. When Acton praised Harrington for having discovered that there existed a great department of human life outside the control of the state, when G. H. Sabine commented that it was strange that a man who saw so far into the economic causes of political power should have placed so much reliance on constitutional apparatus, both made the mistake of assuming that Harrington knew there existed a sphere of economics apart from the sphere of politics and influencing it.[1] Harrington made no such

---

[1] Acton, *Historical Essays and Studies*, p. 380; Sabine, *History of Political Theory* (New York, ed. 1945), p. 505.

assertion; he was studying the military and consequently the political results of a system of dependent tenures, and inquiring what happened when such a system was removed. That is the reason for his inclusion here; it is also his claim to originality as a political thinker.

The second reason for ascribing a peculiar importance to his thought has been the belief that in the century or so before his time there had occurred a major transference of land into the hands of the gentry and a consequent rise of the gentry to political power. Harrington said that this had in fact occurred, and so long as our belief coincided with his it was the fashion to praise him as a man of profound insight into the social developments of his own day, to speak of him as an interpreter of his age and, somewhat less explicitly, to speak as if his discernment of the principle that 'property determines power' were developed from his diagnosis of this process occurring in contemporary English life. But, granting for the moment that a 'rise of the gentry' was going on, we may still legitimately inquire how it was that Harrington—the sources of whose information and the working categories of whose thoughts differed most widely from ours—knew it. The belief that the thought of an age reflects its social developments does not deliver us from the obligation to show how this process of reflexion takes place. Granted that there was a rise of the gentry, and granted also that Harrington says there was, did he mean what we mean by the statement and did he arrive at his conclusion by means of thoughts which have anything in common with ours? If we do not face and answer these questions, we risk inferring that Harrington anticipated in some unexplained and therefore miraculous manner the conclusions of modern economic history and should be praised on this account. This will be no explanation of how he actually thought.

It has been left for a historian who doubts the whole concept of a rise of the gentry—Mr H. R. Trevor-Roper—to ask just what grounds Harrington had for stating that the gentry in his day had engrossed the major part of the land.[1] Now if we examine the manner and the context in which Harrington makes this statement, we shall notice that though it is of course fundamental to his

[1] H. R. Trevor-Roper, 'The Gentry, 1540–1640' (*Economic History Review Supplement*, no. 1, Cambridge, 1954), *passim*.

diagnosis of contemporary England, he nowhere puts it forward as his own discovery or regards himself as having conducted investigations which lead to this conclusion. It is not a conclusion of his thought at all, but rather a presupposition. He does not make himself an authority for the statement, nor does he organize the development of his ideas around it; he merely takes it for granted, as a truth everybody knows, and proceeds to show how it came about and what its consequences must be. In these circumstances, it does not seem very likely that Harrington reached the conclusion that most of the land had passed to the gentry as a result of some train of thought peculiarly his own and was stirred and excited by this discovery to the point of formulating his general theory that landed property determined power. It is perhaps time to remind ourselves of what he actually said, and in so doing to consider by what means he arrived at both the particular and the general conclusion, and what their relation is to one another. We shall then be in a position to decide whether profound insight into contemporary social realities is really the foundation of Harrington's thought, or its most interesting characteristic.[1]

Having enunciated the proposition that landed property determines power, Harrington does not merely select examples to prove it: he goes further and gives a summary account of European history since the second century B.C., designed to show how the unequal distribution of land has determined, since that time, the succession of different types of state. Starting with the presumption that once there existed an 'ancient prudence', in which the form of government was adapted to the existing distribution of land and that distribution stabilized by an agrarian law, he goes on to fix the collapse of this equilibrium in that age of Roman history which preceded the advent of the Gracchi. Like Toynbee, he regards the fatal breakdown of ancient civilization as occurring just after the Punic Wars, and its consequences as felt even at his own day. *Latifundia perdidere Italiam*: the lands which should have been divided among citizen-colonists were engrossed by a few rich men, and by the time of the Gracchi it was too late to restore, even by

[1] All that follows is taken from the 'Second Part of the Preliminaries' in Liljegren (ed.), *James Harrington's Oceana* (Lund and Heidelberg, 1924).

force, the law which defined their proper distribution. For the great men were now able both to subvert the constitution and to defeat the armed efforts of the people; Sulla's dictatorship and Augustus's empire were maintained by settling on the land, which should have been the people's, colonies of veterans who became the clients and the private armies of their patrons. The empire was founded on the emperor's power to settle the armies on lands withdrawn from public control.

> These *Military Colonies*...consisted of such as I conceive were they that are called *Milites beneficiarii*; in regard that the *Tenure* of their Lands was by way of *Benefices*, that is for life, and upon condition of duty or service in the War upon their own charge. These Benefices *Alexander Severus* granted unto the Heirs of the Incumbents, but upon the same conditions: And such was the *Dominion* by which the Roman Emperours gave their *Ballance*.[1]

Harrington proceeds to compare the Roman empire with the Turkish sultanate, which has timariots corresponding to the *beneficiarii*, and a bodyguard of janissaries whose counterpart was the praetorians. But whereas the Turkish is the perfect instance of absolute monarchy—all the land being in the sultan's hands and held of him by military tenants for life—the Roman was imperfect; the senate and people retained some part of their liberty and the emperor, caught between the opposing forces of constitution and army, was in perpetual danger of deposition and death. The empire was an essentially unstable government and continued so until Constantine dispersed the praetorians and until

> the *Benefices* of the Souldiers that were hitherto held for *life*, and upon duty, were by this *Prince* made *Hereditary*, so that the whole Foundation whereupon this *Empire* was first built, being now removed, sheweth plainly, that the Emperours must long before this have found out some other way of support; and this was by *Stipendiating* the *Gothes*...for the *Emperours* making use of them in their Arms (as the *French* do at this day of the *Switz*) gave them that, under the notion of stipend, which they received as *Tribute*, coming (if there were any default in the payment) so often to distrein for it, that in the time of *Honorius* they sacked *Rome*, and possessed themselves of *Italy*.[2]

The historical logic is extremely clear. The advent of the barbarians was not a conquest by a horde of invaders, but an infiltra-

---

[1] Liljegren, pp. 40–1.   [2] Liljegren, p. 42.

tion of over-mighty mercenaries brought into the empire as the result of its own inner weaknesses, weaknesses which Harrington is prepared to trace in logical sequence from a single mistake committed by the later republic; after which power oscillated from one to another of a series of unstable forces, until the introduction and establishment of the Goths came as the natural culmination. With their arrival there ended the transitional period between 'ancient' and 'modern prudence', and 'modern prudence'—which has been defined earlier as an essentially arbitrary mode of government in which the law fails to prevent the establishment of power in the hands of one or a few—is synonymous with 'the Gothic balance'. And the Gothic balance is feudalism: for

> to open the ground-work or *ballance* of these new *Politicians*. *Feudum*, saith *Calvine* the *Lawyer*, is a *Gothick* word of divers significations; for it is taken either for War, or for a *possession of conquered Lands, distributed by the Victor unto such of his Captains and Souldiers as had merited in his wars, upon condition to acknowledge him to be their perpetuall Lord, and themselves to be his Subjects.*

The Goths established three ranks of *feuda*, subinfeudated one to another and held by nobles, barons and vavasors; '*and this is the Gothick Ballance, by which all the Kingdoms this day in Christendome were at first erected*'.[1]

As has already been pointed out, the basic tenet throughout *Oceana* is that a man's tenants must fight for him, while a freeholder will fight for himself; and in the historical section of the work the rise and progress of 'modern prudence'—government by one or a few in their own interest and not according to law—is depicted as the rise and progress of dependent military tenures, of which a simplified version of feudalism is the last and culminating phase. Not only this, but the earlier phases—the devices of military clientage by which the Roman emperors overthrew the republic and prepared the way for the Goths—had all, and more than once, been advanced by the feudal scholars of the sixteenth century as possible origins of feudalism.[2] The possibility that veterans' colonies

[1] Liljegren, pp. 42–3; cf. Calvinus, *Lexicon juridicum juris romani* (Frankfort, 1600), *sub* 'Feudum'. Italics Harrington's.

[2] See ch. IV, above.

or the later *limitanei* were the seed from which the *feudum* had developed was extensively canvassed by Torelli and others, and as extensively refuted by Hotman in the *De feudis commentatio tripertita*, and by Craig in *Jus Feudale*—both works which might very easily have come Harrington's way. Although, as may have been noticed, Harrington ignores Gerardus Niger's belief that the *feudum* had developed from precarious to perpetual after the barbarian settlements, still he locates a similar development of the 'benefice' among the military settlements of the empire. Lastly, the analogy between feudalism and the Turkish system and the emphasis that the timariot holds for life are already familiar to us from Craig. Although Johann Kahl's *Lexicon Juridicum* is the only authority quoted, it looks very much as if earlier discussions on the history of feudalism were behind Harrington's thought in some way. There is good reason to think, first, that Harrington's essential notion of the way in which landed property determines power is derived from consideration of the power which a feudal lord draws from his vassals; and secondly, that in the attempts of sixteenth-century scholars to derive feudalism from Roman military clientage he found instances of earlier institutions embodying the same fundamental principle. Although the Roman dependent tenures had been excluded on technical grounds from the history of the *feudum* itself, they helped him to understand how the power of the emperors had been established among the ruins of the republic, why it too had declined and why, in comparison, the similarly based power of the sultanate seemed to be lasting. Since Harrington was not only writing the history of feudalism, but applying a principle drawn from it to the history of European society, he could combine, where others must compare, the history of Roman clientage with the history of the *feudum* proper; and because he thought of both as instances of what happened when an original balance of property was disturbed, he could see one disequilibrium as leading to another in a dialectical process which continued until, as the result of a miscalculation two centuries before Christ, all Europe became a prey to military nobles in the fifth century of our era. We have here an unorthodox form of historical thought, very unlike that of Craig or Spelman, but indebted ultimately to the same stimulus:

134

the power of feudal institutions to direct the student's thought from the law to the soil beneath it.

When Harrington turns from the history of Europe in general to recount that of England (or Oceana), it is still feudalism that is his guiding and connecting theme. Throughout this part of his work his authority is a single book by John Selden, the enlarged version of the *Titles of Honour* published in 1631. Selden, we have seen, was quoted by the Irish judges in 1639 for the view, as against Spelman, that feudal tenures were older than the Conquest and part of the immemorial law; it was to this book that the judges referred. It is true that he repeatedly refers to Anglo-Saxon thanes as 'feudal'; he says that the king's thanes held of him in chief and by knight-service, and he identifies 'middle thane' with 'vavasor'.[1] Yet, strangely enough, he held a view of the nature of the knight's fee far more in accord with subsequent research than did Spelman, or any contemporary scholar except Robert Cotton;[2] but he does not tell us whether this too existed before the Conquest. Why he adhered to opinions of this sort is uncertain; he was a most careful scholar and it is unlikely that he was actuated by the common desire to represent all English institutions as immemorial. To Harrington, however, who did not of course know Spelman's *Treatise of Feuds and Tenures*, the identification of Norman with Saxon tenures had a definite value. It aided him to think of feudalism as a single and simple body of institutions established everywhere by the Gothic conquerors, and to carry out the simplification of history which his theme required and which probably accounts in part for his choice of a half-mythical form. He wished to write of the rise and fall of the Gothic balance as the key to post-classical history; to have been compelled to depict it as everywhere subject to modification and development would have been no more than a distraction.

He therefore describes the Saxon ('Teutonic') system of government as a simplified form of feudalism, with ealdormen, king's

[1] Selden, *Titles of Honour* (1631), pp. 612, 622, 624–7. None of this matter seems to appear in the 1614 text.

[2] *Titles of Honour*, pp. 691–7. See D. C. Douglas, *The Norman Conquest and British Historians* (David Murray Foundation Lecture, Glasgow, 1946) for a discussion of the views of Cotton.

thanes and middle thanes as the three ranks of feudatories. This society is of course typical of the Gothic balance, with the land dominated by the nobility and the people in dependence on them; and though Harrington finds it necessary to say that the present House of Commons is descended from a representation of the people in the witan—and to employ a positively ultra-Cokean argument to support his claim[1]—it is clear from the context that these Saxon commons must have been virtually powerless. This is a curious passage; an insistence on the antiquity of the commons is unnecessary on a strict interpretation of Harrington's own theory, and its inclusion seems to represent a survival of traditional prejudices in his mind. For, as we shall see, his theory of the rise of the people to power is not clearly connected with a rise of the House of Commons to predominance in the constitution.

To an England already so thoroughly feudalized Norman conquest could make little difference. The Normans ('Neustrians' in the language of *Oceana*) brought an interlude of quasi-absolutism, while the barons who had inherited the lands and tenures of the thanes felt their security in a newly won country to be dependent on the powers of their king; but these

were no sooner rooted in their vast *Dominions*, than they came up according to the infallible consequence of the *Ballance Domesticke*, and contracting the *Nationall* interest of the *Baronage* grew as fierce in the Vindication of the *Ancient rights and liberties* of the same, as if they had beene alwaies *Natives*.[2]

It was still the ancient constitution for which the barons had fought, but to Harrington this was no more than an expression of class conflict. The Norman polity, like the Saxon before it and all other examples of the Gothic balance, was inherently unstable. The nobility had too much land to be properly controlled by the king, yet their own divisions made it necessary that they should have a

---

[1] Liljegren, p. 45 and note, pp. 270–1. The argument (to be found also in Lambarde's *Archeion*) is that the existence of parliamentary boroughs which have been decayed since time out of mind is proof of the existence of borough representation since time out of mind—and consequently before the Conquest. For its use by Hobbes (of all people), see ch. VII, below. See also Coke, Preface to *Ninth Reports* (T.F. vol. v), pp. xxii–xxiii.

[2] Liljegren, p. 47.

king over them. The king therefore was constantly trying to extend his authority, the nobility constantly frustrating him; but as often as they overthrew a king, the necessities of the Gothic balance constrained them to set up another in his place. The establishment of parliamentary government was an expression of this conflict of forces, and at the same time contained the seeds of the Gothic balance's future decay. On the one hand, the barons of Henry III's time exacted the restoration of the ancient parliament of the Saxons; on the other, the kings had by this time found means of introducing into it creatures of their own. So in all government by estates:

> By which meanes this *Government* being indeed the *Master-piece of Moderne Prudence* hath beene cry'd up to the *Skyes*, as the only invention, whereby at once to maintaine the soveraignty of a *Prince*, and the liberty of the *people*: whereas indeed it hath beene no other than a wrestling match, wherein the *Nobility*, as they have been stronger have thrown the *King*; or the *King* if he have been stronger, hath thrown the *Nobility*; or the *King* where he hath had a *Nobility*, and could bring them to his party, hath thrown the *people*, as in *France* and *Spain*: or the *people* where they have had no *Nobility*, or could get them to be of their party, have thrown the *King*, as in *Holland*, and of latter times in *Oceana*. But they came not to this strength but by such approaches and degrees, as remain to be further opened.[1]

Like the Levellers, Harrington condemns the historic constitution as the fruit of Norman misgovernment; but he blames not their tyranny so much as their inefficiency, and regards the Saxons as no better. But if it was in parliament that the people rose to power and overthrew the king—as the foregoing passage certainly suggests—then we should expect to hear that it was through the House of Commons that they did it. We should expect to be told that the new men whom the thirteenth-century kings introduced into the re-founded parliament—in doing which they 'set awry' the balance—were the representatives of the commons. But we are not; Harrington is utterly unable to give any account whatever of the medieval commons and their place in parliament. For an explanation of this remarkable fact we must turn back to Selden's *Titles of Honour*.

In the section of that mighty work that dealt with the English title of baron, Selden wrote an account of parliamentary attendance

---

[1] Liljegren, pp. 47–8.

as one of the distinguishing marks of baronage.[1] Like Spelman in *Archaeologus*, five years earlier, he was aware of the differentiation of the order into barons by tenure, by writ and by letters patent, and thought that Magna Carta's distinction between the modes of summoning greater and lesser tenants in chief marked the decisive moment at which the ancient principle of a baronage purely of tenure had been abandoned. But, as we have seen, Spelman thought that the *summoneri faciemus* clause of 1215 represented a collective re-action of the whole body of tenants in chief against the king's use of the writ of summons to exclude some of their number from his councils. Selden gave a different emphasis and treated *summoneri faciemus* as an attempt by the greater tenants to exclude the less from individual summons and monopolize the title of baron: a fatal breach of feudal principle which prepared the way for the writ to continue undermining the purely tenurial nature of baronage and for the king to exclude from his councils some who were tenants in chief and to summon some who were not, until in Richard II's time the creation of barons by letters patent sealed the divorce between baronage and tenure. Substantially, both men were in agreement, but whether because his brief was only to write about baronage, or because he did not share Spelman's determination to view the history of England as the introduction and decline of feudal principles, Selden did not press his thesis so far as to inquire what became of the parliamentary attendance of the smaller tenants in chief; and neither here nor elsewhere did he advance Spelman's theory that a lower house of small tenants in chief had evolved into a lower house of freeholders.

As we have seen, all Spelman's detailed statements of his theory were contained in writings not published when *Oceana* was written; and Harrington consequently lacked knowledge of a doctrine which his own argument badly needed. His account of parliamentary history follows Selden and makes no mention whatever of the Commons between the Conquest and the reign of Elizabeth I. The passage, earlier quoted, on parliament as a wrestling-ground between king, lords and people occurs as part of an account of the manner in which barons by writ—whom at this point he manages

---

[1] *Titles of Honour*, pp. 701–45, in particular pp. 708–15.

to confuse with the lords spiritual[1]—and barons by letters patent appeared in parliament. It was jealousy between the old barons and the new that led to the deposition of Richard II, and, having once tasted blood, the nobility formed itself into factions and continued to overthrow kings and put up new until the Tudors struck at the roots of their power.

This account of the strange weakness of Harrington's argument, just at the point where we expect it to be most complete, has been given to emphasize his virtual ignorance of later medieval history and inability to chart the decline of the classical feudalism of the Normans. If we now inquire by what stages the people got possession of the land and rose to political power, we shall be given no answer earlier than the reign of Henry VII. This prince, Harrington repeatedly declares, was the first who attacked the power of the nobility and set in train the destruction of the Gothic balance. He did this by means of his statutes of population, retainers and alienations: the first of these—Harrington is following Bacon here—by forbidding the lords to dispossess their tenants holding twenty and more acres, broke their feudal control over the yeomanry and guaranteed the latter in possession of their lands. The second deprived the lords of their cavalry as the former had of their infantry; and, forbidden to keep great households in the country, they resorted to court, became extravagant and began to sell their lands, a course which the statute of alienations thoughtfully encouraged. The next step was Henry VIII's, who

dissolving the *Abbeys*, brought with the declining estate of the *Nobility* so vast a prey unto the Industry of the people, that the *Ballance* of the *Commonwealth* was too apparently in the *Popular party*, to be unseen by the wise

[1] Liljegren, p. 48 and note. Liljegren's comment is interesting. Harrington placed at this point the marginal reference '49 H. 3', the date of the oldest extant summons of knights of the shire to a parliament; and his argument seems so imperatively to demand a discussion of the rise of the House of Commons that Liljegren considers at length the possibility that he is referring to this. But the text at this point contains no mention of knights or burgesses, but only of barons by writ, whom Harrington declares to have consisted of sixty-four abbots and thirty-six priors; and in *Titles of Honour*, pp. 723–4, will be found a list of this number of spiritual persons, whose summons is recorded on a close roll of 49 H. 3. This reference (which Liljegren also gives) is the only one to which Harrington's marginal note can be taken to point.

Councel of *Queen Parthenia* [Elizabeth I], who converting her reign through the perpetuall Love-tricks that passed between her and her people into a kind of *Romanze*; wholly neglected the *Nobility*. And by these degrees came the House of *Commons* to raise that head, which since hath been so high and formidable unto their *Princes*; that they have looked pale upon those assemblies.[1]

This is literally the first mention of the House of Commons since it was observed that a powerless and nominal representation of the people may be presumed to have survived the Norman Conquest. It is clear that, as Harrington was unable to incorporate the history of parliament into his account of the later Middle Ages, so too he believed feudal society to have survived more or less unchanged until the advent of the Tudors. Such was certainly the opinion of that sometime member of the Rota Club, John Aubrey. He wrote:[2]

For the government till the time of Henry VIII, it was like a nest of boxes: for the copy-holders, (who till then were villaines) held of the Lords of the Manor, who held perhaps of another superior lord or duke, who held of the king.... The lords (then lords *in deed* as well as in title) lived in their countries like petty kings, had *jura regalia* belonging to their signories, had their castles and burroughes, and sent burghesses to the Lower House: had gallows within their liberties where they could try, condemne, hang, and drawe.... Then were entails in fashion (a good prop for monarchie). Destroying of petty mannors began in Henry VII to be more common: whereby the meane people lived lawlesse, nobody to govern them, they cared for nobody, having on nobody any dependence; and thus, and by selling the Church landes, is the ballance of the government quite altered, and putt into the handes of the common people.

The thought in the last sentences is obviously Harrington's. Interspersed with these accounts of a feudal world, and forming part of them, are references to the retainer system, the last remnants of which Aubrey's older contemporaries could remember from the closing decades of Elizabeth I's reign: younger sons and servants riding behind some magnate, armed and in his livery, and engaging in riots and rufflings in his cause. It is easy to see how the

[1] Liljegren, p. 49.
[2] A. Powell (ed.), *Brief Lives and Other Selected Writings by John Aubrey* (London, 1949), pp. 2–4.

still living tradition of such customs could blend in the antiquary's mind with the accounts of feudal vassalage given by the scholars, and help create the image of a feudalism surviving until the previous century; but such a confusion could take place only if the means of charting the decline of classical feudalism had not yet been discovered. We have seen how Spelman, unable to give any account of the positive forces which had worked to bring feudal tenures to an end, had written rather vaguely of a general decline; but at least he had insisted on the gradualness of this process, and some of its details of which he had knowledge—such as the replacement of the feudal justiciar by the professional chief justice—he had dated as far back as the reign of Edward I.[1] But Harrington and Aubrey, lacking both Spelman's awareness of the complexity of feudal tenure and (in Harrington's case at least) his concept of the rise of the House of Commons, telescoped history and substituted for the gradual decline of feudalism its sudden and more or less complete overthrow by Tudor legislation.

Now it is the argument of this chapter that Harrington was primarily a historian of feudalism and only in a most rudimentary sense an observer of contemporary social processes. This interpretation seems to be borne out by the account of his thought which has just been given. For when we come to his version of what we call 'the rise of the gentry', it amounts to little more than the statement that under the early Tudors the feudal system was abolished. Henry VII freed the yeomen from feudal dependence and encouraged the nobility to sell land; Henry VIII dissolved the monasteries and threw their estates into the hands of the commons. (To this point, the summary is exactly echoed by Aubrey.) Under Elizabeth I, the House of Commons began to wax in power. That is the most we can justly make of Harrington's account of this alleged development; and it may well seem likely that his 'rise of the gentry' is based simply on a comparison of his own with feudal society, and a very imperfect notion of how the latter in fact disappeared. Mr Trevor-Roper has remarked that Harrington and others who thought like him were singularly vague as to the dates and stages by which their 'rise of the gentry' had come about—as if, he says,

[1] See the article 'Justitiarius' in the 1626 *Archaeologus*.

141

they were trying to derive the present situation from some ideal state of things imagined in the past.[1] In Harrington's case, ignorance of late medieval history seems to explain the vagueness, and the ideal state of things is an extremely generalized description of the classical type of feudalism. Harrington, we may suppose, noted the obvious fact of the political power possessed by the land-holding commons in his own time, and cast back into the past as a means of accounting for it. There he encountered the description of a feudal system in which those who were now the freeholding gentry had been subordinate vassals. Unable to describe the decline of this state of things, he supposed that it had endured through the fourteenth and fifteenth centuries, and guided by Bacon[2] hit upon Tudor legislation—aimed in reality at emasculating the retainer system, checking enclosures and resuming the crown lands—as marking the destruction, almost at a blow, of classical feudalism. The picture thus created was completed by reference to the effects of the dissolution.

It is true that the belief that land had passed or was passing into the hands of the gentry was fairly widespread at this time, and that by no means all its expressions—the statistics of Thomas Wilson the younger, for example—can be explained as resulting from a comparison between a freeholding society and an imperfectly understood feudalism or half-remembered retainer system. It may well be that ideas like Wilson's helped to shape Harrington's thought. But he does not allude to or make use of them; as far as he is concerned, the preponderance of the freeholders is a *datum*, and he is seeking to explain it by contrast with feudalism. It is even not impossible that the study of feudal society—and exaggeration of its longevity—first convinced him of the importance of landed property to the victory of the commons in his own day. But perhaps it does not greatly matter how Harrington arrived at his conviction that a transfer of land into the gentry's hands had occurred during the sixteenth century, because that does not seem to be the most important or interesting part of his thought. It is not the product of an analysis of the contemporary distribution of land,

[1] Trevor-Roper, *op. cit.* pp. 45–6.
[2] For his citations from Bacon see Liljegren, pp. 9, 49, and notes.

because it does not claim to be. As a piece of history, it is fundamentally vitiated by Harrington's ignorance of anything between the establishment of classical feudalism and the legislation of the Tudors. Nor does it seem to have been the origin of the doctrine that the possession of land determines political power, for Harrington expounds that far more convincingly by showing what happens when land is engrossed by an aristocracy: by comparing the history of dependent tenures in general, and feudal tenures in particular, with the land laws of the ideal legislators. The rise of the English freeholders merely makes possible the return to 'ancient prudence'.

It seems reasonable to regard this part of Harrington's political theory as mainly the product of reflexion upon feudal tenures. They provided him with the clearest explanation of how the many, who should be citizen-soldiers, might be converted into the private armies of a few. Roman military clientage provided the link between the Gothic Middle Ages and the ideal republics in which things had been better ordered. The comparison between the tenure for life only of the Turkish timariot and the western benefice's tendency to become hereditary showed him how a despotic monarchy erected on a foundation of military tenures should be maintained, and how it should not. Lastly, the contrast between the vassalage of feudal England and the predominance of freehold about him provided him with a means of explaining his own day, and convinced him that he had lived to see conditions in which the classical republic was once more a practical possibility. These things together amount to the doctrine that the distribution of land determines political power—for no other reason than that it determines whether the soldier shall fight as a citizen for the public power or as a dependent for his patron or lord.

We have now been led to abandon the belief that Harrington was primarily a political economist or a serious authority for a recent or contemporary 'rise of the gentry'. There remain, happily, excellent reasons for holding this amiable man in high respect. If he did not study political power in terms of economics, he wrote its history in terms of land; and he was a very remarkable speculative historian. The 'Second Part of the Preliminaries' to *Oceana* is a connected, logical and consistent history of the transformations of

143

political authority in Europe from the Roman republic to the English civil wars. It starts, admittedly, from an ideal antiquity and it ends with the prospect of an ideal future; but within those limits it is based on the rise and fall of a single phenomenon—dependent military tenures—and it succeeds by means of this generalization alone in accounting for a great many facts and weaving them together in a single narrative. The reader travels far, in Harrington's company, from the allegedly typical humanist historian who searches the past for general principles and the examples which illustrate them; for in Harrington's hands the examples become links in a chain of causation and the principle a key to unlock the whole course of western history. A regular series of causes and effects connects the Gracchi with Cromwell, and since the fundamental idea on which this history is constructed is that of the disturbance of an original balance—of a sometime equitable distribution of the land—the sequence of events that follows the original disturbance is, as has already been observed, dialectical. Excess in one direction produces excess in another, until the oscillations of the 'balance' gather sufficient force to sweep away an inherently unstable system of government. An emperor brings in the Goths, who overthrow both him and his land-hungry armies; a king, to check the nobles, raises up the people, who destroy him and them impartially.

In this dialectic of eighteen centuries the last step—the rise of the people—is, as we have seen, the least satisfactorily explained; and it might be observed also that Harrington shared with Marx the delusion that a historical dialectic might come or be brought to a stop, and a static unhistorical equilibrium succeed it. Just as, in the dialectic of production, the triumph of the proletariat leads to the classless society and the consummation of the historical process, so too, in the dialectic of land distribution, the triumph of the freeholders leads to the foundation of an impersonal machine of government so evenly balanced that there is no reason why it should not last for ever. But these extravagances need not blind one to the fact that the construction of a dialectical process on this scale was a notable achievement of the historical intellect. If it is true that each main point in Harrington's historical thought arose originally from the consideration of feudal tenure, then that branch of study had done as much to broaden his perception of history as it had done for that of Craig or even Spelman.

Another aspect of his historiography can best be appreciated by comparison of his thought with that of his master Machiavelli. The Italian, following Polybius, had spoken of forms of government giving preponderance to the one, the few and the many, each breaking down through the excess of its own peculiar qualities and giving rise to its successor, doomed to perish in its turn. From this sorrowful wheel the legislator might deliver his people by setting up a government so compounded of all three elements that the degenerative tendencies held one another in check. Such a system, like that of Lycurgus, might endure for many centuries; Machiavelli only doubted whether some force, innate human folly or the blind stroke of fortune, would not overthrow even this in the end. But if asked exactly what forces impelled the degeneration of each un-mixed form of government and kept the Polybian cycle turning, he could only reply: the inherent instability of terrestrial things. There was in human affairs, as in everything sublunary, an innate tendency for things to perish by the mere excess of their own being, for each virtue to produce its corresponding vice and for the latter in the end to prevail, for fortune to throw down what it had built up. This cosmology, typical of late medieval thought, lingered on long in humanism, and it has lately been shown how a dominant theme of German historiography in the seventeenth century is that the individual must either struggle with or escape from irresistible fortune.[1] In Harrington there is much of this to be found: riches (including land) are 'the goods of fortune', it is still the legislator's part to found a government immune from change. But for all that an immense alteration has taken place. Governments no longer degenerate because of the operation of a tendency inherent in all nature; they do so because man has ignored, for almost two thousand years, part of the logic of the situation in which he finds himself. The consequences of his blindness follow according to a law of their own, but once they have brought him another opportunity to

[1] Leonard Forster, *The Temper of Seventeenth-century German Literature* (London, 1951), pp. 7–12.

establish stable government, and the process of history is understood, then the original blunder can be remedied and the degenerative cycle brought to a halt. Thus, though history was earlier identified with fortune, the concept of fortune has practically disappeared; history has a law which may be comprehended. Harrington denies Machiavelli's conviction that a people once thoroughly corrupt cannot be saved even by the wisest legislator: the causes of corruption are in an unjust distribution of land, or in the existence of a constitution at variance with the distribution, and its causes being known can be remedied. The dialectic can be solved.

Harrington hints that his conclusions are to be compared to the discovery of the circulation of the blood,[1] and Machiavelli, we may reflect, lived in a closed Greco-medieval universe, Harrington in an expanding scientific one. But that is not all. If degeneration has ceased to be essential and become accidental, that is because Harrington has located its causes, not in man's nature, but in his situation; and he has done this by writing history in terms, not of man's character, but of the social structure. He does not look deeper into agrarian society than the military tenures, but this is far enough to give him a vision of a particular pattern of social relationships, which may be replaced by another and may change from causes lying within itself: a vision to which Machiavelli never attained. Machiavelli lived in a city state, which he could easily identify with Athens or Rome, and where politics could be reduced to the fierce, kaleidoscopic and essentially personal factions and reactions of the piazza; he therefore wrote history in terms of human nature, which he viewed in isolation and thought unchanging. But Harrington lived in a territorial and agrarian community, where law and justice, custom and tenure, mattered and had always mattered more than the logic of the individual's conduct in politics; where institutions, far more than actions, determined the nature of political life. He therefore wrote history in terms of the changing structure of society. Feudalism, as was happening everywhere in English historical thought, helped him to see how the pattern of custom, law and government had changed in modern history, and helped him to see also that law might be largely a matter of land, and

[1] Liljegren, p. 13.

social relationships a matter of tenure. It is the marriage between this and the essentially classical and Italian concepts of the one, the few and the many, of the degenerative cycle, of the legislator, of the citizenry as a voting militia and the militia as an armed citizenry, that produces the thought of the 'Preliminaries', which posterity has agreed to consider the important part of Harrington's legacy. Viewed in this light, *Oceana* is a Machiavellian meditation upon feudalism.

CHAPTER VII

Interregnum: the First Royalist Reaction and the Response of Sir Matthew Hale

I

URING the Interregnum there also occurred the first signs of a royalist reaction in the field of historiography; but this reaction, though it produced some new and valuable criticisms of the traditional accounts of constitutional history, did not of itself lead to a radical reassessment of the whole subject. That could come only when feudal institutions were given their proper place in English history, and the royalist writers before and just after 1660 lacked many of Spelman's works and did not fully understand those which they had. They sought merely to provide a history of the constitution which would emphasize the original and essential nature of the king's authority; and while this was not without its value as a means to criticizing the concept of the immemorial, its power to bring about a deeper understanding of history was limited. It is noticeable, too, that the reinterpretation they did provide depended rather on changes taking place in royalist political theory than on developments in the field of scholarship; and this may help to explain the curious fact that a genuine royalist historiography seems to have been delayed until at earliest the years between the first and second civil wars. Royalists of the school of Hyde, for instance, remained common lawyers in their predilections and consequently believers in the ancient constitution; the limit of their political beliefs was the assertion that a freely functioning royal prerogative formed an essential part of the constitution, and the limit of their use of history was the attempt to find precedents proving its existence. Hyde himself, in his last years and second exile, criticized Hobbes's *Leviathan*[1] partly on the grounds that the

[1] *A Brief View and Survey of the Dangerous and Pernicious Errors to Church and State in Mr. Hobbes' Book Entitled Leviathan* (1676); especially pp. 109, 110.

laws of England were derived from immemorial custom and not from the will of a conquering sovereign, and after his death was himself criticized by Robert Brady, a royalist in a far more radical sense, as one of the school of common lawyers who had built up a myth so dangerous to the crown.[1] But the beliefs of Hyde continued to satisfy many royalists even as late as the Revolution, and they may be found turning the concept of an immemorial constitution to support the doctrine of an immemorial prerogative.[2] From thought as conservative as theirs no new interpretation of history was to be expected.

What Hyde especially disliked in Hobbes was the latter's willingness to believe that William I had ruled as a conqueror, that the laws had continued to exist only by his will, and that his right over them had consequently been absolute and had descended intact to his successors. The theory of conquest, fatal alike to the doctrine of constitutional monarchy and to the concept of the law's antiquity, had for many years been peculiarly odious to common lawyers and parliamentarians, and from Lambarde and Camden far into the eighteenth century they never tired of refuting the suggestion that William I had conquered England. We have seen how the great Spelman himself had thought the idea worth repeated denials. What is curious is that the suggestion seems to have been refuted times without number, but very seldom actually made. Neither James I nor Sir Robert Filmer, normally regarded as the twin dragons of theoretical absolutism, made any serious use of it— Filmer indeed made none—and though it is now and then adduced by figures of no greater stature than Henry Ferne, for a systematic exposition of its meaning we must turn to so untypical and unpopular a thinker as Thomas Hobbes. Conquest struck few roots in royalist thought, though from the writings of its opponents one would think it the most dreaded and ever-present of dialectical menaces.[3]

---

[1] See p. 217, below.

[2] A good instance would be *Antidotum Britannicum*, an attack on Nevile's *Plato Redivivus*, written by one W. W. and published in 1681. This man believes in sovereign monarchy and regrets the abolition of the feudal tenures, yet he transcribes without acknowledgment the passage from Davies's *Irish Reports* in which the immemorial law is extolled. See his pp. 8–9.

[3] Ranke himself seems to have been misled by this anomaly. In his *History of England in the Seventeenth Century* (English edition, 1879), vol. IV, pp. 123–4,

The reasons for its insignificance are probably various; one—brought to light by the mention of Hyde—is that a great many royalists were believers in law and held that in defending the king they were defending the ancient constitution. Others may lie in the nature of the conquest theory itself. Viewed superficially, it seemed to offer royalists the chance of proving that all the subject's liberties were the gift of the king's grace and could not constitute a fundamental law before which he might be brought to book; but under examination it revealed disadvantages. It was essentially an appeal to the sword; if this was no more than an appeal to force, to God's judgment as expressed in success, then it conferred as good a right on Cromwell as on Charles. The royalists sought to establish that kings ruled by a right intelligible to human reason but independent of human consent, and a right ultimately derived from the arbitrament of war could not but seem impermanent and subject to fortune. Furthermore, in the writers on *jus gentium*, by whom the theory of conquest had been most fully worked out, it proved to mean no more than that a conquered people were entitled to derive their laws from the conqueror's will in the absence of any more secure foundation;[1] and Ferne stipulated that the right of conquest could not be alleged where there was a legitimate heir to the defeated king. Royalist thought inevitably turned from the theory of conquest to establish monarchy on the basis of some more permanent principle. Some sought it in *ius divinum* and

he discusses Algernon Sidney's *Discourses on Government* and says that Filmer, against whom Sidney was writing, 'takes his stand upon the Norman Conquest and the right it gave, which he however extends so far as to destroy all national freedom'. In point of fact, Filmer did not use the argument from conquest and, as is shown in this chapter, rather disliked it when he found it in Hobbes. Sidney, however, refuted it at length, as if Filmer had indeed used it; and it is to be feared that in this particular the great German took his notion of Filmer from Sidney.

[1] It was used to justify obedience to a usurping power by several writers during the Interregnum (e.g. Ascham and Dury): Zagorin, *A History of Political Thought during the English Revolution* (1954), pp. 64–73. Hobbes might of course be considered as one of these. It was in this sense that a few 'de facto Tories' sought to justify their acceptance of William III on the grounds that he ruled by right of conquest. The case of the unfortunate licenser of books, Edmund Bohun, in 1692, illustrates the argument's appeal and its dangers.

express divine command, in which case the argument was conducted in scriptural terms and altogether outside the sphere of English history; others, as we have seen, sought it in the immemorial custom of England, and argued from assumptions and presuppositions which did not differ at all from those of the common lawyers.

But the theory that a legislative sovereign was logically necessary, while it did not automatically involve recourse to the notion of conquest, made a wide appeal to royalists and could be couched in constitutional and historical language. During 1648 Sir Robert Filmer began to publish tracts containing the political ideas he had worked out in the still unprinted *Patriarcha*: these were *The Freeholder's Grand Inquest*, *The Anarchy of a Limited or Mixed Monarchy*, and *The Necessity of the Absolute Power of all Kings*.[1] *The Freeholder's Grand Inquest* dealt entirely with constitutional law and history, and there is some interest in the fact that he should have laid it before the public earlier than the tracts which expound his doctrine in the language of political theory; there is a sense, besides, in which it inaugurated the political and historical debate of the next forty years. The work appeared in January 1647–8, a moment at which it was still just possible to hope for an agreed dissolution of the Long Parliament and the issue of writs for a new election by the king's command; and Filmer's purpose in publishing it was to remind the prospective elector of the legal significance of his choice and in particular to convince him that the knights and burgesses he would be electing did not constitute a chamber of unlimited powers. To this end Filmer chose the form of a close examination of the writ which enjoined the sheriff to hold elections, and he undertook to prove three things:

I. That the Commons, by their Writ, are only to perform and consent to the Ordinances of Parliament.

II. That the Lords or Common Council by their Writ are only to treat, and give counsel in Parliament.

III. That the King himself only ordains and makes laws, and is supreme judge in Parliament.[2]

[1] For the order and circumstances in which he published see Laslett, *Patriarcha and other Political Works of Sir Robert Filmer* (Oxford, 1949), pp. 7–9, and the bibliographical notes to the several tracts. From this edition all subsequent quotations from Filmer are taken. [2] Laslett, p. 129.

The argument of the whole tract runs somewhat as follows. By study of the writ of summons, and of the form in which legislation is now and has in the past been promulgated, it can be shown that the king is sole judge and sole legislator; his Lords and his Commons are those whom he summons by writ to aid and advise him in work which is properly his alone. But they do not do this on an equal footing: the writ issued to the Lords summons them 'to treat with us and give us of your counsel' (*tractaturi vestrumque consilium impensuri*), that to the Commons only 'to execute and consent' (*ad faciendum et consentiendum*) to those things which the king and the common council may determine. Filmer concludes that the Commons do not, properly speaking, form any part of the common council, nor, if the terms are interchangeable, of parliament. The Lords alone form the common council and are called to give advice; the Commons are called to stand at the bar ('no magistratical posture'), to present petitions to the king, and to consent and give effect to the decisions arrived at by the king with the counsel of the lords. There may, Filmer says, be many other things which the king permits the Commons to do; but the limit of what they can claim is the function named in the writ of summons, and this too—like the Lords' function of giving advice in the common council proper—has no other origin but the king's command. Therefore, once again, all legislation is the act of the king alone, and as both houses derive from him their mere existence, so their privileges can have no other origin but his grace.

Down to this point in the argument, Filmer is merely extracting from authoritative constitutional documents evidence for his fundamental thesis—that the king must be sovereign and that all law and right must be the work of his will. But in the first few pages of the *Freeholder's Inquest*, he turned aside to meet the inevitable reply that the knights and burgesses had formed part of the common council from time immemorial, so that there was no need for their membership to be made explicit in the writ. He denied the antiquity of the Commons and asserted that there had been a time when the common council had met without them.

For clearing the meaning and sense of the writ, and satisfaction of such as think it impossible, but that the Commons of England have always been a part of the common council of the kingdom, I shall insist upon these points: 1. That anciently the Barons of England were the common council of the kingdom. 2. That until the time of Henry I, the Commons were not called to Parliament. 3. Though the Commons were called by Henry I, yet they were not constantly called, nor yet regularly elected by writ until Henry III's time.[1]

Attacks such as this on the antiquity of the Commons were to be the matter of debate until the Revolution and even after, and it is desirable to see what, in this early stage of the doctrine's history, Filmer meant by it. The reference to Henry I need not detain us: Polydore Vergil and Selden had been inclined to accept a story that 'all the people' had assembled at that king's coronation and made laws, but Spelman had rejected it and it does not figure prominently in subsequent controversy. But the statement that a regular summons by writ began under Henry III presumably alludes to the fact that the first extant summons of knights of the shire by writ to the sheriff was dated in the forty-ninth year of his reign. Filmer indeed mentions '49 H. 3' without suggesting that the commons were sent for,[2] but this was the year fixed on in the angry debates of the next generation between those who wished to date the origin of the Commons and those who wished them to remain immemorial. To all the disputants, the point at issue was less whether the Commons had originated in this year or that, than whether they could be shown to have originated in any identifiable year at all. If they could not, then they were immemorial and their privileges were secure; but if they could, then they owed their being to some pre-existent authority—always assumed to be the king—which must to the end of time retain the sovereignty over them. What the king's remotest ancestor had given, his remotest descendant could take away. There was now no need to prove a Norman conquest, unless that happened to be the best means of

[1] Laslett, p. 136.

[2] Laslett, pp. 139–40. It may be appropriate to mention here that the year 1265 figures prominently in this and the next chapter, but is always alluded to by its regnal dating of 49 H. 3. This was the mode invariably adopted by contemporary writers, and to translate it into *anno domini* would seem to depart from the character of their historical thought, rooted as it was in the English public records.

dating the origin of the Commons, and this may partly account for Filmer's neglect of the argument. As far back as 1581, when they had imprisoned Arthur Hall of Grantham for denying that they were immemorial, the Commons had shown their fear of some such attack as this; but the fact that it had hardly been levelled until now is evidence of the extraordinary sway which common-law historiography exerted over even the royalist mind. Spelman, from his own advanced standpoint, had framed a criticism in 'Of Parliaments' but had probably not meant to argue that the Commons, being late in origin, were in all things subject to the crown. But in Filmer's view this was a necessary consequence; and it was only when a clear doctrine of sovereignty had been framed that royalists, lacking the peculiar impulse afforded by Spelman's thought, began to see the full utility of impugning the antiquity of the Commons. From now on, however, to do so might be to provide arguments for Filmerian absolutism. If the Commons were not immemorial, had they any rights against the crown at all?

The immediate impact of the *Freeholder's Inquest*, however, was rather different from this; but before considering this aspect of the subject, we should observe that to derive the whole constitution from the will of the king did not necessarily bring about a general readjustment of historical ideas. As a statement, it was scarcely susceptible of historical proof, and it could never have the stimulating and deepening effect on historical thought which the discovery of feudalism had had on that of Craig, Spelman and Harrington. Of this branch of learning Filmer was apparently devoid. Though he had been one of the group of scholars who first met at Westminster late in James I's reign, though he had known and could quote Cotton, Selden and Spelman, he shows no sign of knowing that the giving of counsel was an obligation of tenure or that the tenurial relationship was of any special importance in the medieval kingdom. He tells us, for instance, that before the summoning of the Commons the council was composed of barons, but his account of the origin and nature of baronage is given in the words of a peculiarly old-fashioned passage in Coke,[1] and on this subject at least he had clearly read *Archaeologus* and the *Titles of*

---

[1] Laslett, pp. 140–1, with Filmer's reference to Coke.

Honour in vain. Here we may perhaps blame his political philosophy. For Filmer

> the difference between a Peer and a Commoner, is not by nature, but by the grace of the Prince: who createś honours, and makes those honours to be hereditary (whereas he might have given them for life only, or during pleasure, or good behaviour) and also annexeth to those honours the power of having votes in Parliament, as hereditary councillors, furnished with ampler privileges than the commons.[1]

If the difference between one social rank and another comes simply from the sovereign's command, there is no need to investigate the social structure of which they form part; and if the sovereign is an absolutely free agent, we need not inquire whether the relations between him and one class of his subjects are of a special nature and differ essentially from those he has with all other classes. Filmer's absolutism caused him to ignore the complexities of the medieval structure and diminished the extent to which his thought was genuinely historical. He could not see the origin of the Commons as Spelman had seen it, as an aspect of the transition from a feudal to a freeholding society. Filmer's argument means no more than that since the Commons originated late, they are not sovereign but subject to a sovereign.

To us, with the whole of Filmer's political thought before us, the absolutist interpretation of the *Freeholder's Inquest* is evidently the correct one. We need to remember, however, that this tract was first read by a public quite unacquainted with Filmer's doctrine of patriarchalism and none too familiar with that of political sovereignty. To minds such as these, it would be perfectly possible to read it as an essay in constitutionalism rather than absolutism, an appeal to the documents of the ancient constitution rather than a demonstration that the constitution itself was the creation of the king's will. It was in this sense that William Prynne read it; for though this formidable Puritan and common lawyer was profoundly influenced by the *Freeholder's Inquest* and cited it and developed its arguments throughout the rest of his pamphleteering life, he criticized the antiquity of the Commons in order to bring them not

[1] Laslett, pp. 156–7.

so much under the authority of the sovereign as within the bounds of the ancient constitution.

The alliance of two such minds—there is no trace of its having been known to Filmer—seems fantastic to contemplate, but it lay in the nature of the political and constitutional developments of the Interregnum. From late 1647 onwards, the fundamental dilemma of that period became increasingly plain. A single chamber, styling itself parliament, soon claimed sovereign power in the name of the ancient constitution; the only force capable of checking its pretensions was the army, which meant that the power of parliament seemed about to be made subject not to law, but to the sword. To those who wished to end this state of affairs, and were detached from Cromwell's increasingly desperate attempts to do so by means of synthetic constitutions, it was evident that to restore the ancient constitution was the only solution and in time it emerged that the restoration of the ancient constitution meant the restoration of the crown. What was needed was a government not destructive of liberty, but equally not open to the reproach that any man who had not given his consent to its foundation might withhold his obedience, and it might be argued that the monarchy satisfied this need and was beyond the reach of consent as much because it was immemorial as because it was sacred. Every man knew who had made the Protector, but none knew who had made the king unless it were God himself; and if the divine origin of kingship were expressed in terms of ancient English custom rather than of scriptural warrant, it became plain that the immemorial monarchy was the best guarantee of the immemorial law. The Restoration of 1660 was the greatest triumph which the cult of the ancient constitution ever enjoyed, and perhaps the greatest service it ever rendered.

As the theoretical debate of the 1640's and 1650's worked itself out to this conclusion, it became plain that the case for the ancient constitution could be identified with the case for the crown. Possibly none was better placed to discern this conclusion than the conservative Presbyterians, always constitutionalist, monarchist and counter-revolutionary. From the time of the army's march on London and the first expulsions of Presbyterian members of parliament, William Prynne—who was himself to be expelled by Pride—

saw that he was faced with a subversion of the whole parliamentary structure, and he was intelligent enough to see that the root of the trouble was his own house's claim to virtual sovereignty. It was not that the army had dictated to parliament, but that the Commons were taking it on themselves to try the king, abolish the Lords and expel their own members by majority vote. If the right of the secluded members to sit was to be restored, it must be established that the writ under which they had been returned was not within the exclusive control of the lower house acting alone; it must therefore be shown that the summons was issued by the king and that the Commons were not the whole of parliament. At the beginning of 1648, the *Freeholder's Inquest* supplied Prynne with the arguments he needed. It appeared in January;[1] not later than March[2] he published *A Plea for the Lords*, in which he cited Filmer's tract four times and made use of its case against the antiquity of the Commons. (Ten years later he reissued the *Plea* in a greatly expanded form, and the *Inquest* appeared seventeen times amongst his authorities.) The right of the Lords in parliament, he urged, was independent of that of the Commons:

their sitting, voting and judging therefore in Parliament, being so ancient, cleare and unquestionable ever since their first beginning till now; and the sitting of Knights, Citizens, and Burgesses by the peoples election in our ancientest Parliaments and Councells not so cleare and evident by *History* or *Records* as theirs: we must needs acknowledge and subscribe to their Right and Title, or else deny the Knights, Citizens and Burgesses rights in Parliament rather than theirs, who have not so ancient or cleare a Title or right as they.[3]

Next year he pressed the attack further in *The First Part of a Historical Collection concerning the Ancient Parliaments of England, from...673 till...1216.* Throughout these centuries, he wrote,

(and many yeers after), our Parliaments were constituted and made up onely of our *Kings, Princes,* Dukes, Earles, Nobles, BARONS, *Spirituall and Temporall Lords,* and those who in later ages we stile the HOUSE OF PEERS, without any *Knights of Shires, Citizens, Burgesses,* elected by the people as their Representatives, or any House of Commons, not known, nor heard of

---

[1] Laslett, p. 128. [2] Copies are dated 1647.
[3] *A Plea for the Lords* (1647–8), p. 4 (wrongly numbered for p. 12).

in these elder times, though those who now stile themselves the *Commons*, endeavour to cashier both *King* and *Lords* from being Members of our Parliaments, contrary to our *Laws, Statutes, Oathes* and *Solemn League and Covenant*, and the practice of all former ages; at whose Door and Barr themselves have waited, and stood bare upon all occasions, till within these few months, as their professed Superiours, and the onely Judges in Parliament, being but so many *Grand Jurie* men to present the Kingdomes grievances to their Superiour Tribunall and crave their redress and censure of them: A sufficient refutation of their present usurpation over them.[1]

The influence of the *Freeholder's Inquest* is plain, and Prynne now assumed for the rest of his life the role of an historical scholar, the aim of whose researches was to restore the usurped ancient constitution. From 1650 to 1653 he was imprisoned ('of purpose', in his own estimation, 'to debarr me from publishing any thing of this Nature, or against their New *Tyrannical Usurpations*'),[2] but on his return embarked on those labours among the Tower records which were to dominate the last phase of his career. 'In Caesar's Chapel, under the leads of the White Tower', he found great decaying masses of records: writs of summons, returns and other documents relevant to parliamentary elections. These he set himself first to rescue, then to digest and publish; and his toil bore fruit in the *Brief Register of Parliamentary Writs*, published in four volumes and more than two thousand pages between 1658–9 and 1664. In this vast survey of every writ of summons then extant and known we have the repetition on a gigantic scale of the *Freeholder's Inquest*; all the old arguments recur. The writ is issued by the king; it confers a status inferior to that of the Lords; the Commons are formally entitled to discuss only those matters which the king and the Lords lay before them. Above all, the subordinate position of the Commons is proved by the fact that they are not immemorial; Prynne assembled more documentary evidence than had ever been known before to support the view that no summons of knights and burgesses could be traced earlier than the first extant writ in 49 H. 3.

[1] *First Part of a Historical Collection*...(1649), pp. 5–6. No second part appeared and the work's function was carried on (after Prynne's imprisonment) by the *Brief Register of Parliamentary Writs*.

[2] From the preface 'To the Ingenuous Readers' of the *First Part of a Brief Register* (1658–9).

By the time the Long Parliament reassembled in 1660, Prynne could rise to argue that the writs for the new parliament should be issued in the name of Charles II—no decision to recall whom had yet been taken—as a mere matter of obedience to existing law.[1]

But Prynne used the arguments of the *Freeholder's Inquest* to support a view of the constitution ultimately very different from Filmer's. Where the latter maintained a theory of sovereignty which must at bottom mean that all law was the king's creation and consequently had originated at some point in time, Prynne believed in the immemorial constitution with all Coke's extravagance crossed with his own fanaticism. The law he was upholding had been constitutional law since the time of the Britons. The immemorial custom of England was visibly embodied less in the authorities of the common law than in the records of the Tower. The chaotic heaps of documents among which contemporaries saw him labouring assumed in his mind a peculiar sanctity; they were the repository of all constitutional truth, all political wisdom, and he was defending the constitution not merely intellectually by his pen, but physically by protecting these precious evidences and guarding them against neglect, decay and the malice of their enemies. He compared himself to Hilkiah the High Priest, who 'found the Book of the Law in the House of the Lord', and to Shaphan the scribe, who 'carried the Book to the King and read it before the King'. In dedicating the *Third Part of a Brief Register* to Charles II (1662), he told his sovereign that one and the same miraculous resurrection had restored him to the throne and raised up the records of the constitution from oblivion (at Prynne's hands).[2] He was, as usual, fabulously exaggerating his case; but he was only giving expression, in his own way, to a time-honoured belief. He was not therefore stating the view of constitutional history which Filmer had inaugurated and which was to become royalist orthodoxy some twenty years later. In his mind, all that he had proved was that the constitution was immemorial, that the king and the Lords were immemorial, but that the Commons were not. They must therefore

[1] *D.N.B.* 'William Prynne'.

[2] Prynne added that Hugh Peters's proposal to burn the records was the worst deed that sinner had advocated except the execution of Charles I.

accept subordination, not as in Filmer to the will of a sovereign legislator, but to the ancient law of England.

We look, therefore, to Prynne even less than to Filmer for a revival of Spelman's approach to the study of constitutional history. In one respect, it is true, he shows insight superior to Filmer's, but the promise comes to nothing. Filmer, as we have seen, failed to connect baronage with tenure because he thought of it merely as a rank conferred by royal favour; but Prynne wrote the first version (1648) of *A Plea for the Lords* to defend the upper house against Leveller assailants, some of whom had alleged that the Lords owed their title to the king's summons alone and were a nobility foisted upon the country by Norman usurpers. Prynne replied that the Lords had sat in parliament 'by right of peerage and tenure' for centuries before the Conquest, and in the *First Part of a Brief Register* (1658–9) he continued to defend them against the imputation of sitting by the king's will alone, declaring both that their right in parliament was immemorial and that the royal summons alone could not make a hereditary peer, unless the recipient either held *per baroniam* or had a special patent creating a hereditary title. In his anxiety to endow the peerage with a right more august than that of the representatives of the commons, Prynne remembered, where Filmer seems to have ignored, the ancient principle that tenure was a characteristic mark of baronage. He knew that the commons were a late adjunct to the king's council; he knew that before their advent the council had been composed principally of barons; he knew that tenure had been an essential of baronage. But he never quite succeeded in taking the next step and concluding that the barons had given counsel as an obligation incident to their tenures and that the growth of parliament had occurred as society developed away from a condition in which tenure and vassalage had determined the whole network of social relationships.

Prynne's study of the evidence again and again carried him to the point of remarking that before Henry III the council had consisted of barons, that these barons had held land and done homage, and that they had been summoned to give counsel on their homage and allegiance. But he never reached the stage of generalizing from the evidence, and for this we must blame his ignorance of the feudal history of countries other than his own—the basis on which Spelman had built up the concept of certain universal feudal characteristics which could be applied to the history of medieval England. Because Prynne could not do this, he could not explain that before the commons were added to it the council had been a body constituted on the basis of tenure in chief of the crown; and because he could not do this, his thought about parliamentary history continued to be a critical and sophisticated variant of that common-law thought which took the institutions of the present day and sought for their origins in the remote past. Spelman, having concluded that counsel had once been a function of tenure, decided that the parliamentary attendance of the commons had descended to them from the lesser tenants in chief; but when Prynne encountered the *omnes alios qui de nobis tenent in capite* of Magna Carta, or the knights of the shire summoned for specified purposes before 49 H. 3, he invariably argued that these persons could not be the commons, because they attended as tenants of the king and not as the elected representatives of their fellows. Before 49 H. 3 there were no commons; after that date there were the commons summoned in the writ. More than that Prynne could not say.

There was no alternative to an appreciation of the full meaning of Spelman's thought. When he published his last work, *Animadversions on Sir Edward Coke's Fourth Institutes* (1669), Prynne had in his possession Dugdale's 1664 edition of the complete *Archaeologus*, in which 'Parlamentum' had been published for the first time, and he actually quoted several of its most vital sentences; but clearly without understanding their true significance.[1] Spelman—thanks to the *Libri Feudorum* and his Continental learning—had framed a theory of feudalism and by its means established the existence of a feudal phase in the English past; Prynne had not done this, and it does not seem that it could have been done by study of the English evidence alone. He continued to believe that the constitution was immemorial, with the qualification that the House of Commons was not—and this perhaps he owed to Filmer. At the Restoration he was appointed, in recognition of his services to the constitution, to be Keeper of Records in the Tower, a post which he held to his

[1] *Animadversions on the Fourth Institutes* (1669), pp. 2, 6, 7, 8.

death in 1669, inaugurating a period in which the keepers were sometimes appointed for their work in propagandist historiography on medieval and constitutional themes; but significant figure though he is, he yet founded no school and remained in essentials a survivor from the age of Coke. Filmer had denied the antiquity of the Commons as a means to proving the sovereignty of the king, Prynne out of concern for the ancient constitution; their criticisms provided a useful weapon for checking the claims of parliament, but none for altering the way in which Englishmen instinctively thought about their history. For that there was no alternative to Spelman, to the application of feudal knowledge to constitutional history. The appeal to 49 H. 3, however, did much to create a more critical atmosphere: one in which the thought of Spelman, once it re-appeared and was understood, would be taken up and used, as much for its polemical as for its scholarly value. The true royalist counter-offensive, when at last it began, was a mingling of Spelman's ideas with Filmer's.

II

Thomas Hobbes, it is generally agreed, is far from typical of royalist thought—not least in his willingness to make use of the argument from Norman conquest—but, in the field which we are surveying, his writings assist us considerably to understand the case against the common-law mind which a penetrating intellect could build up out of the new historical ideas becoming current in the middle decades of the century. Students of his thought have perhaps neglected to note how much space he devoted to refutation of such ideas as that law is law because it is immemorial custom: several paragraphs of *Leviathan*, the greater part of the *Dialogue of the Common Laws* and much of *Behemoth* are directed to this end, and in all these writings we find English history interpreted in the light of Hobbes's characteristic ideas to form a radical criticism of the traditional beliefs of his countrymen. Coke, as we should expect, was his principal target, and Hobbes set himself to refute two of the chief justice's fundamental contentions: first, that most law was law because immemorial custom, second, that law of this kind constituted an 'artificial reason', the accumulated and refined wisdom of many generations, which none but a professional could comprehend and no individual intellect, however great, could have produced. On the contrary, Hobbes replied, law was two things: first, it was the dictate of a perfectly simple and universal 'natural reason', which enjoined those things which were good for our self-preservation; and second, it was made law by the command of the sovereign, not because he possessed greater or less 'natural reason', but because he had been instituted by men in the state of nature to enforce a certain mode of living which 'natural reason' enjoined.[1] The first part of this argument earned him a highly Burkean rebuke from Chief Justice Hale; it was in connexion with the second that he made most of his allusions to English history. Hobbes's position as regards custom is practically identical with that taken up by Filmer, which may be termed the historical limitation of right: law may be custom, but custom alone has no binding force; for custom to become law requires that there should already exist an authority capable of making law by his injunctions. Therefore no law can be immemorial; before there can be law there must be a sovereign; and every law must have been made at a particular point in time. To state such an argument as this was to give every royalist a vested interest in historical research. Logically, every law must have a beginning in time, the point at which the sovereign commanded it; practically, let that point only be found and the law's derivation from the command of a pre-existing sovereign was demonstrated.

Hobbes, however, did not spend much time in his *Dialogue* searching for the historical beginnings of specific English laws. He was concerned [instead to demonstrate the presence in English history of such a legislative sovereign as he believed must exist on *a priori* grounds, and to this end employed such arguments as that the king made judges and gave them their authority to judge, that the king determined punishments where the existing law prescribed none, and that the king had in past ages made the law of England with the assent of the Lords and Commons in parliament, but without consulting the judges.[2] (It is pleasant to observe that for once in a way Coke was right on a point of history and Hobbes,

[1] Hobbes, E[nglish] W[orks], vol. VI, pp. 5–7, 14–15, 62–3 and generally.
[2] E.W. vol. VI, p. 15.

as many contemporary scholars might have told him, demonstrably wrong; his argument might also tend to exaggerate the antiquity of parliament.) But Hobbes also made use of the concept of a Norman Conquest, and the way in which he did so merits study. He had discussed, in *Leviathan*, conquest as one of the two modes of acquiring dominion over others (the second being the acquisition of paternal dominion by begetting children), and Filmer had deplored his having done so. For—Sir Robert pointed out—Hobbes made it plain that the conqueror's dominion was created, not by his sword but by the wills of the conquered constituting him their sovereign out of fear of his sword, so that all difference between a sovereign by conquest and a sovereign peacefully instituted by social compact disappeared: each was absolute, each was the creature of covenant. This Filmer was unable to understand. How could an absolute sovereign guarantee the well-being of his subjects, and how could a sovereign instituted by the will of his subjects to a specific end be absolute? Moreover, it was clearly at the back of Filmer's mind that an appeal to conquest could not but justify the successful usurper. Hobbes's clarity of mind had exhibited to the perspicacious Filmer the two fundamental reasons why conquest could never be a theory long acceptable to royalists. Under close analysis it proved to be a mingling of force and covenant; and the royalists, especially under the Interregnum, could stomach neither.[1] But to Hobbes nothing could be more acceptable; in his view the will had little to do, at the best of times, but to consent to inescapable force and seek to turn it to its advantage, and the notion that the English kings acquired their sovereignty from William the Norman's conquest of the land was perfectly sensible and not particularly alarming. The mode of acquisition merely illustrated the essential nature of sovereignty. Granted that it must be above the law, it was indifferent how it came there.

> But say withal, that the King is subject to the laws of God, both written and unwritten, and to no other; and so was William the Conqueror, whose right is all descended to our present King....[2]

[1] See Oakeshott (ed.), *Leviathan* (Oxford, Blackwell's Political Texts; undated), pp. 130–3; and Laslett, pp. 239–40.

[2] *E.W.* vol. VI, p. 21.

Statutes are not philosophy, as is the common law, and other disputable arts, but are commands or prohibitions which ought to be obeyed, because assented to by submission made to the Conqueror here in England and to whosoever had the sovereign power in other places.[1]

The quotations fairly illustrate the subsidiary and illustrative character of the Norman Conquest in Hobbes's theory of English sovereignty. Neither in the *Dialogue of the Common Laws* nor in *Behemoth* did he place the fact of conquest at the centre of his argument or attempt, save by way of illustration, to derive the laws and liberties of England from it; but the considerations that made him regard it as not of the first importance made him also unafraid of it. Nor did it necessarily provide him with reasons for criticizing all the allegations of antiquity made about the various institutions of England. In the *Dialogue*'s closing passages the Lawyer and the Philosopher agree that it is in the sovereign's interest to surround himself with the chief men of the realm and make laws with their consent. But what of the composition of this council; what of the antiquity of the Commons? The Lawyer puts forward the old argument, found in Lambarde and Harrington, that the existence of totally deserted and decayed boroughs, still returning representatives to parliament, proves the extreme—and, it is taken for granted, pre-Conquest—antiquity of this right. Consider Old Sarum; its burgesses should be rabbits. The Philosopher agrees: in the time of the heptarchy there were many kings, each with his parliament and burgesses in each parliament; when one parliament met for all the kingdom, each borough sent its representatives. This may account for the preponderance of boroughs in the west, 'being more populous, and also more obnoxious to invaders, and for that cause having greater store of towns fortified'. The *Dialogue* ends on this cordial note.[2] But when the antiquity of the Commons is mentioned in *Behemoth*, an account is given which blends Filmer and Selden with a hint of Harrington:

The knights of shires and burgesses were never called to Parliament, for aught that I know, till the beginning of the reign of Edward I, or the latter end of the reign of Henry III, immediately after the misbehaviour of the

[1] *E.W.* vol. VI, p. 24.   [2] *E.W.* vol. VI, pp. 157–60.

barons; and, for aught any man knows, were called on purpose to weaken that power of the lords, which they had so freshly abused. Before the time of Henry III the lords were descended, most of them, from such as in the invasions and conquests of the Germans were peers and fellow-kings, till one was made king of them all; and their tenants were their subjects, as it is at this day with the lords of France. But after the time of Henry III, the kings began to make lords in the place of them whose issue failed, titulary only, without the lands belonging to their title; and by that means, their tenants being no longer bound to serve them in the wars, they grew every day less and less able to make a party against the King, though they continued still to be his great council. And as their power decreased, so the power of the House of Commons increased; but I do not find they were part of the King's council at all, nor judges over other men; though it cannot be denied, but a King may ask their advice, as well as the advice of any other. But I do not find that the end of their summoning was to give advice, but only, in case they had any petitions for redress of grievances, to be ready there with them whilst the King had his great council about him.[1]

Hobbes, we may take it, was by this time aware of the advantages of proving that the Commons originated late and consequently by the king's will. But it cannot escape notice that the passage just quoted unmistakably associates the decline of the barons' feudal power with the rise to importance of the House of Commons; and this raises the interesting question of Hobbes's knowledge of feudalism and the use he made of it. The opinion of the learned seems to be that these two dialogues were written within a short space of time, the *Common Laws* after 1666, *Behemoth* about 1668.[2] Hobbes could therefore have been acquainted with the complete edition of Spelman's *Archaeologus* that appeared in 1664. However that may be, both dialogues contain a definite and consistent appeal to feudal principles, which occurs first in the context of universal rather than English history.

Then let us consider next the commentaries of Sir Edward Coke upon Magna Charta and other statutes. For the understanding of Magna Charta it will be very necessary to run up into ancient times, as far as history will give us leave, and consider not only the customs of our ancestors the Saxons,

---

[1] *E.W.* vol. VI, p. 261.
[2] J. Laird, *Hobbes* (London, 1934), pp. 35–6, and his references to the work of G. C. Robertson.

but also the law of nature, the most ancient of all laws, concerning the original of government and acquisition of property, and concerning courts of judicature. And first, it is evident that dominion, government and laws are far more ancient than history or any other writing, and that the beginning of all dominion amongst men was in families.[1]

The father of the family—Hobbes does not call him the patriarch, but we may legitimately do so—possesses absolute power over his wife and children. This is in accordance with the principles of *Leviathan*, where it was pointed out that paternity was one of the origins of dominion, but that the father's authority was derived not from the mere fact of his paternity, but from his children's submission to his power (another doctrine which Filmer could by no means accept). Landless individuals may attach themselves to the family for security and submit themselves to the patriarch's authority in exactly the same way as his children. If a family so constituted conquers another and seizes its lands—which the law of God permits if it is the only way of procuring subsistence or removing a just cause of fear—the lands so won become the property of the patriarch. The Lawyer points out that this denies all right of property to the subject members of the tribe. The Philosopher assents: when the subjects placed themselves under the patriarch's authority, they did so for the sake of security; they are entitled to nothing else, and this does not of itself confer a title to land.

Did not Joshua and the High Priest divide the land of Canaan in such sort among the tribes of Israel as they pleased? Did not the Roman and Grecian princes and states, according to their own discretion, send out the colonies to inhabit such provinces as they had conquered? Is there at this day among the Turks, any inheritor of land besides the Sultan? And was not all the land of England once in the hands of William the Conqueror? Sir Edward Coke himself confesses it.[2]

The Saxons and other German peoples—with whose history and institutions Hobbes appears to be identifying those of the Normans —dwelt in families and under patriarchs in this way. When they conquered land in England, it became the absolute property of the sovereign, first of the heads of independent tribes, later of the king. But the subjects were not without definite rights in the land, for—

[1] *E.W.* vol. VI, p. 147.   [2] *E.W.* vol. VI, p. 149.

says the Philosopher—it is necessary to distinguish two sorts of property: the *allodium* and the fee. In a monarchy, none could possess allodial property but the king; all subjects must (as the common law declares) hold in fee, that is by the tenure and service of the king. The king lived, partly by his own demesnes—which Hobbes identifies with the forests—partly by the services which all men owed him. For in addition to the great men of the land, endowed with

much more land than they had need of for their own maintenance; but so charged with one or many soldiers, according to the quantity of land given, as there could be no want of soldiers at all times ready to resist an invading enemy: which soldiers these lords were bound to furnish, for a time certain, at their own charges,[1]

all men took an oath of allegiance to the king in the tithings and hundreds; and those who held 'by the service of husbandry', together with villeins and even women and children, were obliged to help to defend the kingdom in such manner as they were able, by the law of nature. But a special obligation rested on those who held by military service. Hobbes notes with approval the form of words employed in doing both homage and fealty, and looking at them through his eyes we can see how exactly an unlimited and unconditional yielding of one's self and one's services fitted the notion of compact set forth in *Leviathan*. In vassalage royalist thought was beginning to find the irrevocable contract of unqualified and absolute subjection which it had sought for so long. The patriarch was becoming identified with the seigneur, the seigneur with the king, and all three with Leviathan. Thanks to the centralized nature of the English monarchy, it was possible to perform the remarkable intellectual feat of making feudalism an argument for sovereignty.

Hobbes rehearses the feudal services and other rights due to the king; but, he says, speaking of homage and fealty,

both these services, and the services of husbandry, were quickly after turned into rents, payable either in money, as in England, or in corn and other victuals, as in Scotland and France.

[1] *E.W.* vol. VI, pp. 154–5.

However, this could not of itself do away with the military tenant's obligation to serve in person if summoned,

which, methinks, should ever hold for law, unless by some other law it come to be altered....The ancient kings had means enough, by their various feudal rights, to defend their kingdom and keep the peace. And so had the succeeding Kings, if they had never given their rights away, and their subjects always kept their oaths and promises.[1]

These remarks are the nearest Hobbes came to admitting that he was writing after the feudal tenures had been formally abolished, by *rex in parliamento*, in 1660. There were some royalist thinkers, as we shall see, who openly regretted this step, and it may not be unreasonable to attribute a trace of this nostalgia to Hobbes. He had forecast, in considerable detail, the case which royalists of greater erudition were to construct out of English history between 1675 and 1688: the denial of the immemorial, the appeal to a logically necessary sovereign, the attack on the antiquity of the Commons and the attempt to use the king's feudal suzerainty as an argument for his political sovereignty. All these were to be repeated, consciously or otherwise, by later royalists, though his appeal to the Norman Conquest won little favour.

Feudalism might, in addition, be used to demonstrate that parliament and the common law in their present form could have come into being only as feudal society declined. There is something of this in Hobbes: he observes that there seems to have been no Court of Common Pleas before Magna Carta, and

perhaps there was not so much need of it as you think. For in those times the laws, for the most part, were in settling, rather than settled; and the old Saxon laws concerning inheritance were then practised, by which laws speedy justice was executed by the King's writs, in the courts of Barons, which were landlords to the rest of the freeholders; and suits of barons in County courts; and but few suits in the King's courts, but when justice could not be had in those inferior courts. But at this day there be more suits in the King's courts, than any one court can dispatch.[2]

This is not particularly complete, but it shows a willingness to trace the growth of the modern common law from a feudal background. To the history of parliament, however, Hobbes could make

[1] *E.W.* vol. VI, pp. 156–7.   [2] *E.W.* vol. VI, pp. 43–4.

no further application of feudal principles than appears in the passage quoted earlier; he was aware that the barons attended the council as obliged by the homage which they did for their fiefs, but he never quite reached the point of saying that the council was a court of tenants. As the above passage shows, he did not distinguish Saxon from Norman law, and he held that lordship and tenure were institutions common to all the ancient Germans and indeed to all mankind in its primitive age. If, like Spelman, he had realized that a special form of tenure and a body of laws consequent upon it had been brought in and imposed upon England by the Norman conqueror, he might have gone on to reconstitute the early council on a tenurial basis. As it was, this was not done before the rediscovery of Spelman.

III

A reply to the *Dialogue of the Common Laws* was written (but not published or even perhaps completed) by Sir Matthew Hale, Chief Justice of the King's Bench, who also wrote, at an undetermined date before his death in 1675, a *History of the Common Law* which was published in 1715 and is still rightly regarded as one of the early classics of its kind. A train of thought which runs from Hale's reply to Hobbes to its maturity in the *History* deserves study as part of the present work, because in it Hale, one of the finest minds to work within the old legal tradition, revived and developed in a new direction the fundamental premiss of common-law historiography, that law was custom.

This was the point at which Hobbes had attacked Coke's doctrine of 'artificial reason'. Coke, it will be remembered, had presented law as customary and judge-made, the fruit of centuries of constant adaptation, and had argued that each maxim or rule of law embodied reason and experience so great and ripe that no individual mind with its limited horizon could attain to the height of its wisdom. Behind this doctrine there clearly lies the notion that law is custom and custom perpetual adaptation. Hobbes, wishing to deny both that law was immemorial custom and that the judges possessed any esoteric knowledge to which subject and sovereign should defer, had sharply replied that on the contrary law was first, the simple commands of reason, and secondly, the simple commands of the sovereign; no law rested on anything more mysterious than a rule of reason, apparent to any individual who reflected, and the immediate command of the sovereign who had last enjoined it. Hale, therefore, when he came to Coke's defence, was in a position analogous to that of Burke attacking the political rationalists and believers in a simple sovereignty of 1789; and that this is something more than an analogy will be suggested presently.

Hale's reply is printed as an appendix to the fifth volume of Holdsworth's *History of English Law*. The gist of his highly compressed argument is that the wisdom of the law should not be too readily subjected to the criticism and amendment of individual reason. We cannot, he argues, lay down the simple rules of law, if for no other reason than that morals is not an exact science. The reason which we exert in our juridical activity is then a purely empirical one, and we aim at no more than establishing rules of conduct to which all can agree and which will give satisfaction in the greatest possible number of the cases which come before the courts. Yet even in this relatively humble activity we have to bear constantly in mind that the field we are dealing with—human society—exhibits the most unimaginably complex interrelations between all its parts, so that we cannot in fact tell what the outcome of our decisions may be:

it is a thing of greatest difficulty, So to Contrive and Order any Lawe that while it remedyes or provides against one Inconvenience, it introduceth not worse or an equall. A Man that hath a prospect at one, or a few thinges may with ease enough fitt a Lawe to that, or those thinges. Qui ad pauca respicit facile pronuntiat. But the texture of Humane affaires is not unlike the Texture of a diseased bodey labouring under Maladies, it may be of so various natures that such Phisique as may be proper for the Cure of one of the maladies may be destructive in relation to the other, and the Cure of one disease may be the death of the patient.[1]

Life, in fact, overflows the intellect—the image of an organic body is regularly used by Hale when he wishes to suggest the incomprehensibility of the totality of human affairs—and we are compelled to admit that the most we can do in framing a particular

---

[1] Holdsworth, *History of English Law*, vol. v, p. 503.

law is to base it upon experience of as many as possible of the kind of cases it concerns, in order to diminish the probability of an unforeseeable complication appearing and upsetting its workings. This being so, it is immediately evident that the experience of many men outweighs the experience of one; and since the reason of the law is founded on men's experience instead of on abstract reasoning, it follows that the reason of many outweighs the reason of one. I ought to prefer the wisdom of an ancient law even though my reason protests against it.

There are many things especially in Laws and Governments that mediately, Remotely and Consequentially are reasonable to be approved, though the reason of the party doth not presently or imediately and distinctly See its reasonableness. For instance, itt is reasonable for me to preferre a Law made by a hundred or two hundred persons of age wisdom Experience and Interest before a Law excogitated by my Selfe that [am] it may be a Simple unexperienced younge man, though I discerne better the reason of that Law that I have thought of then the reason of the Law of those wise men. Againe it is a reason for me to preferre a Law by which a Kingdome hath been happily governed four or five hundred yeares then to adventure the happiness and Peace of a Kingdome upon Some new Theory of my owne tho' I am better acquainted with the reasonableness of my owne theory then with that Law. Again I have reason to assure myselfe that Long Experience makes more discoveries touching conveniences or Inconveniences of Laws then is possible for the wisest Councill of Men att first to foresee. And that those amendments and supplements that through the various Experiences of wise and knowing men have been applyed to any Law must needs be better suited to the Convenience of Laws then the best Invention of the most pregnant witts not ayded by such a series and tract of Experience.[1]

It is a corollary that no body of existing law can be reconstructed by abstract reasoning:

Now if any the most refined Braine under heaven would goe about to Enquire by Speculation, or by reading of Plato or Aristotle, or by Considering the Laws of the Jewes, or other Nations, to find out how Landes descend in England, or how Estates are there transferred, or transmitted among us, he wou'd lose his Labour, and Spend his Notions in vaine, till he acquainted himselfe with the Lawes of England, and the reason is because they are Institutions introduced by the will and Consent of others implicitely by Custome and usage, or Explicitely by written Laws or Acts of Parlement.[2]

[1] Holdsworth, vol. v, p. 504.   [2] Holdsworth, vol. v, p. 505.

To know the English law, then, there is no other way but to learn what the English have at various times decided shall be law. Since it is essentially an accumulation of judgments, decisions, amendments and refinements of age-old customs, to understand it is to understand the process by which this accumulation has been built up. Hale follows Selden in implying that the lawyer's knowledge is historical knowledge: in knowing the judgments and statutes of the past, he knows what ills they were designed to remedy and what the state of the law was which they remedied. In this way his understanding of the law's content is deepened, and he comes to see a greater part—never, perhaps, the whole—of the accumulated wisdom with which the refining generations have loaded it.

This is what Hale means by 'artificial reason', and it is obvious that he has anticipated and made his own several of the essential points of Burke's philosophy. The distrust of abstract reasoning, the belief that ancient institutions contain a latent wisdom greater than that of the individual, above all the concept of the law as the fruit of a great social process whereby society adapts itself to the consecutive emergencies brought to it by its experience in history—all these are Burke's; but they are foreshadowed, as we have already seen, not by Hale alone, but also by Coke and even by the French sixteenth-century partisans of *droit coutumier*. It is evident that they all arise from the idea of law as custom, or rather from that aspect of the idea of custom which emphasizes its universality and anonymity, the myriad minds who, not knowing the importance of what they do, have, each by responding to the circumstances in which he finds himself, contributed to build up a law which is the sum total of society's response to the vicissitudes of its history and will be insensibly modified tomorrow by fresh responses to fresh circumstances. The philosophy of Burke is descended from the concept of custom worked out in the late Renaissance during the first reaction against Roman law, and Hale marks a definite stage in its development.

But we saw in an earlier chapter that the idea of custom was twofold—men might treat it primarily as that which was continually adapted, or as that which was constantly preserved. The former emphasis would lead, as it does here, to the idea that law was the ever-changing product of a historical process; the latter to the idea

173

that law was fixed, unchanging, immemorial. In Coke and Davies we studied how the cult of the immemorial was built up, through an incautious use of the idea of custom, in the minds of men who had shown themselves equally ready to employ it in its former sense. The interest of Hale is that, following the line established in his reply to Hobbes, he went back in his *History of the Common Law* to the fundamental notion that law was custom and developed it in a reverse direction from that taken by Coke, denying at all points that the law had remained unchanged since time immemorial and asserting instead that it was in continual change in response to circumstances, until he depicted it as altogether a response to history. He lays down a complex and impressive historical theory of law, which has won him, from very competent judges, high praise as a legal historian.[1] But to possess a developed historical sense and apply it to law may not be the same as to solve the actual problems of legal history. It is the argument of the present work that English legal historians in the seventeenth century faced problems which could only be solved by means that Hale did not in fact adopt; and at the end of this chapter it will be asked whether Hale's triumph in the field of legal history was not more apparent than real.

In the first chapter of his *History* Hale treated of the familiar distinction between written and unwritten law, and it is plain that he was warning his readers against making this distinction too rigid. There were, he said, statute laws which were treated as *lex non scripta* simply because they were dated before the coronation of Richard I, which 'according to a juridical Account and legal Signification' marked the limit of 'time of memory'. These were not pleadable as acts of parliament but 'obtain their Strength by meer immemorial Usage or Custom'. The term immemorial, however, is obviously at least in part conventional; and the real status of these laws was that they had been so much expounded by judges as to be 'as it were incorporated into the very Common Law, and become a part of it', absorbed by the body of immemorial unwritten law which it was the judges' business to deliver. If we had the records of the most ancient parliaments, which must be accounted

---

[1] Holdsworth, vol. VI, pp. 584–95.

174

lost, we should no doubt find that much of the *lex non scripta* now regarded as ancient custom was originally statute. Here, it will be noticed, Hale was following his brethren in their common assumption that if we had no records of a certain kind before a given date, that was proof that they had been lost rather than that the courts which preserved them had only then begun to function; but the immediate importance of the argument is that Hale was trying to establish that written and unwritten law were essentially one.[1]

In his second, third and fourth chapters he dealt with the *lex non scripta*, which he showed to have the fundamental meaning of the ancient custom of England; and it was here that his historical thought began to rise to its full stature. He devoted his fourth chapter to arguing that the origins of English law could not be known. In other hands this would assuredly have meant that it was immemorial in the Cokean sense, that there had been no time when substantially the same law had not been in force in England. But Hale's argument is rather that its origins cannot be known because its nature is to be in constant, fluid and largely imperceptible change, a flux in which nothing remains the same for long and the moment and reasons of its alteration are often unmarked and unrecorded. Hale enlarges the old notion of custom into a theory of the nature of law. He draws his principal argument

from the Nature of Laws themselves in general, which being to be accommodated to the Conditions, Exigencies and Conveniencies of the People, for or by whom they are appointed, as those Exigencies and Conveniencies do insensibly grow upon the People, so many times there grows insensibly a Variation of Laws, especially in a long tract of Time; and hence it is, that tho' for the Purpose in some particular Part of the Common Law of *England*, we may easily say, That the Common Law, as it is now taken, is otherwise than it was in that particular Part or Point in the Time of *Hen.* II when *Glanville* wrote, or than it was in the Time of *Hen.* III when *Bracton* wrote, yet it is not possible to assign the certain Time when the Change began; nor have we all the Monuments or Memorials, either of Acts of Parliament, or of Judicial Resolutions, which might induce or occasion such Alterations; for we have no authentick Records of any Acts of Parliament before 9 H. 3, and those we have of that King's Time, are but few. Nor have we any Reports of Judicial Decisions in any constant series of Time

[1] Hale, *The History of the Common Law of England*, 2nd ed., 1716, pp. 2–4.

before the Reign of *Edw*. I, tho' we have the Plea Rolls of the Times of *Hen*. III and King *John*, in some remarkable Order. So that Use and Custom and Judicial Decisions and Resolutions, and Acts of Parliament, tho' not now extant, might introduce some *New* Laws, and alter some *Old*, which we now take to be the very Common Law itself, tho' the Times and precise Periods of such Alterations are not explicitely or clearly known: But tho' those particular Variations and Accessions have happened in the Laws, yet they being only partial and successive, we may with just Reason say, They are the same *English* Laws now, that they were 600 Years since in the general. As the *Argonauts* Ship was the same when it returned home, as it was when it went out, tho' in that long Voyage it had successive Amendments, and scarce came back with any of its former Materials; and as *Titius* is the same Man he was 40 Years since, tho' Physitians tell us, that in a Tract of 7 Years, the Body has scarce any of the same Material Substance it had before.[1]

If the law can remain the same when the whole of its content has altered, it must be the continuity of the process of law-making which counts. Law is made as society adjusts itself to new situations, and under a system of unwritten law little record is kept of the actual moments at which such changes occur. Laws tend to grow more complex and their original meaning to be lost to sight.

It is very evident to every Day's Experience, that Laws, the further they go from their original Institution, grow the larger, and the more numerous: In the first Coalition of a People, their Prospect is not great, they provide Laws for their present Exigence and Convenience: But in Process of Time, possibly their first Laws are changed, altered or antiquated, as some of the Laws of the Twelve Tables among the *Romans* were: But whatsoever be done touching their *Old* Laws, there must of Necessity be a Provision of *New*, and other Laws successively, answering to the Multitude of successive Exigencies and Emergencies, that in a long Tract of Time will offer themselves; so that if a Man could at this Day have the Prospect of all the Laws of the *Britains* before any Invasion upon them, it would yet be impossible to say, which of them were *New*, and which were *Old*, and the several Seasons and Periods of Time wherein every Law took its Rise and Original, especially since it appears, that in those elder Times, the *Britains* were not reduc'd to that civiliz'd Estate, as to keep the Annals and Memorials of their Laws and Government, as the *Romans* and other civiliz'd Parts of the World have done.[2]

[1] Hale, pp. 57–9.   [2] Hale, pp. 60–1.

But the absence of historical records is not the main reason for our ignorance of the origins of our laws. Their history has been such that laws may be altered unconsciously and those who deliberately introduce changes may not realize the full import of what they are doing. A further complication is the fact that England has been several times overrun by peoples of different stocks, and

those Occurrences might easily have a great Influence upon the Laws of this Kingdom, and secretly and insensibly introduce *New* Laws, Customs and Usages; so that altho' the Body and Gross of the Law might continue the same, and so continue the ancient Denomination that it first had, yet it must needs receive diverse Accessions from the Laws of those People that were thus intermingled with the ancient *Britains* or *Saxons*, as the Rivers of *Severn, Thames, Trent*, etc., tho' they continue the same Denomination which their first Stream had, yet have the Accession of divers other Streams added to them in the Tracts of their Passage which enlarge and augment them. And hence grew those several Denominations of the *Saxon, Mercian* and *Danish* Laws, out of which (as before is shewn) the Confessor extracted his Body of the Common Law, and therefore among all those various Ingredients and Mixtures of Laws, it is almost an impossible Piece of Chymistry to reduce every *Caput Legis* to its true Original, as to say, This is a piece of the *Danish*, this of the *Norman*, or this of the *Saxon* or British Law: Neither was it, or indeed is it much Material, which of these is their Original; for 'tis very plain, the Strength and Obligation, and the formal Nature of a Law, is not upon Account that the *Danes*, or the *Saxons*, or the *Normans*, brought it in with them, but they became Laws, and binding in this Kingdom, by Virtue only of their being received and approved here.[1]

Hale has now used three distinct images, suggesting continuity in the midst of change, to convey the historical character of law. This continuity rests ultimately on the continuity of the society itself which constantly makes and unmakes the law, but Hale distinguishes three organs by which it does so—custom, judicial decision and act of parliament. It is never really clear whether these three are all thought essential to the law-making process; if they are, and the process cannot go on without each one of them, then there is clearly some danger that parliament and the courts will be thought immemorial on the grounds that they must have existed from the moment at which society began to make law. We have

---

[1] Hale, pp. 62–3.

seen that Hale was inclined to assume that parliament and the courts must be older than their earliest records. But as regards the content of the law, which is all that concerns him in the book he is writing, Hale's outlook seems entirely historical. Each law is the product of a moment's exigency; as time goes on, new exigencies will arise and the old law will survive or be modified or fall into desuetude, as it gives satisfaction or not in dealing with them. If it survives it will be accounted immemorial, but mainly in a conventional sense. This process may be insensible, for the making of law is partly an unconscious activity, particularly in that part of it which is custom, but the imperceptible formation of custom is one with the conscious activities of interpreting it in the courts and modifying it by act of parliament. Each law is the product of many past moments and is being tested at the present moment by a wisdom which in its turn relies on the past. Each law will change, but society and its wisdom will go on.

This vision of a historical flux seems as far from the thought of Coke as could very well be. Hale seems to have escaped the pitfalls which trapped his great predecessor into treating custom as immemorial and immutable; all his emphasis is placed not on antiquity but on process and continuity. But it is not clear that he has escaped falling into a different error. He can paint the picture of a historical process; but can he study a particular process, date its stages or explain its transitions from one phase to another? There are sentences in the passages just quoted which seem to suggest that the history of law cannot be known. If it is really impossible to trace any particular point of the law back to its origin, it would seem that no means exist of analysing the history of the law in general; we are back at the ancient problem of the unknowability of the flux. If, furthermore, it is unnecessary to do so—as Hale seems to be suggesting—because the courts will maintain the tradition handed down to them, then there is no place for a historian of English law, since nothing will matter except the interpretation which the courts adjudge correct. If Hale has been describing the historical process only to leave its course at the last mysterious and irrelevant, he is after all only half a historian. At this point we must investigate his dealings with the concrete problems of English legal history.

First Royalist Reaction and Response of Sir Matthew Hale

The greatest of these problems to a man of Hale's generation was the Norman Conquest: were we to see in that event the violent imposition of one man's will, or a continuation of the ancient process of custom, judgment and consent? Hale devoted a great deal of space to arguing that it was the latter, and both Maitland and Holdsworth deplored that he should have done so.[1] They regretted it for two reasons: in the first place, it appeared to interrupt the development of his historical narrative; in the second, they felt that a man of so much learning and historical sense should have been able to see the irrelevance and unimportance of the problem. Of the almost obsessive power which the question of the Conquest exercised over contemporary minds we have already had sufficient evidence; but on Hale's own principles there existed a road leading away from the problem, and the strangest feature of his thought is that he set foot on this road only to abandon it. The unhistorical element in most seventeenth-century thought about the Conquest was the assumption that if the laws had at one time existed at the mere will of a conqueror they must continue in some sort to depend on his will even at the present day. The desire to rid the laws of this stigma was Hale's express motive for dealing with the question in his long fifth chapter, but in its course he considered whether it was not possible that a government originally founded on conquest might in time be transformed into a rule of law, and concluded that this might indeed be in certain cases, one of which would arise

when by long Succession of Time, the Conquered had either been incorporated with the conquering People, whereby they had worn out the very Marks and Discriminations between the Conquerors and Conquered; and if they continued distinct, yet by a long Prescription, Usage and Custom, the Laws and Rights of the conquered People were in a manner settled, and the long Permission of the Conquerors amounted to a tacite Concession or Capitulation, for the Enjoyment of their Laws and Liberties.

Hale seems to imply that this tacit concession would in time become as binding on the conquerors as a formal covenant with their subjects. Time and use, custom and history, then, may be

[1] Maitland, *Collected Papers*, vol. II, p. 5; Holdsworth, vol. VI, pp. 584-7.

179

sufficient of themselves to turn the dictatorship of a conqueror into a rule of law:

> But of this more than enough is said, because it will appear in what follows, that *William* I never made any such Conquest of *England*.[1]

Hale made no attempt to bring his concept of gradual transformation out of the realms of hypothesis; abandoning it with obvious relief, he went on to plead the familiar case. William's victory was won over Harold, not over the kingdom; he merely proved by battle his right to succeed to the throne according to English law; he confiscated the lands of none except his active opponents; he confirmed the ancient law of the Confessor. It is evident that Hale's sense of history was not sufficient to convince him that even if there had been a conquest, it had occurred in a remote and alien world and could not possibly confer any rights on Charles II. His concept of law as constantly changing, however subtly conceived and eloquently expressed, remained a theory, not a vision of history in the concrete; he was not able to persuade himself that a right won by the sword did not descend untouched through the centuries; conquest remained an absolute which the history of England as he saw it could not absorb.

If men were to believe in a historic process which could absorb conquest, they must think in a manner more subtle even than Hale. They must see that conquest as occurring in a concrete historical situation, unlike that of their own day, and as capable of being understood only in relation to that situation. Then it would appear that the true problem was the transformation of that past situation into the situation of their own day: a process in which the nature of the conqueror's power could scarcely have escaped being changed. To think with Spelman that the chief effect of the Norman invasion had been to introduce feudal tenure, and that the main features of Anglo-Norman society must be understood as organized upon that basis, must in time bring about such a change in views—even though Spelman himself had found it necessary to go on denying that there had been a conquest. For then William would cease to be that abstract, juridical thing, a conqueror, and become some-

[1] Hale, pp. 81–2.

thing far more concrete and historical, a king whose power consisted largely in his lordship over feudal tenants; and in the effort to explain how the king of England, having been that, had become what he now was, the suggestion that his power might still be that of a conqueror would necessarily be lost to sight. Hale was unquestionably perceptive enough to have followed such a line of thought, but there is nowhere in his work any sign that he considered feudal tenure of any special importance in the history of the law. He can have had no concept that feudal tenure had been introduced at one time, had declined at another, and between those dates had been that in the light of which, above all else, relations of property, personal status, and political rights and obligations must be understood. Therefore there existed a great gap in his perception of history; he studied the Norman period in terms of the problem of conquest because he could not conceive that it could be studied in any other way; and though he was learned enough to see that the reigns of Henry II and Edward I were of particular importance in legal history,[1] his treatment suffered because he was unable to describe these kings as acting upon and modifying a system of tenures, or a system of legal relationships largely determined by the presence of a particular form of tenure. This deficiency prevented his history of the common law from achieving any narrative unity, and it prevented him from transforming his vision of a historical process into terms of concrete history. At the time of Hale's death in 1675, the whole development of constitutional historiography was held up, unable to make progress without the discoveries and the ideas so far peculiar to Spelman.

[1] It was for his treatment of Edward I's legislation that Holdsworth particularly praised him (*Sources and Literature of English Law*, p. 62); and it could be said that his account of Henry II's work is a remarkable piece of insight considering that he could not describe the substratum of feudal customs on which Henry's judges worked.

CHAPTER VIII

The Brady Controversy

I

BUT the royalist version of history was rapidly developing to a point where the ideas of Spelman could be of use to it. Feudalism could be used to prove Filmer's and Prynne's point that the House of Commons was no older than Henry III's reign; it could also be employed, as Hobbes had shown, to vest the monarchy with an authority which was sovereign and paternal rather than contractual. It should perhaps be emphasized once again that to the seventeenth-century English feudalism did not mean a dissolution of the state or even a private agreement between lord and vassal; it implied primarily that all land was held of the king on condition of homage and obedience. The time was not long, therefore, before the ideas of Spelman were revived and employed in party controversy; but the way in which this came about may repay study. In 1675, the year of Hale's death, Sir William Dugdale, the most eminent medievalist of his day, published the first volume of a work entitled *The Baronage of England*, and in the preface gave an account of parliamentary history in which the ideas are plainly Spelman's. Eleven years previously, he had brought out a complete edition of the *Archaeologus*, including for the first time the article 'Parlamentum',[1] and we have seen how William Prynne quoted this without apparently realizing its full significance. The remarkable fact is that Dugdale himself seems to have been distinctly slow to grasp what it really implied. For example, in a work of 1666, called *Origines Juridiciales*, he had opened by declaring the antiquity of the common law in language of which Coke himself need not have been ashamed: it was unwritten, immemorial, rooted in pure reason and had been sworn to by William the Conqueror.[2] Spelman

[1] *Glossarium Archaiologium* (1664). There is an account of how he undertook the task in the life of Spelman prefixed to Gibson's *Reliquiae*.

[2] *Origines Juridiciales*, pp. 3–5.

himself, it will be remembered, had proved unwilling to abandon this myth altogether, and had Dugdale gone on to apply feudal principles to constitutional history, this opening need have been no more than a pious exordium. But in his fifth chapter, 'Of Parliaments',[1] he was guilty of a significant if unconscious distortion of Spelman's meaning. There was sufficient evidence, he thought, of the commons having been represented in the councils of William I and his successors; he cited Anglo-Norman documents which used such terms as *a clero et populo, communitas* and *baronagium*—the last of which, following a suggestion of Lambarde's, he thought should be interpreted to include all freemen. But it was clear, he continued, from the words of Magna Carta that the council of that period had included none but tenants in chief. Yet the charter, as was well known, was no more than a confirmation of the ancient liberties, so that there was a problem of reconciling this restriction of the membership of councils with the right of every freeman to be represented which, Dugdale took it for granted, had formed part of the immemorial law. 'It must necessarily follow', he therefore declared,

that the persons, who held of the King *in Capite*, were the representatives of the rest of the Commons, called by some *Barones Minores*...and that the dependent tenants consent was included in the assent of his immediate superior Lord, whose presence was ever so required in those great Councills, need not I think be doubted.[2]

There was some apparent justification in 'Parlamentum' for this curious attempt to combine the tenurial council with the representative principle. Spelman had undeniably written:

et consentire inferior quisque visus est, in persona domini sui capitalis, prout hodie per procuratores comitatus vel burgi, quos in parlamentis KNIGHTS AND BURGESSES appellamus.[3]

[1] *Origines Juridiciales*, pp. 14–19.
[2] *Origines Juridiciales*, pp. 17–18.
[3] 'and every inferior was considered as giving his consent in the person of his principal lord, just as today he gives it through the representatives of shire and borough, whom in parliament we call knights and burgesses.' *Glossarium* (1664), p. 451, col. 1.

But a passage in the treatise 'Of Parliaments' (still unpublished and presumably unknown to Dugdale) shows what manner of representation Spelman had in mind, and how far the not very happy analogy with knights and burgesses conveys his real thought.

...in those times, it belonged only to the tenants *in capite* to consult with the King on State matters and matters of the Kingdom; insomuch as no other in the Kingdom possessed any thing but under them. And therefore, as in Despotical Government, the agreement or disagreement of the Master of the Family concluded the menial and the whole Family; so the agreement and disagreement of the chief Lord or him that held *in Capite*, concluded all that depended on him or claimed under him, in any matter touching his Fee or Tenure. To this purpose, seemeth that in the Laws of *Edward* the Confessor, ratified by the Conqueror: *Debet etiam Rex omnia rite facere in regno, et per judicium procerum regni.*[1]

Spelman, in fact, had argued from the character of the *feudum* to give a new and quite unfamiliar meaning to the term representation; but Dugdale was employing his master's ideas to suggest that some immemorial right of representation had survived even into the feudal period. Since he was a convinced and lifelong royalist, there can have been no political motive behind these proceedings, and they merely offer one more instance of the astonishing strength and persistence of the common-law habit of mind. Dugdale was a master of feudal learning, and Professor Douglas has commented on his readiness to relate 'the principles of tenure...to the charters in which they were severally expressed',[2] but when he came to the history of the constitution, he could not perform a like feat; the habit of thinking in terms of immemorial liberties was too strong for him, and he attempted to interpret feudalism so as to harmonize it with the imposing structure of ancient law.

The account of parliamentary history which he gave in the preface to the *Baronage* is therefore not quite perfect when considered as a report of Spelman's findings; none the less it conveyed Spelman's essential thesis and was the occasion of the controversy in which this was driven home. From the Conquest to the reign of Henry III,

[1] 'The king ought to do all things in his kingdom in the proper way and by judgment of the chief men.' *Reliquiae Spelmannianae*, p. 58.

[2] D. C. Douglas, *English Scholars* (London, 1943), p. 58.

Dugdale explained, the king's councils had contained none but tenants *in capite*, and these were present not because the House of Lords was older than the House of Commons, but because they were the king's tenants, who owed their lord this service. But though it is right to gloss Dugdale's words in such a way as to emphasize that he was in effect making this latter point, he nevertheless still believed that the tenants in chief had in some way represented the commons, who held as sub-tenants under them. But in 49 H. 3—this date was not Spelman's and, if Dugdale took it from anyone, it could have been from Prynne—there appeared the first direct representatives of the commons in the form of the knights summoned by Simon de Montfort. Here Dugdale departed once more from the full complexity of his predecessor's thought. Spelman had seen the origin of the Commons as occurring in a process of transition whereby a class of lesser tenants *in capite*, promised a general summons in the charter of 1215, had evolved into a class of freeholders no longer confined to tenants *in capite*, who returned their representatives through the machinery of the shire. He had therefore refrained from mentioning any specific date for the first appearance of the Commons in parliament, and had treated the problem as part of the general decline of feudal relationships. But Dugdale assigned the origin of the Commons, almost without qualification, to the year 49 H. 3, and he attributed it to specific acts of deliberate statesmanship occurring in and soon after that year. To his way of thinking, the rebellious barons went in fear of the trains of knights by whose aid they had just defeated the king at Lewes, and therefore brought knights of the shire and burgesses into parliament; and "the Kings of this Realm ever since" saw in this device an admirable means of counter-balancing the power of the barons assembled in parliament. This would present Edward I, as was done as late as the time of Stubbs, as the conscious architect of state who appealed to one class against another.[1] Dugdale's theory of representation implies that the commons already existed and were in some sort represented in parliament; what they

[1] For the historiography of Edward I, there is an article by Mr Geoffrey Templeman, 'Edward I and the Historians', in the *Cambridge Historical Journal*, vol. x, no. 1 (1950), pp. 16–35.

received in 49 H. 3 was a change from indirect to direct representation. Dugdale did not understand, as Spelman did, that the growth of the knights of the shire was one aspect of a general change in social relations, and his historical thought must therefore be placed on a rather lower level.

But whatever its deficiencies as a piece of historical writing, the preface to the *Baronage* had confronted the antiquity doctrine with its most serious challenge to date. Prynne's attack had turned chiefly on the interpretation of documents, and the point that there was no record of a summons older than 49 H. 3 could be met with the usual *argumentum ex silentio*; but Dugdale's preface, and Spelman's 'Parlamentum' to which it soon drew attention, not only alleged that there had been no parliamentary commons before the late thirteenth century, but gave some formidable reasons for thinking that there could not have been. Historical controversy seems to have been relatively dormant for some time, but 1675 was the year of *Shirley* v. *Fagg*, when Shaftesbury and Holles were defending the jurisdiction of the Lords against the attacks of the Commons with arguments drawn in part from their old fellow-Presbyterian Prynne;[1] and perhaps it was in this connexion that William Petyt, a rising Whig barrister, began early in 1676 to collect materials for a reply to Dugdale. Petyt was a Yorkshireman whose career had been built largely on his acquaintance with the public records: it had earned him a new surname, a patent of gentility, membership of the Inner Temple, the friendship of Burnet and Essex and an increasing reputation for learning in circles opposed to the crown—though it is ironical that his first experience had been gained in the office of that more than royalist lawyer and antiquary, Fabian Philipps. In January 1676 three of his clerks were questioned about the writing of libels.[2] By April he was writing to various

---

[1] Shaftesbury, *Two Seasonable Discourses Concerning this Present Parliament* (1675); Holles, *The Case Stated Concerning the Judicature of the House of Peers in the Point of Appeals* (1675), and *The Case Stated Concerning the Judicature of the House of Peers in the Point of Impostures* (1676).

[2] The *D.N.B.* article on Petyt may be supplemented from the following sources. For the pedigree which he made out for himself and his brother, enabling them to take out a patent of gentility and change the spelling of their name, see *Calendar of State Papers (Domestic)*, 5 April, 31 August

correspondents about his reply to Dugdale and inquiring for evidence which might justify the unhandsome accusation that 'Parlamentum' was not Spelman's work but had been foisted into the *Glossarium* by Dugdale or some other enemy of the laws and liberties.[1] However, he did not now publish anything—perhaps for fear of offending John Cotton, Dugdale's friend, in whose care was his grandfather's great library[2]—and the new defence of the immemorial nature of the Commons had to wait until the very different circumstances of the year 1680; so that it appeared both as a contribution to Exclusionist propaganda and after the republished works of Sir Robert Filmer had come upon the scene and transformed the whole polemical situation.[3]

It has long been known that the posthumous republication of Filmer played a major role in establishing that Tory ideology—based almost for the first time on an unhesitating assertion of the crown's sovereignty—to which the theorists of the opposition had to find an answer. But because of the long neglect of that aspect of English political thought with which this book is concerned, it is less often pointed out that, after 1679–80, Filmer was used to attack the Exclusionists on two fronts, with the *Freeholder's Inquest* as well as *Patriarcha*, and that those who replied to him—with the interesting exception of Locke—were at least as much concerned with the origins of the English constitution as with the creation of Adam and the events at the disembarkation of Noah. Yet the facts can easily be established. James Tyrrell, Locke's friend, wrote to Petyt in January 1680, addressing him as his superior in historical learning, and urged him to reply to certain aspects of *Patriarcha* and to the

and 1 September 1676, and (for rumours of forgery) *Historical Manuscripts Commission, VIth Report,* p. 232. The last reference mentions his association with Philipps; see also Philipps to Brady, Caius College MSS. 607, fol. 5. Inderwick, *Calendar of the Inner Temple Records,* vol. III, pp. xvi, xviii, 74. Burnet, *History of the Reformation* (ed. 1865), vol. I, p. 7, gives details of Petyt's help to Burnet. Petyt's *Antient Right of the Commons* is dedicated to Essex. For the incident involving his clerks, see *Cal. S.P.D.,* 16 January 1676.

[1] Inner Temple MSS. (Petyt MSS.) 583 (17), fols. 483 and 483 b.

[2] Petyt to Cotton, Inner Temple MSS. *ibid.* fol. 482.

[3] For what is known of the circumstances of this republication, and a consideration of its effects, see Laslett, *op. cit.* pp. 33–41.

Freeholder's Inquest;[1] and in his own work, *Patriarcha non Monarcha*, he included some discussion of historical and constitutional questions and for the rest referred the reader to Petyt's newly published book.[2] This work, *The Antient Right of the Commons of England Asserted*, seems to have been in circulation as early as October 1679,[3] though it was not published until 1680. Like *Jani Anglorum Facies Nova*, the work which William Atwood, Petyt's pupil and friend, soon produced in its support, it is directed as much against Dugdale and (through him) Spelman as against Filmer, and is irritatingly vague in naming or identifying its adversaries; but the above facts link it unmistakably with the Filmerian controversy. Algernon Sidney also, in his *Discourses on Government*, thought it necessary to answer Filmer at some length on historical grounds. The two branches of the debate were again united in Tyrrell's post-Revolutionary folio, *Bibliotheca Politica* (1694). The many chapters of this work mingle the ideas of Petyt with those of Locke, and this conjoint influence is traceable as late as William Molyneux's *The Case of Ireland Truly Stated* (1698). These facts seem both to establish the dual nature of the Filmerian controversy, and to emphasize how exceptional was Locke in omitting any discussion of English legal or constitutional history from the *Treatises of Civil Government* which he ultimately published.

It was not only the arguments of the *Freeholder's Inquest* which confronted the believers in an ancient constitution; the whole Filmerian thesis was aimed at dissolving and destroying the concept of immemorial law. Such a thing was impossible, wrote Filmer in *Patriarcha*:

for every custom there was a time when it was no custom, and the first precedent we now have had no precedent when it began. When every custom began, there was something else than custom that made it lawful,

[1] Inner Temple MSS. 583 (17), fol. 302; dated 'January 12'. Petyt's work was already complete.

[2] *Patriarcha non Monarcha* (1681), p. 124; cf. pp. 147–52.

[3] See letters in Inner Temple MSS. *ibid.* fols. 291 and 298, dated October 16 and 26, in which Ralph Cudworth and Bishop Thomas Barlow thank Petyt for copies of his book. Cudworth did not cut the pages of his copy, if it was the one shown the present writer in the library of Christ's College in 1949; it was in beautiful condition.

or else the beginning of all custom were unlawful. Customs at first became lawful only by some superior power which did either command or consent unto their beginning.[1]

This superior power, Filmer thought, must ultimately reside in the will of some one man, so that in the last resort the original sovereign was Adam. It was the essence of patriarchal doctrine that the absolute sovereignty enjoyed by the first man must—being by definition inalienable—have descended intact to his successor, the lawfully constituted king of today. Apart from the obvious difficulty of proving that Charles II was descended direct from Adam by primogeniture, it is important that we should recognize that this doctrine did not sound absurd to its opponents; they did not argue, on grounds of historical relativity, that sovereignty in Charles must mean something quite unlike the sovereignty possessed by Melchizedek. This is shown by the fact that, one and all, they angrily denied the occurrence of a Norman Conquest (which Filmer had not asserted). They did so because they unreservedly agreed that if William I in the eleventh century had ruled with absolute power, there was nothing to prevent Charles II in the seventeenth from revoking every law and liberty ever granted by the kings of England. We have been exploring the causes of this lack of historical sense throughout the present volume, and we may agree that if a writer as subtly aware of the processes of history as Sir Matthew Hale could not, when it came to the pinch, bear to admit that there had been a conquest, those causes lay deep and were hard to remove. Filmer is not to be ridiculed for a lack of historical sense all but universal among the Englishmen of his century; and it may be observed that, a few years before Charles's *quo warranto* proceedings and the French king's revocation of the edict of Nantes, there was nothing absurd, from a practical point of view, about the idea that grants made by a sovereign king might be revoked by any of his successors to the end of time. What Filmer did, in the passage just quoted, was to show that, on premises which his opponents accepted as fully as he did, the fact that any law or right must have had a beginning at some point of time within human history was in itself an argument for absolute power. If a man made law, he must

[1] Laslett, pp. 106–7.

have sovereign power; that power must descend to his heirs intact; and all laws, it was contended, must have been made by somebody—if necessary by Adam. Armed with this formula, the Filmerians could tax the battered champions of the common-law tradition with not knowing what they meant by immemorial and ask—as Robert Brady repeatedly did—whether the law of England had existed before the island was inhabited, or before the Flood or the Creation.[1] If the Whig writers could not prove this, must they not admit that the laws had in the first instance been made by some man, empowered by God to do so and consequently sovereign, whose heirs were sovereign to this day? We can now perhaps see why Filmer never thought it worth while proving that there had been a Norman Conquest. He could make his case equally clear without any questionable appeal to the sword, simply by insisting that every law had originated at some point in time and in the will of some man. His influence must therefore have tended to encourage the Tories in historical criticism of the doctrine of antiquity.

But it should still have been possible to meet his arguments by an appeal to custom, along lines similar to those followed by Hale. Laws are the product of custom, it might have been said; they come into being slowly, as the result of many men's agreement tacitly given over many years, and it is insensitive to demand that some established sovereign must have legitimized this process. If you seek a sovereign, some ultimate sanction, it is the people themselves, not indeed met in any legislative assembly, but living their daily lives over the generations; and it is the slow accumulation of their often wordless decisions that makes laws, so gradually that you cannot

---

[1] Brady, *Complete History of England*, vol. 1 (1685), p. xlvii (wrongly numbered lxvii); and *Introduction to the Old English History* (1684), p. 86: Petyt 'lays the great stress of his Argument upon the words, HATH EVER BE. What, were the COMMONS of *England* as now Represented by *Knights, Citizens*, and *Burgesses* ever an essential constituent part of the Parliament, from eternity, before man was created? Or have they been so ever since *Adam*? Or ever since England was peopled? Or ever since the *Britains, Romans*, and *Saxons* inhabited this Island? Certainly there was a time when they began to be so represented. And that is the question between us, which whether this Gentleman, or my self, be in the right, I leave to any impartial Judge.' 'Hath ever be' is correct; Petyt has been quoting a document of the fifteenth century.

say with certainty when any law that we now have first came into being, still less what authority sanctioned it. Hale could assuredly have answered Filmer in some such way as this, as he had answered Hobbes, but he had been dead five years, and no such mode of reply occurred to Petyt and Atwood. Their answer is purely obscurantist; they merely insist that parliament and the law are immemorial —that is, that at whatever time it is suggested that parliament may have originated, it was already ancient: an argument which of course runs straight into the logical absurdities pointed out by Brady. By insisting that the rights of Englishmen must be older than any potential sovereign, they left themselves the more exposed to the Filmerian reply that nevertheless some sovereign must have instituted them in the first place. They made no appeal to custom and do not seem to have understood that the doctrine that a law was immemorial rested ultimately on the presumption that such a law was custom. We have seen that the idea of an ancient constitution was founded, in England, on the customary character of the common law, and that ever since the time of Coke and Davies it had been possible to emphasize either that custom was immemorial or that custom was in perpetual adaptation. The latter idea, brilliantly and elaborately developed by Hale, could have been built into a powerful argument against patriarchalism; but in the Whig controversialists of the 1680's we have only the notion that law is immemorial blindly insisted on by men who seem to have forgotten that it is immemorial because it is custom. If Petyt and Atwood, rather than Hale, are typical of the common-law mind in the last decade of Stuart monarchy, that mind was far gone in ossification and the Filmerian attackers had an easier task than might have been the case if they had had a Hale before them.

Petyt, then, in *The Antient Right of the Commons*, set out to prove once more the traditional thesis that parliament and the laws were immemorial. This is a confused book, hurriedly put together in three sections. The central essay, which we are told was written first,[1] is a group of arguments designed to prove that the Commons were already immemorial, and known to be so, in 49 H. 3; we may perhaps detect in this the reply to Dugdale which Petyt had

---

[1] *Antient Right*, Preface (separately paginated), p. 74.

been preparing since 1676. But a Preface of more than half its length advances the familiar case for the immemorial nature of the law in general, and this as usual develops into a defence of the constitutional character of the Norman Conquest. Neither Filmer, Dugdale nor Spelman had in fact asserted that William had ruled as a conqueror, but a common lawyer defending the immemorial law would soon find himself denying the Conquest, whether an adversary had upheld it or not; and the doctrines of Filmer made a rehabilitation of the immemorial constitution seem a peculiarly urgent need. There is a deeper note, however, in Petyt's treatment of the Conquest, and this is particularly associated with the third section of his book, the Appendix. Earlier, in the Preface, Petyt makes use of the familiar argument that William did not confiscate the land of the whole kingdom, but confirmed much of it in the hands of those who had held it before the Conquest. This assertion had often been made—Petyt quoted Justice Shardelowe in Edward III's reign[1]—in order to demonstrate William's reverence for existing law and rights; but Petyt also used it to suggest that those whose rights were thus confirmed were freemen, who both before and after the Conquest must have enjoyed all the rights which the law accorded to freeholders, including that of representation in parliament[2]—a typical common-law argument, which we have seen was not without its appeal to Dugdale. Its full meaning, however, becomes apparent only when we read Petyt's Appendix,[3] in which an attempt is made to blunt the edge of Spelman's main argument. Petyt admits that the king regularly met his barons in the *curia regis*, which was a feudal court of a lord and his vassals discussing their joint affairs; but in addition to the *barones regis*, he declares, who were tenants *in capite* meeting in the *curia*, there were the *barones regni*, non-feudal freeholders, who met in the *commune concilium regni*, a true parliament of Lords and Commons, to discuss affairs of a far wider range than came before the purely feudal *curia*.

---

[1] *Antient Right*, Preface, p. 27. 'Le Conqueror ne vient pas pur ouster eux, qui avoient droiturell possession, mes de ouster eux que de lour tort avoient occupie ascun terre en desheritance del Roy & son Corone.'

[2] *Antient Right*, Preface, pp. 39–41.

[3] The Appendix (exclusive of documents) occupies pp. 129–48.

This argument was suggested to him by 'friends'—perhaps by William Atwood, who carried it on with a great deal of misplaced ingenuity in his works of this and subsequent years—and while its intrinsic value is emphatically negative, its importance lies in the very extensive concessions which it makes to Spelman's most revolutionary assertions. Petyt had in fact admitted that there was such a thing as feudal tenure, which had been imported into England by the Normans and had exerted a unique form of influence on the way in which the king took counsel and did the kingdom's business. He was merely determined to limit as far as possible the scope both of the phenomenon and of its influence, in order to leave parliament and the freeholders it represented securely immemorial; and this compelled him to adopt a new attitude to the Conquest. Up till now it had been treated, e.g. by Hale, as a purely juridical question, involving the relation of the Conqueror's will to the laws of the land; but when Petyt insisted that the Conqueror had not seized the whole land and that non-feudal freeholders had survived the establishment of Norman rule, he was implicitly admitting that feudal tenants held their land in a special way and would require special institutions for their governance. This was to take a long step in the direction of the new Spelmanist historiography, but Petyt took it unwillingly and was resolved to maintain as far as possible the view that contemporary institutions were immemorial.

II

Petyt wrote this part of his argument because the ideas of Spelman were now being circulated in the context of Filmerian controversy; a man who argued for a feudal phase in the history of law and parliament might be thought to argue against the antiquity of these things, and so for their continuing dependence on the will of the sovereign who had instituted them; and indeed some writers for the crown would soon be willing to argue in this way. It was a question, however, whether the royalists could bring themselves to abandon the traditional historiography to which they had clung for so long; we have seen that Dugdale was far from being detached from the notion of immemorial law. But a new combatant was at hand, who fully understood the thought of Spelman and was Filmerian enough to feel no compunction at throwing over the immemorial. In April 1675, Dr Robert Brady, Master of Caius, had written to Sir Joseph Williamson, then Secretary of State, offering to compose a history of England which would teach the people loyalty and obedience and frustrate the designs of the seditious.[1] Brady was at this time about forty-eight, a doctor of medicine and professor of physic, and had never published a historical work. As a Norfolk royalist, he had suffered a period of exile after the second Civil War, and seems to have been brother to one Edmund Brady who was hanged at Norwich, after an abortive royalist conspiracy, in 1650. The Norwich royalists had been condemned by a High Court of Justice which, like the more famous tribunal at Westminster, could justify its proceedings by appeal either to the ultimate sovereignty of the people, or else to the concept of an ancient constitution in defence of which any action was legitimate—two arguments often confused or used in combination. In so far as the High Courts of Justice and their apologists made use of the latter argument, their claim to jurisdiction had in fact rested on a perversion of history, and Robert Brady could have had his brother, as well as his sovereign, in mind when he declared in his letter of 1675:

Some brave men and such as have done [the crown] and their country eminent service have perished by fragments and partial story (picked out of mouldy parchments and obscure authors which perhaps they never knew of), improved by the artifice of cunning abettors of popular envy, malice, fury or mistake.

[1] *Cal. S.P.D.*, 3 April 1675. For more detailed references, including the manuscript version of this letter, see the present writer's article, 'Robert Brady, 1627–1700. A Cambridge Historian of the Restoration', in the *Cambridge Historical Journal*, vol. x, no. 2 (1951), pp. 186–204, in which an attempt was made to collect all the known facts about Brady's life and writings. It can be consulted for amplification of all that is here said of him. It may be mentioned here that, in the Preface to his *Jus Anglorum ab Antiquo* (1681), Atwood quotes from a letter allegedly written by Brady to Shaftesbury, in which an offer is made to defend the hereditary rights of the House of Lords. If such a letter was ever written, it may have belonged to the year 1675 and the controversies attending the case of *Shirley* v. *Fagg*. Brady was not a man to be approaching Shaftesbury in 1679 or 1680.

He may also have been thinking of Strafford and Laud, for the same historical doctrines had served to substantiate the charges of treason 'against the fundamental laws' on which these ministers had been condemned. The common-law interpretation of history was a powerful and deadly political weapon, and Brady's energies as a historical scholar were to be spent in the struggle against it on behalf of the crown. For the present, however, his letter to Williamson bore no fruit, and it was only the publication of *The Antient Right of the Commons* and *Jani Anglorum Facies Nova* which brought him on the battlefield. He served, therefore, as a combatant on the historical wing of the Filmerian controversy. His auspices now were those of Archbishop Sancroft, who put him in touch with Dugdale; it must have been agreed that Brady's reply to Petyt should be published—it appeared in early 1681, with an appendix attacking Atwood, entitled *A Full and Clear Answer to a Book written by William Petit, Esq.*—while that which Dugdale had prepared should be withheld.[1] The latter survives in manuscript,[2] however, and may be compared with Brady's as a means to estimating the difference in historical mentality between the two men.

Both had now reached the point in the development of royalist thought where it seemed desirable to assert that there had been a Conquest—or rather to deny the traditional assertion that there had not, for neither seems to draw any positive political conclusions from the claim they make. But they set about proving it in significantly diverse ways. Dugdale accumulated instances of William's high-handedness, his violence, cruelty and treacherous dealings, and pointed out that this was not the behaviour of a monarch who felt himself responsible to law. When he dealt with the question of William's seizure of the land and redistribution of it in feudal tenure—which he did at some length, for his knowledge of the evidence was unparalleled—he went no further than to assert that this too was proof that William was bound by no law. It is noteworthy, too, that in this manuscript Dugdale continued his argument

[1] Bodleian Library, Tanner MSS. 37, fols. 22, 70; two letters from Brady dated 11 May and 17 June 1680. Mr Laslett (p. 36) thinks it conceivable that Sancroft was concerned in the republication of Filmer, and it is interesting to find him taking a hand in the ensuing debate.

[2] Bodleian Library Ashmole MSS.; Dugdale MSS. 10, fols. 94 ff.

that the tenants in chief were representative of their sub-tenants. In short, he was still failing to think of the law as altered in its foundations and its structure by the introduction of feudal tenures; and consequently, he thought of William not as the man who introduced new law or changed the society which the law was framed to govern, but as the man whose will was superior to the old law—a law which might not, for all Dugdale indicated, be so very different from the common law of 1681. He continued to think of the Conqueror in terms more juridical than historical.

Brady's treatment marks a radically new departure. Superficially, there is a likeness, and at the outset it may be desirable to emphasize that nearly all Brady's writings are those of a violent, ribald and abusive partisan. He derided his enemies as absurd[1] and hated them as seditious; and in tearing and trampling them, 'baffling and banging them and chasing them like squirrels from tree to tree', as an admirer once expressed it,[2] he not infrequently descended to argument on their own level, so that his essential historical views have to be disentangled from a mass of inessential debating points. Petyt and Atwood had denied that William was a conqueror; very well, it should be asserted in every possible way that he was in every possible sense; and consequently, there is much in the *Full and Clear Answer* that asserts the fact of conquest with no more perceptiveness than Dugdale displayed. But the guiding and connecting thread is of very different stuff. For Dugdale, William's feudalization of the land exhibited his indifference to the law; for Brady, William was the man who introduced feudal tenures and thereby a new kind of law, by altering the pattern of things of which the law must take account. This fact he treats with underlying consistency—whatever the cut and thrust of debate induced him to say on the surface—as of far greater moment than the fact that William ruled by right of conquest:

the Bulk and Maine of our Laws were brought hither from *Normandy*, by the CONQUEROR. For from whence we received our TENURES, and the

[1] Cf. *Introduction*, p. 6: '...he cites *Bede's Ecclesiastick History*, lib. 1. for the Report of this League and Union, where, if he finds it, he hath better luck than I have.'

[2] Fabian Philipps in a letter, 2 August 1684; Caius College MSS. 607, fol. 5.

Manner of holding our Estates in every respect, from thence also we received the CUSTOMS incident to those *Estates*. And likewise the quality of them, being most of them *Feudal*, and enjoyed under several MILITARY CONDITIONS, and SERVICES, and of necessary consequence from thence, we must receive the Laws also by which these TENURES, and the CUSTOMS incident to them were regulated, and by which every mans right in such Estates was secur'd according to the nature of them. But from *Normandy* (and brought in by the *Conqueror*) we received most, if not all our ancien *Tenures*, and manner of holding and enjoying our *Lands* and *Estates*, will appear by comparing our *Ancient Tenures* with theirs.[1]

In asserting so unequivocally that the old law was land law and that consequently a change in the manner of holding land must bring about a general change in the law, Brady was in the forefront of the historical thought of his age; and he could not have risen to such a height of perception if he had not been deeply versed in the kind of thinking of which Spelman had so far been almost the only representative in England. Except William Somner's *Treatise of Gavelkind* (written in 1647 and published in 1662) there had been no work since Spelman's time of his own stature, and Somner's study, excellent as it was on the Kentish tenures, made no application of feudal knowledge to legal or constitutional history in general—subjects with which it did not deal. But Brady followed Spelman—and in certain directions, as was proper, exceeded him— in his willingness to treat feudal tenure as the fundamental reality of Norman and Angevin England and to generalize from it about the nature of law, parliament and the duties of the subject in the whole of that epoch. This was to be his weapon in the Filmerian controversy; it enabled him to upset the notion of the ancient constitution by reconstructing the law and parliament of the past on the basis of an institution which had vanished from English life. It is still largely the business of English medievalists to pursue the line of

[1] *Introduction to the Old English History*, p. 14. The *Full and Clear Answer* is much more accessible as reprinted in this volume of 1684 (see below, p. 203) than in the rather uncommon separate edition of 1681, and references are therefore to the former except where it is desired to compare the two texts. In all quotations from Brady, capital letters are employed to convey some of the effect of the black-letter type that appealed to Brady or his printer (Thomas Newcomb, for Samuel Lowndes).

thought which Brady pioneered, and though they pursue it through modifications and refinements of which he cannot have dreamed, no alternative to feudalism as the starting-point of all thought about Anglo-Norman society seems yet to have been put forward; and the whole argument of the present book has been that there was no other method of curing the ills from which English historical thought suffered in the seventeenth century. The discovery of this method by Spelman and its revival by Brady must therefore be jointly reckoned as one of the most important occurrences in the history of our historiography. For the rest of his active life Brady was occupied in working out the consequences of his fundamental idea and applying them to the intellectual and practical problems of the age he lived in, and it is to this that we now turn.

Brady had to assert that, in consequence of the introduction of feudal tenures, not only was England after the Conquest governed by a feudal law, but this law was determined by the existence of a new class of feudal tenants who were the main governing and governed class; this in his view was the essence of the Conquest. Logically, he should have begun by proving that feudal tenure had not obtained before the Normans came, but though he knew Cujas, Hotman and Craig, he was handicapped by lack of Spelman's *Treatise of Feuds and Tenures* and could do little more than declare that the Saxons had had no military tenures as the Normans understood them.[1] But it was of far greater importance to meet Petyt's assertion that freeholders—men holding neither of the king nor of a lord, and by the same title as in King Edward's time—had survived the Conquest, for the gist of Petyt's argument had become that the freeholder and his rights were immemorial. Here Brady plunged into the thickets of Domesday Book, and his adversaries, notably Atwood, boldly pursued him. Brady sought to prove the single sweeping thesis that there was no land held by an Englishman that was not held of a Norman who held in chief of the crown; his enemies sought to pick holes in this generalization and use them as presumptive evidence that there had existed a class of non-feudal

---

[1] See the article 'Feudum' (which begins without title, telescoped with the preceding article on 'Election'), pp. 39 and 40 of the glossary appended to the *Introduction* and paginated separately.

freeholders who must be further presumed to have enjoyed parliamentary rights. There are well-known difficulties in the way of expounding a purely feudal interpretation of Domesday Book, and if Brady escaped the worst of them, this was because he was not primarily concerned with the manorial aspect of feudal society, or with the nature of rustic or unfree tenures, but with making the assertion that England had been ruled exclusively by and through a class of military tenants and that these alone had performed public services at the level of the shire courts and above. He was establishing the generalization that Norman England was a feudal state and that the relations implicit in military tenure governed and explained the whole conduct of its public proceedings. If it has been necessary for subsequent generations to modify this principle—if his contemporary opponents succeeded in finding anomalies, in Domesday or elsewhere, that could not be fitted into this generalization—we must bear in mind that the Whigs were endeavouring to deny it any validity at all and to maintain that the medieval history of England was intelligible, not on the presumption that feudal relationships had determined political organization, but on the presumption that the law and parliament of the seventeenth century were immemorial. The history of English medieval historiography in and since Brady's time would appear to bear out the thesis that the feudal generalization had to be established first and modified after, and that so long as it was denied or ignored there could be no progress in that branch of historical studies.

He proceeded to establish the feudal character of the Anglo-Norman governing class. In Brady's opinion, Petyt had habitually assumed that wherever he encountered the words *libere tenentes, liberi homines, legales homines,* and so forth, he was in the presence of the freeholder in a sense little different from that of 1681; and he had even tried, following Lambarde and for that matter Dugdale, to smuggle that concept into the term *baronagium.* This habit was characteristic of common-law historiography, but Brady had realized that by systematic use of the feudal generalization it could be set right, and this he now set out to do, reducing the *libere tenentes* to the feudal context in which alone they were intelligible. The freemen of the kingdom, named in the alleged laws of William I, were to perform their Military Services, with Horse and Arms, according to their Fees and Tenures. Therefore they were Tenents in *Military Service*, (which in these times *were the only great Free-men*, and that *Service the only free Service*) which were meant in this *Law*. And how different they were from our ordinary Free-holders at this day...I leave to the Judgment of every ingenuous Reader.[1]

Proceeding with his demonstration that the modern freeholder had not existed in the society governed by the *feudum*, Brady turned next to the shire court. This was the theatre in which the freeholder appeared at his most characteristic, and elected his representatives in parliament; and it was of great importance to Brady to show that its Anglo-Norman constitution must be understood on feudal lines. These, he says of the *libere tenentes*,

were the Men, the only LEGAL MEN that named, and chose *Juries*, and served on *Juries* themselves, both in the *County* and *Hundred Courts*, and dispatched all Country business under the great Officers....The judgment they were to give, and the justice they were to do...(besides that in their own Courts and Jurisdictions) was principally as they were Jurors or Recognitors upon Assizes, *etc.* (though some of the greatest of their *Milites* were often Sheriffs, Hundredaries, and other under Judges, and ministerial Officers of Justice in the several Counties)....This of being Suitors to the County and Hundred Courts, *etc.* was a Service incident to their Tenures: Before them, many times anciently in the County, and Hundred Courts, and not privately in a Chamber, were executed *Deeds, Grants,* and *Donations* of Lands contained in very small pieces of Parchment, Witnessed by *Thomas* of such a Town, *John* of another, *Richard* of a third, *etc.* which were KNIGHTS, *and* LIBERE *Tenentes in Military Service* in those Towns of considerable Estates, and *not the Lower sort of the People*: And this execution of Sales, and Assurances in open Court, was as publick, and notorious, and as secure, as if at that time, there had been a *publick Register* for them.[2]

Here we can see that Brady overreached himself in the feudalization of the past. Not all *legales homines* were knights, and as for the suggestion that the knight acting as juror in a shire court was performing a service incident to his tenure, even the simplified book-feudalism from which Brady was working should have warned him that the only court service a vassal could perform as part of his

---

[1] *Introduction*, p. 18.   [2] *Introduction*, pp. 18–19.

duty as a vassal was service in the court of his lord. Brady certainly did not think that the shire court had been feudalized to that extent, but he did not understand the process by which the knights had settled down as landowners and attended the shire court as local notabilities. But if he was wrong on the technical issue, he was right in his main contention that the early knights of the shire had to be understood as part of a class of military tenants, their actions governed by the requirements of a world of feudal relationships.

The shire court, however, possessed a more critical importance to his thesis. He was proposing to argue that if the first knights representing the county in parliament had been elected in the shire court, they had been elected by just such men as described above. Here he was following Spelman's original contention that the knights of the shire in parliament had originated among the lesser military tenants; but Spelman, arguing from Magna Carta, had supposed that there was in and after 1215 a representation of the lesser tenants *in capite*, which had by degrees evolved into a representation of the freeholders generally, and his failure to make full use of the shire court had inhibited his attempt to explain how this transition had been accomplished. Brady had begun with the shire court, emphasizing its feudal and military aspects and proposing to treat it as the body which had, at a later date, elected knights to parliament. It was therefore important that he should make clear from the start whether he supposed the *libere tenentes* of the shire court to have been confined to the lesser tenants *in capite*, of whom Magna Carta and Spelman had spoken, or to have included military sub-tenants on a more general basis; for the Spelman theory implied the existence of a considerable number of knights holding in chief of the king and receiving in 1215 a general summons to great councils. The problem was complicated by contemporary ideas on the nature of the knight's fee. Spelman had followed Coke in thinking of it as the land which the knight held and in respect of which he owed military service to the crown. It is easy to see how this interpretation might tend to obscure the true nature of knight-service and tempt seventeenth-century scholars to think, as on the whole they appear to have done, that a large number of knights had held direct of the crown and formed a class of lesser tenants *in capite*.[1] But as Professor Douglas has pointed out,[2] the *Posthuma* of Sir Robert Cotton (published 1657) contain an interpretation of the knight's fee exactly in line with that of Round; and Selden in his *Titles of Honour* seems to be moving in the same direction. When it was understood that the knight's fee was primarily the unit in which was reckoned the amount of military service which the tenant *in capite* owed the crown, and the number of knights he enfeoffed with land his own concern, it would be evident that the men who held by a knight's fee, or some fraction thereof, and ranked as knights and appeared in the shire court, would normally be sub-tenants rather than tenants of the crown. Brady's view of the knight's fee seems on the whole to have corresponded with that of Spelman;[3] but since he was following Spelman's thesis that the council had been constituted on a basis of tenure *in capite* until freeholders who were not the crown's tenants had appeared in what was now a parliament, it was necessary that he should decide whether the first knights sent by the shire to parliament had been tenants *in capite* or not. If we now compare what he wrote in the *Full and Clear Answer* with a revised account given some three years later, we shall see that his ideas were changing in favour of allowing an increased role to the sub-tenants. In 1681 he had this to say:

These [the military tenants] in all probability were the Men, that at first *Elected* two *Knights* in every *County*, out of their own number, and only they were *Electors*, when at first the Body of them began to be this way represented. [*In marg.*]—For it cannot be thought but that these blustering men that had the only pretence (as will appear afterward) to be present in the great Councils, would entirely preserve it amongst their own order, and not part with it to people at that time of no interest. Such were the other inferiour sort of people.

[1] Coke, *First Institutes*, lib. 2, c. 3, sect. 95 (7th ed., fol. 69), and elsewhere; Spelman, 1626 *Archaeologus*, p. 259. It is true that in 'Of Parliaments', possibly a late work, Spelman had suggested (*Reliquiae*, p. 64) that the number of lesser tenants in chief had never been very great, and that this would account for there being only two knights for each shire; but his words show that he thought of them as a class of at least sufficient weight to explain the original appearance of a lower estate of parliament.

[2] Douglas, *The Norman Conquest and British Historians* (see above, p. 135).

[3] *Introduction*, Glossary, pp. 42–4.

This points pretty exclusively to the lesser tenants *in capite*; but in 1684 he revised the whole work for inclusion in a larger book, called *An Introduction to the Old English History*, and the corresponding passage now ran:

These with the *Military* Tenents, from whom they derived their Titles, in all probability were the Men, that at first *Elected* two *Knights* in every County, out of the *Tenents* in *Capite*, and only they as Suitors to the *County Court* were *Electors*, when...[while the marginal comment disappeared altogether].[1]

Beyond this opinion, a very partial modification of Spelman's thesis, still suggesting the existence of a large class of knights holding *in capite*, Brady's views did not develop; but the point is not quite vital to the main structure of his argument. It was his task to prove beyond doubt the still-contested thesis that before Edward I the king's council had been primarily an assembly of tenants in chief, and it was more important that he should do this than that he should settle the difficult problem of *omnes alios qui de nobis tenent in capite*. To demonstrate his thesis Brady devoted by far the greater part of his controversial writings, working with the unflagging energy and unpolished style characteristic of his age through every recorded council of the eleventh to thirteenth centuries, and arguing that they were normally composed of bishops, earls and barons, who were the king's greater tenants in chief, and that when it was necessary to suppose the presence of others besides these, it could be proved in a sufficient number of cases that the additional attendance was that of lesser tenants in chief. Assemblies of this kind made up the *communitas regni*, and Brady was one of the earliest English historians to discuss this elusive term. Petyt, in typical common-law fashion, had simply assumed that it meant 'commonalty of the realm', ergo 'House of Commons'; but Brady, true to the underlying principle of his work, busied himself to prove that it must in the thirteenth century be understood first of all in a feudal sense, as a *communitas militum* comprising both greater and lesser tenants in chief.[2] Whether at any time before Edward I's reign the *communitas*

[1] *Introduction*, p. 19; and the parallel passage in the 1681 *Full and Clear Answer*, p. 42.
[2] *Introduction*, pp. 73–6, 80–1, 84 and *passim*.

regni included knights of shires who did not hold in chief, Brady is
not absolutely clear; he deleted from the 1684 edition a passage
which suggests that they rather unwillingly made part of the
communitas which wrote to the pope in 1258,[1] and there are many
passages in which he dogmatically says that the term was confined
to greater and lesser tenants in chief, the latter not being of much
account. On the other hand, in the article on 'Communitas' which
forms part of the glossary appended to the 1684 volume,[2] there are
certain phrases which suggest that Brady was beginning to doubt
whether military sub-tenants should not on occasion be reckoned
with the *communitas*,[3] and this would fall into line with the change
which we have seen was taking place in his views on the first
elections of knights of the shire to parliament. The truth seems to
be that Brady's ideas on the knightly class were still undetermined:
his old-fashioned theory of the knight's fee perhaps predisposed him
to believe in a large class of knights holding direct of the crown,
but his studies of the shire court seem to have opened his eyes to the
importance of knights who held of other military tenants. But, in
common with Spelman, he had perceived, however dimly, that the
key to the future lay in the emergence of the latter class and the
consequent decline of military tenure as a determinant of rights and
duties. On how this came about, however, he had little to say,
beyond the not very helpful suggestion that the fragmentation of
the knight's fee ultimately compelled the legislation of Henry VI
which confined the parliamentary franchise to those having freehold to the value of forty shillings.[4]

On the origin of the House of Commons itself Brady is a leader
of his century; he gives a more thorough and perceptive account of
the events, in and after 49 H. 3, leading to the regular summons of
knights and burgesses, than any historian before, or indeed many
after him. He traces in some detail the events culminating in the
summons of a parliament after Lewes,[5] quotes the crucial writ to
the sheriffs for the sending of two legal and discreet knights, and

[1] *Full and Clear Answer*, p. 127; compare *Introduction*, p. 81.
[2] *Introduction*, Glossary, pp. 26–35.
[3] *Ibid.* pp. 32, 33; these references are to events in 30 and 34 Edw. I.
[4] *Introduction*, pp. 19–20.   [5] *Introduction*, pp. 130–6.

emphasizes first, that it was not stated how these knights were to be chosen, secondly, that there is no record of what this parliament did or what part they played in it.[1] Resuming the narrative after the restoration of normal procedures, he observes that the king for some time after summoned only those barons whom he could trust—there is a hint that it was at this time that the writ of summons began to undermine the purely tenurial composition of the baronage[2]—and that the attendance of knights and burgesses was not at this time continued. Indeed, he argues forcibly that they are not to be found in those parliaments which passed the principal statutes of Edward I. The first knights are encountered in the eighteenth, and the first burgesses in the twenty-third year of that king; and while the knights began now to be elected—presumably according to the procedure described above—it remained with the king to decide how many from each shire were needed to do his business for him.[3] There are writs in which the king dismisses the knights and burgesses, or all such as are not of his council and have not special business to transact;[4] the knights often displayed reluctance to accept the burden of attendance, and arrangements were made to pay them their expenses.[5] As far back as 1258—Brady mentions in an earlier context[6]—there is record of an inquisition to be conducted by four knights in each county, who are to make their reports in person to the king's council in parliament.

Thus the year 49 H. 3 loses much of its prominence, and the picture given by Brady is essentially one in accordance with much later scholarship: improvisation, the shire court being brought gradually and at the king's intermittent will into the transaction of business by the parliament of the realm. There is no revolution; nobody is deliberately founding the House of Commons or altering the balance of forces in parliament by the introduction of a new estate of the realm. Though Brady lacked the information to carry the story into the fourteenth century or investigate the stages by which the knights and burgesses became a single house and rose to prime importance in the constitution, he refrained from antedating

[1] *Introduction*, pp. 140–3. [2] *Introduction*, p. 145.
[3] *Introduction*, pp. 149–51. [4] *Introduction*, p. 154.
[5] *Introduction*, pp. 151, 154. [6] *Introduction*, p. 141.

these things with admirable self-discipline. Though he did not follow the tenurial council past the time of its first decline—his principal concern being simply to establish the fact of its existence— he left his successors what could have been used as a secure foundation for study of the next phase.

While he worked out (always in the course of a brutal controversy, usually in the negative form of refuting his opponents' allegations) his new interpretation of parliamentary history, Brady was evolving a further idea of considerable importance. He had observed how Petyt constantly assumed that *libere tenentes* meant 'freeholders', that *communitas regni* meant 'commonalty of the realm'; and in the course of showing that these words could only be understood by reference to the feudal society of which they formed part, he began to see that the intellectual fallacy at the root of nearly all argument designed to prove the extreme antiquity of familiar institutions was the habit of interpreting words out of their contexts —a practice which could only end in identifying them with their usages at the present day. To us this is a commonplace; to Brady and his generation it was a discovery. Since the first stirrings of philological science a century earlier it had been known in a general way that the form and meaning of words changed with the generations; but not till now—at least in the study of English law—had the tools been available for the systematic reduction of words to a particular institutional context. As Brady composed his arguments and his glossary, it became evident to him that the whole cult of immemorial law was bound up with the fallacy of anachronism. He was now in a position, as hardly any scholar had been since Spelman, to distinguish the feudal law both from that which had preceded and from that which had followed it. He therefore·began to see both that there was a cult of immemorial law and how it might be destroyed; and he even turned his thoughts to the question of how it had grown up.

It was clear beyond argument that the law under which the Anglo-Norman military tenants had lived had been a feudal law; yet there were constant contemporary accounts of how the Conqueror had confirmed the Confessor's law, and constant contemporary demands and undertakings that it be confirmed again.

Brady did not know that several of the relevant documents were unauthentic—he believed in 'Ingulf of Croyland' and in the *leges Edwardi Confessoris*—but it was not of the first importance that he did so. For he pointed out, even more emphatically than Spelman, that most of these documents, purporting to give the law of pre-Conquest England, made use of Norman terminology and described feudal institutions which could not have been in use before William I's reign; and these were the grounds on which later scholars resolved to reject the documents concerned or treat them as quasi-imaginative. Brady believed that there had been a known 'law of the Confessor' and that the Conqueror had confirmed it after amendment, but he insisted that the amendments had been feudal in character and so far-reaching as to convert the old law into Norman feudal law. From this he drew a further conclusion. The Norman kings had claimed to rule by the Confessor's law and in every crisis from 1100 to 1215 or later there had been calls for its confirmation as guarantee of the 'ancient liberties' for which the baronage were fighting. Yet it was obvious that in 1100

Edward the CONFESSOR'S LAWS here desired, were those LAWS WHICH WILLIAM THE CONQUEROR HAD AMENDED; they being very pleasing and acceptable to the *Normans* (who set up *Henry*) having thereby their RELIEFS MADE CERTAIN, THEIR MILITARY FEES HEREDITARY, and FREED FROM ALL EXTRAORDINARY TAXES....[1]

While in 1215,

at this great Solemnity for asserting the *Common Liberties*, which they claimed...the far greatest part of MAGNA CHARTA, concerned *Tenents in Military Service* only, and the LIBERTIES, which our Ancient Historians tell were so mightily contended for, if seriously considered, were mainly the LIBERTIES of *Holy Church*, by which, in most things, she pretended to be free from *Subjection* to a *Temporal Prince*; and the Relaxation of the *Original Rigor* upon which *Knights*, or *Military Fees* were first given by the *Lords*, and accepted by the *Tenents*.[2]

When the baronage demanded the Confessor's laws, they were in fact demanding confirmations of their feudal privileges, or relaxations in their feudal services, in the guise of a pre-feudal 'ancient

---

[1] *Introduction*, p. 29.   [2] *Introduction*, p. 76.

law'; and when the common lawyers of Brady's century called for the restitution of Magna Carta, they were demanding concessions to a parliament of freeholders in the guise of what was in fact a feudal document. Once it could be shown that the laws and liberties of a feudal society were neither those of Anglo-Saxon nor those of post-feudal England, it followed that there had been a double falsification of history, first in the thirteenth and then in the seventeenth century. In explaining the first of these misrepresentations, Brady's Stuart Erastianism came to the fore. He was convinced that the aim of the thirteenth-century insurgents had been as much to win privileges for the church—and, he suspected, to introduce canonist sophistications into the original simplicity of feudal law—as to obtain concessions to the tenants *in capite*; and (perhaps remembering the production of Henry I's charter by Stephen Langton in 1213) he believed that erroneous notions concerning the nature of the Conquest, the ancient liberties, and the right of resistance had first been put about by the medieval clergy and from them had descended to the common lawyers and parliamentarians.[1] Behind it all lay the fallacy of anachronism. In prefacing the *Introduction* of 1684 Brady summed up matters thus:

The old *Romish Clergy* at first, in whose Management were all the Affairs of the Nation, out of Design, to *Bowe* the *Secular Government*, and make it *Truckle* under *Holy Church*, and by that means under themselves, published many Popular Notions concerning Ecclesiastick and Secular Liberty in those Antient Times, and raised up thereby the *Barons* and *Military Men*, to break the King's Power, and lessen his Authority, that by their Assistance they might obtain Dominion over him. These *Popular Notions* have ever since been kept up according to the sound of the Words they were first delivered in, by such as *Succeeded* those *Clergy-Men* in their *Places* and *Offices*. Though many of the Things then contended for, were either for ever sufficiently secured; and others not long after irrevocably vanished; and were all of such a Nature, or so Established, as afterward there could be no Controversie about them, yet the *Words* having been retained, and used, and interpreted according to vulgar Acceptation, 'tis scarce credible what *Mischiefs* and *Bloodshed* they have occasioned in *Successive* Ages, even to our own Days.

Brady was the first to treat the 'Whig interpretation of history' (in its earliest form) as itself an active force in the making of English

[1] *Introduction*, p. 20.

history, and the first to indicate how its fallacies might be set right. Waging the first open struggle against the concept of the ancient constitution, and himself extremely conscious of its explosive political possibilities, he declared that the belief in immemorial rights—the outcome of which must be an elective crown and an omnipotent parliament—could be corrected and nullified by the systematic reduction of the older English laws to their proper historical context. His own work was the elaborate, yet urgently practical reinterpretation of a key period in constitutional history in the feudal terms which alone could render it intelligible. He prefaced the collected edition of his controversial tracts in words which may be taken, together with the passage last quoted, as giving the full measure and character of his historical thought.

I have Intituled these several Discourses, *An Introduction to History*; for indeed so they are, if we observe the Things themselves, and not the Method. *Introductions* I know are Written after another manner; but as to the Matter here treated of, whoever reads our Old Historians and hath not a true Understanding and Apprehension of it, neither can he truly, and as he ought, understand them, nor will he ever be able to *arrive* at the Knowledge of our *Ancient Government*, or of what Import and Signification the Men were that lived under it according to their Several Denominations; of what Power, and Interest they were, what they did, and how they behaved themselves; nor who, nor what they were, that *contended* with our Ancient Kings about *Liberty*, and Relaxation of the Government, nor indeed what truly the Liberties were they contended for.[1]

There is a sense in which these words represent the high-water mark of Spelmanist historiography: the greatest degree of historical insight to which those who wrote as Spelman's immediate disciples ever attained. Having said so much, we must next consider the character and the limitations of the movement which these disciples conducted.

III

From one point of view, it might seem as though the effects of Brady's reinterpretation of medieval politics should have been similar to those which attended the revolution carried out in the

[1] *Introduction*, 'Epistle to the Candid Reader'.

study of Roman law by the sixteenth-century humanists. There should have been a growing realization that the affairs of the eleventh to thirteenth centuries were the affairs of a remote period with a social structure all its own, and could be understood only by constant reference to the main principles of that structure, which now belonged to the past and corresponded to nothing in Stuart England. No one could have put that point with greater clarity than had Brady himself in the passage just quoted; but we should expect to find him, or another soon after him, drawing the conclusion that medieval politics were irrelevant to those of the present day and worth the attention only of those who were interested in studying them for their own sake. We might even— following the analogy of the French sixteenth century—expect to come upon a movement of protest against the uselessness of this study, and hear of men attempting to discover what principles or what political lessons were common to the feudal politics of the thirteenth century and the parliamentary politics of the seventeenth. We might expect to hear admissions that if the main effect of the Norman Conquest had been to introduce a system based upon feudal tenures, then it could not directly determine the rights and liberties of Englishmen who no longer lived in such a system; and even, that if the authority of the monarch had once been primarily that of a feudal lord over his vassals, then this too was the case in England no longer, and that the prime duty of the historian was to discover by what means the monarchy had survived into the post-feudal age and on what foundations its authority now rested. To take the former of these two steps would have been to solve the problem which had been too much for Hale; to take the latter, to bring the systematic scholarship descended from Spelman into line with the conclusions more intuitively arrived at by Harrington. To take both would have imported the historical method into English constitutional thought to a degree never before known. Scholars would first have asserted antiquity's right to be considered independently of the present, and then have passed to investigating the precise nature of the connexion between the two.

None of this happened, however; and there are two principal reasons. In the first place, Brady, and the group of collaborators that grew up around him, were committed to using their new historical conclusions in support of the Filmerian thesis that the laws and liberties of England had come into being at the will of a sovereign king; though, as we shall see, it is disputable how far the new doctrines would support such an interpretation, and even how diligently Brady and his friends tried to make them do so. In the second place, they were at least so far successful in involving the new historiography in the battle between parties that when the cause for which they fought was rejected for ever in 1688, their attitude to history was rejected with it and prevented from exerting its full influence on the course of English thought. To conclude the story of Spelmanist historiography it is necessary to explain more fully the points which have just been made, and to begin with an account of the role which Brady and his friends played in the polemical writings of the 1680's.

By 1684, when Brady revised his *Answer* to Petyt and published it with the other treatises in the *Introduction to the Old English History*, he was no longer immediately engaged in exchanging pamphlets with the Exclusionist opposition. Petyt's only reply to him had been a small and universally ignored pamphlet called *The Pillars of Parliament Struck at by the Hands of a Cambridge Doctor*,[1] and though Atwood in two more works—*Jus Anglorum ab Antiquo* and *The Lord Holles his Remains*[2]—had attempted to sustain the distinction between *barones regis* and *barones regni*, Brady took no notice of them. After 1682, indeed, his adversaries published nothing further —warned, perhaps, by the fate of Algernon Sidney—and Brady's

---

[1] There seems no reference whatever to this work in the writings of Petyt's friends or his enemies, and its existence is known only through the learning of bibliographers. There is a copy in the Bodleian and another in the Advocates' Library, Edinburgh.

[2] Published 1681 and 1682. The latter is a work of some miscellaneous interest. Atwood published a posthumous tract by Holles on the question of the bishops' right of judgment in capital cases in the House of Lords, and added attacks of his own on Thomas Hunt, who had written in support of the bishops, and on a work called *Antidotum Britannicum*, which had been written against Nevile's *Plato Redivivus*. He improved the occasion by making further onslaughts on Brady, and questions of parliamentary history and the Norman Conquest occur sporadically throughout all the works connected by the *Remains*.

larger works appeared on the high tide of royalist reaction that fills the years between Exclusion and Revolution. The *Introduction* is a collection of his controversial writings—the replies to Petyt and Atwood, a demolishing attack on a minor Whig tract called *Argumentum Antinormannicum*[1] and a reprint of a tract on the succession he had written during 1681[2]—designed to supply the reader with a full statement of the feudal interpretation and clear his mind of traditional errors before he went on to read the first volume of the *Complete History of England*, which appeared in 1685 and in which we may perhaps see the realization of the plan Brady had advanced to Williamson ten years earlier. (This volume extends as far as the death of Henry III; a second, reaching the deposition of Richard II, was not published until 1700.) The relation of the *Introduction* to the *Complete History* admirably illustrates that it was through his polemical writings that Brady hammered out his basic interpretation of the medieval past, and these also accounted for his unobtrusive but notable position in the England of James II.[3] By 1685 Brady was a court physician and a man trusted by the government; in July of next year he was awarded the salary usually paid to the keeper of the records in the Tower; and about this time we must note the publication of a group of books by other scholars, all of which reveal his influence and can be shown by correspondence or internal evidence to have been written in his support.[4] Dugdale's last book, *A Perfect Copy of all Summons of the Nobility to Parliament...since*

[1] This is now attributed to one Edward Cook, but Brady thought it to be by Petyt or Atwood. He was right in suspecting it to be associated with them in some way, for a copy in the present writer's possession bears the inscription: 'Silv. Petyt. Ex dono Authoris'. Silvester Petyt was William's brother. It is entertainingly discussed by Professor Douglas, *English Scholars*, pp. 152–3.

[2] *A True and Exact History of the Succession.*

[3] For details of Brady's career during these years, the reader is again referred to the *Cambridge Historical Journal* for 1951.

[4] Dugdale's letters to Brady may be found in Hamper, *Life and Writings of Sir William Dugdale*, and the Preface to *A Perfect Copy of All Summons* is obviously aimed at Petyt and Atwood. Johnston's correspondence with Brady (Johnston MSS., Magdalen College, Oxford) belongs to a later time, the aftermath of the Magdalen College affair, when Johnston was preparing a work called *The King's Visitatorial Power Asserted*; but his earlier book abounds with references to Brady. Philipps's letter to Brady is in Caius College MS. 607, fol. 5.

the XLIX of Henry III, appeared in 1685; Dr Nathaniel Johnston, Yorkshire physician and antiquary, published his *The Excellency of Monarchical Government* in 1686; and the eccentric and quixotic Fabian Philipps his last and largest book, *Investigatio Jurium Antiquorum* (sometimes known as *The Established Government of England*) about the end of the same year. This concerted effort by royalist scholars to express a high-Tory theory of the rights of the crown, by arguments based in different ways upon the feudal interpretation of medieval England, is a noteworthy part of the intellectual reaction of the 1680's, and it also brings to an end the first great phase in the relations of the ancient constitution and the feudal law.

Now if we except Dugdale—whose last book contains few statements of theory or general principle—on the grounds that he never quite shook off a belief in the immemorial, all these scholars wrote under the influence of the republished works of Filmer. That is to say, to prove that parliament and the common law were not immemorial seemed in the context of Filmerian theory virtually identical with proving that these things, and with them all the liberties of Englishmen, owed their being to the will of the king, from which it followed that Charles II might revoke any of them as having been granted by one of his predecessors, no matter how remote. This was the view of the work of the royalist historians adopted by all their adversaries and, in the years when the borough charters were being revised on grounds of *quo warranto*, it seemed evident that Charles was in fact doing precisely what a Filmerian historiography claimed that he might do. We shall see presently that both Johnston and, to a lesser extent, Brady wrote as if the purpose of their historical studies was to present a version of constitutional history in which all was descended and derived from the will or permission of the king. But in actual fact, the Spelmanist technique of reinterpreting medieval history must logically lead, as we have seen, to conclusions of a different sort: if law and parliament had once been feudal in character, then by the same criteria the same must be true of the royal authority, and the problems would arise of determining how the monarchy had become what it now was, and of deciding whether conclusions could be drawn, from its authority in so unfamiliar a past, about its authority in the present.

There were therefore two far from consistent tendencies at work in the thought of the royalist historians, and the problem in interpreting their writings is to ascertain whether one of these tendencies predominated over the other, and with what results.

Johnston's *Excellency of Monarchical Government* is based in approximately equal parts upon Brady and Filmer, and may be taken as expressing the purely Filmerian interpretation which the royalist intellectual in the 1680's placed upon the feudal theory of history. He adopts (at last) the argument which the Whigs had feared for so long: that William I acquired absolute power by his conquest and that consequently all the laws and liberties of England exist as the result of concessions made by sovereign kings. He denies that the effect of his doctrine would be to return the people to the bondage they were in after the Conquest, and asserts that the kings are bound by the laws to which they have consented; but since it is only their consent which binds them, and not the law, he has obviously provided no safeguard against the king's withdrawing his consent at pleasure—nor, in view of his political record, is it likely that he intended to. He uses the fact that the king was feudal suzerain in the age when the great charters were granted as proof that these were no more than unilateral concessions by a sovereign monarch, and proceeds to press Filmer's arguments for the king's sole authorship of all legislation. He employs Brady's feudal interpretation of the period from the Conquest to Edward I to show that the House of Commons, being of late origin and created gradually by a series of royal summonses to men below the rank of tenant in chief, owes its existence to the king's will and must accept the place in the constitution—that of an adjunct to the king's council, a petitioner and assentient in legislation—which the *Freeholder's Inquest* had allowed it.[1] In all this Johnston does not quote or refer to Filmer, whose influence is none the less apparent, but he incessantly cites, quotes and transcribes Brady, with whom he corresponded and who, he does not seem to doubt, held views identical with his. Before we consider whether he was absolutely right in this assumption, there is another aspect of the feudal and Filmerian approach to history which merits attention, and something

[1] See generally Johnston's Introduction and his 22nd to 29th chapters.

should be said of that strangest of figures in contemporary legal erudition, Fabian Philipps.

Craig, and long after him Hobbes—the latter anticipating each main point of the royalist argument of the 1680's—had observed that in a feudal monarchy the king enjoyed the advantage that every proprietor of land owed him the special and personal allegiance of the vassal; and they had supposed that every feudal society was in fact of this sort, a pyramid of dependence upon a sovereign king. This authoritarian interpretation of feudalism was due in part to the impression created by reading the *Libri Feudorum*, the product of a fairly centralized society, which gave scholars the idea that feudalism was a legal system imposed from above; but it also arose from contemplating feudalism through the medium of the English courts of common law, which enforced the principle that all land was held of the king and took the whole system of feudal relations under the king's direct protection. Philipps (born in 1601) had in the first part of his life been an official of the Court of Wards and had there seen the conception that the king was universal seigneur in action. From 1660 to his death in 1690 he devoted himself to pleading on every occasion that the abolition of the feudal tenures had been a disastrous mistake, as they were necessary to the security of the throne.[1] Philipps believed—and it is said that Lord Keeper Guilford was inclined to agree with him[2]—that it was essential that every proprietor of land should have the direct personal relation with the king which tenures *in capite* alone provided; he called them the nerves, sinews and ligaments of society and felt that in any commonwealth where they were absent there was nothing to ensure the obedience of the subject. A freeholding society in Philipps's view was rather like a contractual society as envisaged by Filmer: nothing ensured the subject's obedience except his own will to obey, which he might withdraw at any moment. And just as Filmer endeavoured to represent the royal authority as having the inescapable physical quality of paternity, Philipps emphasized that the vassal's heirs for ever were bound to render the lord's heirs for ever the same un-

[1] The best account of Philipps is that of Professor Douglas, *English Scholars*, pp. 160–4.
[2] Roger North, *Lives of the Norths* (1890), vol. 1, p. 31.

conditional and fervent loyalty as was implied in the original act of homage.[1] He saw feudal society as one in which each proprietor, by the mere fact that he inherited land, was the king's man, with all that this implied; and he thought that the relationship of homage was the only secure social tie—a fabulous vision but not without a certain nobility.

Feudalism, to Philipps, meant patriarchal monarchy. But if he was Filmerian in his interpretation of the social relationships which feudal tenure implied, he was far enough removed from either Filmer or Spelman in his attitude to feudalism's place in history. The disadvantage of having learnt his feudalism as part of the living English law was that he had not passed through the complex adventure of the mind by which Spelman and Brady had discovered it in the past and, conversely, had discovered a past which could only be explained on its principles. Not only, therefore, did he believe that the state of things which he idealized had lasted down to the Civil War and could even now be restored; he was also, at least in his earlier writings, capable of describing the tenures as:

those ornaments in peace and strength in time of war, which have been for so many ages and Centuries since King *Ina*'s time, which was in an. 721 now above 940 years agoe (and may have been long before that) ever accompted to be harmlesse and unblameable, and in King *Edgar*'s Time, by a Charter made by him unto *Oswald* Bishop of Worcester, said to be *constitutione antiquorum temporum*, of antient time before the date of that Charter....[2]

Philipps, in short, had a lawyer's belief in the ancient constitution, with the sole difference that he held the essence of that constitution to be tenure *in capite*. It is true that his last book, the *Investigatio*, written when he was about eighty-five, bears marked traces of the Spelman-Brady influence and shows historical perceptiveness well in advance of the above paragraph; for example, he stresses the gradual and unforeseen nature of the changes which brought the freeholders to predominant power in parliament.[3] Nevertheless,

[1] *Tenenda non tollenda* (1660), p. 13. This (as the date suggests) was the first of Philipps's works upon this subject, and remains his best statement of the case for idealized feudalism.   [2] *Tenenda non tollenda*, p. 25.
[3] *Investigatio jurium antiquorum*, pp. 66–98, 110–13, 116–17, 296–9.

his exceptional background—rather than the eccentricity of his ideas—causes him to stand somewhat apart from Johnston and Brady, showing neither Filmer's desire to prove the whole constitution of the king's making, nor Spelman's interest in reconstructing feudalism as a state of society existing in the past, to such an extent as the Master of Caius, to whom, as the key figure of the royalist school, we must now return.

Viewing Brady's writings as a whole, we see in them the end of that period in which royalists would accept the doctrine of an immemorial constitution and justify the king's prerogatives on the grounds that they were the essence of this constitution and themselves immemorial. There were still royalist writers who clung to this argument,[1] but Brady served notice that he considered it dead when he attacked the whole concept of pre-Conquest ancient law as a heresy of the common lawyers and included the name of at least one eminent royalist among those whom he criticized for upholding it.

What I have here delivered upon this subject [the feudalization of English law at the Conquest] may probably meet with great prejudice, from such especially who have, or may read Sir *Edward Coke*'s Prefaces to his third, sixth, eighth and ninth parts of his Reports, his reading upon the Statute of Fines, or other parts of his Works: Sir *John Davis* his Preface to his *Irish* Reports; Mr *Nathan. Bacon*'s *Semper Idem*. The late learned Lord Chancellor's Survey of *Hobbs* his *Leviathan*, p. 109, 110. And many other works of eminent Persons of the long Robe, or indeed any of our *English* Historians, and therefore I am necessitated to dwell the longer upon it....And beyond them all Sir *Edward Coke* concurs in opinion with Sir *John Fortescue*....[2]

Brady rejected the Clarendon tradition of common-law royalism at least partly because of Filmer's influence; and this raises the problem of the political moral which he expected to be drawn from his historical writings. It would not be difficult to draw up an array of quotations to prove that he meant to teach the same lesson as Johnston: that, as Bémont wrote of him, 'royaliste déclaré...[il]

---

[1] E.g., the author of *Antidotum Britannicum* (1681; see p. 149 n. 2, above).

[2] *Complete History of England*, vol. I, p. 182. 'Semper Idem' is the sub-title of Nathaniel Bacon's *Historical Discourse of the Uniformity of the Government of England* (1647).

s'efforça de prouver que toutes les libertés dont jouissait le peuple anglais étaient un pur don de la royauté'.[1] For example, in the 'Preface to the Reader' of the *Complete History of England* (1685), he claims that from the book as a whole

> there is a clear Demonstration, that all the *Liberties* and *Priviledges* the People can pretend to, were the *Grants* and *Concessions* of the Kings of this Nation, and Derived from the Crown;

and there are other remarks to the same effect. For all this, however, Brady does not tell us how this conclusion is to be demonstrated; he rather leaves it to be inferred, and it never becomes very clear in what sense he supposes it to be true. In those sections of the *Complete History* which are critically written—only a small proportion of the book, as we shall see—he paints the portrait of a feudal monarchy which he supposes to have been centralized, authoritarian and even patriarchal in a very high degree. Since the feudal king was supreme lord of every piece of land, Brady imagines him to have been virtual sovereign; the liberties which he granted were contained in charters of which, since he had granted them, he was sole interpreter; and— Brady intimates—if, as we are constantly assured, the liberties of the people are the same as those contained in the charters of John and Henry III, there can be no doubt that they derive from the concessions of a sovereign will.[2] If the feudal king was sovereign, then all our laws and liberties must be derived from him.

But if this was indeed Brady's case for the descent of liberty from royal concession, it was thin in character and juridical rather than historical. That is to say, he had not proved that the modern liberties —the rights of Englishmen before the common law and in a representative House of Commons—had, as a matter of actual traceable historical development, been created by the king or come into being as a direct result of royal actions; nor did he ever make any serious attempt to do so. The reasons why Brady could not do this are of interest, as they bring us at last into contact with the limitations of Spelmanist historiography. It will be recalled that Spelman was able to reconstruct the main institutions of English

---

[1] Bémont, *Chartes des libertés anglaises* (1892), pp. lv-lvi.
[2] *Complete History*, vol. I, 'General Preface', pp. xxx-xl.

feudalism by arguing from the character of the continental *feudum* to the known characteristics of English law, but could not show how this system of things had passed away—how feudal tenure had ceased to be a key institution in English society—and had contented himself with observing that the process of decay must have been slow and gradual. Brady shared this disability to the full; there is a passage in the *Complete History* on the decline of villeinage[1] which shows clearly that he did not really know what could have brought it to an end except 'time and desuetude' working 'by insensible degrees', and though he has less to say about the decline of military tenure, it would seem as if he regarded this process in a similar light.[2] Now a slow and gradual process of change is nothing if not impersonal; it cannot be thought to flow from the sovereign's will, though its effects in the legal and constitutional fields may indeed require to be legitimized by his permission; and therefore, when Brady was dealing with so essentially post-feudal a phenomenon as the rise of a representative House of Commons, he might argue that the king's permission and even the king's legislative initiative had been necessary to begin and continue the summoning of knights and burgesses, but he could not suggest that the king had been responsible for the position of importance which the commons later assumed in the social structure. He wrote in the *Introduction*, speaking of the first summonings of the commons by Edward I,

...it is most evident, that it was from the [? this] *Kings Authority* and *time* that the House of *Commons* came to be *fixed*, and *established* in the present constant form, it now is, and hath been in, for many Kings Reigns, and that the King in this Age was not altogether *confined* to any *certain number* of *Knights*, *Citizens*, or *Burgesses*, nor were several strict *forms* and *usages* now practised, ever then thought of....[3]

The Filmerian implication is plain enough, but Brady was well aware that the knights and burgesses of Edward I's time were not of the social importance they afterwards assumed, and he thought of the process by which they had become important as one of slow

[1] 'General Preface', pp. xxvi–xxviii.
[2] 'General Preface', p. liii, and *Introduction to the Old English History*, pp. 19–20.
[3] *Introduction*, p. 151.

and gradual change which owed nothing to the king's will except the legitimization of its effects; and there is a passage in Fabian Philipps's *Investigatio* which says plainly that when Edward I began to summon the commons he could not have foreseen the ultimate consequences of what he was doing, because he could not have foreseen the effects of such economic changes as the dissolution of the monasteries, which were to make the freeholders excessively powerful in the state.[1] The king was no demiurge in Spelmanist historiography; much happened that was not by his will, produced by social processes which he could not control; only his legal sovereignty was preserved intact. The royalist historians did not, as they might have done, produce a myth of the king as the wise and benevolent author of each change in the life of his people. Their sense of historical criticism was too strong for that.

But it was a serious limitation on Brady's power to write history that he could build up the picture of a strongly monarchical feudal society, but could not show how this society had declined, except by vague allusions to unspecified general processes. As we shall see, it robbed his *Complete History* of all character as a general narrative. He showed how the feudal monarchy had been created, quite suddenly and catastrophically, at the Conquest; he described its workings—but he could not show, at the same level of historical perception, what happened next. He could not show how the actions of kings, barons and knights, living within feudal society and grappling with the problems with which it confronted them, led to the setting up of institutions which formed no part of feudal society and were bound to transform its character. For him feudal society was something fixed and rigid, and only time which antiquates all things—only a process of gradual decay taking place in the forms of tenure which lay at its root—could account for its ultimate disappearance. His historical thought did not extend as far as the idea that the seeds of change might have been present in feudal society from the beginning; there is no dialectic in history as he conceives it. It is probable that his royalism was partly to blame here. He desired to show that the monarch in a feudal society had been unchallenged sovereign and found it easy to do so by em-

[1] *Investigatio jurium antiquorum*, p. 299.

phasizing the purely feudal nature of that monarch's authority, as recipient of every freeholder's homage for the lands that he held. It did not occur to Brady that there were elements of weakness as well as strength in the feudal monarch's position, or that the ruler might evolve institutions designed to strengthen his control over feudal society, but bound in the end to alter its nature. This is particularly evident in his treatment of the common law in the Middle Ages. His remarks on this subject are scattered and speculative, but they leave the impression that he was inclined to regard the common law of the thirteenth century as the force hostile to monarchy which it appeared to be in its own time. He criticizes the law of Bracton's day as a mass of unnecessary subtleties, produced by the introduction of canonist sophistications into the original purity of feudal custom;[1] and it will be recalled that he suspected the churchmen who had aided the baronial rebels of a design to bring about just this result.[2] Notions of ancient liberty and the lawfulness of resistance, he considered, had come into England through the influence of clerics like Langton, and as he clearly thought of common lawyers as the standard-bearers of such ideas in his own age, he may well have associated them with the cleric-dominated common law of the thirteenth century. At all events, it is plain that he had no notion of the historical importance which we should attach to the name of Henry II;[3] there is no sign that he thought of the founding of the common-law courts as a measure on the king's part to increase his power, or of the substitution of the king's writ for private justice as one of the foundations of royal authority. Brady's failure to grasp the historical character and importance of the common law is one of the principal reasons why he was never able to show that changes went on within feudal society—changes which in the end transformed it—or that there were reasons for these changes occurring.

The name of Harrington should be enough to show that it is not anachronistic to criticize Brady for failing to discover some sort of

[1] *Complete History*, vol. I, 'General Preface', p. lv.

[2] See above, p. 208.

[3] When dealing with that king in the main body of the book he deals with the appointment of itinerant justices (pp. 308–10, 325, 333-4) and gives a translation of the Assizes of Clarendon (pp. 326-8) and the Assize of Arms (pp. 337-8); but allows them to pass without any comment.

dialectic at work within feudal society. We might prefer to emphasize the strength of the medieval English kings, with Brady, rather than their weakness, with Harrington—whom Brady obviously surpassed in his technical knowledge of the *feudum* and its workings—but that does not alter the fact that Harrington knew there were deep-seated causes of tension between the king and his magnates, and that the steps taken by either party to achieve its aims might lead to radically new constitutional developments. And it is not only Harrington, among writers of the later seventeenth century, in whose works we can discover a sense of the medieval dialectic in some ways surpassing Brady's. There is an unfinished study of parliamentary history among the surviving papers of Francis North, Lord Keeper Guilford.[1] Guilford was a Tory common lawyer interested in the feudal interpretation; this essay, however, lays no great emphasis on tenure or vassalage.[2] The point on which he seized was that under that political system the kingdom contained no means of binding a man to observe the oath which he had taken. Accordingly it fell to the Church to punish oath-breakers and to bind and loose the obligations contracted by oath, and in the thirteenth century the aggressive popes made use of this power to obtain increasing control over the realm. But this came to an end with John's surrender of the kingdom to the pope.[3] Henceforward, though he had no power to resist the pope, he could break his oath to his subjects with impunity; but events proved that he had not so much power that he could revoke customs or the grants of land or privilege which he had made to them. His subjects, for their part, found a means of self-protection in associating in *communitates* and finally in the *communitas regni*, and being thus leagued together, determined to obtain a comprehensive and irrevocable grant of liberties, expressed in the charters of Henry III. Only the king's oath guaranteed the charters, and at first the *communitas* stood ready

[1] It occurs (British Museum Add. MSS. 32, 518, fol. 157) among a collection of transcripts of his surviving papers made by his brother Roger. To judge from ch. 389 of his brother's *Life*, Guilford was active in records research between 1675 and 1682, when he received the great seal. There is no mention of his knowing or reading Brady. He died in 1685.

[2] Though he believed in a tenurial parliament (fol. 158).

[3] Fols. 159, 159b–160, 161b–162.

to maintain them by force. When the magnates were summoned to meet the king in *commune concilium*, they were in a stronger position than at any other time to state their wishes and form confederations to enforce them. But this fact was in itself convenient to the king, for he could free himself of his bondage to the pope by protesting that though he desired to do the latter's bidding, the community of his realm would not suffer it. Thus the assembly of the *commune concilium* was in the interest of king and barons alike and the idea of consent to legislation gained ground, not because there was any suggestion that the king could not act on his own authority, but because it strengthened his hand—especially *vis-à-vis* the pope—to have the assent of his barons. The king and the *communitas* accordingly reached an agreement, expressed in a grant under the great seal, that the council should meet regularly and have the right of consent in all great matters. The king was only bound to summon those who held of him and he did this by letters, not proclaiming a common council as a constituted body, but letting it be known that those who wished to give their assent should come and do so; it being clearly understood by all parties that the resolute constitutionalists 'would be sure to come, and would come so strong that the King should not be able to force them to anything they did not approve of '.[1]

Now whether or not this account bears any close resemblance to what actually occurred, it is clearly a remarkable piece of historical writing, holding a place in the late seventeenth century comparable to that occupied by Davies's *Discoverie* in the earlier. Guilford makes no attempt to describe feudal society as a single body of institutions (and thus face himself with the problem of accounting for its decline as a whole); he selects a single point in its system—the difficulty of enforcing an oath—and shows how king and barons, men divided by immediate conflicts yet having certain interests in common, were driven by the inconveniences which either inherited from this

[1] Fols. 162–4. Guilford held a sophisticated version of the 'Dugdale' thesis of the origin of the Commons; he saw their beginning in a revolt against the great men of 'the Comunalty which I suppose were 1st, the kings tenants, & afterwards the freeholders in generall', of which the first sign was the protest of the community of bachelors in support of the prince ('which I suppose were the gentlemen of the kingdom'). Fols. 166–167 b.

weakness to reach a solution of their differences which was at the same time a modification and a strengthening of the constitution. ⁷Je shows how the weakness of one faction, where the other was ₊trong, the measures taken by each to remedy its weakness, and the constant pressure exerted by ·a hostile third party, led by cause and effect to a readjustment of relations in a new system of politics. This is the logic of political development which Brady could not bring into his writings, and it may perhaps be characterized as a Trimmer view of history. Halifax and (as his notes reveal)[1] Guilford himself were interested in political parties, in their tendency to demand too much and in the possibility of bringing them to demand what would be acceptable to their opponents as well as themselves.[2] In the fragment just summarized, Guilford seems to be applying such a *tact des choses possibles* to the history of the thirteenth century and in so doing to move forward from the mere repetition of Spelman's interpretation. But Brady's ultra-Toryism prevented his attempting anything similar.

The main shortcoming of Brady's historical thought, then, was its lack of a pattern of development; and this is reflected in an interesting way in the structure of his *Complete History*. The 1685 volume of this work, which reaches the death of Henry III, is a bulky folio of about a thousand pages, but of this total only a small proportion consists of the kind of critical reconstruction of institutions which makes Brady a figure worth studying. This proportion is subdivided into a number of essays which the author calls Prefaces—the 'Preface to the Reader', the 'General Preface', the 'First Part of the Saxon History', the 'Preface to the Norman History'—and it is in these alone that Brady develops his thesis that Saxon institutions are to be studied on the basis of a pre-feudal form of Germanic land tenure and Norman institutions on the basis of feudal tenure; nor could it be said that these Prefaces, penetrating and instructive though they are, were written in a manner

---

[1] Other papers in the same volume of Add. MSS.

[2] The development of a Trimmer attitude to more recent history has been summarized by Professor Butterfield, *The Englishman and his History*, pp. 86–96. This is the only case known to the writer of its extension to medieval history.

either lucid or methodical. As for the many hundred pages which make up the rest of the volume, they consist almost exclusively of a conflation of the various medieval chronicles to which Brady had access, digested into a single narrative the scope of which naturally does not extend beyond the stories which the various chroniclers had to tell. Some attempt is made at certain points (notably the crises of John's and Henry III's reigns) to illustrate the story by means of records from the Tower; but in general it can be said that the narrative part of Brady's history does not concern itself with tenures, laws, councils or other institutions, and that these are dealt with only in the Prefaces. It was only in the reinterpretation of institutions on the basis of land tenure that Spelman and Brady had developed their critical method, and Brady at least knew of no means of combining this side of his work with the narrative of the doings of kings which he brought together, by strictly scissors-and-paste methods, from the chroniclers. He could not yet show how the conflicting actions of, say, king and magnates in the thirteenth century had led to the setting up of new institutions, or how these had affected the pattern of obligations which arose from tenure and so, in turn, had modified the place of tenure in society. Harrington and Guilford, we have seen, had gone somewhat further towards historical thinking of this kind, but Brady had scarcely begun; and the significance of this fact in the general history of historiography is worth dwelling on. Though he was prepared to reconstruct the whole received picture of medieval institutions on the basis of new principles, Brady had clearly no sense that he ought to apply similar critical techniques to the history of men's deeds. He actually congratulates himself on interpolating nothing of his own in his chronicle material, but on setting the whole of it down as nearly as possible in its authors' words.[1] In short, once he was away from his own field of feudal institutions, he shared the general opinion of his age that the historian's function was merely to repeat or report what his 'authorities' told him—the view which convinced Montaigne and Descartes and Locke and Dr Johnson that history was an altogether inferior branch of intellectual activity. In Brady we have followed to a high degree of development a particular technique of historical criticism

[1] *Complete History*, vol. I, 'Preface to the Reader', last two paragraphs.

that arose in the study of English law and produced in him vigorous and subtle historical insight; but we are compelled at the last to admit that he had no notion of how to combine the reconstruction of institutions with the narrative of men's deeds—how to combine legal antiquarianism with history as a literary art. To this extent, and viewing the matter from this standpoint, we are still in the prehistory, or in a primitive age, of modern historiography; though it is true that as historians we should do better to emphasize how much the scholars of Brady's generation had achieved, than how much they had still to do. But until some marriage between the two branches of study could take place—until some technique of critical reconstruction could be applied to the stories of men's deeds told by the chroniclers, and until laws and institutions could be shown as changing and developing in response to the actions of men, themselves motivated partly by the need to solve problems posed by the character of existing laws and institutions—there was little chance of history's becoming an autonomous science, an independent mode of approach to the structure of human society as a whole. Brady certainly did not envisage history as an independent science; it is significant that he described his essays in the reconstruction of past society not as history, but as introductions to history: 'an introduction to the old English history', 'the preface to the Norman history'. It seems likely that 'history' to him meant still the reporting of what the chroniclers had said, and his use of the definite article before the word suggests that he thought of it as something fixed and unalterable; you could not know more of the past than what the chroniclers had told you. Yet he knew that he had himself reconstructed the institutional and social context in which the Anglo-Norman chroniclers must be read if they were to be understood aright. It was the idea that there existed a science of rewriting the chronicles in the light of new general notions about the structure of medieval society which was still beyond Brady, and which the thought of his generation was only beginning to grasp. Before it could be grasped and employed, the idea of the development of institutions must be explored more fully than Brady's limitations allowed him to do.

If he had failed to solve the problem, he had done much to pose it in the terms on which it must ultimately be solved. He and his friends, working along the same lines as Spelman's unpublished papers, had established that English society had passed through a feudal phase and had described that phase more fully and technically than had ever been done before. It was their description, or one more detailed and thorough still, which would have to be incorporated in future histories of the development of the English constitution. In such histories there might be room for the thought of Harrington or Hale, but it would be with Brady and his allies, and with Spelman, that historians would have to reckon—if, that is to say, the world of English learning was prepared to listen to Brady, and through him to Spelman. It was exactly this condition, however, which was not to be realized. Brady had written as a partisan of the two last Stuarts, and since it was so largely his royalist ardour which had led him to formulate his conclusions, this does him no discredit;[1] but he could not escape the consequences of political partisanship, which in his case included the consequences of defeat. With the downfall of the last king he served[2] came the rejection of his historical ideas. He was deprived of his post as acting keeper of the Tower records and the keys of the office were given to Petyt.[3] Before this occurred, Petyt had figured as one of the legal counsel who advised the Lords in the Convention debates of January 1689, and had had opportunity to associate the doctrine of the ancient constitution with the legitimization of the Revolution.[4]

Dugdale was dead and Philipps at a great age; Johnston, apparently as a Jacobite agent, lived for a time in penury and semi-hiding. Brady returned to his Cambridge mastership, and did not allow his

[1] Byron's verdict on Mitford, the anti-democratic historian of Greece, strikes the present writer as peculiarly applicable to Brady: 'Having named his sins, it is but fair to state his virtues—learning, labour, research, wrath and partiality. I call the latter virtues in a writer, because they make him write in earnest.' (Note on *Don Juan*, Canto XII, stanza xix.)

[2] He took part in a last-minute attempt, promoted by Bishop Turner of Ely, to dissuade James from his second flight. For details of Brady's closing years, the reader is once more referred to the *Cambridge Historical Journal* for 1951.

[3] The warrant is dated 12 March 1689; S.P. Dom. Warrant Book 34, p. 216 (in Public Records Office).

[4] See below, pp. 229-30.

views on hereditary succession to carry him into association with the non-jurors, where we might otherwise expect to find him; in October 1691 he certified that all Fellows of Caius had taken the oaths of allegiance. Non-juring tradition apparently bore him no ill will for this, but the step cut him off from the only cause on behalf of which he might have undertaken further historical writing. In 1690 he published a *Treatise of Boroughs*, a not very satisfactory inquiry into their early history which had probably been in preparation some years earlier, but in general the spate of writings which associated the Revolution with the classic Whig version of parliamentary history went unanswered by the chief of royalist historians. It is significant that the second volume of the *Complete History*, published in the year of his death, contains chronicle matter only; there are no 'Prefaces' or other interpretative comment. The only hint of its author's personal opinions is the bishop of Carlisle's protest against the deposition of Richard II, which, printed in full, closes the narrative part of the volume.[1] Such is Brady's rather unheroic last word to rebels and alterers of the succession. He died on 19 August 1700.

It could be said, then, adapting some well-known words from another context, that the heirs of Spelman 'died beaten and broken men, perishing among the spears of triumphant' Whiggery. With their defeat ended the first serious attempt to give feudalism its proper place in English history, and there was not another until the nineteenth century, when the task was successfully accomplished by historians whom we may feel to be still our own contemporaries. The failure of Brady to convince his countrymen undeniably marked a setback for the course of English historiography. At the same time, the historical thought of the age that followed his was far from being a mere prolongation of the thought of Coke and Petyt, and something more must be said on this subject. There is room for an epilogue in which a little may be done to place Spelman and Brady in perspective as part of the history of historiography.

---

[1] *Complete History*, vol. II (1700), pp. 438–43.

CHAPTER IX

Conclusion: 1688 in the History of Historiography

IT is possible to regard the fall of James II as a triumph, on the plane of historical thought, for the concept of the ancient constitution. As we have already seen, in the microcosm of the Tower records office the Revolution meant the fall of Brady and the substitution of Petyt, who reigned there as a respected scholar to the end of his days; and he had opportunity to assist the House of Lords in their efforts to define what had happened in 1688 by laying his doctrines of English history before them. There is some record of this occasion, and the circumstances are of interest. The House had reached the point, in debating the resolution sent up to them by the Commons, where they were asked to agree that James had broken the original contract between king and people. They had recourse to the legal counsel appointed to advise them and inquired what this original contract might be, 'and whether there be any such or not'. The greater part of this body of counsel—the six judges, Atkyns, Montagu, Dolben, Levinz, Nevill, Holt—were all of the opinion that the contract might be a most liberal and rational concept, but they could not find it in the laws of England. Two of the three additional counsel, Bradbury and Whitelocke, spoke in favour of the contract, but in vague and inconclusive language. Then came Petyt's turn. We have some notes of what he said.[1]

The original of government came from Germany. When they came they settled a heptarchy, and that settled in one. Spelman. Kings should be elected *per sacerdotitium et populum*. There you have laws made by what we call a Parliament, as well the laity as the clergy. All the kings acted and transacted by what we call a Parliament. In Selden's *Titles of Honour* you had the oath before any did homage. The King took the oath to maintain

[1] *Historical Manuscripts Commission, XIIth Report*, Appendix VI, pp. 14 ff.

the Church, to do right between man and man and do justice. The disputes about the crown were treated there thus till William I. Edward Confessor was chosen in a Parliament. D. Normandy comes to be crowned at London; the Archbishop of Canterbury demands of the English, will you be pleased to have this King? They said 'Yes', with one voice, as inspired. Rufus, Henry I, Stephen, Henry II, Henry III, all these claim no right but by Parliament. Two Acts to be read. There was always an agreement in the Saxons' times, and so it continues. 25 Ed. III, that settles (?) the right of the crown. He is bound by his oath to make remedy and law to his people in removing mischiefs.

The part which the ancient constitution might play in the ideology of the Revolution is here made very clear. Petyt is making out a case for the people's right of deposing and, apparently, electing their kings; but he does not ground it upon the original contract as defined in works of political theory, partly no doubt for the reason already given by the judges—the concept cannot be found in English law—but also, we may suspect, because it cannot be cleansed from the suggestion of popular sovereignty, which it was no part of the Whigs' intention to allow lest they should return to the days of the Commonwealth. We can understand Petyt's speech, made in January 1689, better if we bear in mind the efforts of contemporary extremist pamphleteers to suggest that by the deed of James the constitution was dissolved and all power returned into the hands of the people.[1] That could not happen if the constitution were as Petyt describes it. The people indeed recognize the king on hearing him swear to maintain law; they may evidently depose him if he breaks his oath; but there is no suggestion that the law itself is of their making and every reason, having regard to Petyt's earlier writings, to suppose that he meant it to be ancient and immemorial. The remark that 'the original of government came from Germany' is not absolutely compatible with this interpretation; it was easy, in the context of 'Gothic' ideas, to imagine a tribe assembling at the dawn of their history to draw up their fundamental constitution. But the Gothic idea does not appear significantly in Petyt's *Antient Right of the Commons*, where parliament is rather presented as

[1] E.g. John Wildman, *A Letter to a Friend Advising in this Extraordinary Juncture How to Free the Nation from Slavery Forever*. There are other traces of this argument to be found in vol. x of the Somers Tracts.

immemorial within Britain.[1] To all appearances, then, we have
here what Petyt had defended against Brady: an immemorial
constitution, one (we may gloss) which guarantees the people's
rights, of which they are the guardians, but which they cannot
lightly change. The 'original contract' is not 'the original of
government'; it is identified with the coronation oath, an oath to
observe the ancient constitution—which, it seems probable, binds
the people as well as the king.

To this, then, had the ancient constitution come: a conservative
and legalist version of the contract, a sanction—as Brady had pointed
out[2]—by which the doctrines of election and deposition might be
justified. But, in however attenuated a form, it is significant that it
should have been retained in the Whig ideology of the eighteenth
century. Perhaps the notion of fundamental and unalterable law
ceased to be of any serious importance in that age, but to the end of
their *grand siècle* the Whigs—and all Englishmen who took their
stand on the principles of 1688—clung to the habit of appealing to a
supposedly actual English past not less and perhaps more than to
abstract principles of government. There is a doctrine in Bolingbroke, to be found also in men less elaborately sceptical of historical
knowledge of remote ages, which well illustrates this point. He says
that whatever the rights of parliament and the subject may have
been in times past, the Revolution has settled the point beyond
doubt and there is no need to look further back than 1688 for the
foundation of our liberties. Nevertheless, for the satisfaction of

---

[1] There is reference to a supposed British parliament called the Cyfr-y-then,
and phrases like 'hath ever been' and '*a crepusculo temporis*' frequently occur.

[2] *Introduction to the Old English History*, 'The Epistle to the Reader': 'Two
sorts of *Turbulent Men* there are in the World, who under *plausible Pretences*
have appeared for the *Liberty* of the People, or indeed the *Change* of the
Government....One of these sort of Men preach to the *People, That the
Origin of all Power and Government is from them; That Kings or Magistrates
derive their Authority from them...and may be Tryed, Sentenced, Deposed, or put
to Death by them....* The other sort are such as hold forth to the People, *Ancient
Rights* and *Privileges*...and that this was an *Elective* Kingdom, which as often
as they have opportunity they cunningly insinuate, though they do not plainly
assert it in terms....Any Man that shall observe, what the last Men craftily
drive at, and *compare* it diligently with what the former assert, will not find
much *Difference* in their *Principles* and *Designs*.'

such as still desire to feel that Revolution principles are in accord with the remoter precedents of English history—here follows a reasonably orthodox 'common-law' account of history, relating the Revolution to the survival of parliament and limited monarchy from pre-Conquest times.[1] It was still perfectly possible to see the Revolution in terms of the 'myth of the confirmations', ranking 1688 with 1066, 1215 and 1628 in the list of dates on which the ancient and fundamental law had been solemnly reasserted by the nation. The common-law version of history survived, and it survived essentially in the form in which it had been stated by Petyt. There were variations of emphasis and implication from writer to writer and from moment to moment; but in general it remained common ground that law and parliament, having originated in a way usually not specified, could be discovered early in Saxon times and had survived the Conquest, and that certain principles of liberty, deriving from the Saxon forefathers, had animated the English in their resistance to absolute monarchy alike in the thirteenth century and in the seventeenth. The Whiggish idea of the constitution and of liberty continued to rest in part on this version of history, and those who attacked it in the eighteenth century because their idea of the constitution differed from that of the Whigs did not attempt to substitute Brady's feudal interpretation for it. Cartwright and Paine, with their followers and competitors, fought over again the battle waged by Lilburne and Overton; they looked back to a Saxon golden age in which the people had been more than their representatives; they declared that the origins of parliament were in Norman tyranny, and the origins of most governments in conquest and usurpation; and they went on from this last principle to reject history altogether and aver that the criterion by which any government must be judged was not its antiquity, but its rationality. The similarity between their arguments and those of the Levellers is itself evidence of how little the Whig version of history had changed in the intervening century and a half.[2]

[1] *Dissertation on Parties*, 7th ed. (London, 1749); cf. pp. 124–5 and 132–3.
[2] Christopher Hill's essay 'The Norman Yoke' (cited above, p. 54) discusses some changes in emphasis that occurred within the Whig myth

Conclusion: 1688 in the History of Historiography

Nevertheless the concept of the ancient constitution, considered in the setting of eighteenth-century ways of thought, had plainly lost much of its original character. Politically, it had ceased to be principally—perhaps at all—an appeal to the binding force of ancient custom; historically, it had ceased to be essentially a conviction that the law and constitution were immemorial, based upon a too exclusive knowledge of the common law with its dogma that the law was custom and custom immemorial. The reasons why this should have been so are many and various, but we can gain an idea of their character by recapitulating some of the themes of this book.

In Sir Edward Coke's time the concept of the ancient constitution had meant essentially that the whole body of English law—including the customs of the high court of parliament—could be represented as immemorial in the sense that custom was immemorial. Coke had shown himself ready to apply this doctrine to history with a high degree of literalness and actually discover law and parliament in an age before the first written records, on the grounds that they were ancient custom. This delusion had been rooted in the presuppositions of common-law thought, and in a period when the study of the common law did much to determine the character of English thought and learning, it had been accepted and believed by a great many Englishmen of the politically minded classes. But if law and parliament could be represented as immemorial, so too by the same arguments could the prerogatives of the king, and men like Hyde repaired to the standard of Charles I in the belief that by fighting for the crown they were fighting for the immemorial laws of England. There was nothing antimonarchical in a belief in immemorial custom; politically, it represents the medieval concept of an impersonal, unmade and immanent law which defined the just rights of every organ of the community. But when James I was thought to be claiming too wide and undefined a power—and was known to hold, as a point in political theory, that all laws,

during the eighteenth century. Perhaps the most interesting is that Alfred replaced Edward the Confessor as patron saint of the Saxon constitution, apparently because he was supposed to have founded the shire system. *Democracy and the Labour Movement*, pp. 44–50.

customs and privileges were derived ultimately from his will—it became possible to argue that these things were rooted in ancient custom and consequently were not derived from his will, which came to be thought of as a power divorced from custom and standing over against it. Once that which was immemorial and that which was willed were set in sharp contrast to one another, an ideological gap was opened which could not be easily bridged, and the concept of the ancient constitution became alternative to and incompatible with the sovereignty of the king. The idea that it belonged to parliament to define the content of the ancient constitution, and that all actions undertaken in its defence were legitimate, obviously led to the revolutionary sovereignty of that body; yet it is paradoxically significant that parliament should have clung as long as it could to the doctrine that its acts were justified by fundamental law—by a body of ancient custom which it repudiated all claim to have made. The concept of an ancient law which defined the scope of parliament and prerogative alike died hard, and when Prynne denied that the House of Commons was immemorial, his aim was to subordinate it to a law which was. But during his lifetime Filmer and later Hobbes, working from assumptions perhaps incompatible with one another, had seen that the position of parliament could be attacked in a much deadlier way. It was now parliament, rather than the law as a whole, which was being presented as immemorial; and the claim to be immemorial had been virtually identified with the claim to be sovereign. Because parliament was supposed to owe its beginning to no man, it could claim to act as it thought fit in defence of the law; and if it was added that the law too was immemorial, this merely underlined parliament's right to interpret the law by its uncontrolled ordinances and resolutions. The whole concept of ancient custom had been narrowed down to this one assertion, that parliament was immemorial. If parliament was immemorial, parliament was sovereign: if parliament was not immemorial, then he who had made it was sovereign. The medieval concept of universal unmade law, which the notion of ancient custom had sought to express, had collapsed. Filmer and Hobbes each saw that it was possible to argue that every law originated in some man's will and that such a man must have possessed sovereignty and transmitted it to his heirs; and each began to argue that it was possible to prove from history that the House of Commons was not immemorial but the work of the king. When next it was claimed that parliament was sovereign and immemorial, the works of Filmer were re-published; and we have already seen how these revitalized the ideas of Spelman, who had attacked parliament's historical claim from a new angle.

It is plain, then, that the development of parliamentary thought on the ancient constitution had been such as to sap the notion of custom, on which the idea of the immemorial ultimately rested. We saw how law as custom could mean either law in perpetual adjustment or law as unchanging and immemorial, and how the latter idea always tended to predominate, until we could contrast Hale, whose concept of custom as a perpetual process had real profundity, with Petyt and Atwood, in whom the ancient constitution had come to mean nothing but a crude dogma that there had always been a parliament. The conflict between two claims to sovereignty accounts for the degeneration of Cokean thought in the hands of the Exclusionist writers. If Hale had answered Filmer, he might—unless the problem of conquest had proved too much of a stumbling block—have anticipated much of the thought of Burke, but Petyt and Atwood were concerned only to deny the king's sovereignty and smuggle in that of parliament under a thin disguise, and consequently they expressed the problem in the simplest possible terms. If parliament has a known beginning, it must be in someone's will and therefore the king will be sovereign; but parliament is immemorial (and therefore it is sovereign). This formulation underlies all their writing and reduces the concept of the ancient constitution to the point of logical absurdity. Put like this, the argument was one which, even without the battering which they suffered from the Spelmanist historians, the Whigs could hardly help losing. We may now see why a new way out of the dilemma, in non-historical or anti-historical terms, was sought and found in the work of Locke.

Locke answered the patriarchal, not the constitutional arguments of Filmer; or, put another way, he answered him on the plane of sacred, not national history. His concern, however, was to remove the debate from the plane of history altogether. Filmer had cornered the Whigs with the argument that every law must originate in some man's command; since sovereignty was inalienable, that man's heir must have inherited it. Locke, by means of arguments too well known to need repeating, sought to show that law was not derived from the will of any sovereign, whether patriarchal or popular, but from the natural rights of every individual and from his will, as a rational and sociable being, to set up machinery to secure them. Hence it did not matter if law could be traced back to the will of some patriarch or some conqueror; his will had no power to rivet sovereignty on the men of his own generation, still less on their heirs. They retained possession of their rights and these must be the foundation of any government, no matter how it had been instituted. The whole chain of consequences, extending to all eternity, which Filmer and Petyt, and in moments of weakness even Hale, had supposed to follow the introduction of a sovereign into history, seemed by this argument to be dissolved.

Hale's concept of custom had almost led him to the conclusion that no sovereign could impose his power on succeeding generations; only the thought of conquest had been too much for him, and since that was an argument which the royalists could never wholeheartedly accept, we may allow that a reply to Filmer could have been constructed in Hale's pre-Burkean terms. It would have differed greatly from Locke's, for it would have presented custom, the gradual process by which men adjusted their institutions to their needs, as the origin of all law and the ultimate reason why laws could not be derived from the sovereign's will. History would have been turned against the sovereign. But in Locke the ultimate guarantee against sovereign will is located in principles of nature and reason which lie outside history and do not change with its changes: a fact which was to influence the English attitude to the past. Locke's whole cast of mind led him towards a non-historical theory of politics, and there were profound tendencies in contemporary thought pointing the same way. But Hale's ideas, no less than Locke's, are part of the history of their era, and some part in the genesis of Locke's *Treatises of Civil Government* and their reception must be allowed to the fact that the reply to Filmer's version of

Conclusion: 1688 in the History of Historiography

English history was made in Petyt's terms and not in Hale's. Since Petyt's attempt to deny that parliament had been created by the king by asserting that it had been created by nobody at all had manifestly failed, it was the more significant that the *Treatises*, when they appeared, should have shifted the argument to a sphere in which the whole appeal to history seemed irrelevant. The popularity of Locke's theory owes something to the inanition of common-law thought.

This does not make it altogether unremarkable that Locke should have omitted all mention of English history from his writings on politics, or that, so far as can be learnt, the surviving records of his intellectual life contain no sign that the subject of this book had the smallest interest for him. If one thing is certain, it is that the attempt to understand English politics through the history of English law was an all but universal pursuit of educated men in the seventeenth century, so much so that to discover a man who did not engage in it is to discover something of a rarity. Yet Locke appears to be such an exception, perhaps the only one among the important political writers of the age. He seems to have taken no interest whatever in the historical aspect of the controversy about Filmer's works—it is true that he owned Atwood's books written against Brady,[1] but he nowhere mentions him—and his chapter on conquest in the *Second Treatise*, though it is full of discernible allusions to the juridical problems which his contemporaries feared would arise had the Normans conquered England, makes only the most cursory attempt to prove that this did not happen. Locke does not so much deny that William conquered England as assert that it is absurd to suppose the question of any importance; even if it were true, he says, 'as by history it appears otherwise', a conqueror can acquire only the most limited rights, which cease to be valid within a generation, for reasons which he proceeds to expound at length and which are rational, not historical, in their character. Once again, Locke is removing the debate out of the field in which history appears relevant, and this may well seem a sufficient explanation of his refusal to discuss it. But he was not the only man of these years to attempt a non-historical theory of politics, and most of those who

[1] I owe this information to Mr Peter Laslett.

did ended by drifting back to English history by way of some such parenthesis as Locke's 'as by history it appears otherwise', magnified to much greater length. Algernon Sidney, for example, having unequivocally stated that what mattered was whether a government was good or evil, not whether it was old, instantly added:

> But if that liberty in which God created man, can receive any strength from continuance, and the rights of Englishmen can be rendered any more unquestionable by prescription, I say, that the nations, whose rights we inherit, have ever enjoyed the liberties we claim, and always exercised them in governing themselves popularly, or by such representatives as have been instituted by themselves, from the time they were first known in the world.[1]

He then, in many pages, set forth the familiar version of early English history (emphasizing the idea of a common 'Gothic' origin to a degree beyond most of the writers of whom we have been treating). The appeal to ancient liberty was hard to abandon. Even Tyrrell and Molyneux, men who knew Locke well at different times, based their writings on Petyt's as well as on his and acknowledged the former as their master in a degree second only to Locke. It may be that Locke was more clear-headed than these lesser figures and refused to drag history back into an argument from which it had just been eliminated; or he may have thought that the appeal to the past was losing its hold on the public—though it is doubtful if it was; but as likely an explanation is that Edward the Confessor and Magna Carta and the rest of it simply did not interest him.[2] After all, for

---

[1] *Discourses concerning Government*, 3rd ed. (1751), p. 380; see generally pp. 375–98.

[2] Dr von Leyden remarks (John Locke, *Essays on the Law of Nature*, ed. W. von Leyden, Oxford, 1954, p. 37 and elsewhere) that Locke's view of natural law differed from those of Grotius and Selden in being 'chiefly epistemological, [while] theirs was mainly legal or historical'. He dwells on Locke's denials that that natural law can be known from tradition or the general consent of men. Mr E. A. Olssen of the University of Otago has suggested to me that Locke's 'chiefly epistemological' attitude may account for his lack of interest in custom, precedent or prescription. I find this suggestion illuminating; yet it probably does not altogether explain why Locke should have been uninterested in seeing his principles reflected in the positive law of England. Tyrrell shared Locke's views on natural law and tradition (von Leyden, p. 86), yet wrote copiously on the ancient constitution.

those capable of taking an interest in history, when one has proved
that a certain mode of government is the most conformable to reason
and abstract justice, there is at least an illustrative value in showing
that this constitution has been normally observed in time past—
even in time immemorial.

'Our constitution is rational', it might now be said; 'that
substantially the same constitution existed among our Saxon
ancestors proves both that the principles of reason on which it is
founded are eternal, and that our ancestors in their unpolished way
were rational beings too, as all free men should be.' Something like
this must have been the thought underlying many of the appeals to
the ancient constitution made in the age of political rationalism;
and in so far as this was the character of eighteenth-century constitutional antiquarianism, it was clearly unlike that of the seventeenth century. The concept of immemorial custom, founded on
the interpretation of the common law, was—let us repeat it—in
decay. Ideas of sovereignty had undermined belief in an ancient
custom binding on both king and community; the concept of custom
itself had hardened into an obscurantist insistence that parliament
must not be known to have had a beginning. In addition to all this,
and for reasons many of which lie outside the scope of this book,
the first decades of the new century witnessed a wave of historical
scepticism—Bolingbroke is its best-known English exponent—in
which both the possibility and the utility of knowing what had
happened in remote ages were called in question.[1] In creating this
mood of doubt it is possible that Spelmanist criticism played some
part. Very shortly after Petyt had identified the original contract
with the coronation oath, that oath itself was re-worded by the
statute 1 W. & M. c. 6, and the traditional reference to the laws of
Edward the Confessor removed,

forasmuch as the oath hath heretofore been framed in doubtful words and
expressions, with relation to antient laws and constitutions at this time
unknown.[2]

[1] See P. Hazard, *La Crise de la conscience européenne*, and for Bolingbroke,
Douglas, *English Scholars*, ch. XIII, 'The End of an Age'.

[2] There is a discussion of this aspect of the oath in relation to the reign of
James II in A. Taylor, *The Glory of Regality* (1820), pp. 335–42.

Conclusion: 1688 in the History of Historiography

'The rationalists of 1688', Professor H. M. Cam has called the instigators of this measure;[1] but are we in the presence of a rationalist indifference to the past, of a general scepticism as to the possibility of historical knowledge, of an uneasy awareness of the telling criticisms launched by Spelman and Brady, or of a mixture of all three? It is hard to tell, but we may note the words in which Evelyn denounced the legal and historical education dispensed by the Inns of Court: he declared that young lawyers and students of law were 'shamefully ignorant in the Feudal [Law] and our own', and that they must be taught 'whence our holding by Knight's service and Feudal Laws have been derived, whether from Saxon or Norman'.[2] Similarly Thomas Madox, the greatest medievalist of the next generation, permitted himself the remark:

> One may justly wonder that *Feudal* Learning (if I may so call it) should be so little known or regarded as it seems to be by the Students (I ask their pardon) of the Common Law of *England*.[3]

Evelyn and Madox were echoing Spelman's criticism of Coke, and it would appear that neglect of feudal history aroused dissatisfaction and furthered the decline in the intellectual reputation of the Inns of Court; but this is only one small aspect of that little-studied and important phenomenon, the way in which the Inns ceased to teach, ceased to be a third university for the gentlemen of England and ceased to exert a determining influence on English historical and political thought. Perhaps this development, more than even that decline in medieval scholarship which Professor Douglas detects about 1720,[4] may be taken to mark the end of the age of Coke and the transformation of the concept of the ancient constitution. In the days of Coke, of Prynne and Hale, even of Petyt and Atwood, the idea of immemorial law had sprung direct from the Inns of Court; it had been shaped by historical presuppositions implicit in the common law, and had been the ideology of a period in which

---

[1] *England before Elizabeth* (1950), p. 55.
[2] *Letters on Various Subjects to and from William Nicholson*, ed. John Nichols (1809), pp. 137 ff.
[3] Madox, *Formulare anglicanum* (1702), Preface, section VIII.
[4] *English Scholars*, ch. XIII.

that law exercised an influence on education, scholarship and political thought greater than it possessed at any other time in English history. In the age of the Inns' decline the presuppositions on which it was founded must have undergone radical change. The minds which believed in it now had not been formed by an exclusive study of the common law, and consequently must have believed in it for reasons differing from those analysed in this book.

Italian historians concerned with the political and historical thought of the *mezzogiorno*[1] speak of a process, which they date about the year 1700, whereby the kind of thinking which attempted to solve problems in political thought by reference to existing and ancient law (the 'tradizione giuridica') was largely replaced by political thought which they describe as Cartesian, and which brought about corresponding changes in the contemporary attitude to history. In so far as the period following 1688 witnessed a transference of emphasis from ancient custom and precedent to unhistorical reason, we may be in the presence of something similar in the history of English thought; and it is suggested that the concept of the ancient constitution was itself transformed, to a considerable extent, by being based on reason rather than custom. But the appeal to the Saxon and medieval past did not altogether lose its original significance when prolonged into the eighteenth century. As Burke was to point out, it was of no small importance that Englishmen of the great Whig epoch preferred, as often as not, to describe their liberty as an inheritance from their ancestors than as a thing rooted in abstract reason; and a foreign observer, de Lolme, remarked of the whole question that

there was a far greater probability of success, in raising among the people the notions (familiar to them) of legal claims and long-established customs, than in arguing with them from the no less rational, but less determinate, and somewhat dangerous doctrines, concerning the original rights of mankind, and the lawfulness of at all time opposing force to an oppressive government.[2]

[1] See the works of Romeo and Marini, cited in ch. 1, pp. 16 n. and 18 n.
[2] *The Constitution of England* (ed. 1816), p. 8 n. It is interesting that this should be part of a comment on Spelman's remark that at the Conquest 'novus seclorum nascitur ordo'.

Conclusion: 1688 in the History of Historiography

De Lolme had seen the conservative and anti-theoretical character of the appeal to the past; but, true to his age, he supposed this to be the result of a shrewd calculation by those who had elected to use this argument rather than its alternative. The present book contends, however, that its use in the seventeenth century is better interpreted as arising from habits of thought deeply rooted and almost instinctive in the English mind; and there is reason to believe that its prolongation into the eighteenth century indicates, after all, some survival of these traditional habits. The great masters of common-law thought, when all is said, continued to be read and studied in the age that succeeded their own; so too did their opponents, Spelman and even Brady; and the ideas of Burke, which close the eighteenth century as an age in the history of English political thought, can be fully appreciated only if we realize, first, that he had studied the controversy between the partisans of the ancient constitution and those of the feudal law,[1] and come to the conclusion that this controversy was of importance in the history of English politics; secondly, that his own thinking was saturated in the ideas of Coke and Hale. Burke's essential ideas are that institutions are the products of history; that history consists in an unceasing and undying process, in which the generations are partners and in which men perpetually adapt themselves to new needs and new situations; that existing institutions are the fruits of this process and, whether because they represent the latest adjustment or because they have been retained through many adaptations, embody the wisdom of more men, in a higher state of refinement, than the individual intellect can hope to equal or exceed; and that political wisdom lies in participating in this process—which can be identified with order and nature—not in attempting to reconstruct institutions on *a priori* lines. In all this we cannot be mistaken in recognizing the voice of

[1] The evidence for this is to be found in his fragment 'An Essay towards an History of the Laws of England', *Works*, Bohn ed., vol. VI (1877), pp. 412–22. See also Butterfield, *Man on his Past* (Cambridge, 1955), pp. 18, 68–9, with a quotation from Acton. Acton was much impressed by Burke's sympathy for the Middle Ages, as compared with Bossuet and the eighteenth-century writers; but should he not have compared him rather with the English legal historians of the seventeenth century? Professor Butterfield remarks that Acton's knowledge of these writers seems deficient (pp. 65–6).

the great tradition of common-law thought, and in particular of those men who had conceived the law of England as custom and custom as perpetual adaptation. Every one of Burke's cardinal points, as just enumerated, can be found in Hale rebuking Hobbes, in Coke rebuking James I, or in Davies rebuking the partisans of written law; and in Hale we have seen an adumbration of Burke's philosophy developed to a high pitch of subtlety. It is as if the concept of custom, and of English institutions as founded on custom, ran underground about the time of Hale's death, to burst into sunlight again in Burke's letters and speeches. From what sources Burke derived it, and with what elements of eighteenth-century thought and his own genius he enriched it, are questions for the specialist; but that Burke's philosophy is in great measure a revitalization of the concept of custom and the common-law tradition may be safely asserted as part of the present study's contentions.

By the time of Burke, however, the historical outlook of Englishmen was very different from what it had been in the time of Hale or Brady. In order to understand this difference, we must first consider whether the feudal interpretations founded by Spelman played any part in the historical thinking of the eighteenth century. The full investigation of this question remains a task for future researchers; but it would appear that, while after 1688 there was general determination not to allow the presence of feudal elements in English medieval history to upset the dogma that parliamentary liberty was pre-Conquest in character, the existence of those elements as a field of possible study may have been neglected but was not actually denied. Whig bishops of the Revolution settlement—Gibson, White Kennett and Nicholson—completed the editing of Spelman's unpublished works and commented learnedly on his feudal investigations; all through the century he was acknowledged and quoted as one of the greatest of authorities, and even Brady's writings did not go unread. Eminent writers on the common law were in time able to admit the importance of Spelman's doctrines: Wright and Blackstone, Gilbert and Sullivan expounded the derivation of English law from a feudal origin, while in Scotland Kames and Dalrymple carried on the tradition of Sir Thomas

Craig.[1] But the writings of these sound and conservative scholars leave one wondering (though the point requires further investigation) whether anything important had been added to the knowledge of feudalism since the early seventeenth century. Dalrymple, for example—still considered a writer worth reading on Scottish feudal tenures[2]—had not advanced beyond deriving feudalism from a Lombard origin and, though there are clear signs in some writers of the influence of Montesquieu on this topic, it does not seem that eighteenth-century British scholarship had entirely reached the point of treating feudalism as a plant of Frankish and Carolingian growth.[3] Compared with the times of Spelman, Brady or Madox (d. 1727), the high eighteenth century appears to have seen the exploration of feudal society at a standstill. For this there are various reasons; the unpopularity of the subject in an age still wedded to the ancient constitution was one of them. Blackstone, for instance, though his whole account of the origins of common law presupposes a knowledge of feudal society, is bent on treating Norman feudalism as a mere intrusion on English constitutional history. For him the driving force of thirteenth-century politics is still the desire of 'the nation' to recover its ancient liberty, which the Conquest had submerged. Many writers of his age, having apparently given all due weight to the importance of the Norman introduction of feudal tenure, then undermined their own writings by insisting on treating feudalism as a mere interruption of the true course of the national life, and the habit of presenting 'feudalism' and 'the nation' as opposite and antagonistic concepts coloured much of

[1] Sir Martin Wright, *An Introduction to the Law of Tenures* (1729); Sir Geoffrey Gilbert (d. 1726), *Treatise of Tenures* (1754); Blackstone, *Commentaries on the Laws of England* (published 1765–9); F. S. Sullivan, *An Historical Treatise on the Feudal Law* (1772); Henry Home (later Lord Kames), *Essays upon Several Subjects concerning British Antiquities* (1746); John Dalrymple, *An Essay towards a General History of Feudal Property in Great Britain* (1757).

[2] H. M. Cam, *Liberties and Communities in Medieval England* (Cambridge, 1944), p. 220, n. 4.

[3] But cf. Robertson's *History of Scotland* (*Works*, collected ed., London, 1824, vol. I, p. 35 n.), which does not, however, clearly state that feudal tenure originated in Frankish society. See also Hume, *History of England* (1762), vol. I, p. 263.

the historical thought of the nineteenth century, in a way no longer thought illuminating. It seems that we must look to the age of Kemble and Palgrave for signs of fresh life in this branch of thought.

But there is another way in which this apparent slowing-up of feudal studies is important. It would seem as if feudal society was not being investigated as part of a live movement of research, based on the recovery, editing and interpreting of charters and other forms of evidence; as if, in short—and this seems the general opinion among scholars—the great movement of seventeenth-century antiquarianism had come to an end. We have seen how the concept of custom and the intellectual ascendancy of the common law both lost importance at the end of the Stuart period, which may help to explain the general decline. It is as if the security of the Whig state and Church after 1714 loosened the ties which bound England to her past. The foundations were felt to be solidly established and fairly recent, and what had happened in remoter ages, while it remained in doubt, could no longer so vitally affect the present. If this generalization can be maintained, we may say that we draw to an end of the first great age of modern historiography: that in which the structure of society is authoritatively determined by the laws and sacred books of the past; in which means exist of interpreting these authorities by canons which are those of modern historical criticism, and so of reconstructing the past of which they formed part; but in which the structure of the present is still thought to be vitally affected by the reconstruction which is made of the past. In such a period the writing of history is inevitably partisan, but may not be much the worse for that; there is an intimate and passionate concern with the details of the past, and the organic unity of past and present is vigorously asserted. But in so far as the eighteenth century was an 'age of reason', in so far as it supposed itself to be securely based on principles independent of history— neither generalization is of course absolutely true—its whole attitude to the past must have been very different; and in this alteration there was both loss and gain.

The past tended to lose its immediate and controversial relevance to the present, so that there was some slackening of partisan zeal

Conclusion: 1688 in the History of Historiography

among English medievalists; but on the other hand we observe not only a tendency to lose interest in the whole subject, but the rise of a new and unfamiliar problem. Of great stretches of past time it could now be said that the way in which they were interpreted could not make any difference to the lives of men in the present. What then was the point of studying them at all, and what was the attitude which the modern intellect should adopt towards them? It is the same problem, though differently arrived at, as that which had been more remotely discerned by the critics of Cujas. Bolingbroke's *Letters on the Study of History* attempt to answer such questions as these, but by universal consent the solution they propose is an unsatisfactory one. Bolingbroke cannot imagine any cultivated man studying the remoter and less sympathetic periods of history with the idea of finding out what they were like or how they worked. For him the function of historical study is not to discover how men have lived—thinking nothing human alien to its inquiries —but to inculcate the moral and practical lessons of statecraft, and the man of affairs need concern himself only with those periods likely to contain examples relevant to his own situation, a definition which ends by ruling out the greater part of recorded history. This is certainly a deplorable attitude, and there is something peculiarly unpleasing about the spectacle of Bolingbroke blotting out vast tracts of human experience as unworthy of serious attention. But he had called attention to a real problem: if it was no longer thought that the form of the modern state was directly determined by what had happened in the eleventh century, why should that period be studied at all, except by dry-as-dusts cut off from their own age and incomprehensibly interested in the past for its own sake? Concepts of custom and sovereignty, of the origins and ultimate authority of law, had once bound the present to the past; if these were abandoned, what was called for was virtually a new conception of the unity of history—with the disappearance of historical study as an alternative. It was the achievement of the eighteenth century—of Vico and Voltaire, of the Göttingen and Edinburgh professors—to formulate general ideas and construct schemes of universal history; and if their work points in some respects to the intellectual disasters which befell and are befalling the human race

246

with the advent of historicism, this does not alter the fact that, in replacing the intense but limited concern with the past that characterized the antiquarians with a set of general ideas that made it possible (however inadequately) to see the present state of mankind as emerging from the whole of its past experience, they were doing what had to be done if historiography was to survive. There is a certain case to be made for Bolingbroke against the antiquarians who surpassed him in scholarship and whose scholarship he said he despised. He was detached from the past as they could never be, and though his detachment made him often superficial and obtuse, it also gave him the power to reflect on the historical process and on the problem of a man's defining his own place in it; and here he often displayed a subtlety of perception which was beyond better scholars. He knew that historical situations did not exactly recur, so that we must beware of applying too rigidly any generalizations we formed from past experience;[1] and he had a sense of historical relativism—he liked to observe that arguments about the nature of the constitution had been used in the seventeenth century which it would not be appropriate to use in the circumstances of his own day.[2] Bolingbroke could appreciate ideas of this kind because he had an awareness, beyond anything possessed by Spelman, Harrington or Hale, of living in a generalized historical process. His generalizations were often unsound and superficial; but generalizations, and perhaps even superficiality, were what the age needed. They were necessary to the construction of schemes of universal history which alone could give an 'age of reason' a sense of oneness with its past.

Even in Bolingbroke's most cocksure judgments about those periods of history in which a polite statesman will, or will not, find anything deserving his attention, we catch a hint of that aspect of eighteenth-century historical thought which was, for good and ill, to be of greatest importance for the future. This is the habit of generalizing about the periods of history, of supposing each of them

---

[1] This point is discussed in Professor Butterfield's *The Statecraft of Machiavelli* (London, reprinted 1955), ch. IV, where Bolingbroke's debt to Guicciardini in this matter is emphasized.

[2] *Dissertation on Parties*, 7th ed., pp. 124–31.

to have been governed by certain general characteristics, so that it could be further supposed that there was a certain logic about the way in which one period succeeded another, and that the dominant characteristics of one period might help to explain how it had been transformed into another or replaced. Thought of this kind—which certainly belongs to the eighteenth century, whatever used to be said to the contrary—points the way to historicism and to the idea that the entire process of history can be abstracted and turned into a single set of laws, and as such we may deplore it; but we ought also to admit that such a habit of generalization provided a solution to the problem which had been too much for Brady. He had been able to reconstruct the institutions of a past time, but he had not been able to show how these institutions had evolved into something different, to combine a narrative of the evolution of institutions with a narrative of the deeds of men, or to apply the techniques he used upon legal and governmental records to the study and interpretation of chronicles; and consequently he had apparently not conceived of history as a single unified discipline. His limitations were, it seems probable, those general in his age. But eighteenth-century historians—Vico, Voltaire, Montesquieu, Millar, Schlözer[1] —were able, each in his way, to observe that in a period supposedly governed by certain characteristics it was natural that certain social institutions, certain habits of thought and forms of art should exist in conformity with the dominant characteristics, and that they should fall and be replaced by others as the character of the period changed. It remained only to show how the actions of men might contribute to altering the whole pattern of the age, and the problem was solved. In comparison with their predecessors of the seventeenth century, the difference between Voltaire's 'rationalism' and Vico's 'historicism' loses some of its importance. The writers of the eighteenth century converted history into a

---

[1] The present writer derives virtually all his knowledge of the Edinburgh school from a series of articles by Mr Duncan Forbes in the *Cambridge Journal* ('*Historismus* in England', April 1951; 'James Mill and India', October 1951; 'The Rationalism of Sir Walter Scott', October 1953; and 'Scientific Whiggism: Adam Smith and John Millar', August 1954), and of the Göttingen school and Schlözer from Professor Butterfield's *Man on his Past*.

unified science, capable (at least in theory) of looking at the whole of human life from a standpoint distinctively its own. It had not been in that condition when they found it.[1]

They carried out this great change in ideas partly because they were willing to engage in sweeping generalizations, many of which were naturally unsound. Craig and Spelman may have been too ready to deduce all the phenomena of feudal tenure from a single Lombard origin, but in spite of Maitland's famous remark, Spelman did not speak of a 'feudal system', a phrase which seems to belong to eighteenth-century terminology; it was Robertson, writing between 1753 and 1759, perhaps under Montesquieu's influence, who could say 'the genius of the feudal government, uniform in all its operations, produced the same effects in small, as in great societies'.[2] If the English and Scottish writers of this age did little new research on feudalism, it was because they were making an 'ism' of it; they were reflecting on its essence and nature and endeavouring to fit it into a pattern of general ideas. In so doing they committed and perpetuated many great fallacies; they transmitted some of the mistakes of their predecessors and did not always profit by their best work. It is true that the best in the older tradition did not altogether die out. The thought of Burke, it is suggested here, owed far more to the common-law concept of custom than to the system-building historicism of the eighteenth century; and, in our own times, is it too fantastic to suggest that the contrast between Fisher ('one emergency following another') and Toynbee represents a continuing conflict between the two traditions? It is not yet certain that when feudal studies came to be revived in the nineteenth century, Spelman, who was still read, was altogether without his influence. However all this may be, it is nevertheless fairly certain that the eighteenth-century historians failed to continue, to appreciate as they should, or to learn as they might from the work of the seventeenth-century legal historians; and it is irritating to find Bolingbroke's facile contempt for the antiquary occasionally

[1] It may be worth mentioning that 'the eighteenth century' is here, as always, an elastic term. It could well be extended to cover the period of Hazard's 'crise de la conscience européenne', beginning about 1680.

[2] *Works*, vol. I, p. 62.

repeated by Robertson and Gibbon.[1] But it is hard to shake off the feeling that their superficiality was perhaps an essential part of their real achievement, which was to generalize history and make it universal. Generalizations are necessary and must be permitted some inaccuracy.

The commonest approach to the history of historiography is one more likely to do injustice to Coke and Hale, Spelman and Brady, than to the great men of the next age. In Robertson's hands history was its modern self, capable of attempting to narrate the whole evolution of a human society;[2] in Brady's it was not, and there is an obvious and natural temptation to begin the history of historiography at the point where it became a unified and independent science and treat all who lived before that time as forerunners, collectors of material for others to use, voices crying in the wilderness. But this seems a fallacy, of the same order as that committed when the history of the subject was taken to begin only with the rise of German *Historismus* and the men of the eighteenth century were relegated to a sort of prehistory—the view still prevalent in most general histories. Mr Duncan Forbes and Professor Butterfield have both reminded us that *vixere fortes ante Germanos* and encouraged us to look for concepts of universal history and subtleties of historical perception in the eighteenth century; the present study simply seeks to extend the subject a stage further back. Mr Forbes in particular warns us against the danger of a 'Whig interpretation' in this field; he suggests that we ought not to look merely for the precursors of the fully fledged German romantic concept of history.[3] Similarly, it may be sug-

[1] Professor Momigliano (*op. cit.*) sees Gibbon as carrying out a great synthesis of philosophical history and antiquarian erudition in the field of ancient history. It was as well for Europe, then, that he abandoned his idea of writing on the English barons' wars, for no such synthesis was likely to be achieved there.

[2] This is not to deny that there was much of an unhistorical character still surviving in eighteenth-century practice, or that the German historical movement carried out a vast deepening of perspectives. But eighteenth-century historiography proposed to itself the object of treating the evolution of society as a whole and, whatever its defects, it had not been thought before that this could be done.

[3] In '*Historismus* in England', cited above, pp. 389–90.

gested that the moment when history became a distinct and self-conscious way of looking at things is indeed of the greatest importance, but that there was historical thought which we must take seriously long before that date. The history of historiography is not only the history of the rise and perfection of a particular manner of thought—tremendous subject though this is—it is the history of all the ways in which men have felt committed to their past and bound to find out what it was and how they are related to it, and all the attempts they have made to deal seriously with the problems in which this inquiry involves them. The men who form the subject of this book felt bound to their past by the law under which they lived, and their interpretation of the law and their interpretation of the past depended upon and influenced one another. Through their law, historically interpreted, they could learn much about their past; but to think of their law historically was rendered difficult by the character of that law itself and by many ideas about the present, to some of which it had given rise; and to succeed in this aim would alter their attitude to both the law and the present. That was the problem with which they were faced by their sense of being bound to the past. That they thought about it seriously, and often fruitfully, is the justification for treating them as a chapter in the history of historiography. At last the age in which law was supremely important in determining men's thought about the past was succeeded by another in which that importance had been lost.

THE
ANCIENT CONSTITUTION
REVISITED

A Retrospect from 1986

Dedicated to participants in the seminars conducted at
the Folger Shakespeare Library
by the
Centre for the History of British Political Thought
between 1984 and 1987

CHAPTER I

Historiography and Common Law

THE 'COMMON-LAW MIND', CONSIDERED AS MENTALITÉ

THE book published in 1957 belongs to two fields of historical enquiry: the history of British political thought, which has grown and changed dramatically since that date, and the history of historiography, whose development has not been so rapid. The term 'historiography' is frequently employed in the preface and throughout the text,[1] but the use of 'English historical thought' in the sub-title conveys— or seems to convey now—the message that writing about the past was not always carried on or developed by the writing of 'histories', as that plural might in the seventeenth century be used to denote a certain literary form. One may seek to distinguish between 'historical thought' and 'historiography'; perhaps better—since the word 'historiography' can be used to comprehend more than one genre—one may say that the writing of 'history' was not always carried on by the writing of 'histories'. It is a further question, however, whether the history of a diversity of genres recognizable (to us) as 'historiography' can be written as though it were a single 'history'. To say that the 'history of historiography' should be written as proceeding through a diversity of channels may well be prudent; but it does not prevent our saying that these channels can be seen, at various points and in various combinations, to flow together.

There is a moment in the present book from which it is possible to follow the separate course and ultimate confluence of

---

[1] This seems a convenient point at which to state that the term 'historicism,' as found at pp. 247–8, is employed only (but only there) in the sense at that time given it by Sir Karl Popper.

255

two such channels. Robert Brady drew a distinction between 'history' and 'introductions to history'[2] and used it to distinguish between two differently constructed books of which he was the author. He was probably not the first to make this distinction, and certainly not the last. Explicitly in David Hume or William Robertson, implicitly in Edward Gibbon, one can trace the duality between the construction or compilation of narratives (Collingwood's 'scissors and paste history') according to fairly precise classical or medieval canons, and the provision of 'discourses', 'digressions', 'reflections', or otherwise-named species of commentary, designed to illuminate the narrative without being incorporated into it. The activity of being a historian (in Oakeshott's phrase) might be restricted to that of providing the original narratives; it is linguistically quite possible that Brady did not consider himself a 'historian' either when writing 'discourses' in his *Introduction* or when compiling narratives in his *History*. 'The English history', as the phrase was used far into the eighteenth century, might denote only the corpus of narratives written by contemporaries (William of Malmesbury or Matthew Paris, Thomas More or Lord Clarendon), reinforced by that of classically constructed 'histories' written by humanists at later times (Bacon's *Henry VII* or Herbert of Cherbury's *Henry VIII*). During the nineteenth century 'historiography' took on its modern meaning, in which the formal distinction between 'history' and 'discourse' or 'introduction' was supposed to have disappeared; yet the debate between 'narrative' and 'scientific' modes of historiography continues to this day, and is regularly found to have real and significant implications.

This book has not entered into that debate, but it has dealt with what may be seen as a moment in the history of English historiography when narrative and discourse were still clearly distinct, but the latter was undergoing a certain development. To state the case in these terms, however, is to expose oneself to two criticisms. The first is that of writing whiggishly, i.e., of presenting every moment in the history of pre-modern historio-

---

[2] Above, p. 209.

graphy as a station along the way of its modernization. The second is that of neglecting a series of problems of which nothing has indeed been said in the last two paragraphs: those which arise as we become aware that 'discourses' interpretative of history have in the history of historical writing been written by many kinds of author with many kinds of purpose, and have sometimes contributed to the interpretation of history without being intended as, or becoming, part of 'historiography' at all. These problems are so great that they have given rise to a doubt whether 'the history of historiography' can be written as a unitary sub-discipline; possibly the phenomena which it offers to study are inherently discrete.

There are doubtless passages in *The Ancient Constitution and the Feudal Law* which are whiggish in the sense that they treat seventeenth-century writers as not yet having acquired capacities which were acquired later on. It can only be replied that the history of how these capacities were acquired has to be written somehow, and that there is much to be said for starting at a time when they did not exist and showing why they did not yet exist and what the changes were which led to their being acquired subsequently. One has only to avoid the 'vulgar whiggism' of regarding the time when they did not exist as thereby impoverished; I hope I avoided it in 1954–5, as I certainly intended to. With regard to the second criticism, I believe I was already developing the argument, which I subsequently elaborated,[3] that the study of past states of society or social arrangements has arisen from so great a diversity of modes in which thinking beings may be involved in the present institutions of their societies, and thereby in the real or supposed pasts of these institutions, that it is highly unlikely that the histories of all these writings about pasts can ever be unified in a single *histoire totale de l'historiographie*.

The history of political thought has developed far more

---

[3] In 'The Origins of Study of the Past: A Comparative Approach', *Comparative Studies in Society and History*, vol. IV, no. 2 (1962), pp. 209–46, reprinted in P. B. M. Blaas (ed.), *Geschiedenis als Wetenschap* (The Hague: Martinus Nijhoff, 1980), pp. 53–94.

rapidly than the history of historiography, and this may have
been because the former sub-discipline has accepted and exploited
the extreme plurality of its subject matter instead of seeking to
unify it. Nevertheless there is always a case for construction
alongside that for deconstruction. There cannot be a unified
'history of historiography' and it might be whiggish to seek to
provide one; but it may be possible to detect patterns of
confluence between modes of writing history, occurring from
time to time in such ways that they come to define and prescribe
the practice of whole communities of those recognized as
writing history; and the term 'history of historiography' might
be acceptable as shorthand for the histories of such quasi-
Kuhnian processes. In the field of study to which *The Ancient
Constitution and the Feudal Law* addressed itself, there have been
at least two historiographic developments of this order. The
account given in chs. I and IV of the growth in France of a
historiography based on Roman law has been greatly enlarged
by the works of Donald R. Kelley, Julian H. Franklin and
J. H. M. Salmon[4]—to restrict myself to those writing in English
—and it is seeming possible that the interactions between French
and English scholarship in the late sixteenth and seventeenth
centuries may appear increasingly close and complex; perhaps to
the point where the antithesis which I have drawn between them
may have to be modified.

As for the history of English historiography itself, a hypothetical model has begun to appear in the writings of F. Smith

---

[4] Donald R. Kelley, *Foundations of Modern Historical Scholarship: Language,
Law and History in the French Renaissance* (New York, 1970); *François Hotman: A
Revolutionary's Ordeal* (Princeton, 1973); *The Beginnings of Ideology: Consciousness
and Society in the French Reformation* (Cambridge University Press, 1981); 'Civil
Science in the Renaissance: Jurisprudence Italian Style', *Historical Journal*, vol.
XXII, no. 4 (1979), pp. 777–94; 'Civil Science in the Renaissance: Jurisprudence
in the French Manner', *History of European Ideas*, vol. II, no. 2 (1981), pp.
261–76; Julian H. Franklin, *Jean Bodin and the 16th-Century Revolution in Law and
History* (New York: Columbia University Press, 1963); *Jean Bodin and the Rise of
Absolutist Theory* (New York: Columbia University Press, 1973); J. H. M.
Salmon, *The French Religious Wars in English Political Thought* (Oxford
University Press, 1959); J. H. M. Salmon and Ralph E. Giesey (eds.), *François
Hotman: Francogallia* (Cambridge University Press, 1972).

Fussner, F. J. Levy and Arthur B. Ferguson,[5] which can be briefly stated as follows. The endeavours of English humanists in the first half of the sixteenth century, coinciding with the development of the printed book, led to a revival and imitation of Roman and Hellenistic narrative historiography, conceived and presented largely as a literature of counsel to princes. At the end of Elizabeth I's reign and during that of James I, a mood of disillusionment overtook the community of would-be counsellors and courtiers, and gave rise to a 'Tacitist' literature—including a historiography—with satirical and occasionally republican overtones. The humanist literature of counsel, however, had already generated, alongside narrative historiography, a non-narrative genre of dialogues and discourses concerning the commonweal, of which Thomas More, Thomas Starkey and Thomas Smith were in their very different ways exponents. It is possible to regard this both as one of those revivals of interest in the vernacular which classical humanist movements were capable of generating, and as an intensification of the ideal of counsel: an intensified awareness of those features of the realm or commonweal which should and could be brought to the prince's attention. With important contributions from ecclesiastics in search of the native and imperial origins of the English church, there developed the striking topographic and archaeological surveys carried out by the Elizabethan and Jacobean antiquaries, which Ferguson encourages us to consider a characteristic outgrowth of English humanism and Fussner considers so massive an addition to the conventions of narrative historiography as to justify the term 'the historical revolution'. If we may consider the common-law scholars as following, with William Lambarde, in the footsteps of the antiquaries, *The Ancient Constitution and the Feudal Law* may take its place in this

[5] F. Smith Fussner, *The Historical Revolution, 1580–1640* (London: Routledge & Kegan Paul, 1962); F. J. Levy, *Tudor Historical Thought* (San Marino, Calif.: Huntington Library, 1967); Arthur B. Ferguson, *The Articulate Citizen and the English Renaissance* (Durham, N.C.: Duke University Press, 1965); *Clio Unbound: Perception of the Social and Cultural Past in Renaissance England* (Durham, N.C.: Duke University Press, 1979).

account of how a mode of 'discourse', archaeology and 'the study of the past' came to be added to a mode of 'narrative', example and counsel, in a pattern of confluence helping to form the history of English historiography.

I have found it possible to use this model in an attempt to describe a set of general characteristics belonging to the study of 'history' in Elizabethan and Jacobean times.[6] It has, however, been forcefully criticized in a review by G. R. Elton;[7] partly on the general grounds that the notion of a 'historical revolution' is a whiggish exaggeration and the enterprise of 'history of historiography' itself prone to whiggism, but also on grounds which call for modification of a central thesis of *The Ancient Constitution and the Feudal Law*. Arthur B. Ferguson, the target of these criticisms, had contended that by the early seventeenth-century history written by ecclesiastics was being encouraged to a fluid and dynamic vision of secular change by the Church of England doctrine that the sovereign might legislate for the church in things indifferent to salvation; whereas history of property and institutions, written by lawyers and legally educated laymen, was hamstrung by the 'common-law mind' with its insistence on customs that were immemorial, unwritten, founded on usage and hardly to be altered by legislation. Elton challenged this by arguing, first, that Ferguson's antithesis fell into whiggism through failing to recognize that ecclesiastics and common lawyers were not engaged in comparable enterprises and could not be said to have succeeded or failed in reaching the same goals; second, that Ferguson's and my account of 'the common-law mind' was exaggerated because—as Elton has long been arguing—the capacity of the crown to alter and create law, in courts by judgment and in parliament by statute, was much better established and understood than the doctrine of

---

[6] 'The Sense of History in Renaissance England', in John F. Andrews (ed.), *William Shakespeare: His World, His Work, His Influence* (New York: Scribner's, 1985).

[7] G. R. Elton, review of Arthur B. Ferguson's *Clio Unbound: Perception of the Social and Historical Past in Renaissance England*, in *History and Theory*, vol. xx, no. 1 (1981), pp. 92–100.

immemorial custom allowed for. He was able to make (though not, for once, to document) the quite correct assertion that I had already agreed that the doctrine set out in chs. II and III above was in need of re-inspection. I shall now endeavour to carry out that inspection in the light of recent research.

The two chapters which deal with 'the common-law mind' are premised on two sets of assumptions. In the first place, it is asserted that 'the ancient constitution' was an 'immemorial' constitution, and that belief in it was built up in the following way. The relations of government and governed in England[8] were assumed to be regulated by law; the law in force in England was assumed to be the common law; all common law was assumed to be custom, elaborated, summarized and enforced by statute; and all custom was assumed to be immemorial, in the sense that any declaration or even change of custom—uttered by a judge from his bench, recorded by a court in a precedent, or registered by king-in-parliament as a statute—presupposed a custom already ancient and not necessarily recorded at the time of writing. Record and memory, action and precedent, written and unwritten law, therefore enacted the roles of Achilles and the tortoise racing each other back into the mists of antiquity. The time of memory, in which men could be seen acting on their own authority, could never overtake the 'time beyond memory...whereof the memory of man runneth not to the contrary', in which they found authority for their actions, and it tended to be assumed that the forms and institutions of action—juries and courts, shires and parliaments—were as immemorial as the customary law which they maintained. My second and third chapters assume that Jacobean Englishmen made these assumptions, but do not assume that

[8] It may be conceded here that the term 'constitution', as used throughout this book, has not been systematically cleared of anachronism. There will have been a time when it was more usual to speak of 'the laws' as 'ancient', after which a practice of speaking about 'the constitution of government' became one of using 'constitution' and 'government' as interchangeable terms, hardening finally into the more modern practice in which 'the constitution' (unwritten rather than written) could be spoken of as 'ancient'. The chronology of such a process has not been attempted here.

they amounted to either a description or a caricature of the way law had been practiced in early Tudor or pre-Tudor England. On p. 31 it is indicated that the way of thinking described here was consolidated in the second half of the sixteenth century, and is not necessarily to be found at earlier times; but I made the further claim that by the reign of James I it was so widespread as to be practically universal. The assumptions on which it was based—I seem to have been saying—came to be so generally accepted as to be unexamined. There is clearly the possibility of an Eleatic paradox here; the process by which they came to be unexamined may prove very hard to free of any moment at which they were not being examined by someone. Criticism of my position, however, as I shall try to show, goes beyond criticism of a rhetorical device which I might be said to have adopted; it seeks to transform what I said were assumptions into assertions, and essentially contestable assertions at that, made by identifiable actors in identifiable circumstances for identifiable reasons. It seeks, that is, to transform a *mentalité* into a series of 'moves'—a historiographical strategy typical of our times.

In the second place, there is a set of assumptions (found especially in ch. III) which offers to explain the alleged general acceptance of the presumption of immemorial custom by alleging a high degree of insularity in 'the common-law mind'. Jacobean Englishmen, it is claimed, lacked the knowledge which would have obliged them to see the common law as co-existing and interacting with other legal systems, undergoing in a historical dynamic changes incompatible with the presumption of immemorial custom and explicable only as the product of contact with other laws. There are two kinds of 'insularity' envisaged here, which could have existed together but ought to be distinguished and perhaps are not sufficiently distinguished in the chapters under review. Englishmen may have been so thoroughly insular as to know nothing whatever about law outside their part of the island; alternatively, they could have known a good deal about other systems of law and yet maintained the 'insular' conviction that no law but common law had ever obtained in England. I have been so often accused of making the former statement that I have almost come to believe the accusation myself, and it would be vainly attempted to clear myself of the charge of having used language that justifies it; but I think it can be pleaded that ch. III rests on statements of the latter kind. A key figure of that chapter is after all Sir John Davies, who when comparing common law with brehon law in Anglo-Irish history wrote what David Hume recognized as 'philosophical history' in the Scottish Enlightenment's sense,[9] and yet was capable of those statements quoted on pp. 32–4 and 41 as classical expressions of the doctrine of immemorial insular custom. More should have been made (I now think) of the circumstances that Davies wrote to vindicate the use of English law in Irish courts,[10] and dedicated his text to Lord Chancellor Ellesmere, who was no admirer of Coke; but though I selected Davies as an ideal type of 'the common-law mind' rather than an authority in its making, I did so with a view to showing that the same man might write with great sophistication about history shaped by the conflict of laws and, at almost the same moment (1612, 1614), deny that such a conflict had shaped English law or history. My claim cannot be upset by showing that Davies knew Roman civil law;[11] it could be upset by showing that he knew Roman law to have played a

---

[9] See Hume's citation of Davies's *Discoverie* in those chapters of the *History of England* which deal with the condition of Ireland in the seventeenth century; edition of 1762, vol. v, ch. 11, pp. 40–2.

[10] Mr David Baker of Johns Hopkins University draws my attention to the interesting fact that Edmund Spenser, in his *View of the State of Ireland* (1596), wants English common law established in Ireland by conquest and argues that it was similarly established in England by the Normans. Davies, engaged in establishing it after the conquest of Ireland, argues (1614) that in England it is custom and not conquest.

[11] Hans S. Pawlisch, in 'Sir John Davies, the Ancient Constitution, and Civil Law', *Historical Journal*, vol. XXIII, no. 3 (1980), pp. 689–702, showed that Davies knew civil and canon law, and used them in arguing both English and Irish cases. This tells against the argument (if I put it forward) that common lawyers knew no Roman law, not against the argument (which I know I put forward) that nothing they knew about Roman law compelled them to revise what they held about their own. See further Pawlisch, *Sir John Davies and the Conquest of Ireland: A Study in Legal Imperialism* (Cambridge University Press, 1985).

part in the history of English law, and either accepted or repressed that knowledge. This is the point where—with regard to others than Davies—the debate becomes interesting, and it may be that the issue as just stated has been transcended.

The central case against the argument of chs. II and III is that it makes 'the common-law mind' (I shall not readily be persuaded that there was no such thing) more monolithic than it was. This I should not resist, but criticism has not ended there. There has been an objection (to which I do not attach much weight) that the book is whiggish in the formal teleological-progressive sense given the word by Butterfield: i.e., that it traces the development towards a predetermined modernity. I show the critical historiography of 'the feudal law' being intruded upon the presumption of 'the ancient constitution' first by antiquarian writers (Spelman above all) in the 1630's, and then by polemic controversialists (Brady and his associates) in the 1680's; there are sentences in which I describe writers preceding these developments as impeded or inhibited from arriving at a subsequent position. It does not seem, however, that a propensity to write in this way supplies the structure of the argument, which is that belief in 'the ancient constitution' existed because of conditions which were broken down in the ways described; this is the argument about which readers of the book were and are required to make up their minds, and I am reviewing it here. In addition to the contention that the book is 'whiggish' in the sense given above, there have been criticisms, rather more interesting in character, which suggest that it is 'Whiggish' in the sense that it contains positions and attitudes which are those of the 'Whig interpretation' of English history as it was recognized as existing even before Butterfield published *The Englishman and His History* in 1944.[12]

Whig (as distinct from whiggish) history was constitutionalist before it was progressive; and though my book was a study of a constitutionalist myth and its overthrow, the possibility is not

---

[12] H. A. L. Fisher had published a Raleigh Lecture on *The Whig Historians* in 1912 (*Proceedings of the British Academy*, vol. XIV, pp. 297–339).

thereby precluded that the book rests on constitutionalist assumptions. When it says that 'the ancient constitution' rested on an assumption, deeply rooted in 'the common-law mind', that all law was common law and all common law custom, it may seem to be asserting that 'the law' or 'the constitution' did, in some ideal or universally assumed sense, consist in a body of custom, common law or *jus non scriptum* which preceded and underlay statute; that *jurisdictio* preceded *gubernaculum*, that statutes were judgments in the high court of parliament declaratory of existing law, or even that the common law might control and adjudge statutes and find them to be utterly void. As far as I am concerned, the ghost of judicial review was laid by J. W. Gough in 1955,[13] and there may have been exorcisms more effective even than his; but one sometimes hears the doctrine being rebutted still. Professor Elton, I suspect, regards me as a closet McIlwainian to this day, and he would not merely be reiterating his conviction—uncontroversial as far as I am concerned—that statute was a source of law, capable of bringing about radical changes in custom and obliging judges to follow its language to a point where even Coke would not seek to assimilate it to precedent and usage. He would also be repeating his warning against letting the study of law guide the study of history to such an extent that it becomes the latter's purpose to find out what 'the law', or the state of 'the law', was at a given time.[14] This is a trap into which one may fall as a result of representing 'the common-law mind' as monolithic; but could the trap not be avoided if it should turn out to have been monolithic after all? Much research has been done since 1957 on the *mentalité* of Jacobean common lawyers, both as regards their equation of law with custom and as regards the role which other legal systems played in their thinking; and some of this should now be reviewed.

When Davies wrote in his *Irish Reports* that the common law

---

[13] J. W. Gough, *Fundamental Law in English Constitutional History* (Oxford: Clarendon Press, 1955).

[14] See most recently his 'Herbert Butterfield and the Study of History', *Historical Journal*, vol. XXVII, no. 3 (1984), pp. 729–44, esp. 734–5.

of England was 'nothing else but the common custom of the realm', that it could be 'recorded and registered nowhere but in the memory of the people', and that it originated in the use and practice of the people reiterating 'a reasonable act once done... time out of mind', he obviously did not mean that it was the function of practicing lawyers to go out among the 'people', consult grey-bearded village elders as to their customs and report them back to the courts. Davies had in fact done just that in his researches into brehon law in Ireland, where he wrote these words, and knew very well that he had been engaged in destroying Irish customs and converting them into common law. He must have meant something other than a narodnik populism in writing thus of English law, and it is clearly not enough to say that he thought of custom as local and exceptional; the common law is 'the common custom of the realm'. One is obliged to say that he knew the common law to have been shaped in courts, and that his language somehow denotes a process whereby the courts ascertain or determine law and declare it to be common custom. The 'people' present no problem (given the chronic indeterminacy of the word and concept), since they may be thought of as appearing in court, possibly as jurors of witness, and establishing their 'customs' through interaction with the determining justices; even the 'customs' in 'use' among the 'people' may have to be such as the courts will recognize as in use and having 'obtained the force of law'. The question is rather why Davies said that the law established in courts consisted in usages 'recorded and registered nowhere but in the memory of the people', even if he thought that the records and registers of courts were 'the memory of the people'. We cannot, without falling into the trap against which Elton warns us, say that Davies was wrong (or even untypical), and that common law was more correctly (or typically) described in other terms. The point is that he did use this language, and that other jurists in and out of court used it too. What can perhaps be established is that there were alternative ways of speaking about the common law, ways which were variant whether or not they came into conflict. To establish this would be enough to modify the notion of a monolithic 'common-law mind', if not necessarily enough to upset the argument of this book.

The terms *usus* and *consuetudo* are of course ancient in the vocabulary of English law. Ellesmere found them in Bracton, though he was quick to note that they occurred also in Roman law and to conclude that common law agreed with civil in containing the concept of unwritten law rooted in usage.[15] There remained the problem of determining in what community *usus et consuetudo* were said to operate, and what juridical or social processes they were said to presuppose. They might be the *usus et consuetudo* of courts alone, and there was often no need to look further; or they might be the usages and customs of lay or popular communities existing outside the courts and extending on occasion to 'the whole realm'.[16] The probability that 'courts' and 'people' were thought of as interacting and were not carefully distinguished should warn us against dichotomizing, but an important social and philosophical distinction arises here. The royal courts were communities of the learned, hard to imagine as engaged in unreflective or unsophisticated reiteration of a reasonable act since time out of mind until they discovered its reasonableness; the 'people' could and must be thought of as

[15] Louis A. Knafla, *Law and Politics in Jacobean England: The Tracts of Lord Chancellor Ellesmere* (Cambridge University Press, 1977), pp. 217–18.

[16] In a paper read to a colloquium on 'The Ancient Constitution Revisited' at the Folger Institute Center for the History of British Political Thought (March 1985), Professor Knafla drew attention to the multiplicity of communal and corporation courts locally held outside the structure of royal common law. These courts seldom kept written records and their customs were certainly 'recorded and registered nowhere but in the memory of the people'. Their existence helps explain the prevalent definition of custom as local and not general; but can it help explain the counter-definition of common law as 'the common custom of the realm'? If we could suppose that the courts of common law were endeavouring to annex these local courts to themselves, we could also suppose that they would tend to annex the latter's self-definition. We might also imagine how local officers like Gerrard Winstanley—constables, overseers and church-wardens—might come to see the common law as the fruit of the Norman Conquest, and decide that the gentry and royal officers were still implementing the Conquest which the Normans had begun. These are only speculations, but may be worth exploring.

exercising intelligence (if at all) in precisely this unreflective way. The two in conjunction might even form an Aristotelian relation of few and many, except that English courts were emphatically not given to submitting their determinations to the authority of popular custom; in the end, 'custom' was a term of art, employed in courts to legitimate their proceedings.

Once a court was left alone to apply the relatively sophisticated intellect of those 'learned in the law', the hydra reason raised its many heads and 'custom' no longer operated (if it ever had) in unreflective isolation. The *usus et consuetudo* of the courts might be indistinguishable from the 'ley et resoun' of the Year Books, or at a later date from the 'artificial reason' of which James I heard from Coke, and which was obviously more than the experiential reiteration of acts found reasonable. The 'use' of a court might be nothing other than the reason it used, and there might be varying definitions of judicial reason, not necessarily excluding one another and not necessarily entailing custom in the sense in which Davies used the word. We catch sight of occasions on which courts proceeded not by declaring or determining customs, but by establishing maxims; and what a maxim was in common law might be defined in several ways. In Fortescue's *De Laudibus*, it is said to be a self-evident principle from which rules of law can be syllogistically derived,[17] but commonly it is a gnomic and authoritative summation of a train of legal reasoning which has been going on for some time. Such a maxim does not depend on the authority of whoever formulated it, but appeals to reason, precedent, judgment and whatever other antecedents it successfully mobilizes. It need not establish an antecedent body of popular custom in order to become part of the *usus et consuetudo* of a court, but it is essentially a moment in a process; from this point of view, Coke's habit of citing as maxims what it is hard to find so cited before was not altogether as outrageous as might appear. The ongoing reason of the courts contained custom but was not

[17] Sir John Fortescue, *De Laudibus Legum Anglie*, ed. and trans. S. B. Chrimes (Cambridge University Press, 1949), ch. VIII, pp. 20–3.

limited to it; it need not cite custom, but might do so whenever it saw fit.

Once the giving of judgment was held—as there was no time at which it was not—to entail the exercise of reason, there was a route along which it could move at will away from declaration towards determination, away from the giving of law towards the making of it; towards such dicta as the famous 'Do not gloss the statute; we know it better than you do, for we made it.' A judge on his bench, expounding *usus, consuetudo* and *jus non scriptum*, was not in the least precluded from thinking of law as decreed by the king's authority in the king's courts, from discerning the affinity between what he was doing and the sovereign reason by which the king-in-parliament made statutes binding on him and the whole nation, or from moving with ease between what was done in the king's courts of common law and what was done in the king's courts of equity and conscience. Hence the firm conviction of Lord Chancellor Ellesmere—established in the work of Professor Knafla—that the ultimate authority in law was that of statute, that the common law was not the whole of the *lex terrae*, but that the practice of Chancery contained nothing which common lawyers need regard as a threat.[18] Yet customs and statute remained a Janus with two faces; linguistic usage allowed so perfectly of all being called custom which was not statute, or (alternatively) which was not obliged to rely immediately on the authority of reason, and of all being called custom which a court had long chosen to recognize, that any judge—even one thinking just as did Ellesmere—might choose a route the reverse of the one just described, and proceed towards an account of all law as custom rooted in popular usage if he desired, without committing himself to one side or the other in the dispute which was to break out between Coke, Ellesmere and Bacon in 1616.[19] This, combined with the tactics of the moment, is what must account for Davies's dedication to Ellesmere of the language of the *Irish Reports*, which I have cited as displaying the foundations of ancient-constitution thinking. It

[18] Knafla, *Law and Politics*, pp. 164–7.   [19] Knafla, ch. VII.

is not at this point, consequently, that 'the ancient constitution' appears as a doctrine necessarily opposed (as Davies certainly was not) to the royal sovereignty or even prerogative; only in 'Whig historiography'—it could be argued—does it play that role.

Once we see that the step from 'common custom' to 'common (or legal) reason' was a short one, which could be quite casually taken and easily retraced, we see that the making of new law and the changing of old were entirely compatible with the persistence of old law since time immemorial; I believe that this is and was the proper reading of my text of 1957. Thomas Hedley, in a remarkable speech to the House of Commons in 1610, used language which illustrates how men could think in this way. He was wholly clear about the authority of parliament:

> I affirm that the parliament hath power over all arts, sciences, mysteries, and professions, practiced in the commonwealth, and may make laws for reformation of any abuse in the practices therein. . . . And even the law itself presumeth that men that profess not law, by the assistance of lawyers, may judge of matters in law, as judgments in the King's Bench (the highest court of justice) are examinable and reversible by writ of error in parliament, and that in the higher House only, where the judges are but assistants, and have no voices. So judgments in the Exchequer are examinable and reversible before the chancellor and lord treasurer, calling unto them certain of the judges, and they to be only assistants unto them. For as the rules and maxims of all arts are agreeable to reason, and grounded thereupon, so especially is that of the common law.[20]

After developing this argument so as to reach Fortescue's position that all legal reason was deducible 'from the original or radical rule or maxim of law',[21] Hedley continued:

> But then you will say, the parliament, which is nothing else in effect but the mutual consent of the king and people, is that which gives

[20] Hedley's speech is given in Elizabeth Reed Foster (ed.), *Proceedings in Parliament 1610:* vol. 2, *House of Commons* (New Haven: Yale University Press, 1966), p. 172.   [21] *Ibid.*

matter and form and all complements to the common law. No, nor that neither, for the parliament hath his power and authority from the common law, and not the common law from the parliament. And therefore the common law is of more force and strength than the parliament, *quod efficit tale maius est tale....* The parliament may find some defects in the common law and amend them (for what is perfect under the sun) yet the wisest parliament that ever was could never have made such an excellent law as the common law is. But that the parliament may abrogate the whole law, I deny, for that were includedly to take away the power of the parliament itself, which power it hath by the common law. And no parliament can take away the power of any one succeeding parliament or make a law for certain years, which may not be revoked by parliament within those years, much less can it take away the power of it forever.[22]

This is not a doctrine of judicial review. No court, custom or maxim sets limits to the power of parliament to alter the common law by statute; parliament itself may not limit the power of parliament to do so. All that Hedley was saying was that parliament and statute were part of and inseparable from the ongoing reason of the common law, 'which is the life and soul of the politic body of the commonwealth',[23] and could not annihilate the law without annihilating parliament and commonwealth themselves. It was a doctrine of consubstantiality, like denying that God the Father could annihilate God the Son. We see why every exaltation of the antiquity of law was an exaltation of the authority of parliament. This common law, furthermore, was the union of reason and custom, which no man such as Hedley would think of as opposed; ancient usage gave the law its antiquity and thus much of its authority, yet usage would have no meaning without the constant workings of reason in courts and parliament. Hedley proceeded to tell how

I entered into consideration with myself what that was that could try reason better than the parliament. I found it could not be the judges of the law, for they are all joined to the parliament and there is besides the whole wisdom of the whole realm, the king, his nobilities, clergy and

---

[22] Pp. 173–4.   [23] p. 174.

commons, and yet the wisdom of all these united cannot be so true triers as that which we must find to be the essential form of the common law; that then that can only try reason, and is the essential form of the common law, in a word, is time, which is the trier of truth, author of all human wisdom, learning and knowledge, and from which all human laws receive their chiefest strength, honor, and estimation. Time is wiser than the judges, wiser than the parliament, nay wiser than the wit of man. We see when the parliament hath long debated a bill or act and at last concluded to pass it, yet to have continuance but for some certain time, hereby to see and try by the wisdom of time and experience whether it be good and profitable for the commonwealth or no. But this time must not be such as statute laws are tried by, for 7 years or till the next parliament, but such time whereof the memory of man is not to the contrary, time out of mind, such time as will beget a custom.[24]

The time which begets a custom is also the time which begets common law. It is other than the time which tries a statute, but Hedley's language is not altogether clear about the difference between them. Formerly 'time out of mind' or 'beyond memory' had been a term of art, to which courts and parliaments had been quite willing to assign a term of years; it was in process of being enlarged into a *spatium historicum*, and Hedley was not perfectly in control of this process. The term 'custom' was also undergoing enlargement. We see it being magnified into 'time and experience', 'time and reason', in which usage is transformed by the reason of courts and parliaments; the root of the concept is not lost and gives 'time' much of its meaning, but an older and more limited significance of 'custom' is being isolated and left behind.

Having now found the matter and form of the common law, namely reason and time. . . which for antiquity is not unlike Melchisedek, so old that no man knew his father, and the final being obvious as all men know, *salus populi suprema lex*, I will now define it thus: the common law is a reasonable usage, throughout the whole realm, approved time out of mind in the king's courts of record which have jurisdiction over the

[24] p. 175.

whole kingdom, to be good and profitable for the commonwealth. But here because I make custom a part in my definition of the common law, I would not be mistaken, as though I meant to confound the common law with custom, which differ as much as artificial reason and bare precedents. Customs are confined to certain and particular places, triable by the country, but their reasonableness or unreasonableness by the judges, to be taken strictly according to the letter and precedent, and therefore admits small discourse of art or wit; whereas the common law is extended by equity, that whatsoever falleth under the same reason will be found the same law.[25] And it hath not custom for his next or immediate cause, but many other secondary reasons which be necessary consequence upon other rules and cases in law, which yet may be so deduced by degrees till it come to some primitive maxim, depending immediately upon some prescription or custom,[26] in which secondary reasons and consequence appear as much art or learning, wisdom and excellency of reason as in any law, art or profession whatever.[27]

We must either separate usage and custom (*usus et consuetudo*) altogether and declare that they bore radically different meanings; or (which seems more reasonable) we must acknowledge that the latter term could either be read as having a local and particular significance or be enlarged and enter into the former. When we transfer our focus from the 'people' postulated by Davies to the 'courts and parliament' emphasized by Hedley, we see 'custom' in a simple form being constantly worked on, generalized and transformed by reason in the legal sense, and the apparent polarity of 'custom' and 'statute' is seen never to have been there. We may also examine Richard Tuck's assertion that

ideas...according to which...the laws operating in human societies were to be construed in terms of developing social utility [were] not the revolutionary development that Pocock thought [them] to be in *The Ancient Constitution and the Feudal Law*: a number of practising English lawyers in the period (such as Lord Ellesmere) were perfectly capable of

[25] This pithily informs us why Coke was unlikely to win his struggle against Chancery some years later.

[26] This clause seems to betray confusion or circular argument, but the confusion (if it is one) is itself significant.

[27] *Proceedings*, vol. 2, pp. 175–6.

contemplating historical change in the English law, and in a way the real puzzle is why men like Edward Coke did not do so.[28]

Tuck—who ascribes this capability to an early reception by English lawyers of the French legal humanist ideas of 'men like Alciato and Connan'—quotes Ellesmere as saying:

> Some lawes, as well statute lawe as common law, are obsolete and worne out of use: for all humane lawes are but *leges temporis*; and the wisedome of the iudjes found them to bee unmeete for the time wherein they were made.[29]

But there is nothing in this dictum to which Hedley would have objected, and it was after all Coke who proclaimed that

> the laws have been by the wisdom of the most excellent men, in many successions of ages, by long and continual experience, (the trial of light and truth) fined and refined.

I submit it is not a proper reading of *The Ancient Constitution and the Feudal Law* that Coke held the whole body of English law to be immemorial, static and unchanging. His notion of custom (and usage) was more flexible than that. Certainly he could regard the survival of an ancient custom as proof that having survived the test of usage it had given evidence of its modernity, and no doubt he could be criticized for arguing that this had happened when in fact the custom had undergone change (though this is not the gravamen of Ellesmere's observations on his *Reports*).[30] But I stressed incessantly that the notion of custom was ambiguous in that it implied both preservation and adaptation, and the central ambiguity I now find in my own language occurs on p. 36, where I state that 'the common lawyers, holding that law was custom, came to believe that the common law, and with it the constitution, had always been

---

[28] Richard Tuck, *Natural Rights Theories: Their Origin and Development* (Cambridge University Press, 1979), p. 83.

[29] Tuck cites this from *A Complete Collection of State Trials*, ed. T. B. Howell (London, 1809), vol. II, p. 674.

[30] Knafla, *op. cit.*, pp. 297–318.

exactly what they were now, that they were immemorial.'

It will be found that I stated this as a 'paradox', meaning that the notion of custom, which could imply adaptation, was employed to imply preservation; and there are many cases where this was precisely what occurred. Yet my intention seems to me now (and has long seemed) to have been to state less that the whole body of the law was held to be immemorial than that any element in it could be held immemorial at will; and if there is confusion, it can be resolved by taking up and developing, from the sentence just quoted, the words 'and with it the constitution'. These offer us the opportunity of saying that it was less (though it always could be) the content of the law than the juridical process itself—usage, judgment and statute—that was immemorial; that the reform of obsolete laws and the making of new ones were perfectly compatible with the view that common law rested in ancient usage; and that (as against Tuck) the notion of refinement and reform was inherent in common-law ways of thinking and could be derived from Fortescue no less effectively than from Alciato (if an English reception of Alciato occurred earlier than I suggested, this would indeed not have been a 'revolutionary development'). This is the thrust of ch. VII, part III, which deals with Sir Matthew Hale (and of which Tuck is also critical, for reasons which I will consider later). I have never quite understood (though the reader must be judge) why I have been taken as saying there that Coke thought the law had always been the same, Hale that it had always been in adaptation.[31] Though I state (p. 174) that Hale proceeded 'in a reverse direction from that taken by Coke', I would now (and I think I did then)[32] read the statement in the context of my argument that 'the common-law mind' was Janus-faced, could always proceed in either of two directions, and could look in both at

[31] The comparison between them I would endorse has been excellently stated by Charles M. Gray in the introduction to his edition of Hale's *History of the Common Law of England* (Chicago University Press, 1971, pp. XXI–XXVII).

[32] The historian engaged on a retrospect of his own work is perpetually tempted to join in Edward Lear's Pelican Chorus: 'We think so then and we thought so still'; a statement in itself redolent of 'the common-law mind'.

once without distraction or contradiction. The 'revolutionary development' I had in mind was not, as Tuck thinks, the perception that law underwent change and adaptation; it was the growth of critical and archaeological tools whereby its past states could be reconstituted and shown to have been discontinuous with its present.

I have now indicated a strategy, involving a partial shift of emphasis from Davies's 'common custom of the realm' to Hedley's 'time and reason', which enables us to see custom and reason, judgment and statute, as existing in a Fortescuean symbiosis and the appeal to time immemorial not indeed as rigidly and uniformly compulsive, but so perpetually available to the point where its employment, when properly triggered, would be instinctive and practically unavoidable. This improves on my earlier account of 'the common-law mind' but does not seem to replace it. However, I have not yet cleared myself of an Eltonian charge, of a kind mentioned earlier, that might possibly be brought against me: the charge of allowing the state of the law, or of legal interpretation, at a given time, to dominate the account being offered of either English politics, or English political self-understanding, at that time. Obviously I was, and am, not arguing that 'the law was' thus or thus at the time being examined. I am arguing (a) that English political discourse was for a long time conducted largely by minds trained in the common law; (b) that such minds were for a long time trained to proceed from certain assumptions, and follow certain patterns of argument, conducive to belief in 'an ancient constitution'. The salutary Eltonian warning now becomes, in my case, a warning against exaggerating the stability and duration of the institutions and mental habits which constituted 'the common-law mind'. At the end of the period with which I deal, minds as sophisticated (but still not modern) as that of Edmund Burke are to be found contending that even if the constitution is not immemorial, the habit of treating it as if it was is very ancient indeed;[33] to treat 'the common-law mind' as proceeding from

[33] See my 'Burke and the Ancient Constitution', in *Politics, Language and Time*, pp. 206–7.

fixed and unchanging assumptions might lead in a similar direction.

The question is how far the assumptions I sought to isolate were institutionalized and ingrained in minds by the training they had received; alternatively, how far they were assertions, more or less successfully propounded by actors whose moves and utterances can be identified and assigned to momentary contexts which explain them.[34] How far was belief in an ancient constitution a matter of *durée*, how far of *evènement et conjoncture*?

It will be found at pp. 31–2 that I leant strongly towards the former, but that at the same time I did not want to extend the *durée* further back than the middle of the sixteenth century and was fairly explicit about leaving room for the explanation that the Cokean *mentalité* was the product of forces not older than Coke himself. This was in some measure a precautionary move, and I continued to write of the foundations of common-law thinking as lying in medieval practice; but I was aware of Coke as a product of his age and his own eight decades of life, and the figure sketched on p. 31 of 'a common lawyer who was a mature man at the time of Coke's birth [and] would not have thought quite as Coke was to do half a century later' has since taken on flesh and bone in J. A. Guy's studies of Thomas More and Christopher St German.[35] Perhaps the evident importance of Fortescue to Hedley in 1610 and other parliamentary speakers in 1628 can be explained by saying that Jacobean common lawyers had to go back to the *De Laudibus* in search of the kind of authority they needed. A history of 'the common-law mind' (if there was one) from Fortescue to Coke would be a valuable possession;[36] but there are historians of deserved authority who would not wish to accept that belief in the ancient constitution

[34] An intermediate possibility is that medieval concepts of custom underwent further sophistication after contact with humanist and neo-Bartolist ideas. The subject awaits investigation.

[35] J. A. Guy, *The Public Career of Sir Thomas More* (New Haven: Yale University Press, 1980); *Christopher St German on Chancery and Statute* (London: Selden Society, suppl. series, 6, 1985).

[36] Dr Christopher Brooks is at work on one such, not primarily concerned with attitudes towards history.

took shape as the result of processes accruing over the second half of the sixteenth century and the first quarter of the seventeenth. Such an explanation would smack of the currently unacceptable belief that parliament and the House of Commons became steadily more autonomous and assertive over the whole of that tract of time. It is not my concern to argue against wind and tide that this happened after all, but it does seem worth pointing out that the anti-whig reaction in historiography has now reached a point where all processes are to be dissolved into moments and all long-term explanations dismissed in favour of short-term ones. The ideological implications are fairly clear: all history is to be reduced to high politics, to the actions of those close enough to power to disregard change, unless they are its authors, and act only in the short run. There is much to be said for such a view; actors in history are usually motivated by short-term considerations, and English political history has been a pretty oligarchic affair. It remains a question, however, whether short-term actions are not sometimes undertaken in contexts stabilised by structures having a longer *durée* behind them, and whether changes in such structures are not sometimes slow and continuous enough to merit the name of 'processes'. All that has been inveighed against, since Butterfield, as 'whig history' is simply a mistaken way of identifying the processes.

We seek to escape the dilemma of chicken and egg by viewing the act as performed in context, as both modified by and modifying the context in which it is performed; nothing new, of course, in that. The kind of anti-whig excess which I am addressing is typified by the tendency one now hears voiced—which Richard Tuck's words quoted above hint at though they do not illustrate—to treat Sir Edward Coke as an eccentric, a maverick lawyer in opposition to his colleagues and their thinking, and obtaining authority as the 'oracle of the law' only when his works were posthumously published in full by order of the Long Parliament. This will never do; Coke is too tough a baby to be thrown out with the Whig bath-water; yet it is salutary to be reminded that his brother judges by no means always agreed with him, and that in that part of his life which we most associate with Magna Carta and the ancient constitution he was no longer sitting on the bench *cum fratribus* but had been dismissed from office to display great activity on the benches of the House of Commons.[37] If 'the ancient constitution' is a product of 'the common-law mind', we do not mean by the latter simply that which was articulated by the judges roaring in chorus as lions under the throne, or even enjoyed their approval and authority in that capacity. We may mean something which Sir Edward Coke succeeded in communicating to those members of the Commons who could hear him speak. But this does not reduce it to triviality. Thomas Hedley reminds us that it was sound doctrine that men not learned in the law might judge of matters of law in parliament, and it is usual to suppose that gentlemen as well as 'men of the long robe' who sat in the Commons knew some common law and were used to thinking in its terms. 'The common-law mind' was not confined to the profession of judges and serjeants; it can also be thought of as taking shape along the lines of communication linking the Inns of Court, the county communities and the houses of parliament, as a creation of utter barristers and utter amateurs led by Sir Edward Coke, a judge in exile from his bench. In *The Ancient Constitution and the Feudal Law* I was at pains to emphasize that we were dealing with an ideology as well as a practice.

But I argued that the ideology was also a *mentalité*, rooted in habits of mind bred by education and practice. It is the thesis of a common-law *mentalité* which appears to me to have been challenged by the most interesting criticisms to which my book has been subjected; and I think it can be maintained that, intentionally or not, these criticisms also conform to the pattern of an anti-whig revisionism that has been pushed to considerable lengths. Parliaments were occasional and individual gatherings; consequently, if one were to develop the thesis that the doctrine of an ancient constitution took shape largely through acts and arguments performed by Coke and others in parliament, one

---

[37] The most recent study of his parliamentary role is Stephen D. White, *Sir Edward Coke and the Grievances of the Commonwealth, 1621–28* (Chapel Hill: University of North Carolina Press, 1979).

could see these acts as 'moves' carried out in special circumstances and for tactical reasons. One could thus avoid both the macro-whiggism of presenting 'the common-law mind' as itself immemorial and (if so desired) the micro-whiggism of present-ing parliament or commons as 'winning the initiative' and pressing towards greater power throughout the reigns of Elizabeth I and James I, while maintaining the hypothesis of a common-law *mentalité*, founded in insularity and the cult of custom (or time and reason), which made it possible to articulate such 'moves' and get them widely accepted. But if the notion of a *mentalité* were itself overthrown and there were no ideological matrix within which these acts could have been performed, nothing would be left but a series of moves of the most occasional character. This is the problem raised, though not invariably intended, by the criticisms directed against the more monolithic features of my account of common-law insularity and ancient-constitutionalism.

THE 'ANCIENT CONSTITUTION' AND THE STRATEGIES OF DEBATE

It will be remembered that my hypothetical common lawyer of 1552 'would have been far more aware of the civil law as a part of the English fabric';[38] I left unanswered the question how his successors might have lost this awareness. In *Past and Present* during 1974 and 1976, there occurred a debate beween Donald R. Kelley, Christopher Brooks and Kevin Sharpe,[39] which illustrates this problem. Kelley, whose work has lain among the *mos gallicus* and *mos italicus* of French legal humanism,[40] endorsed my thesis that common-law thinking was so highly insular that nothing but the philological researches of Sir Henry Spelman sufficed to upset it, and my explanation that the causes of this

[38] See p. 31, above.

[39] Donald R. Kelley, 'History, English Law and the Renaissance', *Past and Present*, vol. LXV (November 1974), pp. 24–1; Christopher Brooks and Kevin Sharpe, 'History, English Law and the Renaissance'; Donald R. Kelley, 'A Rejoinder', *Past and Present*, vol. LXXII (August 1976), pp. 133–42, 143–6.

[40] See n. 4 to this chapter.

insularity lay in an English refusal to admit that the civil law had anything to do with the history of law in England. It is worth reiterating that neither Kelley nor I contended that common lawyers knew no civil law—he indeed gave far more wealth of detail about the civil law in England than I had[41]—but that they were not obliged to compare the two in such a way as to duplicate the French realization that civil and customary law had been agencies in one another's history. In their jointly written reply, Brooks and Sharpe contended that there were many Elizabethan common lawyers anxious to apply systematic reason to the reform of the common law; that some of these were sympathetic, and none hostile, to what they knew of the *mos italicus* through the teachings of Alberico Gentili;[42] that the members (and after its dissolution the former members) of the Society of Antiquaries were developing a conception of a Norman importation of feudal tenures not less clearly than Spelman (who was of their number); and that willingness to admit this view of the Conquest died away only because of the political conflicts of the 1620's, in which Coke took a leading part.

It will be seen from p. 96 of this book that I did not assert, but on the contrary denied, that Spelman played a role isolated from the other members of the Society of Antiquaries; I gave reasons there for deciding to focus attention on him. I was inclined to think that the Society's growing interest in feudal tenures could have come about only through correspondence with Peiresc and other French philologists of *mos gallicus* antecedents, and Brooks and Sharpe do not seem to me to have fully substantiated their hint that a generalized knowledge of civil law gained through Gentili is enough to account for it. The real interest of their essay lies elsewhere. Though I have not claimed that common lawyers

[41] See further B. P. Levack, *The Civil Lawyers in England, 1603–1641: A Political Study* (Oxford: Clarendon Press, 1973).

[42] See also Diego Panizza, *Alberico Gentili, Giurista Ideologo nell' Inghilterra Elisabettiana* (Padua, 1981). Panizza argues that the longer Gentili lived in England, the more he drew away from the strictly neo-Bartolist position and adopted positions derived from legal humanism of a French pattern.

knew no civil law—my central claim has always been that '*as a key to their past* the English knew of one law alone'[43]—the more one insists that they knew a good deal but rejected its significance for their own law, the less 'the common-law mind' resembles a self-explanatory closed ideology. We examine instead a series of reasons, whether ideological or accidental, for their not seeing, or refusing to see, its significance, and *mentalité* gives place to contingency as the object of our study. For this reason, the suggestion put forward by Brooks and Sharpe, that denial of the Conquest was not a reflex rooted in tradition but an assertion put forward in the tactical circumstances of the 1620's, exerts a claim on our attention.

Research and publication has occurred which enables us to meet that claim in several ways: by re-examining the theory of conquest, by scrutinizing the role of John Selden, and by examining the all-important parliamentary debates surrounding the Petition of Right (recognized since study of the 'ancient constitution' began as a cornerstone of the doctrine). In an article published in 1965,[44] Quentin Skinner contended that there was far more awareness, and willingness to admit, that the Normans had conquered England than I had allowed for. Because his argument was already thrusting towards the interpretation of Hobbes, he tended to conflate the use of conquest theory after 1649 with its use before the civil wars; I shall try to show in this and the next chapter why the two uses need to be distinguished.

---

[43] P. 30. Italics added in this quotation. It may be justifiable to add the following, for which I am grateful to Mr Neil Kamil of Johns Hopkins University. The writer is a merchant of La Rochelle interested in legal studies, and the year is 1593, when Alberico Gentili was already Regius Professor of Civil Law at Oxford: 'Apres i avoir demeuré quinze jours (i.e. in London), je m'en allay à Oxford tres celebre et fort ancienne université, ou on list en toutes sciences, excepté en droit, d'autant qu'on ne s'i gouverne pas le droit escrit ains seulement par coustumes et ordonnances des roys. A raison de quoy, voyant que je m'en revins à Londres, ou par conseil de Monsieur de la Fontaine (a Rochelais minister) et de quelques autres gens d'honneur je m'embarquay pour venir à Leiden en Hollande', where he remained from 1593 to 1597 (Leopold Chatenay, *Vie de Jacques Esprinchard Rochelais et Journal de ses voyages au xviᵉ siècle*, Paris: S.E.V.P.E.N., 1957, p. 86).

[44] Quentin Skinner, 'History and Ideology in the English Revolution', *Historical Journal*, vol. VIII, no. 2 (1965), pp. 151–78.

He did not produce many writers before 1640 who had argued from the fact of a Norman conquest to the present absolute prerogative of a king of England, which was what I had contended was nearly unknown; but he did pose an awkward question for my interpretation in asking how this argument was refuted or dismissed. If there had been no conquest and William I had acquired the throne by ancient English law, no problem arose; but if he had conquered the land, the question of how the English laws had been re-affirmed was even more difficult than the question whether they had been. Conquest was a term known to the *jus gentium*, which was an outgrowth of the natural and civil law; the processes by which conqueror and conquered might capitulate or contract for restoration of the laws preceding conquest belonged to the *jus gentium* no less unequivocally. A conquest in 1066 would therefore have intruded upon the insular laws of the English not merely the brute power of the sword, or the alien realities of feudal tenures, but the inescapable authority of *jus gentium*, a form of law either Roman or natural but not English. Here was a better reason than I had known of why so many English writers might have denied that such a conquest had ever taken place; but there was the added circumstance that more of them than I had recognized were prepared to acknowledge that, under *jus gentium*, it had. How, if at all, had they reconciled this admission with the claim that the common law guaranteed and explained its own immemorial antiquity?

In 1610 as in 1628, it is evident that those who used this argument relied heavily on the text of Fortescue's *De Laudibus Legum Anglie*, perhaps because Fortescue, instead of distributing the royal authority among several jurisdictions, had distinguished between a law of England, consisting of reason, custom and statute, and a royal authority exercised *regaliter tantum* where it was not conjoined with that law. But in that text the lawyers encountered the spectre who was to haunt their dreams for a very long time: the spectre of the conqueror, Nimrod or Nembroth as Fortescue named him,[45] who won power by the

---

[45] Sir John Fortescue, *De Laudibus Legum Anglie*, ed. S. B. Chrimes (Cambridge, 1949), ch. XII, pp. 28, 29.

naked sword and used it to constitute a kingdom in which the enforcement and interpretation of the law of nature belonged to him alone. Nimrod is a figure of primeval nature rather than civil history; as builder of the Tower of Babel, he is older than the *jus gentium* which grew up following its fall, and no civil law—not even the law martial—can be traced directly to him. Yet, as a figure of *lex naturae*, he survives in both gentile and covenantal history; conquerors may from time to time appear whose power is of the sword and not of the law, and Fortescue's dualist theory of kingship might mean that outside the *leges Anglie*, a king could claim to rule England only by Nimrodic authority.

It could thus become a disturbing implication that insofar as any king—and a king of England was no exception—was not bound to observe the forms of law, he enjoyed such an authority and could claim to have acquired it by conquest. This assertion need not be made good by demonstrations drawn from secular history. James VI of Scotland and I of England, to whom it was axiomatic that a king derived his power immediately from God, did not attach much importance to the processes of secondary causation by which he might have acquired it, but had no objection to considering conquest as a normal and typical method of acquisition. It was not unthinkable that he might have had to overcome armed opponents on his way south in 1603. As king of England, however, he declared that a king was bound, not only to observe any compact which he might have made with his people to leave them in possession of their laws, but even to enter into such a compact as a thing good in itself, following the promise which God had made to Noah in exhibiting the rainbow to him.[46] For all this, the dichotomy was clear: a king who did not rule by compact ruled by conquest; a

---

[46] James I, *The Political Works of James I* (ed. C. H. McIlwain) (Cambridge, Mass.: Harvard University Press, 1918), p. 309, cited in Paul Christianson, 'Young John Selden and the Ancient Constitution, ca. 1610–18', *Proceedings of the American Philosophical Society*, vol. CXXVIII, no. 4 (1984), pp. 271–315, at 274 and n. 18. I am much indebted to Professor Christianson's essay for this part of my argument.

king ruling *politice et regaliter* ruled by both compact and conquest, and so might claim to rule as Nimrodic conqueror where he did not rule *politice*. This was one of the insoluble conceptual problems which frustrated James's attempt to bring about the legal union of his kingdoms. If there was to be a kingdom of Great Britain, which he should rule neither by the law of England nor by the law of Scotland, he could rule it only as a conqueror; and the absorption of either kingdom into the new one must be not only a conquest but a wrongful conquest, since it would entail a breach of the compact by which the king was bound to observe the ancient English, or Scottish, law.[47] The merger by codification of the two legal systems might indeed create a new 'law of Great Britain' which the king might compact to observe, but the compact would lack the authority of antiquity, since neither the people nor the law of 'Great Britain' had enjoyed any antecedent existence. Britain therefore remained uncreated as any kind of corporate entity, until 1707 if then, and the laws of England and Scotland are distinct at this day. As Machiavelli had observed, nothing was more difficult than innovation; if ancient customs existed, they were almost impossible to change; if they did not, they were almost impossible to create. The problem of conquest was part of the problem of the 'Machiavellian moment'; the 'Nimrodic moment' envisaged by both scripture and *jus gentium* was, as Machiavelli had indicated, almost impossible to define in terms of secular time.[48]

[47] See Brian P. Levack, 'English Law, Scots Law and the Union, 1603–1707', in Alan Harding (ed.), *Law-Making and Law-Makers in British History* (London: Royal Historical Society, 1980), pp. 105–19, and 'Towards a More Perfect Union: England, Scotland, and the Constitution', in Barbara C. Malament (ed.), *After the Reformation: Essays in Honor of J. H. Hexter* (Philadelphia: University of Pennsylvania Press, 1980), pp. 57–74. A full-length study of the Union debates in and after 1603 would be an invaluable contribution to the 'unknown subject' of British history; it is hoped that Professor Levack will complete one. See also Arthur H. Williamson, *Scottish National Consciousness in the Age of James VI* (Edinburgh: John Donald, 1979).

[48] Nimrod, unmentioned by Machiavelli, would have to be classed with 'Moses, Cyrus, Romulus, Theseus and their like' in ch. VI of *Il Principe*: the founders of states who owe nothing to *fortuna* and can impose any form they think good on

John Selden was aware that both Machiavelli and the civilians had warned against the unwisdom of attempting to make new laws for newly conquered peoples,[49] and his writings designed to deal with this problem appear to be datable from as early as 1610. It has always been necessary to admit[50] that Selden's absence is a significant weakness in the structure of this book, and to re-introduce him to it must be to encounter problems. As an internationally recognized expert on natural law, *jus gentium*, common law and Talmudic law, he clearly will not do as a representative of blinkered English insularity, and the breadth of his learning has to this day denied him a thorough intellectual biography.[51] We know that from about 1610 he was studying the introduction of feudal tenures into England by the Normans, and Richard Tuck has felt able in consequence to relegate Spelman to the status of Selden's 'methodical but less inspired senior'.[52] The relation between the two men was by no means as simple as that. But when we find such an intellect as Selden's asserting in 1628 the supremacy of common law over all other forms of law in England, it is evident that the massive simplifications we attribute to Coke can be neither the full explanation nor the full content of what he was saying. The relation between the two men calls for investigation, and we may even have to ask whether Coke's mind has been over-massively interpreted.

If we follow Paul Christianson in tracing Selden's writings on the problem of ancient law and conquest from their beginnings in *Jani Anglorum Facies Altera* (1610), we need ascribe to their author no constitutionalist or parliamentarian intention beyond that of keeping the Fortescuean image of bi-fronted kingship

the unshaped matter of their subjects. For the near-impossibility of such situations see Pocock, *The Machiavellian Moment: Florentine Political Thought and the Atlantic Republican Tradition* (Princeton University Press, 1975), pp. 167–72.

[49] Christianson, p. 280 and n. 57, draws attention to Selden's allusions to Machiavelli.

[50] P. VII.

[51] The late David S. Berkowitz left his massive study of Selden uncompleted at his death; but Paul Christianson's essay may lead to a full-length monograph.

[52] Tuck, *op. cit.*, p. 83.

alive in the changing intellectual circumstances of the times. This is all that is necessary in order to understand a very important move which Selden can be seen making: one whose character has perhaps been obscured by the emphasis which my work, among that of others, has laid upon the problems of the Norman Conquest. The primeval conqueror was Nimrod; but to make William the Norman bastard, not Nimrod the grandson of Ham, the central figure in the discussion was to remove the problem of conquest from the context of sacred and patriarchal history to that of secular and legal, minimizing its implications and bringing it under the control of custom and convenience, by a strategy essentially the same as Selden was to carry out in the *Historie of Tithes* in 1618.[53] Nimrod, looming titanically at the dawn of politics, might display power unfettered by custom—in Machiavellian terms, *virtù* uncommitted to *fortuna*; but William, coming with his sword late in the history of nations, occurred in a context of known laws and customs and was to that extent more of a *principe nuovo* and less of an *ordinatore*. England was not inert matter on which he could impose form. To declare—as Selden was at times not unwilling to do—that William had carried out a conquest over the laws of England[54] was to declare by implication that there had been known and ancient laws preceding his conquest; it was rather compatible than otherwise with the claim—to which Selden subsequently moved[55]—that at a date later than the conquest he or his successors bound themselves by compact to observe the laws over which he had reigned as a conqueror. Fortescue's kingdom *regale et politicum* was a Janus, and this must be part of the meaning of Selden's emblematic title; its two faces were conquest and compact, and William both had and had not ruled by conquest. To go on—as soon began to be done, even by Selden—to the claim that he had never been a conqueror, or possessed the authority to enter into a compact, was to go beyond Fortescue altogether, whether or not this was done with the intention of lending him added

[53] Christianson, pp. 299–305.
[54] *Ibid.*, pp. 279–80, 285, 289.
[55] *Ibid.*, pp. 80, 285–6, 297–8, 306–7.

emphasis. Conquest on the field of Senlac was a less formidable matter than conquest on the plain of Shinar.

It is a strategy typically Seldenian to reduce law to matter of local particularity, and by seeming to place it in subjection to contingency to leave it in the end under the authority of custom, statute and local sovereignty. By focussing attention on the question of '1066 and all that', he had rendered the existence of the Fortescuean kingdom in England a matter of English history rather than of *jus gentium* and the same strategy is paradoxically evident when we find him conceding—in the light of whatever may have been his sources in contemporary legal erudition—that William I had introduced feudal tenures into England,[56] and thereby brought about some profound changes in the law. For Selden was preparing himself to argue that these changes could have been brought about only by the authority of custom and statute, of the resources which the English possessed to recognize and make their own law; and at the moment when the sword of the conqueror, by which perhaps feudal tenures had been introduced, encountered and compacted with the gradual authority of custom or the legislative authority of primitive parliaments, it became the sword of a monarch ruling *regaliter et politice*. Selden further strengthened this mode of argument by advancing early in his writings the thesis that the tenures introduced by the Normans were not much unlike those already in use among the English. The status of a knight was only a more rigorous elaboration of that of a thegn, and the history of feudal tenures could be traced back to the first interactions of Roman and Germanic peoples.[57] Here, as over the question of tithes, Selden's arguments were to confront directly those of Sir Henry Spelman, for whom Norman tenures were so sharply discontinuous with any hitherto found in England that their introduction must not only be an act of conquest, but must subvert and profoundly change the institutions of court and parliament, custom and statute, by which in Selden's sophisticated reconstruction of the Fortescuean model, they were

---

[56] *Ibid.*, pp. 279, 280. [57] *Ibid.*, pp. 293–5.

recognized and accepted in England. A conqueror did not merely compact with subjects the conditions of whose existence he had violently and radically changed.

But the debate between Selden and Spelman was slow to develop, and although Selden's brand of ancient-constitutionalism is as important as Coke's in the parliaments of the 1620's we are not to look there for any confrontation between 'the ancient constitution' and 'the feudal law'. There is confrontation between the antiquity of the law and the possibility of conquest, but the advocates of the former do not negate the introduction of feudal tenures and their adversaries do not affirm it. Conquest is debated in the context provided by *jus gentium* and the Fortescuean model, but this does not entail consideration of William I's possible role in introducing either new laws or feudal tenures. Selden himself is extremely active but is not called upon to display or defend his views on feudal history; these in no way become relevant to the debate. Because the problem of ancient law and the problem of conquest are not linked to one another by the problem of feudal tenures, they are even more loosely linked than I recognized in 1957. Since they remain important, however, it is valuable to study their role in the debates attending the Petition of Right in 1628.[58]

It is noteworthy that when the House of Commons chose a delegation to present the Petition of Right to the Lords, the contention—so often associated with Coke—that the Petition confirmed Magna Carta, and Magna Carta the laws of Henry I and Edward the Confessor, was entrusted to Sir Dudley Digges.[59] Littleton and Selden were commanded to show that the Petition was grounded in common law and precedent—a task which the latter performed at mind-destroying length[60]—while Sir Edward Coke, by express command of the House, was to show that it was in accord with the reason of the law, and

---

[58] Now available as *Commons Debates 1628*, edited by Mary Frear Keeler, Maija Jansson Cole and William B. Bidwell for the Yale Center for Parliamentary History (New Haven: Yale University Press, 4 vols., 1977–8).

[59] *Commons Debates 1628*, vol. II, pp. 332–4.

[60] *Ibid.*, pp. 342–56.

did so by citing a series of fourteen maxims.[61] Once again, the antiquity of custom is seen as a cornerstone, but not the sole foundation, of 'the common-law mind'. Selden's mind, more-over, was more than the factory of precedents which it showed itself to be on this occasion.

Drawing upon the writings of Richard Tuck, Conrad Russell, Kevin Sharpe, and other scholars whose work has appeared since 1957,[62] we may construct an interpretation of the arguments used in 1628, and of Selden's role in them, somewhat along the following lines. During the lifetime of Sir Edward Coke, lawyers in the service of the crown—judges, chancellors, solicitors, serjeants—found nothing repugnant in arguing that the common law was one of several jurisdictions by which the king governed his realm. Others were equity, ecclesiastical law, 'the law martial' (sometimes spelt 'marshall'[63]), the civil law where it was exercised, and possibly others. In an ill hour for himself, Sir Robert Ashley, a king's serjeant in 1628, mentioned a 'law of state' and was rebuked by the Lords because they had not heard of it before.[64] This episode, late in the story, illustrates the point that it was not usual for the law's great officers to think of common law as threatened by, or even in competition with, other modes of jurisdiction; Ashley was set down for threatening their symbiosis by innovation. The royal prerogative might be thought of as a necessary power unrestrained by the ordinary course of law, or as the king's right to move freely among his various jurisdictions; the two meanings were linked, in much of the discourse that went on, by the recognition that the common law was of all laws the most

---

[61] *Ibid.*, pp. 324, 356–8.

[62] Conrad Russell, *Parliaments and English Politics, 1621–1629* (Oxford: Clarendon Press, 1977); Russell, (ed.), *The Origins of the Civil War* (New York: Barnes and Noble, 1974); Kevin Sharpe, *Sir Robert Cotton, 1586–1631* (New York: Oxford University Press, 1979); Sharpe (ed.), *Faction and Parliament: Essays on Early Stuart History* (New York: Oxford University Press, 1978).

[63] It is so spelt by Francis Bacon or his amanuensis in a manuscript 'The Charge Against Mr Whitelocke' in Hardwick MS 51. I owe this information to Mr Mark Neustadt of Johns Hopkins University.

[64] *Commons Debates 1628*, vol. II, pp. 528, 530–1.

procedural, the most bound to the strict observance of rules. It could be said that the king needed lawful modes of jurisdiction not bound by rules, whether their own or the common law's; but even a jurisdiction as swift and draconian as the law martial, which observed little in the way of due process and allowed few objections or appeals against the marshal's decisions, was not less for that reason a form of jurisdiction or of law.

What was not so clear was the juridical foundations enjoyed by the king's various jurisdictions, and how far these foundations were to be found in history. To proclaim 'martial law' in the ordinary sense of the term[65] was to invoke the immediate severity, not irrational but not pleadable either, of the terrible swift sword; but to speak of 'the law martial' might be to speak of a known form of jurisdiction, which the king exercised and derived from somewhere. It was of course usual—especially if one were James I—to say that it was of the nature of regality, so that he derived it from heaven or the deputizing will of God, to which the law of nature and of nations did no more than testify. But it was also usual—notably if one were John Selden—without formally negating the authority of heaven, to differentiate the law of nations or *jus gentium* into the uses of various nations recorded in history, and to ask from which of these the law martial as exercised in England might be derived. A possible answer seems to have been that it was of Roman origin, along with the civil law, and was exercised by the king as *imperator in regno suo*—*imperator* being a martial as well as a civil office. However, the kings of England did not usually derive their authority from Roman emperors, if only because it was a cardinal point in post-Reformation historical orthodoxy that Pope Eleutherius had told King Lucius of Britain that he had no need of Roman law, having laws of his own whereby to erect a Christian kingship in his dominions.[66] How far the king was

---

[65] The normal definition may be found in Sir Thomas Smith, *De Republica Anglorum* (1583 ed., p. 44), ed. Mary Dewar, (Cambridge, 1982), p. 86. See also John Cowell, *The Interpreter* (Cambridge, 1607), s.v. 'Martiall lawe'. Smith's spelling is 'marciall'.

[66] The tale of King Lucius is to be found in Bale, Parker and Foxe; see Levy,

simply *imperator in regno suo*, how far God's immediate lieu-
tenant, was a question as old as Henry VIII's reign.

The lack of a secular national history which might be ascribed
to modes of jurisdiction other than the common law put these
modes at a disadvantage whenever it was desired to assert that
they could not be used to set rules of the common law aside, or
that the common law enjoyed priority or superiority over them.
This happened from time to time—there is no need to decide
here whether or when these occasions amounted to a cumulative
process—notably when it seemed that the king was using other
jurisdictions to impinge upon his subjects' *meum et tuum*, or
claiming his authority as defender of the realm to regulate (say)
the movement of goods in and out of the seaport towns. On
such occasions, 'the common-law mind' organized itself to
claim that the law of real property possessed an authority which
was that of time itself, that it was co-eval with the kingdom and
was consequently *lex terrae* in a sense to which no other law
could lay title. This was the argument urged in parliament
against royal officers—judges and chancellors included—who
argued that *lex terrae* extended to all the jurisdictions by which
the king might rule and judge his realm.[67] We have found it in
Thomas Hedley's speech of 1610, and I am leaving open (though
I hope not unexplored) the question of when and why it first
took shape.

The House of Commons spent much time that session in
debating the character of martial law, which had been employed
both to discipline Buckingham's unpaid (and partly Gaelic)
soldiers and to quarter them on the civil population.[68] On all
sides it was agreed that the way to deal with soldiers was to 'pay

---

Tudor Historical Thought (cited above), pp. 91, 101, 112, 121, 137.

[67] See Secretary Coke in 1628; *Commons Debates 1628*, vol. III, p. 24.

[68] Lindsay Boynton, 'Billetting: The Example of the Isle of Wight', *English Historical Review*, vol. LXXIV, no. 1 (1959), pp. 23–40; 'Martial Law and the Petition of Right', *English Historical Review*, vol. LXXIX, no. 2 (1964), pp. 255–84; Lois G. Schwoerer, *'No Standing Armies!' The Anti-Army Ideology in Seventeenth-Century England* (Baltimore: Johns Hopkins University Press, 1974), ch. II, pp. 15–22.

well and hang well';[69] the question was by what authority this might be done, if the power of martial law extended so far over the rights of property as to intrude soldiers into men's houses. The king had also been imprisoning, by act of state and without cause shown, those who had refused forced loans, and this action raised the question of liberty of the person as well as *meum et tuum*. It is not easy to find much suggestion that the king had been acting, in this latter respect, in the exercise of his martial authority; but the martial law became a major component of the contention that he possessed a diversified and lawful authority to act outside of the procedures of common law. As Sir John Coke, the Secretary, put it:

There is no man but desires to live under the law, and we all hold the common law our inheritance that does preserve us. We are in the government of a state. The martial law touches kings highly. It is their very original. They are God's captains and leaders of his people. The name of kings is sacred, and the foundation of the commonwealth depends on them. All civil government may pass well and have a happy success. And for arms and conducting of armies, it can admit of no formal law. I must tell you that martial law is an essential law of the kingdom, and the whole government consists not in the common law, but in others. The King is supreme head and governor in all causes, and all causes are governed by the common law, not excluding other laws. We all admit and subscribe to the ecclesiastical law; we have the martial law; also Westminster Hall itself has a law of equity in every ordinary cause, and shall we not say in military matters must there not be concurrence of martial law, without which a commonwealth cannot be governed in peace or war?[70]

But the counter-statement had already been made, in characteristic language, by Sir Edward Coke:

I shall ever be as ready to maintain the King's prerogative as any man. I have been twice sworn to it, and it was resolved *3 Jac.* at the parliament that the King's prerogative is the supreme part of the laws of

[69] *Commons Debates 1628*, vol. II, p. 363: 'Sir Peter Heyman. For the soldiers, if they be paid well and hanged well, what hurt do they?' Cf. pp. 369, 371.
[70] *Commons Debates 1628*, vol. III, p. 24.

the realm. No other state is like this. *Divisos ab orbe Britannos*. We have a national appropriate law to this kingdom. If you tell me of other laws, you are gone. I will speak only of the laws of England. This question is a question of law. That Mr Attorney may have something to answer, I will say somewhat, and I shall speak with reverence; and I would not speak were it not that my gracious King I hope shall hear it. It is not I, Edward Coke, that speaketh it. I shall say nothing, but the records shall speak.[71]

Sir Edward spoke a month before Sir John, and the speeches have their own contexts; the earlier occasion dealt not with martial law, but imprisonment. Nor is it my concern here to enquire how far the debates in the Commons reveal the political realities of the crisis of 1628; it is patterns of speech and argument that we are seeking to understand. The two quotations are confronted to reveal two recurrent strategies of argument; in reply to the crown's contention that England was governed by a plurality of laws in varying states of formalization, Sir Edward Coke and other speakers in the Commons made it their first move to assert the insularity and uniqueness of the common law. That this was a strategic move in debate is obvious; that it appealed to a long-standing habit of 'the common-law mind' is, to say the least, possible.

It is from the assertion of insularity—*divisos ab orbe Britannos*—that we should deduce all the subsequent argument that the Petition of Right was a confirmation of Magna Carta and Magna Carta of the Laws of Edward the Confessor, the whole constituting the fundamental and immemorial *lex terrae*. We cannot weigh move against *mentalité* in assessing how this argument was constructed unless we understand what counter-argument was possible on the other side; and here the records of debate do not suggest that the king's officers in the Commons were equipped to strengthen Secretary Coke's doctrine by

[71] *Ibid.*, vol. II, pp. 100–101. *Cf.* p. 17 (the Speaker's address to the king): '*Et penitus toto divisos ab orbe Britannos* is a name of advantage to this island if the division be not amongst ourselves, which the God of unity for his mercy's sake forbid.' The line is from Virgil, Eclogue I, line 66.

producing a counter-history with which to answer the assertion of insularity. To find what history might have brought laws other than the common law into England we must turn to Selden; and Selden was arguing for the common law's supremacy over others.

First let us consider the general nature of martial law, and how this law is in England. If the question were what the law of England is, we must say what is done in the courts at Westminster. Thus here, if we could know this law, see what is done in the Marshal's court. In England we have common law, the canon law, and the martial law, all in due time and place. As the canon and civil law we have from Rome, and out of the Empire, so is the martial law out of the law of the Emperor. In the title of the civil law they have titles *de re militari.* Those laws were at the pleasure of the Emperor or general of the army. And there is no certain *leges militares.* As in the Empire they had *leges militares,* so have we our martial law, which is according to the pleasure of the kings of England; at divers times, divers laws. Some particular laws are by custom, and have been usually heard before the Marshal and Constable, and that is truly and properly the martial law....[72]

We have divers laws, as canon law, civil law, etc., and these are *leges terrae* in our sense, that is, such as by the law of the land are in force, but in acts of parliament they are not meant but only the common law.[73]

Selden not only knew there was plenty of Roman law in England; it actually suited his essentially insular argument to emphasize—even to exaggerate—its extent. Once the martial law ceased to descend from the sword placed by God in the king's hand, and became instead a foreign law migrating from the Roman Empire, the question must be asked how it came to be of authority in England, practiced not simply on a drum's head in the field but by a court at Westminster. Selden does not seem to have had to meet the argument of an eighteenth-century *thèse royale*—that the first English kings, like Clovis in Gaul, had been lieutenants of an emperor then reigning at Rome; Angles and Saxons (if not Picts and Scots) were held to have extinguished Roman authority in the island. He was able to take

[72] *Ibid.,* vol. II, pp. 462–3.   [73] *Ibid.,* p. 464.

it for granted that only custom and statute could make or receive law in England, and that these two together made up the common law.

Sir John Coke spoke of the several laws of the kingdom. All the law you can name, that deserves the name of law, is reduced to these 2: it is either ascertained by custom or confirmed by act of parliament.[74]

In another transcript of the same speech:

I know Secretary Coke speaks with great integrity, yet in matters of law I know will give place. Name what laws you will—ecclesiastical, marine, the law of Oleron, or others—they are all to be reduced to these two foundations: either ascertained by custom, or established by acts of parliament. There is not a third.[75]

The greater the diversity of laws obtaining in England, the greater the supremacy of the common law which alone could have received them; the longer the history of their naturalization, the more ancient the custom and statute which must have antedated them. Selden was no doubt able to envisage very early law as consisting of primitive and particular acts of reception; it is noteworthy that he came to believe that much unwritten law from ancient times had probably been statute rather than custom in the first instance. Yet a statute presupposes a parliament, and perhaps some antecedent custom as well; these institutions must have been more ancient than the first laws. Selden's ancient-constitutionalism was sophisticated by comparison with a monolithic 'common-law mind', but used the same assumptions and arrived at the same conclusions.

Sir Edward Coke chimes in, replying to the admiralty judge Sir Henry Marten:

Good sir, keep your circle; next mine own profession I love yours very well. Our common law bounds your law martial. Tell me of this or that or what you will, but show me such a law as the common law;

---

[74] *Ibid.*, vol. III, p. 33 (Grosvenor Diary).
[75] *Ibid.*, p. 35 (Newdegate MSS.).

no nation hath any like it. We are *toto divisos*, etc. If there be never so little canon law mixed with the common law, the common law carries it. That is armor of proof.[76]

Marten was once heard to say that 'the common law is the daughter, the civil law is the mother',[77] but he was arguing only that some swift jurisdiction there must be to deal with packs of hungry soldiers and sailors. Civil law was not an alternative *lex terrae*, if those words were to be construed as meaning a law of landed property, of *meum et tuum*; and if the common law was the only *lex terrae*, there could be only one history of tenure, property and jurisdiction over them. Marten's apophthegm could not therefore be developed into a history of common law deriving from civil. This is why I have contended that until it was recognized that feudal tenures had been imported into England and imposed upon land and law, a history of English law could not be written; and the debates of 1628 do not seem to give us the clue to how this recognition occurred. To begin with, the study of Roman law as such would not give rise to a concept of the origins of feudal tenure; some of the reasons are to be found in ch. IV. It is true that the Lombard *Libri Feudorum* formed part of the civil law; but they were *novellae*, later in date than the Norman Conquest, and though the account they furnished of the growth of hereditary *feuda* was used in the dating of knight service to Norman times, there is no image I have found of William I as a kind of Frederick Barbarossa, invading England with the imperial law and the *Libri Feudorum* in his baggage. On the other hand, it is true that the debates of 1628 contain recognition that the performance of military service in England was once an obligation which men owed their lords and their lords the king, and that this obligation may be dated from the Conquest.[78] It is instantly to be added,

---

[76] *Ibid.*, vol. II, p. 550; *cf.* p. 555 for another report of his words.

[77] *Ibid.*, p. 568 (Stowe MSS.); *cf.* p. 572 (Grosvenor Diary): 'Reason is the mother of the common law. Though I know not the law, yet no stranger to the mother, reason.'

[78] *Ibid.*, vol. II, pp. 80 (Coke: 'it was an excellent law that the poor man went

however, that this recognition has nothing to do with the derivation of martial law, which is depicted as Roman and civil, but not as Norman or feudal. Bacon in 1610 had remarked that the obligations of the *Libri Feudorum* had been unknown to the Romans themselves;[79] and the thrust of argument in 1628 was towards the position that if, as one speaker put it, 'we are all soldiers to serve the king' and this had been or still was an obligation incident to property, it must for that very reason be, as it always had been, subject to common and not to martial law. 'I beseech them that are near the chair', said Digges, 'to consider how long this kingdom was governed without this military law. There's no need of it'.[80] And in another transcript:

> We have had, since the Conquest, trained bands; let us not disgrace them. God and nature have defended this island; if the King will believe as well in them as they in him we cannot fail of a blessing. Yet let any man consider if martial law should be used in these bands whether it would not be a means to overthrow them.[81]

We are close here to the long-standing belief that the militia of the kingdom was ancient but not feudal and the post-Conquest order less feudal than might appear; but we are not at the point where a conquest by the Normans could be identified with a feudalization of landholding. It is not easy to say why or how a recognition that feudal tenures had entered English law from Normandy appeared in the writings of Selden and the Society of Antiquaries, or by what stages Selden arrived at the conviction (which he voiced in 1628) that they were even older than the Conquest; but the evidence of parliamentary debate does not

---

with his lord and master.... In E. 3 times there came a new line, men were pressed'), 280 (Selden, who thinks some such obligation older than the Conquest).

[79] *Proceedings in Parliament 1610*, vol. II, p. 52. The historical implications of the arguments used in the Great Contract debates would repay detailed study. James I remarked that he held his rights of wardship and tenure as a great lord, but not as a king (*ibid.*, p. 104).

[80] *Commons Debates 1628*, vol. III, p. 25 (see also Coryton: 'we are all soldiers to serve the king'). Both from 'Proceedings and Debates' text.

[81] *Ibid.*, p. 28 (Stowe MSS).

suggest that a recognition that civil law was present in England, or that both civil and martial law formed part of the king's imperial jurisdiction, had very much to do with it.

As for the theory of conquest, we hear a good deal about it in 1628, but the notion of feudal tenure forms hardly any part of what we hear. Our authors are Robert Mason and John Pym, developing the charge which became an impeachment against Dr Roger Maynwaring for his sermon in favour of the king's right to require aid of his subjects. They accused him of perverting the text of Suarez which sets forth how a conqueror may compact with his subjects to leave them in possession of their former laws, and be bound by the compact which he has made. The immediate context in which they spoke was the Lords' proposal that the Petition of Right be interpreted with a 'saving' that would leave the king's 'sovereign' power 'entire', and the remarkable feature of their argument is their admission that 'sovereign' and 'prerogative' power might very easily be grounded in a right of conquest. 'A conqueror,' said Mason,

is bound by no laws but has power *dare leges*. His will is a law. And although William the Conqueror at first, to make his way to the crown more easy and the possession of it the more secure, claimed it by title; yet afterwards, when there were no powerful pretenders to the crown, the title of conquest—to introduce that absolute power of a conqueror—was claimed; and the statute of Magna Carta and the other statutes mentioned in our petition do principally limit that sovereign power.

He reviewed the text of Suarez and Maynwaring's alleged omissions from it, and continued:

The statutes then mentioned restraining the absolute power of a conqueror—if we recite those statutes and say we leave the sovereign power entire, do we not take away the restraint which is the virtue and strength of those statutes, and set at liberty the claim of the sovereign power of a conqueror which is to be limited or restrained by no laws? This may be the danger of the word 'entire'.[82]

[82] *Ibid.*, p. 528.

Mason was more explicit than Pym in admitting that only the statutory force of Magna Carta prevented the king of England from claiming sovereignty by right of conquest; he left it uncertain whether William had been a conqueror, but not whether he had claimed to be one. Pym, impeaching Maynwaring a fortnight later, used a more conventional language in averring

> True it is that time works alterations in all states, but when on the one side it is endeavored to maintain old laws, and on the other new frames are desired, states fall to confusion; and those states are found to be of best continuance which make the shortest and easiest recourse to their ancient laws.
>
> Concerning the second position: these laws are ancient, original, and essential. William the Conqueror swore in person to maintain and observe them. And the Great Charter of England, and the other 6 statutes which your Lordships have heretofore heard of were always claimed and petitioned for as of right, and no otherwise.[83]

He very clearly charged that in perverting the text of Suarez Maynwaring had denied that the king was bound to observe the laws of his kingdom, and had therefore offended against his lawful authority. The alarming implication seemed to be that only a power limited by compact or statute was a lawful power, while a sovereign power was rooted not in law but in conquest. Pym did not clarify the relation between custom and statute in making laws 'ancient, original and essential'; but it could be argued on his own grounds, and on Mason's, that every king possesses an absolute sovereignty, which is rooted in conquest until it is limited to law by compact. This might be 'the original contract between king and people', of which Phelips spoke in 1628[84] and which James II was said to have broken in 1689; a popish successor, it had been argued in favour of the Bill of Exclusion, was incapable of entering into compact with his

---

[83] *Ibid.*, vol. IV, pp. 103–4.

[84] *Ibid.*, vol. II, pp. 61 (Phelips), 150 (Cresheld, quoting Sir John Davies); vol. III, p. 110 (Noy: 'We do not come to make a new contract but to establish the old').

people by reason of his subjection to the Pope, and could therefore rule only as a conqueror.

But it is worth observing that in all the 1628 debates there is very little to suggest that William the Conqueror brought feudal tenures with him and imposed them by right of conquest. A few references by Selden to the 'three aids' reserved to the king by Magna Carta are all that we have touching that document's feudal content,[85] and there is nothing about undue burdens imposed on the subject by the Conqueror and remedied by appeal to the laws of the Confessor. Yet we know that there was to be plenty on that theme in discussion for the rest of the century. The conclusion must be that the debate of 1628 was not a debate concerning the history of the king's various modes of jurisdiction, not yet a debate between 'the ancient constitution' and 'the feudal law', and in that sense not a historical debate at all. We see here the strengths and the weaknesses of 'the common-law mind' as described in chs. II and III above. On the one hand, only the common law could claim the authority of 'time out of mind' necessary to make it the *lex terrae*; the civil law and the martial law could not provide themselves with a history in England. In consequence, the royal lawyers found it harder to make out their case for a plurality of laws enjoying authority as *lex terrae*, and Coke and Selden in their several ways could argue that custom and statute were the only law. But it followed next that any 'prerogative' or 'sovereignty' outside the common law was not a jurisdiction at all, but an absolute power claimed from the gift of heaven, the law of nature, or a theory of 'conquest' so abstract as hardly to be a phenomenon of history. The common law, monopolizing history, was left face to face with conquest as its only possible alternative: a *jus conquestus*, imposed on rather than arising from the events of 1066. It was a dialectical threat so alarming as to make it more important than ever to argue that William I had claimed the crown by title and not by conquest; and the law's immemorial antiquity was used to argue, not that conquest could not prevail over custom—that

[85] *Ibid.*, p. 534.

301

was manifestly false—but that it had always been possible to allege a better title than a conquest standing outside law.

The doctrine of an 'ancient constitution' had not yet become— if it ever became—a simple claim to prescriptive legitimation through the immemorial antiquity of custom; still less, of course, was it a means of alleging the legislative supremacy of parliament or the House of Commons acting alone. In 1628 it was a means of alleging that the common law, by reason of its antiquity, was the *lex terrae* which protected the property and liberty of subjects, and through which the royal authority was bound by its own legality to proceed in matters touching property and liberty. The antiquity of the common law rendered it 'fundamental' in the sense that any other laws obtaining as part of the royal authority did so by its sanction, and did not provide the crown with alternative modes of jurisdiction through which 'the prerogative' might choose to proceed. Parliament—as was often claimed in the House of Commons and elsewhere—was as ancient as the common law itself (this could be affirmed by the same strategies of appeal to precedent as established the antiquity of the law), and because it was the assembly in which were made the statutes by which the law was altered (as was denied by none) it was peculiarly charged with maintaining common law as well as with altering it. No issue as between legislative sovereignty and judicial review troubled anyone's mind; the antiquity of the law underwrote the authority of the king-in-parliament.

In the debates surrounding the Petition of Right, we have followed the development of this argument about as far as it could go. Coke and Selden encountered no serious opposition: none, that is, capable of investing the civil law, the martial law, or the hardly mentioned feudal law with histories of their own by which they could be said to have shaped the governance of England. Insofar as they possessed histories, these operated to make them appear aliens, naturalized in England by an authority which could only be that of common law—whether by this term was meant the customs collected by Edward the Confessor, or the statutes of the ancient parliaments whose existence Selden suspected. Custom or statute, said Selden; there was no third way. Defenders of the view that royal authority operated according to a plurality of *leges terrae* had no counter-history to offer: no *thèse royale* which would invest an Anglo-Saxon *bretwalda* with the authority of a Roman emperor; no theory of Norman rule which would show William the Conqueror altering the nature of English law by the introduction of feudal tenures. Selden, among the first to suspect that this might have happened, was already moving to neutralize the possibility by claiming that feudal tenures were older than the Conquest.

There were many, of course, who could not see how to deny that William I had in some sense conquered England; but what this might mean constitutionally has to be understood by reading the charges which Pym and Mason brought against Maynwaring. The issue here was ceasing to be that of a royal jurisdiction free to choose among a plurality of laws, and was looking more like that of a prerogative which need not be identified with any particular procedure. Pym and Mason therefore chose to accuse Maynwaring of denying the process by which a king might bind himself to observe the antecedent laws of his people, and leaving him with nothing but the prerogative which he might claim by right of conquest. Any king, as bearer of the sword, might claim to rule by *jus gladii* or *jus conquestus* insofar as he had not bound himself by an 'original contract between king and people'; the distinction was Fortescue's and the type of conqueror was Nimrod. If the king had entered into such a contract—as William would have done by any promise to maintain the laws of the Confessor—it did not automatically convert the ancient laws into statutes enacted by the assemblies in which the contract was made, though clearly Selden did not object to the suggestion that this might have been the case. The laws might retain their character as custom in use since time beyond memory, and we know how this could be exploited so as to suggest that William had succeeded according to known law, and so had never possessed a *jus conquestus* or the freedom to enter into an original contract.

What is significant is that Pym and Mason, though they knew

of this argument, did not rely exclusively upon it, and so left it strongly to be inferred that any king might be a conqueror (in respect of his prerogative) insofar as he had not bound himself as a contractor (in respect of the laws). We should be reluctant to attribute this to their entertaining historic doubts as to the reality of ancient custom or the events of 1066. It was important to assert that William had bound himself to observe the laws of the Confessor; but the alternative would not be a different reading of the circumstances of the Norman invasion, so much as a decision to leave the English kingship in that historical category where contract was the only alternative to conquest. What was happening was that common law (which had a history) was failing to bind prerogative (which had none); the common-law argument was failing because it had reached the limits of its own strength.[86] It was not that one reading of history was being countered by another; a historical discourse had exhausted itself and was giving way to discourse of another kind.

All this would change once it was possible to present the Norman Conquest as a feudalization of landownership rather than a Nimrodic occurrence in the universe of *jus gentium*. Meanwhile, the debates in the House of Commons during 1628 appear to provide reasons for maintaining the thesis, put foward in 1957, that the common law still furnished the only historic past which could be visualized by those engaged in English government. Outside it lay not history but *jus gentium*, and that 'nature' in which 'rights' were coming to be seen as generated.

There are those anxious to pursue the discourse of politics in England as conducted in terms of the latter kind, and for this may be found a significant ideological explanation. Over the last twenty-five years, 'Britain' has aspired to be part of 'Europe', and there is a disposition on both left and right to deny that it has any history which is not European history. Those who share this disposition are suspicious of 'insular' interpretations of the

---

[86] Margaret A. Judson, *The Crisis of the Constitution* (New Brunswick, N.J.: Rutgers University Press, 1949) remains the best study of this confrontation and dilemma.

history of England, and tempted to deny the assertions of its insularity which have from time to time been put forward—as certainly happened in 1628. Here it may be observed that *The Ancient Constitution and the Feudal Law* was written at the University of Otago, which is the southernmost on this planet. To a subject of the queen who surveys the world from the Southern Hemisphere, the proposition *divisos ab orbe Britannos* makes an oceanic, not an insular statement about British history; one which is obviously true. We may take it as probable that the interactions between island and continent have been understated, and as certain that there is much yet to be learned by investigating them; in an important sense, that is what this book has been about.[87] But there have been occasions on which the assertion of insularity has been made—by the cosmopolitan Selden no less than by the provincial Coke—and it is possible that the operations of so idiosyncratic an institution as the common law (among others) have had something to do with it. We do not dismiss this possibility by treating the discourse of the Stuart kings and their parliaments as a mere incident in a European debate over sovereignty and natural right; provincial colorations are important to a cosmopolitan history, and the coherence of the latter is not to be taken for granted.

---

[87] Alan Macfarlane's *The Origins of English Individualism* (Cambridge, 1979) seems to argue that they have been overstated. His book is a remarkable attempt to revive the thesis of insularity, in which the present writer is attacked from an 'off-shore' position, as by others from a 'continentalist'.

CHAPTER II

Civil War and Interregnum

THE opening paragraph of ch. VI of this book is undeniably whiggish. It treats the middle decades of the seventeenth century as the interval between Spelman's death and his resurrection; as a period during which English scholars were preparing themselves to receive the doctrine of a historian far in advance of his time. The best that can be said of this is that it is untypical of the book as a whole, and that the interval it posits is inhabited by characters—Harrington, Prynne, Hobbes and Hale—who do not exactly fit the role of watchers by the sepulchre. In this part of the retrospect, an attempt will be made to review the mid-century in the light of modern research, and consider what was happening to the 'common-law mind' and the 'ancient constitution' in this rich and tormented period in the history of English political discourse.

The Petition of Right of 1628 brought us to a moment at which it may be said that the doctrine of an ancient and fundamental law had been unchallengeably defined, and yet had failed, or rather had not attempted, to define the prerogative in other than absolute terms. The parliamentary debaters had articulated the demand that the prerogative should act in certain all-important matters only through channels known to the common law, but had left it as possible as ever to present the power which the king exercised *regaliter* as derived from God and from Nimrod. Like David Hume in the eighteenth century, or a diversity of historians in the twentieth, we may say that two unrelated conceptions of authority were being presented side by side, and that it is wrong to call the Fortescuean tradition a doctrine of mixed monarchy,[1] precisely because the *regale* and

---

[1] *Cf.* R. W. K. Hinton, 'English Constitutional Theories from Sir John Fortescue to Sir John Eliot', *English Historical Review*, vol. LXXV (1960), pp. 410–25; Donald W. Hanson, *From Kingdom to Commonwealth: The Development*

the *politicum* persisted in association but not in admixture. We need not assign this theoretical confusion its place (though doubtless it had one) among the 'causes' of the Civil War; it is enough for our present purposes to assert that it persisted until the breakdown of political relations in 1641–2, but that its capacity to supply language for the analysis or resolution of what was happening was both inherently limited and rapidly overtaken by events.

This does not mean that contemporaries lacked such a language; on the contrary, they were an articulate generation and modified or evolved language at remarkable speed, though they did not succeed in averting civil war by doing so. Once it became apparent that the House of Commons was claiming to exercise powers which had normally been exercised by the king, those not content to argue that this was an emergency measure necessitated by the doings of evil counsellors were obliged, perhaps by the sheer habit of appealing to precedent and history, to construct an image of the past in which the king and parliament were seen as having exercised these powers conjointly. This could not be done by the appeal to precedent alone, and the Commons did not therefore go to war in the name of a merely prescriptive constitution; indeed, the notion of ancient and fundamental law might well be made a weapon in the king's armoury of discourse, since it reinforced by implication the companion notion of his separately sanctioned prerogative. Hyde perhaps went to war at the king's side in the name of such a strictly Fortescuean ancient constitution, while the strategy of reducing everything to terms of contingency, custom and convenience left his fellow common lawyer and Great Tew habitué John Selden in a position at once intellectually authoritative and politically impotent.[2] This is not the place, however, to trace the

of Civic Consciousness in English Political Thought (Cambridge, Mass: Harvard University Press, 1970).

[2] Tuck, *Natural Rights Theories*, pp. 98–110; J. P. Somerville, 'John Selden, the Law of Nature and the Origins of Government', *Historical Journal*, vol. XXVII (1984), pp. 437–48. There has been no close study of Hyde's position to surpass B. H. G. Wormald, *Clarendon: Politics, History and Religion, 1640–61* (Cambridge University Press, 1951).

notion of 'the ancient constitution' through the intricate confusions of pre-Civil War argument, but—at some risk of whiggism—to examine the leading revision of the idea which was put forward in these political circumstances; and here we encounter the by now well-known but still startling fact that the doctrine of mixed and conjoined power, and a version of history to go with it, which we might expect to have been the move the Commons were forced by their position to make, was most lastingly and authoritatively put foward in the king's name and by two of his counsellors.

His Majesty's Answer to the Nineteen Propositions of Parliament has been established as a cardinal document of English political thought by the writings of Corinne C. Weston, first in her *English Constitutional Theory and the House of Lords, 1556–1832*, published in 1965, and later in *Subjects and Sovereigns: The Grand Controversy over Legal Sovereignty in Stuart England*, written jointly with Janelle R. Greenberg and published in 1981.[3] The second of these works will be examined in more detail as part of the concluding chapter of this retrospect; of more immediate concern is to show why the first must be considered among those which, having appeared since *The Ancient Constitution and the Feudal Law* was published in 1957, have modified the understandings with which it must be read. *The Answer to the Nineteen Propositions* was issued on June 18, 1642, having been written by Sir John Colepeper and Viscount Falkland, who did not take much trouble to secure the approval of King Charles or Edward Hyde, the authors' closest associate. It contended that, there being three forms of government known among men, monarchy, aristocracy and democracy, each having its characteristic virtues and vices, the wisdom of the English ancestors

---

[3] Corinne Comstock Weston, *English Constitutional Theory and the House of Lords, 1556–1832* (London: Routledge & Kegan Paul, 1965); Corinne Comstock Weston and Janelle Renfrow Greenberg, *Subjects and Sovereigns: The Grand Controversy over Legal Sovereignty in Stuart England* (Cambridge University Press, 1981). For a new view of the prehistory of the *Answer* and its leading concepts, see Michael Mendle, *Dangerous Positions: Mixed Government, the Estates of the Realm and the Answer to the XIX Propositions* (University of Alabama Press, 1985).

had combined these three, so far as it was possible to do so, in a balance which aimed to prevent excess on the part of any one of them. This balance consisted of king, lords and commons; the law-making power reposed in all three jointly, while the king was entrusted with a prerogative, the House of Lords with a judicatory power, and the House of Commons with the right to propose grants of money to the crown and the right to impeach evil-doers. The document closed with a warning to the Commons against demanding more than was their due by the terms of the balance, and a prophecy of the evils (chiefly popular turbulence) which would follow if it was disturbed.

The *Answer* is an extremely rich document, and can be read from several points of view. In all her writings Professor Weston has concentrated on the implications of a conjoint legislative power, and has of course been right to do so; but it is also possible to see the *Answer*, in the most paradoxical of lights, as the introduction by Charles I's counsellors of a republican component into English constitutional theory. The conception of three forms of government, distinguished by the number of their holders, each possessing an inherent tendency to degeneration which must be checked by combination with the other two, is unmistakably Aristotelian and Polybian and could carry with it (though in the *Answer* it may not) the idea of an *anakuklōsis politeiōn*; all formal theory of republican government, ancient and modern, was theory about the combination of these imperfect powers. If the king's power was *per se* imperfect, it could not be the earthly representative of the power of God, and only the wisdom of the ancestors had succeeded, 'as far as humane Prudence can contrive', in combining it with the aristocratic and democratic powers which were its equals. It was this, no less than the admission of conjoint legislative authority, which gave the *Answer* the effect of reducing the king to an estate of his own realm: the great *lapsus calami* which English constitutional theorists were to debate for the next century and a half.[4]

[4] Mendle stresses that a traditional idiom, in which the church, or the bishops as a component of the House of Lords, occupied the status of one of the three

While Professors Weston and Greenberg have pursued the implications of conjoint legislative power, therefore, I have in a series of writings published since 1957[5] been concerned to show that the *Answer to the Nineteen Propositions* imported the possibility of a republican alternative into English political thinking; that English theorists briefly followed up this alternative between 1649 and 1659, and American founders put it into effect between 1776 and 1789. Perhaps this is the place to reiterate that I see this reading as an alternative to Professor Weston's, but in no way as a refutation of it. The notion of a legislative power exercised conjointly by king, lords and commons is a notion of legislative sovereignty undeveloped in classical republican theory; its presence in the *Answer* is a reminder that the notion of a 'separation of powers', though invented largely in England, could not be effective there and could be realized in the United States only after a rejection of parliamentary government. Yet the *Answer* is ambivalent; it explains why the republican experiment must fail in England, but also why it would be tried.

From the point of view with which this retrospect is more immediately concerned, we must see June 1642 as marking the moment when 'the ancient constitution' became authoritatively identified with the 'mixed' or 'balanced' constitution. Much though not all previous talk of 'mixed government' in England had been talk of 'mixed monarchy': of the combination (if indeed it was a mixture) of prerogative with liberty and *regale* with *politicum*, of the compact or custom which bound the king to observe the forms of parliamentary procedure and common law. We have found evidence of uncertainty as to how far this compact was binding or this combination a stable 'mixture'. A

---

estates, was already being challenged by another in which the three were king, lords and commons, and shows how the controversy over the bishops' seats in the Lords helped to shape the language of the *Answer*. The phrase about 'humane prudence' is at p. 263 of Weston, *English Constitutional Theory*.

[5] *Politics, Language and Time*, p. 130; *The Machiavellian Moment*, pp. 361–6; *The Political Works of James Harrington*, edited with an introduction by J. G. A. Pocock (Cambridge University Press, 1977), pp. 19–22.

Polybian theory of mixed government, in which the king was one of three modes of power, three estates, or three conjoint agents in legislative sovereignty, was something else again; and what we must lose no time in perceiving is that such a balance could not be justified merely by appeal to immemorial custom, or imagined as coming into existence merely through the operations of reason and usage, or custom and statute. It had been established, said the authors of the *Answer*, by 'wisdom' operating according to 'prudence' in a situation inherently problematical; and problem-solving looked more like legislation than like custom. The theory of the 'balanced constitution' was not simply the product of a 'common-law mind', and Selden, who in 1610 had favoured the idea that the king was an estate (*ordo*) of the realm, seems to have rejected it later in life when he saw where it had led.[6] In the eighteenth century, as we shall see, the 'balanced constitution' became part of the idea of an 'ancient' but not necessarily a prescriptive 'constitution', and circumstances had to be imagined in which the rude if sturdy ancestors had employed their 'prudence' to bring it into being. These had more and more to do with the image of a king with his greater and lesser followers establishing themselves in a region by occupation and appropriation; their ancient customs preceding their act of conquest.

The assertion of balanced government and conjoint legislative sovereignty is a reminder that the language of 1628 was no longer adequate in 1642. We have so far been concerned with the doctrine of an immemorial and fundamental law, of which parliament was the principal organ and guarantor; but the shift of emphasis from the antiquity of law to the antiquity of parliament, which I see I adumbrated on pp. 124–5 above, means more than that this doctrine was being reiterated (though no doubt it was). Especially if we follow the readings of Weston and Greenberg, we must suppose that any assertion of the

[6] Weston and Greenberg, *Subjects and Sovereigns*, pp. 5, 269. The rejection is recorded in *Table Talk*. See Mendle, *Dangerous Positions*, pp. 153–4, and for the earliest known appearances of 'mixed government' as 'ancient constitution', pp. 98–102.

antiquity of the House of Commons made after June 1642 was put forward in the context supplied by the *Answer to the Nineteen Propositions*, and amounted to a claim to equal status with the king and the House of Lords in the conjoint exercise of sovereignty. This, for example, supplies a proper approach to the career of William Prynne, whose *Sovereign Power of Parliaments and Kingdoms* asserted the antiquity of both houses in 1643, just as his writings after 1648 denied that of the Commons in the way shown in ch. VII. Weston and Greenberg have presented their case with a wealth of evidence that conjoint legislative sovereignty was more than formally the centre of debate, and have been right to do so. Yet there are at least two other contexts in which Prynne's writings and those of others must be read, and these directly or indirectly modify our understanding of the *Answer to the Nineteen Propositions*.

In the first place, it is of course obvious that the First Civil War was not fought to determine the location of the power to make statutes, though it was in some measure a consequence of the claim that ordinances of the two houses of parliament might enjoy the same authority as statutes in the absence of the royal assent. If by 'legislative sovereignty' we mean the statute-making power, there was no question before 1646 that this normally resided in the king and parliament now unhappily estranged, whose reunion was being sought (on either side) by the ultimate argument of the sword. The issue before the subject during these years was not where the legislative power justly lay, but which component of a sundered sovereignty might command his allegiance in the struggle to restore it to unity. This was a problem in conscience and casuistry,[7] rather than in constitutional theory; tracts of the Civil War period deal repeatedly with 'the grand case of conscience', 'the grand case of allegiance', 'the subject's duty'. The location of legislative sovereignty and the antiquity of parliament's participation in it were indeed exhaustively discussed, but as means of guiding the conscience in this grand case and problem in casuistry. The term

[7] *The Machiavellian Moment*, pp. 366–8; *Works of Harrington*, pp. 22–4, 28–33.

'casuistry' did not exclusively bear the contemptuous signification, of jesuitry and equivocation, which was in process of
becoming attached to it; it still meant the guidance of the
conscience in morally difficult and ambiguous cases. In this
context, the message of the *Answer to the Nineteen Propositions*
was that since king, lords and commons were parties to an
ancient distinction and conjunction between modes of legitimate
power, the conflict now raging between them was a conflict
between authorities of which each had a good title to legitimacy.
The problem before the individual conscience was to determine
where its allegiance lay in this war between legitimacies, this
'unnatural' war as it was termed on all sides. The location and
antiquity of legislative sovereignty might be discussed in the
search for guidelines in this problem; but the reunification of the
warring partners in a conjoint sovereignty could not be achieved
by the definition or the exercise of that sovereignty, but by the
sword. The call to allegiance was a call to take up the sword; the
call to conscience was the call to justify taking it up, in and by
the act of doing so, in the form of what was termed an 'appeal to
heaven'. As late as Locke's *Second Treatise*, whenever that was
written, the appeal to heaven was an appeal to civil war; it
transcended the ancient constitution by affirming the immediate
sovereignty of the sword and the ultimate sovereignty of God.

In these circumstances, the concept of a balance between three
autonomous forms of authority, which is one principal message
of the *Answer to the Nineteen Propositions*, was seen to offer no
solution to the problem of conflict between them. That was the
conclusion drawn by Philip Hunton in his *Treatise of Monarchy* of
1643; when a tripartite balance broke down, he said, no one of
the three authorities might claim the general allegiance in
restoring it, or the balance would not have existed in the first
place. To Sir Robert Filmer, publishing a few years later, this
meant one thing only: *The Anarchy of a Limited or Mixed
Monarchy*;[8] but the compelling power of tripartite theory in

[8] Reprinted in Peter Laslett (ed.), *Patriarcha and Other Political Works by Sir
Robert Filmer* (Oxford: Basil Blackwell, 1949).

defining the problem, even if it defined it as insoluble, is shown by the fact that Hunton and so many others retained it. Responsibility, they thought, now returned to the individual conscience, which must choose, declare its allegiance, appeal to heaven and submit to the judgment of God, even if pronounced by the issue of a trial by the sword. But this choice was not to be taken in existential randomness; it had need of all the resources of human prudence and personal piety. Hunton now reverted to the concept of conjoint legislative sovereignty, and explored it in search of guidance to the conscience in its dilemma; but the tentativeness with which he did so, and of which Weston and Greenberg make a good deal,[9] may be taken as showing that he thought of it as a source of relatively weak arguments. In Hunton's mind the conscience had access only to weak arguments in the politics of this world; neither divine nor human authority had unequivocally declared themselves in matters of government and allegiance, which consequently belonged to the province of casuistry. If the conscience desired stronger arguments, it must escape from the casuistry of mixed government altogether, and bind itself by concepts of political authority, under God, which could oblige it to obey. Some of these obligatory concepts might be found by critically exploring the notion of balance; as I have argued elsewhere, and will try again to show lower down, they might include the widely differing notions of conquest, reversion of power to the people, and the reconstruction of the balance in a true republic. Alternatively, solutions might be found by abandoning the tripartite scheme altogether, and establishing a unitary authority, sovereign, prescriptive, or both. This may be how Filmer and Prynne found themselves arguing on the same side after 1648: a divinely established monarchy or an immemorially established constitution might equally deliver the conscience from the intolerable burden of choice. There is evidence that suggests that neither man found the two concepts absolutely incompatible; each seems to have explained the notion of conjoint legislative

[9] *Subjects and Sovereigns*, 53, 48–61.

sovereignty in such a way as to deny the House of Commons antiquity, and therefore equality, within it.

But in order to understand the writings of Prynne, it is necessary to situate them in the second of the two contexts mentioned earlier, and to do so will open up the theme of a massive re-evaluation of mid-seventeenth-century thinking about law and history, a good deal of which has been carried out since 1957. This is the context supplied by apocalyptic and millenarian language, in which England appeared as an 'elect nation' with a role to play in prophetic history; it was established in the minds of a generation of historians and literary scholars by a famous book which William Haller published in 1963[10] and which has been much debated ever since. However, Haller did not possess any monopoly of the subject, and it was in the same year 1963 that William M. Lamont published his study of Prynne in this context, the first of a trilogy of works which he has devoted to the politics of English millennialism.[11] The problem which he raised was that of understanding Prynne as simultaneously, or perhaps concurrently, an exponent of 'elect nation' and 'ancient constitution', and to confront this we have to state the problematics of the former concept. Haller contended that John Foxe's *Acts and Monuments* depicted England as a second Israel, a nation, like its antetype, chosen by God for a special role in the fulfilment of prophecy and the struggle against Antichrist under the leadership of a 'godly prince'. The ensuing debate[12] has centred on the question of how far Foxe, or any subsequent writer, intended that it was England, the secular national community, that was so 'elect', and how far election to

[10] William Haller, *Foxe's Book of Martyrs and the Elect Nation* (London: Jonathan Cape, 1963).

[11] William M. Lamont, *Marginal Prynne, 1600–1669* (London: Routledge & Kegan Paul, 1963); *Godly Rule: Politics and Religion, 1603–1660* (London: Macmillan, 1969); *Richard Baxter and the Millennium* (London: Croom Helm, 1979).

[12] Paul Christianson, *Reformers and Babylon: English Apocalyptic Visions from the Reformation to the Eve of the Civil War* (University of Toronto Press, 1978); Katherine Firth, *The Apocalyptic Tradition in Reformation Britain, 1530–1645* (Oxford: Clarendon Press, 1979).

the role of second Israel fell upon the true church of Christ, which must be universal and of which England could be no more than the local vessel. Too rigorously to identify church with nation might be to expose oneself to the charge of judaizing, unless the mechanisms of typology could be employed to prove one not guilty of such a revision; and always there must be the question of how militant English Protestants stated their relation to the church universal. Clearly, a wide variety of attitudes could take shape along this front; and it may aid our present purposes to suppose them arranged upon a spectrum. The more the church was identified with its laity, the less *jure divino* the authority of its clergy, the more its membership would appear co-terminous with the membership of the national community and responsible to the latter's authority; the more, it may be added, would any separation within the church be a separation within the social and political community. We may therefore pursue the argument in the direction taken by Haller, while leaving open the question of how far theorists in general or in particular had proceeded in that direction.

Prynne, in Lamont's reading, believed the sovereign national authority of the 'godly prince' to be what distinguished England as 'elect' for the struggle against the papal Antichrist. He was a common lawyer and militant Protestant, who was at his most apocalyptic when at his most erastian and recognized the elect nation by its bearing the marks of the ancient constitution. When the faction of clergy headed by Laud began to deny that the Pope was Antichrist and affirm that the Church of Rome was no worse than a true church fallen into corruption, Prynne's first response was that this implied a *jure divino* clergy independent of the authority of the godly (but secular) prince, and was therefore a conspiracy against the latter. His second and third moves were typical of that projection into the past which has been said to be characteristic of the 'common-law mind'. In *The Antipathy of the English Lordly Prelacy* he declared that not merely the Laudian group of bishops now, but the whole order of bishops back through time, had consistently betrayed the English godly prince and his elect nation to their Romish enemies. When reluctantly convinced that Charles I, conniving with the prelates, was false to his vocation as godly prince, Prynne wrote *The Sovereign Power of Parliaments and Kingdoms* to demonstrate that parliaments had always enjoyed an authority co-ordinate with the king's, so that they might at need rescue him from himself. At this point Lamont's reading comes together with Weston's: the elect nation with the ancient constitution and the *Answer to the Nineteen Propositions*. The fifth chapter of *Subjects and Sovereigns* is entitled 'The curious case of William Prynne'.

In and after 1648, Prynne—confronted with a Commons which had fallen under army control, abolished the king and the House of Lords, and as he saw it sold out its authority to independents and sectaries whose claims were as much *jure divino* as Rome's itself—changed his front but not his base. He was still the apocalyptic erastian, convinced that Levellers and Quakers were secret agents of the papacy, but he now began two decades of indefatigable and fanatical research into the records in the Tower, aimed at bringing to light every precedent which would substantiate the true character of the ancient constitution. In the process he became convinced that the House of Commons—by now in his eyes the principal agent in the betrayal of godly erastianism—was no older than the forty-ninth year of Henry III; but this, as shown in ch. VIII, in no way lessened his conviction that the government of the elect nation was immemorial. It seems then entirely possible to reconcile the interpretation of Prynne I put forward in 1957 with that advanced by Lamont in 1963, unless it be thought that the language of medieval law drowned out that of apocalyptic and typology. Prynne might compare himself with Hilkiah the high priest, who 'found the Book of the Law in the House of the Lord', but what was to be found under the leads of the White Tower was the past of the ancient constitution, not the covenant and prophecies vouchsafed by God to his Englishmen. Yet the sovereignty of the godly prince, exercised through parliament and common law, was in Prynne's mind England's bulwark against Rome, and its antiquity may have been the

317

assurance of an enduring covenant. There was at least nothing
monarchomach about the 'common-law mind' of this uncon-
querably moderate fanatic; the ancient constitution was the
expression of national sovereignty.[13]

In Prynne's sequence of publications can be glimpsed a
process studied in more detail by Lamont in his second volume,
Godly Rule, 1603–1660: the ease with which church, king or
parliament could be perceived as false to the mission to which
each had been elected, and as falling by the wayside to be
replaced by another instrument. In his case the process was
circular: godly rule ended as the ancient constitution restored;
but there was an antinomian potential in the notion that the
mission was greater than its agents who claimed authority in its
name. In the church at Putney they debated the possibility that
the Lord's work might outwear the covenants in which it was
from time to time embodied; and if it were objected that
covenants were with the Lord and that it was not for men to
declare them superseded, the reply might come that each man
covenanted with the divine within himself, and that the process
by which God entered into men to dwell with them was not yet
at an end. Once the ancient constitution came to be the form of
England's covenant with the Lord, there began to be the
possibility that the Spirit might transform it from within; and a
considerable part, though not the whole, of the radicalism of the
World Turned Upside Down can be thought of as an antinomian
revaluation of the ancient constitution. Christopher Hill's essay
'The Norman Yoke' was known to me from a volume of essays
published in 1954, and came fairly early in his long and rich
rediscovery of the sectarian mind.[14] I made use of it in order to

[13] *Cf. The Machiavellian Moment*, pp. 344–8.

[14] Christopher Hill, *Democracy and the Labour Movement: Essays in Honour of
Dona Torr* (London: Lawrence and Wishart, 1954); *Puritanism and Revolution*
(London: Secker and Warburg, 1958). 'The Norman Yoke' may be found in
either volume. See further Hill, *God's Englishman: Oliver Cromwell and the English
Revolution* (London: Weidenfeld and Nicolson, 1970); *Antichrist in Seventeenth-
Century England* (Oxford University Press, 1971); *The World Turned Upside
Down* (Harmondsworth: Pelican, 1975); Hill, (ed.), *Winstanley: The Law of
Freedom and Other Writings* (Cambridge University Press, 1983); and Hill, *The*

distinguish between the propositions that the existing laws were laws of liberty, older than the Norman Conquest, and that they were laws of deprivation and repression, imposed on the nation at the Conquest and possibly replacing older and juster laws which had preceded it. Since ancient constitution doctrine sometimes makes use of the idea of a temporary Norman usurpation, followed by a restitution of ancient law, it is possible to confuse the two propositions, and Hill and I may now and then have become entangled in this muddle; but our task will be made easier if we can retain 'the Norman Yoke' as a phrase designating the radical proposition that the laws are unjust, Norman and still in force. Gerrard Winstanley employed this doctrine to attack the English system of landed property, Thomas Paine to attack the British constitution.

In a very short account of this matter (pp. 125–7) I described an anti-Normanism which I attributed mainly to the Levellers. This was a good deal too simple. Recent research has made much of the Leveller propensity to advance their radical claims under existing law,[15] and propound a version of the ancient constitution which guaranteed the birthright of a freeborn Englishman to the 'poorest he' as to the 'greatest he'; the assertion that the entire fabric of the law was a usurpation of that birthright may have to be sought for in other groups. I can claim only that the account I gave of anti-Normanism is valid as far as it goes, irrespective of to whom the anti-Normanism is attributed; and I draw attention to Winstanley's very remarkable assertion that 'custom'—by which he seems to mean the 'custom of the manor' to which copyholders and those with still less security of tenure were obliged to appeal—is itself a fruit of 'conquest' and guarantees the tyranny of the freeholders.[16] It was not my business in 1957 to say very much about the social

---

Experience of Defeat: Milton and Some Contemporaries (London: Faber & Faber, 1984).

[15] R. B. Seaberg, 'The Norman Conquest and the Common Law: The Levellers and the Argument from Continuity,' *Historical Journal*, vol. XXIV (1981), pp. 791–806.

[16] Hill (ed.), *Winstanley*, pp. 107, 121, 123, 133, 135, 137.

protests of the Interregnum; but I would now make far more of the extent—revealed by Hill's researches on Winstanley, and paradoxically (I think) by my own on Harrington[17]—to which anti-Normanism was antinomianism, part of the Spirit's indictment of the as yet unsanctified flesh. Feudal tenures, landed clergy, appropriation of the common lands: all were types of the old Adam not yet burned away in the fires of 'the great spirit Reason'. To Winstanley, Christ's resurrection and return would mean the perfect possession of the earth by its creatures; to Harrington, the harmony of property and power, and the perfect union of reason with matter in government which was the expression of the divine in man. Both, while differing in class outlook, are applying the concepts of spirit and reason to the redistribution of property in land. If the Norman yoke is the antinomianism of the ancient constitution, do not both spring from a consciousness universal among Englishmen that property was the distribution of land by law and law the distribution of land as property? Poor and underprivileged men were intensely aware that the existing law excluded them, but could for that reason imagine that there might be a law which would not. I am close here to saying that the Law begat the Spirit: the dialectic of Christians both radical and orthodox, like Joachim of Fiore and the Spiritual Franciscans. *Filioque*. Small wonder if the presupposition that Interregnum radicalism must embody a 'bourgeois' perception of movable property and wage relations produces tensions among English Marxists.

The Norman yoke seems to encounter the ancient constitution when Rainborough and Ireton hold their debate at Putney.[18] Rainborough indeed does not make much use of anti-Normanism—though the Conquest is mentioned from time to time—but he is manoeuvred by Ireton into making use of both an English birthright and a natural right which command relations between franchise and property very different from

[17] *Works of Harrington*, pp. 70, 72–3, 75–6, 86, 91–3, 112–3, 120–1, and the textual references given at these points in the Introduction.

[18] The best edition of the Debates still seems to be that of A. S. P. Woodhouse, *Puritanism and Liberty* (London: Dent, 1938).

those established by the existing laws. From this it would not be far to asserting that the existing laws were not just, and that—if the notion of England's birthright were to retain any meaning— there had been a time when they were more just than they were now. It was the function of anti-Normanism to make these assertions. Ireton in reply goes beyond any mere vindication of the existing arrangements for parliamentary franchise on the grounds of their antiquity; he affirms that all government must be founded in property—in a right to things possessed—and that the nature of *meum et tuum* is such that it cannot be deduced from original right or natural right, which may vindicate it but cannot supply it with rules of law capable of determining disputes. Property must therefore be anchored in systems of particular law, which may be in harmony with natural law but do not simply arise from it in ascertainable processes of history; and if governments are to be founded in property, they must be anchored in systems of law of their own generating and therefore ancient. Ireton was appealing to prescription against principle, and we have yet to find anything but the 'ancient constitution' and its foundations in 'the common-law mind' which made it possible for him to do that. This is why, in writing *The Ancient Constitution and the Feudal Law*, I was already interested in Ireton's affinity with Edmund Burke.

Chapter VI, 'Interregnum: the *Oceana* of James Harrington', was the first of a series of studies of that author published between 1957 and 1978.[19] Its concluding dictum, that '*Oceana* is

[19] 'Machiavelli, Harrington and English Political Ideologies in the Eighteenth Century', *The William and Mary Quarterly*, 3rd Series, vol. XXII, no. 4 (1965), pp. 549–83, reprinted in *Politics, Language and Time*; 'The Only Politician: Machiavelli, Harrington and Felix Raab', *Historical Studies: Australia and New Zealand*, vol. XII, no. 46 (1966), pp. 165–96; 'Civic Humanism and Its Role in Anglo-American Thought', *Il Pensiero Politico*, vol. I, no. 2 (1968), pp. 172–89, reprinted in *Politics, Language and Time*; 'James Harrington and the Good Old Cause: A Study of the Ideological Context of His Writings', *Journal of British Studies*, vol. X, no. 1 (1970), pp. 30–48; *Politics, Language and Time* (1971); *The Machiavellian Moment* (1975); *The Political Works of James Harrington* (1977); 'Contexts for the Study of James Harrington', *Il Pensiero Politico*, vol. XI, no. 1 (1978), pp. 20–35.

a Machiavellian meditation upon feudalism', is one which I have elaborated but see no reason to modify; though perhaps there is still need to add that when I say that '*Oceana* is this', I do not mean that it 'is this' and nothing else. Under-sophisticated critics in the history of literary discourse often ascribe to the historian an essentialism which is more theirs than his; they accuse him of having said that his interpretation contains 'the' true meaning of a text, in order to burn up this man of straw by pointing to the validity of some other possible interpretation. Over-sophisticated critics, on the other hand, first endeavour to dissolve all previous interpretations into their interpretations, and then, when challenged, behave as if all interpretations were of independent value, so that their own become invulnerable to any challenge brought against them by the implications of others. The effect is that history and the agents in it disappear, and only the interpreter is left, indulging in the eternal and irresponsible play of a Hindu deity and wielding nearly as many arms. I have no interpreter of Harrington in mind as I write these words, yet they need repeating. The historian will continue to insist that there are questions to which some interpretations respond better than others; some meanings which were fed into a text by its author or other agents in the past, others which were not. It is with the actions—in this case, intentions and interpretations—of agents other than himself that the historian is concerned.

It was therefore not the case, as Christopher Hill supposed, that I represented Harrington as 'an armchair theorist who got all his ideas from Machiavelli'.[20] To call him a 'Machiavellian' was indeed a means of liberating him from the vaguely constructed contexts of immature social realism: from those who would posit a 'rise of the gentry', and at the same time (if at all possible) a 'rise of the bourgeoisie', and interpret his writings as momentary 'reflections' of these macroscopically conceived processes. It was to claim that the categories which he used to organize his perceptions of what was happening in his time were specific and mediated, not intuitive and immediate; and at the

---

[20] Hill, *The Experience of Defeat*, p. 200.

same instant to ask whether these categories, once we recovered and explicated them, would ever make contact with the categories employed by Tawney or Hill to interpret the age in general and Harrington in particular. As the reader will have seen, I did not in 1957 find much contact between Harrington's categories and theirs, and I do not find much today. The lively debate over the interpretation of Harrington put forward in C. B. Macpherson's *The Political Theory of Possessive Individualism*[21] has not altered my position, because it has not sufficiently addressed the methodological concerns with which I was already beginning to write in 1957. The question has never been whether Harrington employed perceptions of the social changes occurring in his day, but what categories of thought gave shape to these perceptions and, in consequence, what the changes were that he perceived. To shift from the possible social context to the actual intertextual context of Harrington's theses—which was what I did by calling him a 'Machiavellian'—was an attempt to reconstitute his discourse: to discover what he was saying by reconstituting the concepts and vocabulary in which he was saying it. It further entailed the assumption—of which I was far from unconscious—that the contexts of practical action and social process, so heavily privileged in contemporary historiography, must in the first instance be those rendered accessible by the structures of seventeenth-century discourse; and that the moment we are incessantly adjured to seek, at which 'language' is modified by 'reality', had better be deferred to the point at which we could see something forcing innovation within those structures. I was maintaining, from one point of view, that language and social experience are interdependent, not colliding billiard balls of different magnitudes and weight; and it surprises me that I am still sometimes called a Platonist for my pains. I was maintaining from another point of view that we had to know the 'normal science', in Kuhnian terminology, before we

[21] C. B. Macpherson, *The Political Theory of Possessive Individualism: Hobbes to Locke* (Oxford: Clarendon Press, 1962); the best of the ensuing exchanges are in Charles Webster (ed.), *The Intellectual Revolution of the Seventeenth Century* (London: Routledge & Kegan Paul, 1974).

could understand the 'scientific revolutions', and it was being borne in upon me, in Cambridge and Dunedin, that we did not yet know very much about what the normal structures of discourse in seventeenth-century England had actually been. It surprises me when I am accused of indifference to what these structures were.[22]

Research and interpretation carried out by several hands, since 1957, on the political literature of the post-regicide Interregnum, has enlarged in a number of ways the contexts, of both theoretical concern and practical action, in which Harrington's writings may be situated and interpreted. We have already seen that the drastic restatement of ancient-constitution doctrine carried out in the *Answer to the Nineteen Propositions* made it possible to speak of the English government as a 'balance' and to state the problem of civil war as the problem of what happened when such a balance broke down. In Hunton's *Treatise of Monarchy* we found the possibility considered that the doctrine of balance precluded any governmental solution to this problem, and that all that was left was necessarily an appeal to heaven, performed by a drawing of the sword. If the ancient constitution was not a balance but a simple sovereignty, this dilemma might be avoided; but saying that it was a simple sovereignty might entail saying that it was not an ancient constitution at all. Hence, in some measure, the appeal of the *Answer to the Nineteen Propositions* with its doctrine of conjoint sovereignty, which might help to keep the constitution ancient; but to retain the doctrine of the balance was to retain the dilemma of the sword. In a period beginning about 1647 or 1649, this dilemma was incessantly debated, in terms which sometimes entailed rejection of the notion of balance and sometimes did not.

In writings by Perez Zagorin,[23] Quentin Skinner,[24] John M.

[22] Nancy S. Struever, "Historical Discourse," ch. 10 of *Handbook of Discourse Analysis: Disciplines of Discourse* (New York: Academic Press, 1985).

[23] Perez Zagorin, *A History of Political Thought in the English Revolution* (London: Routledge & Kegan Paul, 1954).

[24] Quentin Skinner, 'History and Ideology in the English Revolution', *Historical Journal*, vol. VIII (1965), pp. 151–78; 'The Ideological Context of

Wallace,[25] Margaret A. Judson,[26] Julian H. Franklin[27] and others, we now possess an extensive literature on what is called either the 'Engagement Controversy' or the '*de facto* controversy', and came about when the regicide regime set out to impose an 'engagement' to do nothing against it. There ensued a debate on how far the injunction of Romans XIII, 'let every soul be subject to the higher power, for the powers that be are ordained of God', obliged the conscience to obedience when 'the powers that be' exercised authority *de facto* and not *de jure*. In this setting there was no point in debating the antiquity of the government, since to discuss what was ancient was by definition to discuss what was *de jure*. The *factum* which set up a regime with no legal title was necessarily modern, the deed of a *principe nuovo* or a naked sword. Filmer and Prynne, even had they disagreed regarding what was ancient, would have been bound together by their agreement that there could only be government *de jure*, that to explore antiquity was to go in search of it, and that to debate authority *de facto* was to plough the shifting sands of anarchy. But the most incisive theorists of the *de facto* entered into the state of anarchy—which like Harrington later they knew to be a state of 'pain and misery'[28]—and sought a way out of it. They postulated an individual in this 'state of nature' and inquired what there was in his nature which might oblige him to obey a government, even if (given the state of nature) he

---

Hobbes's Political Thought', *Historical Journal*, vol. IX (1966), pp. 286–317; 'The Context of Political Obligation', in Maurice Cranston and R. S. Peters (eds.), *Hobbes and Rousseau: A Collection of Critical Essays* (New York: Doubleday Anchor, 1972); 'Conquest and Consent: Thomas Hobbes and the Engagement Controversy', in G. E. Aylmer (ed.), *The Interregnum: The Search for a Settlement, 1646–1660* (London: Macmillan, 1972).

[25] John M. Wallace, *Destiny His Choice: The Loyalism of Andrew Marvell* (Cambridge University Press, 1968).

[26] Margaret A. Judson, *From Tradition to Political Reality: A Study of the Ideas Set Forth in Support of Commonwealth Government in England* (Hamden: Anchor Books, 1980).

[27] Julian H. Franklin, *John Locke and the Theory of Sovereignty* (Cambridge University Press, 1978).

[28] *Works of Harrington*, p. 838 (*A System of Politics*, ch. IV, aphorism 18).

had to constitute it in order to obey it. The most wretched of beings, binding himself to servitude and obedience to a despot for the preservation of his right to existence, was nevertheless a constituent of government, a legislator of the natural world. In the 'pain and misery' which followed the seeming collapse of the ancient constitution was born much of the radical natural-rights individualism which in the opinion of most is the seventeenth century's lasting achievement in political theory, and in the opinion of many (though not this author) decisively displaced the political humanism of the Renaissance.

In this condition the individual came face to face with Nimrod the conqueror. It might well have been the sword that had brought him into the 'privation of government', as Harrington called it; it was very probably by the sword that he would perish if he could not escape from this condition; any power claiming to rule him *de facto* must necessarily be ruling, and claiming to rule, by the sword; the only way to the establishment of a government *de jure* was to invest the sword with a foundation of right, even if this meant deriving all rights from the sword. For all these reasons emphasis fell on the notion of a *jus gladii* or *jus conquestus*, which the law of nations or *jus gentium* was found to contain: a right which, all else failing, the bearer of a conquering sword might claim from the mere fact of conquest, whether as the outcome of an appeal to heaven or by the assertion that authority must exist somewhere in nature and must be lodged in the sword if it could be lodged nowhere else. This was the authority long ascribed to Nimrod, but conquest was not being made the foundation of monarchy. The point at issue was not the authority of a single person—Oliver Protector was too cautious to claim a princely role requiring complex legitimation, and in the years of rule by the Army the conquering sword might be borne by a covenanted band calling itself God's people—but the stark fact that a point might be reached where only the sword which gave protection might command obedience, all other titles having disappeared. When this point was reached, it devolved upon the individual to reconstitute government, reconstituting himself a subject in the process; he must encounter the sword at this point, but the conqueror's command was given meaning less by the sword than by the individual's submission to it. Leviathan, accordingly, is something of a corporate Nimrod; his sword commands, but it commands the people to incorporate themselves by covenanting to obey it. The two halves of the Fortescuean formula become a single expression, but Leviathan is rendered the 'artificial sovereign' and 'mortal god' which the sword alone could never make him. The biblical figure of Nimrod is drawn into the geometry of submission; and if we hear less about him openly expressed than implied, we hear still less about that minor conqueror William the Norman, who was worth discussing only when the fabric and antiquity of government *de jure* were worth discussing, as was not the case given the assumptions of this controversy.

In the republican theory which makes its appearance during or just after the *de facto* controversy, we encounter a conquering sword, but one very different from Nimrod's. In the next paragraphs I shall be recapitulating and abbreviating interpretations developed in the introduction to *The Political Works of James Harrington* (1977). Marchamont Nedham,[29] writing in 1650–2, contended that in a balanced system of three powers, it was conceivable that one component might claim more than was its due by the balance, and that civil war might follow. There could be no human arbiter over this war, which was of the nature of an appeal to heaven, and the victor would emerge possessed of a *jus conquestus*, reinforced certainly by the now proved injustice of the vanquished's original claims. This had happened in England, but the *jus conquestus* now lay with the democratic component in the original balance, embodied in its armed force rather than in its representative the House of Commons. Nedham thus found Hobbesian arguments for submission to the protecting authority of the sword, and these

---

[29] *Works of Harrington*, pp. 13, 33–7; Philip A. Knachel (ed.), *The Case of the Commonwealth of England Stated: By Marchmont Nedham* (Charlottesville: University Press of Virginia, 1969); Joseph Frank, *Cromwell's Press Agent: A Critical Biography of Marchamont Nedham, 1620–1678* (Washington: University Press of America, 1982).

could lead him in due course towards justification of the Protectorate; but more immediately he had lodged that sword in the hands of a conquering democracy. At this point, however, we observe him repudiating the Levellers, and by implication any suggestion that power had reverted to an undifferentiated 'people'; his 'democracy' was that of classical theory, one of several components which together made up the 'people', but one which had acquired by war a right of conquest over the others. Following the logic of this theory, he saw that the democracy-in-arms could use its sword only to establish a republic, in which it would be one component in a balance; but he endorsed the proclamations which had followed the regicide in 1649, declaring that monarchy and the House of Lords had proved themselves inconvenient and were now abolished. King, lords and commons had never furnished the stable balance claimed for them in the *Answer to the Nineteen Propositions*; barons' wars, wars of York and Lancaster, and now wars of king and parliament had marked this regime at least since its foundation at the Conquest of 1066; and there are hints of anti-Normanism about Nedham's insistence that all forms of 'kingly' (in which he includes noble) power must vanish from England and Scotland if stability is to be attained. His assertions (it is of course useless to speak of his beliefs) in 1650–2 were radically republican, though never quite populist; even the democratic conquest was not the same as a 'reversion of power to the people'.

Criticism of the historic constitution must entail an alternative view of the English past. We find this in Harrington's *Oceana*, published in 1656, where the scenario sketched out by Nedham is reiterated in greater detail. The conquering army of Oceana sets up its general as chief legislator and embarks upon the creation of a republic. But a republic is *ex hypothesi* a relationship between an aristocracy and a democracy; and the fundamental problem of Oceana is that aristocracy in its feudal form—the power which one armed man exercises over another by retaining him in dependent military tenure—has vanished for ever and taken monarchy with it. The practical necessity is therefore the reconstitution of aristocracy in some other form, to play its part as a component of the republic; and it may be said of Harrington that he did not believe that aristocracy could have any material foundation in social relations other than the feudal control of land and the sword, of which he was so intensely aware. His reconstituted aristocracy was to be nothing other than a natural aristocracy, a naturally superior few whose parts and talents would be recognized and voluntarily deferred to by the many. He thought there would be social foundations of this superiority: property, leisure, gentility; but he was only minimally interested in legislating these foundations into the orders of the republic, so that they became necessary qualifications for membership in the few. Harrington was not troubled by the need to restore a ruling elite; like John Adams after him, he took its presence for granted, and was concerned only with the form it would take and the conditions under which it would exercise leadership. The elite he looked for would attain its position through the votes of others.

We know that there were many ways in which the aristocracy exercised social control that had nothing to do with feudal tenure, and Harrington a few years after 1656 saw the restoration of a historic constitution in which a peerage exercised a conspicuous and increasing power on the basis of these controls. There may be little reason to suppose that they had been more than momentarily challenged, or that their nature after the Interregnum was radically different from their nature before it. However that may be, it is Harrington's single-minded isolation of feudal tenures as a force in history and a factor in political theory that arrests our attention and makes him important in this retrospect; it was this which was meant by calling *Oceana* 'a Machiavellian meditation on feudalism'. What is based on Machiavelli at this point is the perception that the immediate control of arms is necessary to make the individual a political being or citizen; what is based in contemporary English understandings of feudalism is the perception that arms may be borne by the individual either as independent freeholder or as dependent tenant. Harrington is interested in feudalism as supplying the historical sociology, and indirectly the politics and ethics, of the sword now ruling England, which he desires to reconstitute as the *milizia* of an arms-bearing citizenry in an expanding republic. This means that he takes part in the historiography of the ancient constitution, but not in the debate over that constitution's existence.

In the debates of 1628 we found signs of an already existing perception that property and arms were connected with freedom and military virtue, but not much sign that the introduction and decline of feudal tenures were perceived as part of the problem whether there existed an ancient law or constitution by which property was guaranteed. Harrington was entirely uninterested in that problem; having lived through civil war and regicide, he held that the ancient constitution had never supplied stability or civil order and had now utterly disappeared. Though the genesis of his writings owes something to the debate over *de facto* power, he was equally uninterested in *conquestus* as a source of *jus*, as a means of seeing how the sword as the source of protection could be a source of the obligation to obey; he was not a legalist writer at all, and the lexicon of *jus* is altogether absent from his vocabulary. He was most Machiavellian in his concern for *verità effettuale*: for showing how various distributions of land and arms could effect or occasion various distributions of power and authority, in which human capacities for government and virtue would be fulfilled in different ways; but we must look elsewhere than in Machiavelli for the sources of his specialized awareness of the relations between arms and land. Harrington was also most English in his intense consciousness that the 'ancient constitution' of king, lords and commons had (whatever one thought of it) existed for centuries but had at last fallen 'with such horror as hath been a spectacle of astonishment unto the whole earth'.[30] He very urgently desired to know how this had happened, and he found an explanation in the hypothesis that feudal tenures had been introduced into England by the Saxons and Normans, and then had disappeared

[30] *Works of Harrington*, p. 235.

during the reigns of the Tudors. He developed this thesis in such a way as to make him the first social-change historian of the causes of the civil wars, as opposed to May[31] and Clarendon, for whom they lay in a failure of counsel and confidence and were moral rather than material in character; a mode of explanation at present in vogue once more.

Chapter VI explains how Harrington took his understanding of the decline of feudal tenures in England from Bacon: specifically—though I do not seem to have been very specific—from the *History of the Reign of King Henry VII*. In 1957 the debate over 'the rise of the gentry' was in full swing[32] and that over 'the crisis of the aristocracy' was to follow it a little later;[33] both are now out of fashion, though Harrington seems to me easier to connect with the latter than with the former. As I have throughout insisted, he was more concerned with the transformation of military relationships than with that of either constitutional or productive relationships; and while 'the rise of the gentry' had much to do with historians' perceptions of changes in pasturage, agriculture and the cloth trade, 'the crisis of the aristocracy' had more to do with the decline in magnate military power, of which Bacon, Raleigh and others are witnesses that there was a contemporary perception. It was a cardinal point with Harrington that the Civil War came about, and took the course it did, because magnates with their armed tenants and retainers were no longer a serious military force; the war was therefore a contest for control of the militia, and both sides were driven to rely on men who were neither tenants nor mercenaries, a new and revolutionary phenomenon. Harrington made use of the term 'a standing army', but wrote twenty years

---

[31] Thomas May, *The History of the Parliament of England Which Began November the Third MDCXL* (London, 1647); *A Breviary of the History of the Parliament of England* (London, 1650).

[32] J. H. Hexter, *Reappraisals in History* (London, 1961; 2d ed., University of Chicago Press, 1979), pp. 117–62.

[33] Lawrence Stone, *The Crisis of the Aristocracy, 1558–1641* (Oxford: Clarendon Press, 1965); J. H. Hexter, *On Historians* (Cambridge, Mass.: Harvard University Press, 1979), pp. 149–226.

(at most) before it came to denote an army of long-service professionals, paid and maintained by the fiscal and administrative machinery of the state. This was to bring about a major change in European practice, and in historical and political thinking. To Hume and Macaulay it was to seem the central problem with which Harrington's generation had to do; Harrington himself neither diagnosed nor predicted it, but he provided the conceptual means by which it came to be diagnosed and criticized.

There are two other respects in which Harrington seems to have contributed to the later growth of political economy. His account of how barons became courtiers and, instead of maintaining vassals on the land, maintained servants as a form of conspicuous consumption, is prominent in Adam Smith's account of the transition from a military to a productive economy: a reminder, perhaps, that the part played by the concept of the court in the history of the concept of the market is even now not fully worked out. Tenants who were no longer subject to the calls of military service, but had not become unproductive servants in courts or great households, could play a leading role in this scenario, devoting their energies to industry, production and exchange; but I continue to find very little sign of their presence in Harrington's scheme, and those who claim that they are there seem rather to be insisting that they must be. However, the unidentified pamphleteer R. G., who anticipated Harrington's theses shortly before the publication of *Oceana*, does allow a leading role to the growth of trade among the people and indebtedness among the nobility;[34] such a reading of history, dominant through the eighteenth century, was therefore possible in 1656. If, as I contend, it is not to be found in Harrington, the circumstance is of more than negative significance. *Oceana*, the 'Machiavellian meditation on the history of feudalism', is at the same time a 'civil history of the sword', which in one light is what links it with the Engagement Controversy of 1649–51. In another, what situates it at a

---

[34] *Works of Harrington*, pp. 11–12.

'Machiavellian moment' is both the breakdown of the ancient constitution and Harrington's perception that he was living at a moment when feudal armies had disappeared and mercenary armies were succeeding only in bankrupting the kings who hired them. The New Model encouraged him to believe that the future lay with militias of self-employed and self-motivated citizens, and he married Machiavellian politics with feudal scholarship to provide a history of which they were the recurring motif. As it turned out, his revolutionary expectation was utopian; for the next century and a half, until the age of the democratic revolutions, and perhaps for long after that, the military and political future lay with the professional armies that served the states. The immediate point, however, is that the Machiavellian and Harringtonian thought whose history it is possible to study was focussed on military relationships first and on commercial and productive relationships a good deal later; this was my theme throughout *The Machiavellian Moment*.

What, meanwhile, of *The Ancient Constitution and the Feudal Law*? We are clearly not concerned, at this point in the story, with a simple antithesis between the two terms making up its title: the importation of feudal tenures is not being employed to refute the antiquity of common law (which Harrington never mentions) or parliament. He visibly does not believe in such an ancient constitution, but his motives are not those of Spelman or Brady. We may think of him as concerned with the breakdown of that balance between king, lords and commons into which the *Answer to the Nineteen Propositions* had transformed the ancient constitution, and as explaining it by demonstrating that it had never been a stable balance and must now be replaced by a better one. The Engagement debate over the sword as a pre-juristic source of authority provides necessary background to his thinking, but he was more concerned with the *verità effettuale* of the swords of a popular army. This furnished his explanation of why the historic balance had been feudal and therefore unstable, why it had collapsed in the interval between Henry VII and Charles I and what the problems were which must attend its re-placement. To complete his picture he blended Machiavelli's

333

account of the history of Roman arms, Selden's account of the importation of feudal tenures into England, and Bacon's account of their decline, dated as late as the end of the fifteenth century. Since in Selden's version of history military tenures were not particularly dependent on a Norman Conquest to introduce them, but had originated among the barbarian invaders of the Roman empire, Harrington replaced the ancient constitution not with a Norman yoke but with a 'Gothic balance', whose characteristic was its instability. From the concerns of the generation among whom the ancient constitution had taken enduring shape—Selden had died aged seventy in 1654—Harrington moved out towards both a myth of republican historiography and an enquiry into the military, economic and ecclesiastical conditions of Roman and post-Roman society, which in many ways was to bulk larger in the history of historiography than the straightforwardly Whiggish interpretation with which I was originally concerned. The history of Coke, Spelman and Brady has in many ways to be situated in a context shaped by the writings of Selden, Harrington, Hume and Smith.

CHAPTER III

Restoration, Revolution and Oligarchy

THE ANCIENT CONSTITUTION'S ROLE IN CONTROVERSY
TO THE SETTLEMENT OF 1689

IN the remainder of this retrospect I shall review the closing chapters of the book, in particular those which deal with the controversy of the 1680's and proceed to consider the role of historic constitutionalism in the period from 1690 to 1790 (and after). A great deal of research and publication has gone on since 1957, and is still going on; it is not too much to say that our understanding of John Locke, of the Revolution of 1688–9, and of the main lines of English and Scottish political argument in the eighteenth century, has been transformed and is still fluid. The last chapter of my 1957 text, 'Conclusion: 1688 in the history of historiography', is now less a conclusion than a curiosity, and in re-issuing the book an attempt must be made to bring it up to date. This in turn cannot be done without some review of the penultimate chapter, which deals with 'the Brady controversy', 'the Filmerian controversy' or 'the Exclusionist controversy'—terms which are never quite interchangeable— and with the still-vexed question of the relation between John Locke's role as an actor in these controversies and his role as a publicist and author after 1689. The richness of the historical material, furthermore, has brought to light many discussions of important questions in which Locke played no part even when he might have; and if these cannot merely be dismissed as unimportant because they did not interest him, it follows that his own role in the history of discourse has had to be re-assessed.

In ch. VII of *The Ancient Constitution and the Feudal Law*, I considered the writings of William Prynne as an author of the

Restoration period—he lived until 1669—as well as of the Civil Wars and Interregnum. The significance of his denial of immemorial antiquity to the House of Commons was not examined in as broad or as exact a context of debate as I might now wish; but two important attempts have since been made to supply a context in which Prynne may be considered. One, that of William M. Lamont, has been reviewed in the preceding chapter of this retrospect; it consists in treating Prynne as an apocalyptic erastian, obsessed by the relations between ancient constitution and elect nation. The second, that of C. C. Weston and J. R. Greenberg in their *Subjects and Sovereigns*,[1] has been more briefly mentioned but will hold much of our attention henceforth, as we move past 1660 into an era when elect nation and 'godly rule' were emphatically if not finally rejected by large sectors of opinion in the English governing classes. Weston and Greenberg in effect propose a model in which constitutional debate from the end of the Protectorate to the fall of James II can be considered as a series of responses to the *Answer to the Nineteen Propositions*. The restoration of both king and parliament in 1659–60 might be looked on as a return to the conjoint exercise of sovereignty by king, lords and commons; within this framework the Houses of Parliament might—depending on the polemical needs of a changing political situation—be accorded antiquity as a means of bringing them within the ancestral constitutional balance, or denied antiquity as a means of preventing them from exceeding its limits. At the same time, however, a powerful dissent was levelled against the doctrine of conjoint or co-ordinate sovereignty by those who held that the *Answer to the Nineteen Propositions* had disastrously and absurdly reduced the king to equality with the estates of his realm. These exponents of the king's sole and undivided sovereignty—whether or not it be accurate to call them apologists for 'absolute monarchy'—might be and often were interested in a view of English history in which lords and commons, courts and parliaments, came into being at known

[1] See ch. II, n. 3, in this retrospect.

times, by the king's permission or at his initiative. The authors of *Subjects and Sovereigns* contend that most constitutional and historical debate in England between Restoration and Revolution can be interpreted within this scheme.

I did not apply this or any other general pattern for the interpretation of Restoration political debate in completing my seventh and proceeding to my eighth chapter; perhaps it would have been better if I had. I went on instead, in parts II and III of ch. VII, to examine the confrontation between Hobbes's *Dialogue* and Hale's *History* of the common law;[2] a confrontation which I hope I did not suggest was exhaustive, or even representative, of political thought between 1660 and 1675. I did so partly because Hale was clearly a leading exponent of 'the common-law mind' in the generation following Coke and Selden; partly because I was already interested in the role later played by common-law immemorialism in Burke's formulation of a doctrine of pre-scriptivism. In an article published a few years after *The Ancient Constitution and the Feudal Law*,[3] I was able to show that Burke was well aware of Coke and Hale, though his attitude towards their understanding of history changed during his lifetime, and the link between Burke and 'the common-law mind' seems to me to have been established. In claiming, however, that Hale used 'prescriptivist' argument in reply to Hobbes and in the construction of his *History of the Common Law*, I do not (and I hope I did not) suggest that the second half of the seventeenth century was an age in which proto-Burkean arguments were used to a point where we can speak of a 'Burkean' theory of government as existing at that time; only that it is one in which we can discern the historical sources from which such arguments and such a theory could be and later were assembled. This point

---

[2] There have now appeared modern editions of both these works: Joseph Cropsey (ed.), *Thomas Hobbes: A Dialogue between a Philosopher and a Student of the Common Laws of England* (Chicago University Press, 1971); Charles M. Gray (ed.), *Sir Matthew Hale: The History of the Common Law of England.* (Chicago University Press, 1971).

[3] 'Burke and the Ancient Constitution: A Problem in the History of Ideas' (1960; see Preface to the 1986 Edition, n. 4).

will recur when we come to consider the debates of 1689.

In *A Dialogue between a Philosopher and a Student of the Common Laws of England*, it is not clear that we have Hobbes at his best. He wanted to deny that either custom or Coke's 'artificial reason' possessed authority sufficient to make a law, but went so far further as to deny—or so it seemed to his readers—that either possessed sufficient rationality. There could be no law-making reason other than sovereign reason, and this reason, though vested in an artificial person, must not be artificial reason but the practical reason of the natural man. Hale replied that both custom and judicial reason played important parts—he did not say sovereign parts—in the creation of law; we might almost think of him as saying that while the sovereign's authority is of course decisive in the promulgation of law, the sovereign's reason, as that of a natural man or men, does not adequately explain to us how law comes into being. He went on to show that both custom and judicial reason were 'artificial' in the sense that they were based not on deductive reasoning from a principle, but on the institutionalized presumption that precedents, usages and (by all means) statutes adequate to the formation of a decision (or a rule, or a statute) already existed. Since presumption presumed an antecedent presumption, a law so created presumed itself immemorial, and was so to the extent that its practice could show itself to be ancient; whether the laws presumed to exist in antiquity were presumed to be customs or the statutes of unrecorded parliaments was to Hale—following Selden in this matter—more interesting than important. Presumptive law was by definition immemorial; no beginning other than presumption need or could be found; but since presumption and application were two faces of the same medal, the law which was always ancient was always in process of adaptation. Hale was thus led to those images of English law—more Seldenian than I recognised thirty years ago[4]—as a river always the same though its water was always changing, a ship always the same though its timbers were always being

---

[4] For Hale's relation to Selden, see Tuck, *Natural Rights Theories*, pp. 113–18.

renewed. Though I had written a few pages earlier that to Coke 'law is custom and custom perpetual adaptation',[5] I slipped at this point into writing a sentence which describes him as 'treating custom as immemorial and immutable',[6] which has suggested to some that for Coke the immemorial was always static, while for Hale it was always fluid. I regret a lapse which runs counter to what I argued at other points; Coke, Selden and Hale could perfectly well have agreed that custom was *tam antiqua et tam nova*, though the two latter would have stated it with greater sophistication.

But it is less Hale's relation to Coke that is at issue here than the role which he accords to custom. Richard Tuck has written:

Pocock slides from talking (in the context of Hale) about the constant change and adaptation of law to new circumstances, to talking about *custom*, that is, the creation of law without the deliberate decision of a law-making authority. (It is for this reason above all that he wants to associate Hale with Coke, who undoubtedly did want to protect the common law from such an authority.)[7]

I am in fact not at all sure that Coke wanted to protect the common law from the legislature, and I certainly do not 'want' to assert that Hale did; though doubtless both of them did 'want' to protect it from the natural reason of a sovereign acting outside due process. My reason for 'talking about custom' is that Hale talks about it a great deal himself, and 'in the context' of 'the constant change and adaptation of law to new circumstances'. In a passage quoted by Tuck as well as by me, he says that the laws of England cannot be ascertained by philosophy or comparative jurisprudence

because they are Institutions introduced by the will and Consent of others implicitly by Custome and usage, or Explicitly by written Laws or Acts of Parliament.[8]

---

[5] P. 170 above. [6] P. 178 above.
[7] Tuck, p. 133. [8] *Ibid.*, p. 137; also above, p. 172.

Tuck, I think, 'wants' to minimize or eliminate any suggestion that custom could be an independently acting force in the making of law, as if it had been suggested that this meant it could act independently of control by courts or parliaments. (Perhaps the ghosts of Bonham and McIlwain are walking once more.) He therefore emphasizes that law can be adapted by means other than usage or custom (which is true but irrelevant), and proceeds to suggest that Hale sees custom as 'simply' one of the various ways in which the common law 'could be *known*, rather than *made*'[9]—which is a little hard to reconcile with Hale's quoted statement that English laws may be 'introduced... implicitly by custom and usage'. Although

an element in his argument which looks extremely Burkean...has led Pocock to think that Hale was putting forward a theory of the gradual and insensible modification of the common law through the decisions of innumerable private individuals...Hale's case is in fact perfectly compatible with the complete denial of the genuinely customary status of the common law.[10]

I think the last sentence is a little more startling than necessary. Hale nowhere denies 'the genuinely customary status of the common law'; as well as the words already familiar, Tuck quotes him as saying 'Usage and Custom generally receiv'd, do *Obtinere vim Legis*.'[11] What he would have denied, if anyone had ever, anywhere, asserted it, is the *exclusively* customary status of the common law: any proposition that custom alone had created the common law, without the necessity of any judgment by a court or statute by a parliament.[12] It was obviously necessary that judgment or statute should declare that custom *obtinuerat*

---

[9] Tuck, p. 134.

[10] *Ibid.*, p. 137.

[11] *Ibid.*, p. 134. I am not quite sure what Tuck meant by 'genuinely'.

[12] My occasional phrase 'all common law is custom' encapsulates the phrases 'all law is recognized as custom' and 'the law-making process is founded upon custom'. I do not see it as negated—and neither did the seventeenth-century common lawyers—by the undoubted truth that many statutes are made without having been custom.

vim legis, that this implicit law-making should be explicitly recognized. That custom *obtinuerat vim legis*, however—and this we must take Hale to be conceding—was precisely what judgment and statute sometimes recognized; and it was because this happened that the 'implicit' authority of usage and custom could be reinforced and added to, without being absorbed or annulled by, the 'explicit' authority of court and parliament. This was the 'artificial' reason, known to Hedley and Davies and Coke and Selden, which Hale was concerned to vindicate against Hobbes.

All of the foregoing is a significant side-issue. It does not establish what Weston and Greenberg aptly call 'the idiom of Restoration politics',[13] and propose to consider as the idiom of a debate over co-ordinate sovereignty. As this goes to press we are awaiting the publication of Mark Goldie's *The Tory Ideology: Politics and Ideas in Restoration England*,[14] which is expected to propose, as an alternative idiom, that of persecution, comprehension, indulgence and toleration, the ecclesiology of the royal supremacy, and the problem of sovereignty as occasioned by debate over all these questions. We have not yet adopted agreed guidelines for the interpretation of Restoration political argument, and certainly none are to be found in *The Ancient Constitution and the Feudal Law*, though the evidence it presents will probably have to form part of any such interpretation. It has been left to Weston and Greenberg, so far, to propose a context of debate in which 'the controversy over the origin of the Commons, 1675–88'[15] ought to be read, and we must now move towards considering how far their proposal is satisfactory.

Before doing so, however, I should like to re-emphasize some evidence regarding the state of political argument in 1675–7, which I have used more than once[16] in developing a thesis—

---

[13] The title of their sixth chapter; *Subjects and Sovereigns*, pp. 149–81.

[14] Announced by the Cambridge University Press as forthcoming in the series Ideas in Context.

[15] I venture to cite the title of my doctoral dissertation (1952).

[16] *Politics, Language and Time*, pp. 115–26; *The Machiavellian Moment*, pp. 406–16; *The Political Works of James Harrington*, pp. 128–33.

subsequent to that first put forward in the present book—regarding the character of oppositional thought for the next hundred years and longer. This evidence included a speech by Shaftesbury to the House of Lords, *A Letter from a Person of Quality to His Friend in the Country* (1675), and somewhat more at a distance Andrew Marvell's *Account of the Growth of Popery and Arbitrary Government* (1677). These accuse the king's ministers, Danby in particular, of plotting to subvert the constitution by introducing standing armies and using the influence of the crown to corrupt members of the legislature; they propose to remedy these evils by an immediate dissolution of parliament and the holding in future of more frequent parliaments (triennial if not annual). As Shaftesbury's close advisor, Locke must have been involved in preparing this polemic, and he has been named as a possible author of the *Letter from a Person of Quality*.[17] Arguments of this kind, however, are not to be found elsewhere in his writings—though this does not prove that he was not in sympathy with them; they appear to prefigure the 'country' arguments which became standard with all eighteenth-century oppositions, whether the 'country' was currently supposed to be Whig or Tory, and in emphasizing the danger that the representative legislature will become corruptly dependent on the executive, they look in the direction of a 'separation of powers' which could lie on the republican side of the conjoint sovereignty otherwise envisaged in the *Answer to the Nineteen Propositions of Parliament*. With this stress on the need for frequent parliaments and the dangers of a standing army, indeed, these arguments contain echoes of the 'good old cause' of the 1650's and even the Army manifestoes of 1647, when the New Model had called for frequent parliaments and denied that it was a mercenary instrument of state. We begin to see evidence that Shaftesbury's supporters included old soldiers and republicans, among whom Andrew Marvell, John Wildman and

[17] K. H. D. Haley, *The First Earl of Shaftesbury* (Oxford University Press, 1968), pp. 390–6. My own view would be that I doubt his authorship of the 'neo-Harringtonian' passages in the *Letter*, but do not doubt that he was very close by when it was written.

Henry Neville might figure with others. There could be a republican as well as parliamentarian reading of the idea of mixed government, and the debate over co-ordination of sovereignty does not cover the argument at every one of its points.

This group of writings has its significance in the history of the ancient constitution. To hark back to the 'good old cause' might easily be to hark back to Harrington, who was not without reputation; yet Shaftesbury—who was exploiting the quarrel between the Houses in the case of *Shirley* v. *Fagg*—informed the House of Lords that only they stood between the nation and the alternatives of a 'Democraticall Republicque'[18] and rule by a standing army. In this I have found evidence that Harrington's doctrines were being adapted to a situation in which monarchy had been restored and a peerage which no longer possessed feudal military power was exercising weighty political authority. The ancient constitution had returned, particularly in the form ascribed to it by the *Answer to the Nineteen Propositions*, and a Harringtonian reading of the political importance of the possession of arms—more than ever necessary in the face of the new 'standing army'—must be located in English history: not merely in the classical antiquity or the imminent millennial future where Harrington had located his republic of armed freeholders, but in the past of the ancient constitution. I have called this 'neo-Harringtonianism' and it will recur in the context of the 'Brady controversy'.

Weston and Greenberg offer to locate this controversy almost wholly—it might be too much to say 'exclusively'—within the context of the debate about co-ordination of sovereignty, and advance a considerable weight of evidence in support of their thesis. I am glad to agree that the text of *The Ancient Constitution and the Feudal Law* does not do enough to establish the pattern of a constitutional debate which explains why the antiquity of the Commons became a question of importance in 1680; I welcome their attempt to supply one, and I find their arguments at many

---

[18] *Politics, Language and Time*, p. 116.

points convincing. As they tell the story, William Petyt—an antiquary of more learning and authority, and an agent a good deal closer to the Earl of Essex, than I made him appear in 1957[19]—initiated the controversy by writing *The Antient Right of the Commons of England Asserted* in 1679–80. He did so in reply to Dugdale's *Baronage of England* in 1675, and also to the republication in 1679 of *The Freeholders Grand Inquest*, which Weston and Greenberg hold was not the work of Sir Robert Filmer but of Sir Robert Holbourne.[20] He was moved throughout by the fear that to deny antiquity to the Commons was to deny them a share in the legislative power, leaving them only the authority named in their writs of summons: '*ad faciendum et consentiendum*' to what the king and his council might resolve to enact. To argue this very case, Weston and Greenberg continue, was what moved Robert Brady and his allies to argue against the antiquity of the Commons and advance their feudal interpretation of the Norman Conquest; 'and they go so far as to pronounce that this new vision of English history was of little importance in providing either the motive or the substance of Brady's writings, in comparison with his theory of the location of sovereignty.

Given these themes in his writings, Brady may be termed a political theorist of Bodinian leanings who made skilful use of the records of early English history in the service of a greater cause, namely, the high power of the later Stuart kings. To this cause his historical scholarship was subordinate. Whatever admiration may be felt for Brady as a pioneer in modern historiography, he formed part of a dwindling minority in the political nation to which he belonged, his scholarly finding about early history an imposing barrier to the intellectual acceptance of a theory of legal sovereignty in king, lords and commons.[21]

[19] *Subjects and Sovereigns*, pp. 197–9, 252, 344–5. The publication of *A Catalogue of the Petyt Library at Skipton, Yorkshire* (Gargrave, England, 1964) has done much to illuminate the learning of William Petyt and his brother Silvester.

[20] *Subjects and Sovereigns, passim* (see index, s.v. 'Holbourne, Sir Robert') and Corinne Comstock Weston, 'The Authorship of the *Freeholders Grand Inquest*', *English Historical Review*, XCV (1980), pp. 74–98.

[21] *Subjects and Sovereigns*, pp. 196–7. See also Weston, 'Legal Sovereignty in

Even if we disregard the evident 'whiggishness' (and 'Whiggishness')[22] of the last sentence, I think these remarks carry their authors a little too far. They smack of what Hexter calls the fallacy of 'the conservation of historical energy',[23] in which two possible 'factors'—in this case 'political theory' and 'historiography'—are placed in opposition to one another, and every strengthening of the one explanation is held to entail a weakening of the other. They also leave it unexplained just how the losing cause in political theory could command the high ground in determining the future of historiography. However, we can avoid both these traps, first by ceasing to regard 'political theory' and 'historiography' as mutually exclusive categories, and second by exploring what did become of Brady's reading of history in the age which followed his political defeat. Furthermore, it is possible and may be preferable to disregard all of the issues raised by the passage just quoted. I did not supply an adequate polemical context for the controversy over the origins of the Commons during the 1680's; Weston and Greenberg have done so, and it is in a great many ways both convincing and satisfactory. My only doubt is whether it accounts for all the events taking place in the narrative available to us; whether there are not other contexts which must be reconstructed in order to account for other features of the story.

'The Brady controversy' was also 'the Filmerian controversy', and 'the Filmerian controversy' was also 'the Exclusion controversy'; each time one alters the label the context expands and changes, and we have to ask whether the debate over co-ordinate sovereignty is more than one conspicuous and important phenomenon of the field before us. We know that Petyt was moved to complete and publish his *Antient Right of the Commons* by the republication of the *Freeholders Grand Inquest*, as

the Brady Controversy', *Historical Journal*, vol. xv (1972), pp. 409–31.

[22] For this distinction see the discussion in ch. 1 of this retrospect and the reference in n. 12 to that chapter.

[23] For this term see J. H. Hexter, *Reappraisals in History*, 2d ed. (University of Chicago Press, 1979), pp. 40–41. One may also speak of the 'two-buckets fallacy'; water placed in one must come out of the other.

well as by Dugdale's work on the baronage four or five years
before; and there is a letter to Petyt from James Tyrrell, the
friend of Locke, which tells us this and a good deal more. I
mentioned this letter—as did Laslett in his edition of Locke's
Treatises[24]—at pp. 187–8 above, but did not give the full text as
transcribed in my doctoral dissertation. Perhaps it is time to do
so. It bears the date January 12, and the year must be 1680.

I sent up last week to Mr Marsham some Papers which I desired him to
communicate to you: but since he sends me word that you were about
the same designe your self, I cannot but assure you that had I known
your intentions sooner, I should have bin so far from undertaking it,
that I should have bin one of the first that would have importuned you
to the performance of it: since I know none more able to doe it than
your self: and therefore if you still hold your resolutions as I hope you
doe, If you please to think any thing I have writ in those papers may be
of the least use to you: I freely offer it you. (For as for the greatest part
of the Records I have quoted you may justly challeng them for your
owne, since I must owne my self beholding to you for them.) I have
likewise made observations upon all the rest of those treatises of Sir
Robert Filmer, which if you intend to answer the whole book shall be
altogether at your service; since not intending to put my owne name to
them if ever I publish them: I should be very glad to contribute my mite
to so good a work, especially when undertaken by so worthy, and
ingenious a friend, to whom I wish all happyness and good successe as
well upon his owne as the publick account, which is the hearty prayer of

Your obliged friend, and humble servant
J. Tyrrell.

There is lately come to this towne a new treatise of Sir Robert Filmers
called Patriarcha, which I am now considering of, and I desire you
would be pleased to look it over. For the 3d. chapter conteins as
dangerous errors as are in the Freeholders Inquest, (though most are the
same) especially as to the opinion of the extravagant power of the privy
Counsell, which you know best how to answer.[25]

---

[24] Laslett (ed.), *Two Treatises on Government*, p. 60.

[25] Inner Temple MSS 583 (17), vol. 302; as transcribed in my 'The
Controversy over the Origins of the Commons, 1675–88', Ph.D. dissertation,
Cambridge University, 1952, pp. 101–2.

Several things are clear from this letter. Tyrrell is referring to a work of his own in reply to the *Freeholders Grand Inquest* and is offering not to publish it since Petyt is engaged on one; he believes the *Freeholders Inquest* to be the work of Filmer, with whose tracts it has been reprinted, and is anxious to see the whole Filmerian corpus answered; he has not at the time of writing begun, or at least completed, his reply to *Patriarcha*, later published under the title *Patriarcha Non Monarcha*, but regards *Patriarcha* (at this point almost exclusively) as continuing the harmful intent of the *Freeholders Inquest*. The question whether the latter's author was Filmer or Holbourne is therefore not relevant to its impact in 1680. We also know from other evidence that Tyrrell and Locke were living in the former's house at Shotover when Tyrrell wrote *Patriarcha Non Monarcha*, and were jointly engaged on a reply to Edward Stillingfleet's *Unreasonableness of a New Separation*; there is a strong probability that Locke's *First* if not his *Second Treatise of Government* was composed about the same time.[26] I confess to a persistent if unverifiable suspicion that the reply to Stillingfleet constituted 'the Papers that should have filled up the middle, and were more than all the rest', mentioned by Locke when he published the two *Treatises* in 1690 as 'the Beginning and End of a Discourse concerning Government';[27] he had by that time recast the argument they contained as the *Epistola de Tolerantia*.

If this were demonstrable, we should be able to tell a single story concerning Locke's and Tyrrell's collaborative efforts in 1680 and thereabouts. As it is, however, we are able to say that Tyrrell looked on Petyt and himself as concerned to refute the *Freeholders Grand Inquest*, as the work of Filmer, at the same time that he and Locke were engaged on the refutation of *Patriarcha*. Petyt's *Antient Right of the Commons*, the supporting works written by William Atwood, and the counter-attack by Robert Brady and his allies, are therefore part of the Filmerian controversy to the extent that they were occasioned by the

---

[26] Laslett, pp. 60–61.
[27] *Ibid.*, p. 155.

347

denial of antiquity to the Commons; and James Tyrrell was as anxious to see Filmer refuted on the historical front as he was on the patriarchal. This is true not only of his activities in 1680, but of the *Bibliotheca Politica* which he published in 1694; and the same may be said of Algernon Sidney's *Discourses of Government*, published by John Toland in 1698 but written (assuming the genuineness of the published text) between 1679 and the author's execution in 1683.[28] As against this, we have the fact that Locke, who became renowned as Filmer's chief opponent, is not known to have written anything concerning the antiquity of parliament; there is debate whether this silence is accidental or significant.

The immediate point, however, is that 'the Brady controversy' was part of 'the Filmerian controversy' to the extent that Petyt, Atwood and Brady wrote in consequence of the republication of the *Freeholders Grand Inquest* among the works of Filmer. We have next to ask whether this modifies the contention of Weston and Greenberg that 'the Brady controversy' is to be read in the context of the debate over co-ordinate sovereignty. That it is to be read in that context we may take them to have established; but is there no other context? Did the *Freeholders Inquest*, supposed to be the work of Filmer, have no other effect than to refuel debate over the location of sovereignty? Is there no relation between the debate over the meaning of the Norman Conquest and the origins of the Commons, and the debate over the patriarchal theory of kingship descended from Adam? Tyrrell and Sidney thought that 'Filmer' should be refuted on both counts in the same book.

In closing ch. VIII above, I refer to Brady and his associates as 'Filmerian' writers, but do not go so far as to refer to them as 'patriarchalists'. By 'Filmerian' I seem to have meant little more than the argument which derived all liberties from the will and condescension of the monarch; and though this is to be found in the *Freeholders Inquest*, we do not have to go there for it and there

---

[28] Blair Worden, 'The Commonwealth Kidney of Algernon Sidney', *Journal of British Studies*, vol. XXIV, 1 (1985), pp. 1–40.

is no need to draw on patriarchal theory to substantiate it. For these reasons the late James Daly, in the only book so far devoted entirely to the study of Filmer,[29] queried how far the Tory feudalists ought to be called 'Filmerian' at all[30] (it was in general his intention to minimize Filmer's importance and suggest that we knew him chiefly from the writings of his opponents). Certainly, if there is no more to 'Filmerian' historiography than the *Freeholders Inquest*'s denial of antiquity to the Commons, we have—the question of authorship apart—little enough to build on, and might be pressed back towards the position advanced by Weston and Greenberg. There remains, however, the question whether the feudal interpretation of Norman kingship is, as they would have it, no more than a tool in denying the Commons a share in sovereignty.

A feudal king—even one who was lord of the whole land—was not really a patriarch; he was not even metaphorically the father of his vassals, since oaths counted for more in homage than birth or kinship. I recall thinking as I wrote that if historians had wanted to discover patriarchal rule in the British past, they would have done better to focus on the Gaelic chief, supposedly the lord over a name or kindred; and recently I have been gratified to discover that the same thought occurred in the eighteenth century to the Jacobite historian Thomas Carte, a warm supporter of Brady.[31] But if we are prepared to move out of national history into *jus gentium* (as we did in order to elucidate the notion of conquest), the patriarch may be made to look a little more feudal; it can be argued that God granted the whole earth to Adam as *dominium*, so that the subjects of a king enjoy their property only as *usus*. This theme, and much besides,

---

[29] See, however, Gordon J. Schochet, *Patriarchalism in Political Thought* (Oxford: Basil Blackwell, 1975).

[30] James Daly, *Sir Robert Filmer and English Political Thought* (University of Toronto Press, 1979), pp. 182–90.

[31] Thomas Carte, *A General History of England, vol. 1, Containing an Account of the First Inhabitants of the Country, and the Transactions in It, from the Earliest Times to the Death of King John, A.D. MCCXVI* (London, 1747), pp. 47, 48, 77–8, 176–7, 361–2, 365, 372, 376.

occurs in James Tully's *A Discourse on Property: John Locke and His Adversaries*,[32] where the debate between Filmer and Locke is returned to the context of *jus gentium* established by Suarez, Grotius and other jurists. But the discussion of *dominium* and *usus* is not only a very abstract and universalized way of talking about feudal property; it may even be doubted whether the discussion of feudal property is more than incidental to it. The great jurists did not as a rule feel obliged to take the long stride from *jus gentium, dominium* and *usus* to *jus feudale* and the *Libri Feudorum*, to the Roman, Gothic or Lombard origins of the *feudum*, to the processes whereby it became inheritable and subject to services, or to the relation between the sword of the conqueror and his grant of lands to his companions. Their problems could best be discussed in Roman terms without venturing into barbaric, and the study of barbaric jurisprudence remained correspondingly autonomous.

Sooner or later, we must confront the question whether the nature of feudal tenure played any part, and if so what part it did play, in 'the Brady controversy', 'the Filmerian controversy' or 'the Exclusion controversy' of the early and middle 1680's. The ghost of the Marxist 'transition from feudal to bourgeois social relations' hangs over our thoughts still, but ought to be challenged by exorcists. Nobody was threatened with a re-imposition of feudal obligations and, outside the widespread but special categories of those who owned former monastic lands or forfeited lands in Ireland, nobody's property in land was threatened at all; this was not 1628 and the debate was about something else. The aged Fabian Philipps, a former official of the Court of Wards, might long for the days when tenure *in capite* had carried the obligation to knight service; but James Duke of York, that very modern military administrator and energetic promoter of mercantile empire,[33] cannot have had

---

[32] Cambridge University Press, 1980.

[33] See Stephen Saunders Webb, *The Governors-General: The English Army and the Definition of the Empire, 1569–1681* (Chapel Hill: University of North Carolina Press, 1979) and *1676: The End of American Independence* (New York: Knopf, 1984).

much desire to find himself at the head of a feudal host. Matthew Wren twenty-five years earlier had seen well enough that the case for absolute monarchy was best made on the basis of commercial property, a standing army and a Hobbesian theory of social relationships.[34] If a nostalgia for feudalism could be felt by monarchists for whom it meant the days when every proprietor was the king's sworn vassal, it could equally be felt by neo-Harringtonian republicans for whom it meant the days when every free man kept and bore his own arms. The one thing agreed upon by all serious students of feudal relationships was that they had disappeared from England a long time ago, probably under the early Tudors. What makes Brady 'a pioneer in modern historiography' is that he knows he is resurrecting a past that is dead, and it is the role of modernism in his political argument that we have to understand.

Henry Neville's *Plato Redivivus*,[35] which appeared in 1682, must have a place in any study of these controversies. It has little to do with the refutation of patriarchalism, but something to do with the antiquity of the Commons. I have proposed calling Neville a 'neo-Harringtonian'[36] because, though a close friend of Harrington for the whole of their active lives, he now carried out a drastic revision—hinted at by Shaftesbury in 1675—of the Harringtonian historical scheme. For Harrington the republic of armed proprietors had existed in classical antiquity, but had been subverted first by the Caesars and then by the feudal lords of the 'Gothic balance'; with the decay of feudal tenures after 1485, it was now in process of being restored, and contemporary political institutions were unstable in so far as they failed to adapt themselves to its return. Neville, faced with the return to

---

[34] *The Political Works of James Harrington*, pp. 83–9.

[35] There is a modern text in Caroline Robbins (ed.), *Two English Republican Tracts* (Cambridge University Press, 1969).

[36] For doubts concerning this term, see J. R. Goodale, 'J. G. A. Pocock's Neo-Harringtonians: A Reconsideration', *History of Political Thought*, vol. I, no. 2 (1980), pp. 237–60; J. C. Davis, 'Pocock's Harrington: Grace, Nature and Art in the Classical Republicanism of James Harrington', *Historical Journal*, vol. XXIV, no. 3 (1981), pp. 683–98.

power of the monarchy, the peerage and the ancient constitution, all of which Harrington had supposed obsolete, now proposed to locate the polity of armed freeholders in the *communitas militum* of the thirteenth century. He conceded that barons had enjoyed great authority over their vassals and that the Commons in a medieval parliament had followed the will of the Lords (as so often with English historians, he did not consider the representatives of boroughs to have been of much account as a separate class); it had taken the works of Petyt and Atwood, he said, to convince him that the Commons had attended at all.[37] But this was of secondary importance. Baronial or knightly, the exercise of political power by armed men seated on their own lands had been the guarantee of medieval liberty, and the problems of modern government were the consequence of the decay of feudal tenures. Kings and their ministers were now tempted to such expedients as standing armies and the corruption of parliaments, and the solution must lie in recognizing the increased independence, and therefore the increased power, of the post-feudal lords and commons. Neville thus came into line with the 'country' demands for more frequent parliaments, and at the same time joined Petyt and Atwood in asserting the antiquity of the House of Commons; he may be said to have supplied 'neo-Harringtonian' arguments for the place of both Houses in a system of co-ordinate sovereignty.

In one respect, however, Neville is closer to Brady: the reconstruction of feudalism is for him a means of reconstituting a past which history has left behind, and only superficially does he support Petyt and Atwood in minimizing feudalism's role in making that past different. In so far as the debate about the Bill of Exclusion raised the problem of co-ordinate sovereignty, it made sense for Petyt and Atwood to assert the antiquity of the Commons and for Brady and the agents in republishing Filmer to deny it; but Neville was less concerned about the popish successor than about the problems of the post-feudal monarch.[38]

[37] *Two English Republican Tracts*, pp. 119–20.
[38] *Ibid.*, pp. 160–75.

In so far as the Exclusion crisis raised, especially after 1681, serious dangers of rebellion and civil war, it made sense for the party of order to revive, in patriarchal and possibly in feudal terms, the argument that property entailed obedience and carried no rights that could justify resistance. The debate about the feudal interpretation of the English past was an analysis of both conquest in the eleventh century and baronial rebellion in the thirteenth; and here the thrust of Brady's writings does seem to have been towards the argument from anachronism, the argument that the liberties the barons wrote into their charter were feudal liberties and had nothing to do with the rights of parliament or people in a post-feudal age. We cannot, simply by calling him 'a Bodinian political theorist', dismiss the force of this argument, or ignore the possibility that he was read as a conservative modernist, enhancing the power of the crown by situating it in a context of incessant change. Atwood by contrast, with his distinction between *barones regis* who held of the king and *barones regni* who held of the community of the realm, may seem to have been denying anachronism and maintaining that there were rights and liberties which were prescriptive and immemorial. Had the sword been drawn— might it again be drawn—in their defence? It is hard to extract from any of these tracts a clear allusion to the possibility of civil war in the 1680's; Brady's charge that his adversaries 'insinuate' the English monarchy to be elective is about as close as we come to it. 'Two Sorts of Turbulent Men there are in the World', he wrote,[39] meaning those who affirmed a right of resistance and those who affirmed the antiquity of the constitution; but neither they nor he wished to return to the Middle Ages.

John Locke was only one sort of turbulent man, but turbulent he undeniably was. As I was writing *The Ancient Constitution and the Feudal Law*, Peter Laslett was executing a revolution in Locke scholarship by demonstrating that both *Treatises of Civil Government* must be work of the early 1680's,[40] with the result

---

[39] Above, p. 231, n. 2.
[40] Peter Laslett, 'The English Revolution and Locke's *Two Treatises of*

that the *Second* unequivocally calls for an 'appeal to heaven' and a 'dissolution of government' at a time when both terms must imply a rebellion and civil war which had not taken place and never did, and not the miraculously bloodless confrontation of 1688 which the *Treatises* were published to justify. The Protestant wind blew England many things, one of them being Locke's reputation as a great political moderate. The *Treatises* have therefore to be considered an item of the 'Filmerian controversy', of which the 'Brady controversy' was another, and their genesis can be traced back as far as Tyrrell's letter to Petyt of January 1680; yet the *Second Treatise* envisages action so drastic that some would prefer to date it as near to 1683 as possible. In this setting one's attention must be drawn to the fact that Locke displays little or no interest in the antiquity of the Commons, not much more in the problem of the Norman Conquest, and none to speak of in the history of feudal tenures.

One might explain the absence of English history from the *First Treatise*—which is directed against *Patriarcha*—by supposing that, even more unequivocally than Tyrrell in writing *Patriarcha Non Monarcha*, Locke had decided to leave all such matters to Petyt. Yet we know that Tyrrell would have tackled the historical issue if Petyt had not done so, and that he did return to it after the Revolution in *Bibliotheca Politica* and the *General History of England*;[41] there is no evidence that it interested Locke at any time. One may explain the absence of history from the *Second Treatise* more simply still, by pointing out that the subject of the latter is the origin and dissolution of government, and that the ancient constitution has no origin and contains no provision for its own dissolution. Yet this will not satisfy those who

Government', *Cambridge Historical Journal*, vol. XII, no. 1 (1956), pp. 40–55; *idem*, (ed.) *John Locke: Two Treatises of Government: A Critical Edition with an Introduction and Apparatus Criticus* (Cambridge University Press, 1960; reprinted with amendments, 1963; New York: Mentor Books, 1965).

[41] *Bibliotheca Politica; or, An Enquiry into the Ancient Constitution of the Government of England... In thirteen dialogues* (1694), 2d ed. (fourteen dialogues), 1701; *The General History of England, as well Ecclesiastical as Civil...* (1696–1704, 3 vols.).

start—as to some extent we all do—from the premise that Locke is what has been termed an 'epic theorist',[42] a master intellect in whose writings the currents of the age are summed up and transformed. On this premise his refusal to enter the debate about English history must mean something, and even Quentin Skinner has raised the possibility that his silence intentionally conveys the message that the subject is not worth debating.[43] I incline to the view that Skinner raises this for methodological reasons, as a specimen of the kinds of problem we have to consider, a specimen in particular of the problems of *argumentum ex silentio*; for certainly, if Locke intended to convey any such message he was singularly unsuccessful. The debate about the ancient constitution continued for the next two centuries. One recoils, all the same, from the alternative explanation that the reasons for Locke's silence are trivial and idiosyncratic; he did not write about English history because he just wasn't interested.[44] There was clearly a convention among his close friends of finding it very interesting indeed, and if he had been a political agent for Shaftesbury he must have known its importance in argument. We should like to find an interpretative framework in which his not writing about it would have some significance.

Without having recourse to a strategy of trivialization, it is possible to ease our predicament by suggesting that the *Treatises* are not "epic theory" in the sense that, say, *Leviathan* is: a piece of theory in which the intellectual trends of an age are summed up and brought to bear on its major crisis. It is possible to contend that they are *pièces d'occasion*, which moreover missed their *occasion* and were published years later, in a political context very different from that for which they were written. It can be

[42] The term is Sheldon S. Wolin's; see his 'Political Theory as a Vocation', *American Political Science Review*, vol. LXIII, no. 4 (1969), pp. 1062–82, and *Hobbes and the Epic Tradition of Political Theory* (Los Angeles: William Andrews Clark Memorial Library, 1970).

[43] Skinner, *The Foundations of Modern Political Thought* (Cambridge University Press, 1978), vol. I, p. XIV.

[44] I entertained this possibility at p. 238, above.

shown, as we shall see, that in that context they failed to have
the effect hoped for them when they were published. In
addition, they were published anonymously and their author
never admitted to having written them.[45] Only in the next
generation did it come to be recognized that the *Treatises on
Government* were the work of 'the great Mr Locke' and ought to
be read in the context furnished by the *Essay on Human
Understanding,* the *Letter Concerning Toleration,* and other works
which he published (and in some cases owned to) after he
published the *Treatises.* We have been trying to read the *Treatises*
in that context ever since, and it is very right that we should do
so; anything which John Locke has to say about the significance
of revolutionary events in which he was himself involved ought
to be studied very seriously indeed. But to read the *Treatises* in
the context of a *corpus Lockeanum* and a view of Locke's historical
significance formed by that corpus is one thing, and to read
them in the context of immediately contemporary debate is
another. This may be a case in which to return texts to their
immediate practical context is to restrict their significance rather
than expand it, and we must be careful not to mix the two
contexts up in ways which lead to the asking of *questions mal
posées.* What Locke meant by not saying anything about English
history may prove to be such a question.

I have stressed more than once that 'the Brady controversy' is
not co-terminous with 'the Filmerian controversy' and the latter
not co-terminous with 'the Exclusion controversy'. At the time
when *The Ancient Constitution and the Feudal Law* was published,
I had access to only two articles[46] which offered to survey the
literature and the argumentative structure of 'the Exclusion
controversy', and there has not been very much written on the

---

[45] Laslett, p. 79.

[46] B. M. A. Behrens, 'The Whig Theory of the Constitution in the Reign of
Charles II', *Cambridge Historical Journal,* vol. VIII, no. 1 (1941), pp. 42–71, and
O. W. Furley, 'The Whig Exclusionists: Pamphlet Literature in the Exclusion
Campaign, 1679–81', *Cambridge Historical Journal,* vol. XIII, no. 1 (1957), pp.
19–36. I was not then aware of F. S. Ronalds, *The Attempted Whig Revolution of
1678–81* (Urbana: University of Illinois Press, 1937).

subject since.[47] My book was therefore necessarily confined to
the two lesser fields, and what it says about Locke's lack of
interest in English history amounts to the statement that as a
participant (which he certainly was) in 'the Filmerian controversy' he was not at all a participant in 'the Brady controversy',
meaning that aspect of 'the Filmerian controversy' which
followed the publication of *The Freeholders Grand Inquest*.
However, it is obviously desirable to view the 'Brady' and
'Filmerian' controversies as aspects of 'the Exclusion controversy'. Weston and Greenberg have proposed to treat the last-
named as principally a debate about co-ordinate sovereignty, but
it may be possible to go further still.

Richard Ashcraft, the author of the latest (and very impressive) attempts to consider Locke as a revolutionary, indeed as a
'bourgeois revolutionary', theorist,[48] has proposed to dismiss
the problem of Locke's non-use of historical argument by
claiming that the use of historical argument was not typical of
'the Exclusion controversy' as a whole. I do not recall asserting
that it was; I contended merely that it was crucial to the conduct
of controversy by Locke's close associates at the time when he
probably began writing the *Treatises*. But Ashcraft collects a
great deal of evidence about the use of argument in favour of the
Bill of Exclusion, and the right of the two Houses to pass such a
bill, which presents kingship as conditional and contractual and
looks in the direction of action without the royal assent. There
was of course argument which carried such implications, which
is why there was serious fear of civil war in 1679–80. Ashcraft

---

[47] J. R. Jones, *The First Whigs: The Politics of the Exclusion Crisis, 1679–83*
(London: Oxford University Press, 1970) and K. H. D. Haley, *The First Earl of
Shaftesbury* (n. 17, above), are useful but do not study the literature in detail.
[48] 'The *Two Treatises* and the Exclusion Crisis: The Problem of Lockean
Political Theory as Bourgeois Ideology', in J. G. A. Pocock and Richard
Ashcraft, *John Locke: Papers Read at a Clark Library Seminar, 10 December 1977* (Los
Angeles: William Andrews Clark Memorial Library, 1980); 'Revolutionary
Politics and Locke's *Two Treatises of Government*: Radicalism and Lockean
Political Theory', *Political Theory*, vol. VIII, no. 4 (1980), pp. 429–86;
Revolutionary Politics and Locke's Two Treatises on Government (Princeton
University Press, 1986).

makes two further moves. He emphasizes the extent to which such arguments indicate the presence in London, Southwark and Wapping of radical, green-ribbon, commonwealth-minded tradesmen, artisans and labourers (who were therefore 'bourgeois', whatever that may mean); and he avers that these arguments do not make much reference to history in the sense of the antiquity of the Commons. Very likely they do not; we know that there were ways of appealing to history a good deal more radical than those which produced indications of the ancient constitution. Ashcraft, however, has got himself close to arguing that unhistorical theories about contract, natural right and deposition are indicators of bourgeois radicalism, whereas any appeal to history and the antiquity of parliament is an indicator of genteel conservatism. Locke's *Second Treatise*, accordingly, places him on the bourgeois-radical side of the ledger.

That Locke was a good deal more 'radical' (though 'bourgeois' he was not[49]) than most Whigs, and than historians have till recently allowed, we may all join in affirming; yet there are important ways in which Ashcraft can be challenged. He is quite rightly resolved to dispel a reading of Locke as an author of a conservative and respectable revolution in 1688–9, and he is right in seeing that the use of history is important to both this reading and its replacement. But if he has allowed himself to suppose that the use of historical precedent is necessarily a sign of Burkean caution and conservatism, this is not perfectly correct. There are two reasons why he may have thought so. One is that Macaulay constructed a 'Burkean' reading of the debates in the Convention Parliament during 1689, in which the speakers' use of antiquarian precedents and the ancient constitution was extolled for having saved England from the horrors of

---

[49] He was a gentleman, the son of a gentleman, a member of the client gentry from whom the trusted advisers and servants of great houses were drawn, and a member of the educated clerisy not in orders. This did not stop him investing his capital; it merely proves that one did not need to be a bourgeois in order to have capital to invest. The terms are not synonymous, and should not be used interchangeably.

Jacobin intellectualism.[50] Macaulay made no mention of Locke one way or the other, and neither did Burke, but we may concede that there has been a 'Whig interpretation' of Locke which makes his *Treatise* fit into this pattern, thus constructing what Ashcraft more than once calls 'the myth of Locke's political innocence'[51] and suspects all historians of conspiring to uphold. That there has been a myth of Locke as the accredited Whig apologist of 1688–9 is known to us all.

The second foundation on which Ashcraft's argument rests may be this. When Locke returned to England from the Netherlands, in the wake of William's expedition and the flight of James, he set about publishing the *Treatises* (anonymously) in their incomplete form, ending with an account of how a government might be dissolved and a people resume the right to preserve or alter it as they thought fit. There is reason to suppose that this aligned him with hard-line 'radical' Whigs who wanted the Convention to maintain itself as such and assume the role of a constituent assembly.[52] What the Convention did, however, was to declare itself a parliament, with the clear intention of maintaining that the entire historical fabric of king, lords, common law and church as by law established—in other words the ancient constitution—remained in being as legitimating the Convention Parliament's proceedings and by implication all that had been done in the months since William landed. In short, no

[50] Macaulay, *History of England from the Accession of James II*, ch. x.

[51] Ashcraft, *John Locke*, pp. 45, 46; *Political Theory*, p. 466. For my own views, see 'The Myth of John Locke and the Obsession with Liberalism', in *John Locke, op. cit.*, n. 48, and 'Recent Scholarship on John Locke and the Political Thought of the Late Seventeenth Century', *Theoretische Geschiedenis*, vol. XI, no. 3 (1984), pp. 251–61. That the *Treatises* are activist was settled by Laslett; that they are bourgeois is not settled yet. *Cf.*, of course, C. B. Macpherson, *The Political Theory of Possessive Individualism* (Oxford University Press, 1962).

[52] See Julian H. Franklin, *John Locke and the Theory of Sovereignty: Mixed Monarchy and the Right of Resistance in the Political Thought of the English Revolution* (Cambridge University Press, 1978), pp. 98–126; Lois G. Schwoerer, *The Declaration of Rights, 1689* (Baltimore: Johns Hopkins University Press, 1981); Charles D. Tarlton, ' "The Rulers Now on Earth"; Locke's *Two Treatises* and the Revolution of 1688', *Historical Journal*, vol. XXVIII, no. 2 (1985), pp. 279–98.

dissolution of government, and no reversion of power to the people, had occurred. It would not be easy, and was in any case totally unnecessary, to interpret the *Second Treatise* as meaning that an appeal to heaven could be made without a dissolution of government; and this is why William Atwood—one of the few publicists of the Revolution Settlement to pay attention to the *Treatises on Government*—applauded them as philosophy, but added that there was fortunately no need to make use of their arguments.[53] All that had been done could be justified by the necessity of preserving and transmitting the constitution inherited from time immemorial;[54] the way was open to the assertion, later made by Burke, that the constitution had not been altered at all.

These arguments probably arose less from a spirit of Burkean prescriptivism than from a grim certainty that dissolution of government meant civil war, that only a succession of miracles had averted civil war, and that civil war might still very possibly occur. It is therefore far from certain how far we are to project such considerations back to the circumstances of authorship obtaining in 1680–3. It is clear that, whenever Locke wrote the *Second Treatise*, he was willing to contemplate civil war, and that the need to answer the shade of Sir Robert Filmer is not enough to account for this willingness; but it is not so clear that because Tyrrell, Petyt and others used arguments about the antiquity of the Commons, they were therefore unwilling to contemplate extreme measures and were preparing to use the

---

[53] William Atwood, *The Fundamental Constitution of the English Government* (London, 1690). See Franklin, *op. cit.*, pp. 105–8; J. P. Kenyon, *Revolution Principles: the Politics of Party, 1689–1720* (Cambridge University Press, 1977), pp. 18–20; and more generally Martyn P. Thompson, 'The Reception of Locke's *Two Treatises of Government*, 1690–1705,' in *Political Studies*, vol. xxiv (1976), pp. 184–91, and Mark Goldie, 'The Revolution of 1689 and the Structure of Political Argument', in *Bulletin of Research in the Humanities*, vol. lxxiii (1980), pp. 473–564. Goldie classes Atwood as a 'radical Whig'; I contend that he is in this respect less 'radical' than Locke.

[54] On 1689 as an achievement of 'the common-law mind', see Howard A. Nenner, *By Colour of Law: Legal Culture and Constitutional Politics in England, 1660–1689* (University of Chicago Press, 1977).

ancient constitution to preclude the dissolution of government. And if that is not clear, it is not clear either that Locke did not use historical arguments because he was a more logical revolutionary than his associates were. It may have taken 1681, 1683, 1685 and 1688 to bring matters to the point where the *Treatises on Government* could be dismissed by Locke's former associates as irrelevant and possibly subversive.

Ashcraft is mistaken, finally, in suggesting that the appeal to history was necessarily ancient-constitutionalist and conservative, and that it was the mark of the green-ribbon radical to abstain from making it. There was an argument from history, as old as the Norman yoke and the good old cause and with a future before it reaching as far as the People's Charter, which grounded annual parliaments, the rights of boroughs and the people's militia in pre-Conquest antiquity. This was the style of argument favoured by the London commonwealthsmen and old soldiers to whom Shaftesbury, and very likely Locke, had made appeal; and a group of old Shaftesbureans and associates of Locke—Robert Ferguson, Samuel Johnson and others—revived it in criticism of the Revolution settlement as soon as they saw what this amounted to.[55] Locke may have kept up contacts with these people after his return to England; but in the published text of the *Second Treatise* he went out of his way to repudiate their arguments, insisting that it was for the prerogative alone to decide upon the duration of parliaments, to abolish corrupt boroughs and charter new ones, that such matters could not be regulated at the first institution of government, and that the only thing needful was that the prerogative should be exercised for the common good.[56] Locke was neither a 'good old cause' man nor a True Whig.[57] To understand the role of historical argument after 1688–9, we must understand that the Gothic liberties and the Norman yoke, as well as the ancient constitution and the feudal law, persisted into the coming century.

[55] Mark Goldie, 'The Roots of True Whiggism, 1688–94,' in *History of Political Thought*, vol. I (1980), pp. 195–236.

[56] *Virtue, Commerce, and History*, pp. 226–8 and notes 42, 43.

[57] *Ibid.*, p. 229.

Restoration, Revolution and Oligarchy

The concluding chapter, '1688 in the History of Historiography', is shaped by the debt it owes to D. C. Douglas's *English Scholars*, still one of the best of the few books we have on late Stuart erudition. From Douglas I drew the image of an efflorescence of medieval studies which came to an end about 1720 and was not again equalled until the age of Stubbs and Maitland. To adopt such an image was, for its day, an anti-whig move in the politics of historiography; the whiggish assumptions on which it continues to rest were less apparent then than they are now. The Saxonists and medievalists portrayed by Douglas were students of ecclesiastical history rather than the history of parliament and common law; they were the great clerical scholars of the post-1688 'crisis in church and state'[58]—Wake and Gibson on the Whig side, Hickes, Collier and Atterbury on the non-juring and Tory—and the disputants over ancient constitution and feudal law who appear in *English Scholars* figure in the company of divines. In his final chapter, 'The End of an Age', Douglas showed clerical erudition retreating before an offensive in the name of 'polite learning': a significant episode in eighteenth-century politics of culture,[59] but one of which I knew little more than could be associated with the name of Bolingbroke. I was, furthermore, trying to work out a theory of 'past-relatedness', designed to inquire what elements in a society's culture operated, from time to time, to generate the image of a past and seek to maintain contact with it;[60] and I dimly saw that the

---

[58] I take this phrase from G. V. Bennett's study of Francis Atterbury, *The Tory Crisis in Church and State, 1688–1730: The Career of Francis Atterbury, Bishop of Rochester* (Oxford: Clarendon Press, 1975).

[59] For this see Joseph M. Levine, *Dr. Woodward's Shield: History, Science and Satire in Augustan England* (University of California Press, 1977) and 'Ancients and Moderns Reconsidered', *Eighteenth-Century Studies*, vol. xv, no. 1 (1982), pp. 72–89; Lawrence E. Klein, 'The Third Earl of Shaftesbury and the Progress of Politeness', *Eighteenth-Century Studies*, vol. xviii, no. 2 (1984–5), pp. 186–214.

[60] 'The Origins of Study of the Past: A Methodological Approach', *Compara-*

campaign for 'polite learning' might imply, among other things, the demise of the county communities of the seventeenth-century gentry, with their antiquarian culture generated at the Inns of Court.[61] I therefore proposed a search for the sources of an inanition of the 'common-law mind' and its view of history, based on assumptions about custom, precedent and charter; but at the same time I was looking for explanations of its survival or revival in the prescriptivism of Edmund Burke. I do not think I was wrong in applying myself to this apparent paradox; but I may have left readers with the impression that the eighteenth century was an age of unrelieved ancient-constitutionalism from Petyt and Tyrrell to Blackstone and Burke, and that Boling-broke's contempt for the critical minutiae of erudition served to keep feudal scholarship in oblivion and repression. This would certainly be far from an adequate account of what really happened. Chapter IX of *The Ancient Constitution and the Feudal Law* must therefore be deemed very tentative, and some of its initiatives are now obsolete.[62]

There have been two major developments since 1957 in fields of scholarship relevant to the history of the ancient constitution after 1688. In 1959 Caroline Robbins published *The Eighteenth-Century Commonwealthman: Studies in the Transmission, Development and Circumstances of English Liberal Thought from the Restoration of Charles II until the War with the Thirteen Colonies,*[63] which deeply changed our awareness of the character of radical thought between the English and French revolutions. We now

tive Studies in Society and History, vol. IV, no. 2 (1962), pp. 209–46, reprinted in P. B. M. Blaas (ed.), *Geschiedenis als Wetenschap* (The Hague: Martinus Nijhoff, 1980).

[61] Peter Laslett's article, 'The Gentry of Kent in 1640', *Cambridge Historical Journal*, vol. IX, no. 2 (1948), pp. 148–64, was the only account of such a community then known to me. The works of Alan Everitt, J. S. Morrill, and other exponents of the 'county community' interpretation of the Civil War, were still to come.

[62] The remainder of this chapter follows the argument of 'The Varieties of Whiggism', *Virtue, Commerce, and History*, pp. 215–310.

[63] Cambridge, Mass.: Harvard University Press, 1959; another edition appeared in 1968.

see it as maintained by the activities of a succession of minority Whigs—Old, True, Independent and Honest in their own estimation—who were discontented with the settlement of 1689 and repelled (in one sense or another) by the oligarchic politics to which they saw it giving rise, and who may by one affiliation be traced back to those who (like Locke) wanted to keep the Convention Parliament a convention. These came to be called Commonwealthmen for a variety of reasons, one of them (in Robbins's narration) being the activities around 1700 of John Toland and others in publishing what she calls 'the Whig canon': Ludlow, Milton, Nedham, Marvell, Harrington, Sidney, Neville and Locke, all of them too radical for the settlement of 1689 and nearly all of them associable with the regicide Commonwealth and the republican literature of the 1650's. Junto Whigs, Court Whigs, Modern Whigs, or whatever the politicians of the increasingly Whig regimes of 1690–1720 may be called, had no desire to take responsibility for this Whig (or rather Commonwealth) canon. They were more anxious than ever to escape regicide and revolutionary (to say nothing of Dissenter) associations, and it is from this time that we may date the appearance of the famous (but little studied) 'Whig interpretation of history', which was based upon extolling the parliamentary oppositions to Charles I while condemning the Independent revolution of 1647–9, and upon condemning the unsuccessful revolutionaries Shaftesbury and Monmouth while extolling the bloodless, preserving and glorious revolution of 1688–9, and which made use of the ancient constitution at precisely those points in the story which we would expect. James Tyrrell and White Kennett were among its architects, and it was carried on by Laurence Echard, John Oldmixon and Paul de Rapin Thoyras.[64]

Mark Goldie's article 'The Roots of True Whiggism, 1688–94' has pushed the story further back than the foundation of

[64] For Tyrrell, see n. 41 above. White Kennett (ed.), *A Complete History of England* (London, 1706); Laurence Echard, *The History of England from the First Entrance of Julius Caesar and the Romans . . .* (London, 1708–18); John Oldmixon, *The Critical History of England, Ecclesiastical and Civil* (London, 1724); *The History of England during the Reign of the Royal House of Stuart* (London,

Toland's canon, by isolating the writings of a group of old Shaftesburean radicals—John Wildman the sometime Leveller, Robert Ferguson the Scottish conspirator, Samuel Johnson the degraded clergyman—who thought the Revolution Settlement inadequate because it had not made provision for annual parliaments, and were soon to think it inadequate because it had not made sufficient provision against standing armies. It is with this group that Locke's *Treatises* cannot convincingly be associated, and their existence sets limits to the enterprise of showing him to have been a 'radical'. Locke was not a True Whig, and the True Whigs were originally men of the 'good old cause'; they proclaimed an 'ancient constitution' in which not only was the House of Commons ancient, but its annual re-election had been guaranteed since Anglo-Saxon times. Their affinities were with the Commonwealth if not with its regicide; in their writings we catch echoes from Nedham, Milton, Harrington and others who had stood to the left of the *Answer to the Nineteen Propositions*, and their call for annual parliaments was intended to reinforce the autonomy of the House of Commons in either a system of co-ordinate sovereignty or—more radically—a 'separation of powers' in which every part of the constitution must be independent of every other. Once again we see the 'ancient constitution' liable to assimilation with the 'balanced constitution', and the 'balanced constitution' putting down republican and democratic roots which some could assert while others denied.

Arguments of the True Whig kind had since at latest 1675 carried overtones of opposition to standing armies and executive patronage which were not without their appeal to country gentlemen, and it is one of the most remarkable features of the story that such arguments, without losing their ancient constitution and good old cause components, became increasingly in

1730); Paul de Rapin Thoyras, *The History of England as well Ecclesiastical as Civil*, trans. N. Tindal (London, 1725–31). For an excellent account of these writers, which restores Echard to his proper place with Kennett and Gibson, see D. J. Stephan, 'The Early Eighteenth Century Reviews Its Seventeenth-Century Past', Ph.D. Dissertation, University of Sydney, 1986.

365

favour with Tories who were not far from being Jacobites as well as with True Whigs who were not far from being republicans. It became a Whig cliché that Jacobites and republicans had formed an unholy alliance, and cases are known of extreme True Whigs who (like Ferguson) became Jacobites, though Jacobites who became republicans are for obvious reasons harder to find. The formation of a Junto, maintaining a large standing army, exercising political patronage, and expanding a system of public credit, in order to prosecute the wars in which William III and his political heirs had involved the three kingdoms, is enough, as far as concerns our present purposes, to account for these phenomena. The effect on which it is most important to focus our attention is that the ancient constitution tended to drift into opposition control and became a means of furthering True Whig and Tory programmes and slogans. It came to denote an 'ancient' state of affairs in which standing armies had been unknown (because arms had been in the hands of sturdy barons and their landholding vassals), parliaments had met every year (because King Alfred had so provided) and executive corruption had been unknown (because placemen had been few, excisemen and stockjobbers unthinkable, in a manorial economy where the king was merely the master of the greatest household). It came also to denote a version of the 'balanced constitution', authoritatively expressed in 1642, which supposedly represented the 'principles' on which the ancestors had based English government and liberty. From these principles there had been departure, which might have occurred as late as 1688 or as far back as 1485; that departure represented 'corruption', and the cure lay in a 'return to original principles'.[65]

---

[65] I have written a number of accounts of these matters: *Politics, Language and Time*, pp. 104–48; *The Machiavellian Moment*, pp. 423–61; 'Radical Criticisms of the Whig Order in the Age between Revolutions', in Margaret Jacob and James Jacob (eds.), *The Origins of Anglo-American Radicalism* (London: George Allen & Unwin, 1983). As this book was being prepared for the press, there appeared J. C. D. Clark's *English Society, 1660–1832* (Cambridge, 1985), which argued powerfully for the persistence of high-church and divine-right doctrines which preserved many Tories and Jacobites from temptation by these semi-republican

The ancient constitution, when we first met it a means of asserting the privileges of law-courts and parliaments against the prerogative, and subsequently of asserting that there existed a co-ordinate sovereignty capable of regulating the succession, had now become a means of indicting an executive government exercised through parliament, and of articulating the grievances of discontented parliamentary and extra-parliamentary opposi-tions. These asserted the antiquity of their political preferences on grounds which had less and less to do with the 'time beyond memory' of 'the common-law mind', and were more and more often the expression of a quasi-republican fundamentalism. Less was heard of ancient customs, and more of original principles; but for all that, the myths, shibboleths and arguments of the seventeenth century, in favour of the ancient constitution as we have known it, could be marshalled by the opposition all the more effectively because they still formed part of the vocabulary of legitimation maintained by the regime. The common law continued to be taught and practiced, and its vocabulary continued to be part of the political vocabulary of Englishmen. In these circumstances, the apologists of the Whig regime had in theory two strategies open to them. They could argue, as Burke was to do in 1781,[66] that since the constitution was immemorial and prescriptive, it had no original principles and ancient usage necessarily legitimated the present state of affairs; or they could boldly abandon the appeal to antiquity and argue that only in modern times—in 1689 with the Declaration of Rights or in 1716 with the Septennial Act—had liberty been rendered stable and the constitution arrived at perfection, This might not be quite so drastic a departure from tradition as may appear; given

doctrines. I do not question this at all; yet I should still argue that language of the above kind was adopted by Tories and even Jacobites on occasion. Stephan (see n. 64) quotes (p. 403) a letter in which Thomas Carte worries about Tory use of 'old whig' arguments. See further J. A. W. Gunn, 'The Skeleton at the Feast: The Persistence of High Tory Ideas in the Eighteenth Century', in *Beyond Liberty and Property: The Process of Self-Recognition in Eighteenth-Century Political Thought* (Montreal and Kingston: McGill–Queens University Press, 1984).

[66] *Politics, Language and Time*, pp. 225–30.

the doctrine of custom as perpetual adaptation, it was theoretically possible for quite radical innovation to carry on the continuities of history, and even Locke had been prepared to consider that, when there occurred a dissolution of government and power reverted to the people, they would probably return it to those institutions and procedures in which they were accustomed to see it exercised.[67] Nevertheless, those about to argue in favour of the constitution that it was modern would find their hand strengthened if it could be shown that an alternative 'ancient constitution' was historically impossible; and this is where we find the arguments of Robert Brady re-entering the picture.

There are aspects of Brady's *fortuna* after 1688 which I did not consider. In 1690 he published a work on ecclesiastical history,[68] and a *Treatise of Boroughs* of which more might indeed have been said, seeing that we find it figuring in controversies over borough history a century later.[69] Nor is much known about his posthumous role as a source of authority in the interminable debates among Revolution supporters, non-jurors and Jacobites, and by the time we come to his notable successor, the Jacobite historian Thomas Carte, we are among historians of a mentality very unlike that of 1680–5. Carte's *General History of England* cites Brady and follows him against such Whig shibboleths as Magna Carta, the antiquity of the Commons, and the coronation oath;[70] but he seeks the origins of feudalism in the clan chieftainships of the modern and ancient Celts, whose ancestry he is willing to trace back to Gomer the son of Japhet and the

---

[67] Laslett, *ed. cit.*, p. 432.

[68] *An Enquiry into the Remarkable Instances of History . . . Used by the Author of the Unreasonableness of a New Separation*; see *Cambridge Historical Journal*, vol. x, no. 2 (1951), p. 203, n. 63.

[69] Brady, *An Historical Treatise of Cities and Burghs or Burroughs* (London, 1690); cited, together with Thomas Madox's *Firma Burgi; or, An Historical Essay Concerning the Cities, Towns and Boroughs of England* (London, 1726), by Josiah Tucker, *A Treatise Concerning Civil Government* (London, 1781). See also *Virtue, Commerce, and History*, p. 182.

[70] Carte (n. 31 above), vol. I, pp. x–xi, 47, 361, 394–5, 833; vol. II, pp. 151, 241–60.

colonization of the European forests after the Flood.[71] Carte is closer to Filmer than Brady was in his readiness to telescope feudal kingship with patriarchal; but his equation of dependent tenure with the common law of all post-diluvial mankind obliges him to admit that the hereditary *feudum* which the Normans brought into England carried with it a *jus feudale* much more sophisticated, and feudal services much more burdensome, than any to which the English were accustomed as part of the law they shared with other Germanic and Gothic peoples.[72] Carte, in short, is of the school of Selden rather than of Spelman, and though he endorses Brady's account of the feudalizing effects of the Conquest, his desire to suggest covert parallels between William I and William III makes it seem that both imposed foreign yokes which the English were anxious to cast off.[73] He is to be taken seriously, as a precursor of John Whitaker and James Macpherson,[74] the historians of Celtic Britain who were to appear in the next generation; but it is not here that we are to look for the lasting effects of the kind of history written by Brady. Nevertheless, it was his aim to keep his readers on paths which Brady had indicated, and keep them from straying to those to which Bolingbroke had deceptively pointed.

Isaac F. Kramnick in his study of Bolingbroke[75] was the first to show how Walpole's defenders in the paper war against *The Craftsman*—Lord Hervey, James Pitt and William Arnall,[76]

---

[71] *Ibid.*, vol. I, pp. 20, 48, 77–8, 153, 176–7, 360–8.

[72] *Ibid.*, vol. I, pp. 363–6, 372, 376.

[73] *Ibid.*, vol. I, pp. 426, 450–2.

[74] John Whitaker, *The History of Manchester* (London, 1771–5); James Macpherson, *An Introduction to the History of Great Britain and Ireland* (Dublin, 1771; London, 1773).

[75] Isaac F. Kramnick, *Bolingbroke and His Circle: The Politics of Nostalgia in the Age of Walpole* (Cambridge, Mass.: Harvard University Press, 1968), pp. 111–36.

[76] Hervey's *Ancient and Modern Liberty Stated and Compared* was published in 1724; see ch. II of Reed Browning, *Political and Constitutional Ideas of the Court Whigs* (Baton Rouge: Louisiana State University Press, 1980). Pitt and Arnall wrote chiefly in the *London Journal* (Kramnick, *loc. cit.*). See Thomas Horne,

writing in the late 1720's and early 1730's—argued that the constitution was modern and could not have degenerated from a set of original principles, on the ground that England had once been a feudal kingdom in which parliamentary liberty had been impossible, and that it had taken until 1688 at earliest to establish modern liberty on secure foundations. The name of Brady is now and then mentioned, and those of Harrington and Neville could not have been far from the thoughts of informed readers. The Whigs and their opponents—True Whig, Country, Patriot or Tory—had changed roles and arguments, to the extent that the doctrines of the Charles II Tory Brady were now being used by defenders of the Whig regime under George II to confute the Queen Anne Tory Bolingbroke. It is true that the ground had shifted; where Brady had argued that because the constitution was not ancient there could be no challenge to the authority of a king placed above his estates—it emphasizes the point if we follow Weston and Greenberg here—the Walpoleans were arguing that there could be no challenge to a co-ordinate sovereignty in which the executive maintained a controlling influence in parliament. Subsequent writers of this persuasion— Viscount Egmont and Bishop Squire[77]—contended that it was precisely because the vertical network of feudal tenures had disappeared that the crown now needed the compensating influence of patronage. Yet hindsight does keep in view the possibility that Brady was not trying to impose on England a prerogative derived from an Adamic or Norman antiquity, so much as seeking to destroy antiquity and defend kingship as necessary and modern. Certainly by the time of Walpole there was a regime which could claim modernity as readily as antiquity, an opposition less anxious to break with tradition than to return to principles allegedly rooted in the English past.

'Politics in a Corrupt Society: William Arnall's Defence of Robert Walpole', *Journal of the History of Ideas*, vol. XLI, no. 4 (1980), pp. 601–14.

[77] Egmont, *Faction Detected by the Evidence of Facts* (London, 1743); Samuel Squire, *An Enquiry into the Foundation of the English Constitution* (London, 1745) and *A Historical Essay upon the Balance of Civil Power in England* (London, 1748). There is a study of Squire in Reed Browning, *op. cit.*, ch. v.

To understand more fully what was going on, we must look beyond England and turn to the second of those major developments in scholarship mentioned as having occurred since 1957. This is the rapid development of scholarship concerning the Scottish Enlightenment, and it is worth repeating that in 1957 the subject was known to me mainly through a series of articles by Duncan Forbes in the *Cambridge Journal*.[78] A great deal has been done since then, by Forbes and by others,[79] and it will not again be possible to write the history of ancient constitution and feudal law in the eighteenth century without taking account of the Scottish appropriation of a previously English discourse. There had been no 'common-law mind' in the Scotland of James VI, and consequently no 'ancient constitution' as I have argued the term was understood in England,[80] though the impact on both Scottish and English thought of Sir Thomas Craig, and the Union debates attending the accession of James I, await re-assessment;[81] and the uses of secular history in

[78] Forbes, '*Historismus* in England,' *Cambridge Journal*, vol. IV (1951), pp. 387–400; *idem*, 'James Mill and India', *ibid.*, vol. V, pp. 19–33; 'The Rationalism of Sir Walter Scott', *ibid.*, vol. VII (1953), pp. 20–35; 'Scientific Whiggism; Adam Smith and John Millar', *ibid.*, vol. VII (1954), pp. 643–70.

[79] The recent literature is very large, and rather supplies the context for Scottish Enlightenment historiography than exposes it in detail. The following may be mentioned as relevant to the present work: W. C. Lehman, *John Millar of Glasgow* (Cambridge University Press, 1960); Duncan Forbes, *Hume's Philosophical Politics* (Cambridge University Press, 1975); Donald Winch, *Adam Smith's Politics: An Essay in Historiographic Revision* (Cambridge University Press, 1978); Istvan Hont and Michael Ignatieff (eds.), *Wealth and Virtue: The Shaping of Political Economy in the Scottish Enlightenment* (Cambridge University Press, 1983); John Robertson, *The Scottish Enlightenment and the Militia Issue* (Edinburgh: John Donald, 1985); Richard B. Sher, *Church and University in the Scottish Enlightenment: The Moderate Literati of Edinburgh* (Princeton University Press, 1985).

[80] H. R. Trevor-Roper, 'George Buchanan and the Ancient Scottish Constitution', *English Historical Review*, suppl. 3 (1966); Arthur H. Williamson, *Scottish National Consciousness in the Age of James VI* (Edinburgh: John Donald, 1979); Roger Mason, '*Rex Stoicus*: George Buchanan, James VI and the Scottish Polity', in John Dwyer, Roger Mason and Alexander Murdoch (eds.), *New Perspectives on the Politics and Culture of Early Modern Scotland* (Edinburgh: John Donald, 1982).

[81] Above. pp. 79–80.

Covenanting and Restoration Scotland remain unexplored. But those historians of the eighteenth-century Scottish Enlightenment who place historical thought at the centre of their interpretation—there are other possible approaches—assign a highly important role to the neo-Harringtonian Andrew Fletcher of Saltoun,[82] a leading critic of the parliamentary Union of 1707 who had earlier, in 1697–8, taken part (along with two Anglo-Irishmen, John Toland and John Trenchard) in the familiar but recently revived English debate concerning militias and standing armies, and in so doing posed important questions about Scottish history in the context of European.

Because Fletcher was concerned with the role of arms rather than laws in the history of government and liberty, his approach owed more to Harrington than to Coke; it was neo-Harringtonian in the sense that he accepted the feudal and 'Gothic' roots of modern liberty, and at the same time accepted that he was living in a post-feudal and commercial world, where liberty faced new opportunities and at the same time new dangers. In language that recalls Neville and perhaps also Atwood, he posited a 'Gothic' past in which arms and government had been in the hands of the occupiers of land, and played down the subjection of lesser tenants to greater to the point where he could affirm that the former had played their part in the maintenance of liberty. Because he thought this political order had been everywhere established by the invaders of the Roman empire, his sense of 'the feudal law' was Selden's rather than Spelman's, and his sense of 'the ancient constitution' was Selden's (or Harrington's) rather than Coke's. He held monarchical government to have been less powerful and menacing under medieval

---

[82] The fullest account of Fletcher is currently in Robertson, *The Scottish Enlightenment and the Militia Issue, op. cit.* See also N. T. Phillipson, 'The Scottish Enlightenment', in Roy Porter and Mikulas Teich (eds.), *The Enlightenment in National Context* (Cambridge University Press, 1981); Robbins, *The Eighteenth-Century Commonwealthman* (1968 edition), pp. 88–109; Pocock, *Politics, Language and Time*, pp. 138–40; *idem, The Machiavellian Moment*, pp. 427–35. Fletcher's *Discourse of Government in Relation to Militias* (1698) is reprinted in David Daiches (ed.), *Selected Political Writings and Speeches of Andrew Fletcher of Salton*, (Edinburgh University Press, 1979).

than under modern conditions; it was the growth of commerce and culture about 1500 which had encouraged the arms-bearing freeman to accept specialization, permitting himself to be defended and governed by others while aiming at the maximization of his own satisfactions. With this, the critique of modern society may be said to have begun in Britain.

Fletcher was neither nostalgic nor reactionary; there was no past to which he, or any other Scot, desired to return; but he held that there was no substitute for the foundation of liberty in arms-bearing and landed property, so well understood in both ancient and medieval times, and that therefore a militia system must be instituted to conserve ancient freedom and virtue under modern commercial conditions. He is among the ideological ancestors of the Second Amendment to the Constitution of the United States, and of the *Marseillaise*. To the arguments of Trenchard and Fletcher, the Englishman Daniel Defoe[83] retorted that liberty was much better preserved by freedom to pursue one's own ends in a trading society than by being tied to the defence of one's own lands or the cultivation of another's in a feudal, and that representative government controlling the flow of revenue to government had little to fear from a standing army. By implication, Defoe was affirming that freedom encountered no problems under modern conditions, his adversaries that there were problems some of which required ancient solutions. The apparently bourgeois Defoe was a defender of the Whig Junto; Trenchard, Toland and Fletcher with their apparent nostalgia for the Middle Ages were as much heirs of the good old cause as he was.

This debate of 1698 between ancient and modern views of the constitution permits us to see two faces of the British Janus. To the north, students of the Scottish Enlightenment[84] affirm that it was after the failure of Fletcher's militia-based opposition to the Union of 1707 ensured an end of independent military and

---

[83] *The Machiavellian Moment*, pp. 432-5.

[84] Robertson (n. 79); Phillipson (n. 82), and other articles cited in Robertson's bibliography and *Virtue, Commerce, and History*, p. 237 (n. 64); cf. Sher (n. 79).

political virtue in Scotland that Edinburgh and Glasgow intellectuals began to develop a philosophy of history based on the progress of commerce, the specialization of labour and diversification of the personality, and the limited participation in free but aristocratically controlled polities, which in their view constituted the difference between ancient and modern society. In the course of doing so they developed a four-stage scheme of history,[85] in which feudalism played an important part in the pastoral and agricultural stages, but which may have owed more to the modernization of Roman law and *jus gentium* by Netherlands and German theorists than to English debates over the ancient constitution (and all that). Scots were a self-consciously cosmopolitan people, and we should not regard their Enlightenment as a mere by-product of English cultural domination.

On Janus's south face, it is evident that Fletcher's historical thinking has strong Harringtonian and neo–Harringtonian roots, and presents—especially when taken in conjunction with the Commonwealthmen Trenchard and Toland—a link in the chain between the First and True Whigs and the intellectual opposition to Walpole. With suitable modifications to allow of distinctively English preoccupations, it belongs (as was recognized[86]) in the literature of opposition with works like Bolingbroke's *Remarks on the History of England*, which stressed the antiquity of the Commons, the liberty of the armed proprietor, and the dangers of corruption by the monied interest and the executive. In short, Fletcher supports a version of the ancient constitution much like that which Walpole's modernists set out to deny; and they employed Brady's account of feudalism in order to reach conclusions much like Defoe's. It was the desire for union with the kind of England Defoe defended and Walpole governed which Fletcher failed to deflect in Scotland; and if we think of the Scottish Enlightenment as the effort to continue intellectual

[85] R. L. Meek, *Social Science and the Ignoble Savage* (Cambridge University Press, 1975); Peter Stein, *Legal Evolution: The Story of an Idea* (Cambridge University Press, 1980).

[86] E.g., by Josiah Tucker; see *Virtue, Commerce, and History*, p. 178.

growth from the moment of that choice, it will fail to surprise us that a major part of the Scottish intellectual enterprise was to write the history of English government as well as that of the progress of human society. The two histories were in their perspective one. It was because the Scots understood this that they could write English history better than the English could; but the terms in which they wrote it were already drawn in part from the vocabulary of English discourse.

Indirectly, therefore, David Hume's *History of England*[87] is a product of the Walpolean decision to make the defence of the Whig regime a defence of modernity. His Stuart volumes appeared before his Tudor and medieval, and it is not anything he wrote about 1066 and 1265 which makes him an important historian of the ancient constitution or the feudal law; it is what he wrote about the emergence of the society which replaced them. Hume follows Harrington in contending that the distinguishing characteristic of 'the Gothic government' was its incoherence. The liberties of the baronage were entrenched; the authority of the king was without formal limits. Such a system could not endure change and must fall apart when the minds of men altered.[88] Hume had before him the theses of Bacon and Harrington, which located the sources of change as far back as the reign of Henry VII, but early informed Adam Smith that he would begin with the accession of James I because only then did the English political outlook begin to alter.[89] He was inclined to explain this by unrelated changes in the field of religion, but wrote also of 'a revolution in manners'[90] connected with the transition from a feudal to a commercial society. There are hints also of an explanation as old as Defoe, to which Macaulay still

[87] See Victor C. Wexler, *David Hume and the History of England* (Philadelphia: American Philosophical Society, 1980); also Duncan Forbes's introduction to the Penguin Classics edition of Hume's seventeenth-century volume: *The History of Great Britain: The Reign of James I and Charles I* (Harmondsworth, 1970).

[88] David Hume, *The History of England from the Invasion of Julius Caesar to the Revolution in 1688* (London, 1762), vol. v, p. 14, 110–11, 156–7, 203–4, 459.

[89] Letter to Smith, September 24, 1752; J. Y. T. Greig (ed.), *The Letters of David Hume* (Oxford: Clarendon Press, 1932), vol. i, p. 168.

[90] *History of England*, vol. iii, pp. 66–7; vol. iv, p. 336; vol. v, pp. 68–9.

subscribed a century later: once a standing army became a possibility, history became a race on the part of the subjects to seize control of supply and taxation before the king could make himself absolute by paying the army himself.[91] But the Stuart kings had lacked the arms with which their feudal prerogatives might be asserted under post-feudal conditions, and the civil wars had been fought by amateurs and enthusiasts. If, then, Hume is the first 'whig historian' who imposes an explanation in terms of long-range social process, he is certainly not a 'Whig historian' who justifies action by the need to maintain the ancient constitution. He employed the feudal interpretation to destroy any such hypothesis, and wrote with relish that a series of at least three 'ancient constitutions' could be distinguished in the English past.[92] In Forbes's terms, Hume was a 'scientific', not a 'vulgar whig'.[93]

A 'vulgar whig' means, among other things, an uncritical defender of the ancient constitution.[94] But there was a great deal of life in the old dog yet, and the indignation with which Hume's *History* was widely received (though without injuring its sales) was due in part to the fact that Walpolean modernism had lost much of its value as polemic by the time Hume's volumes were appearing. The political actions ascribed to George III and his advisers made it convenient to accuse them of both reviving the prerogative and increasing the influence of the crown, and the resources of Whig and Old Whig rhetoric were utilized to the full on both sides of the Atlantic. The king's aristocratic opponents saw themselves playing the roles of Russell and Somers, Pym and Hampden, Simon Montfort and Stephen Langton; the Whig interpretation of history entered its third volume; and much again was heard (as it had never ceased to be) about the liberty-loving and sturdy (if uncouth) barons of

---

[91] Macaulay, *History of England from the Accession of James II*, ch. 1.

[92] Hume, *History of England*, vol. IV, p. 314n; vol. V, p. 238n.

[93] Forbes, n. 78, above; *Hume's Philosophical Politics*, pp. 125–92 and *passim*; 'Sceptical Whiggism, Commerce and Liberty', in A. S. Skinner and T. Wilson (eds.), *Essays on Adam Smith* (Oxford: Clarendon Press, 1976).

[94] Forbes, *Hume's Philosophical Politics*, ch. 8, pp. 233–307.

Runnymede.[95] The borough and county radicals of the 1760's and 1770's, who seized the opportunity of assailing royal and aristocratic 'influence' and 'corruption' in a single polemic, developed historical argument about the antiquity of boroughs,[96] hundreds and tythings,[97] which depicted them as original Saxon folkmoots to which recourse might be had to remedy the corruptions of parliament. The Norman yoke and the good old cause, never very deeply buried, stirred again; though to the malign effects of the Norman Conquest must now be added those of the more recent growths of 'boroughmongering' and 'the monied interest'.

Even when it came to be argued, in Massachusetts, Pennsylvania and Virginia, that the emigrant ancestors had retained no more of English law than was compatible with the rights of nature, or that the earth belonged to the living who were under no authority derived from the past, there was no reason not to acquire legitimacy by praising the liberty and independence of primitive Teutonic freemen, who had exercised their rights when they were the living generation. Thomas Jefferson wanted to place Hengist and Horsa on the Great Seal of the United States, and he argued in *The Rights of British America* (1775) that American settlers held their lands by conquest like the Angles and Saxons, and therefore held them allodially, under no allegiance to the king. History and natural right were by no means always the opposed arguments we take them to have been. Paine's *Common Sense* arrives at its savage repudiation of England and English institutions by way of such familiar devices of 1649 as the instability of kingship ever since the Conquest and

---

[95] This image of the barons—as representing both sides of the "Gothic" personality—had been around for some time and had a long life before it. John Cleland's Fanny Hill on one occasion—which it is unnecessary to describe in as much detail as she does—is reminded of their ancient vigour, and their battle-axes.

[96] T. H. B. Oldfield's *The Representative History of Great Britain and Ireland* (1816) was a *History of the Boroughs* when it first appeared in 1792.

[97] Herbert Butterfield, *George III, Lord North and the People, 1779–80* (London: Bell, 1949), pp. 337–51, is still an excellent account of the historical arguments of the Yorkshire Association.

the claim that God had condemned kingship in his words to Samuel.[98] We may indeed debate how far Paine believed in the premises of his own rhetoric; the point is that, given those premises, to affirm rights based in antiquity was perfectly compatible with affirming rights based in nature and rationality. As Lilburne had seen, the birthright of the free-born Englishman was both his inheritance and his reason.

It was therefore a bad time for Hume to be constantly revising and polishing his case for the defence of Charles I, and he was most inappropriately called a Tory for his pains. His fellow Scottish and scientific whigs—Robertson, Ferguson, Smith and Millar—continued, in some detachment from the party debates in England and America, to develop (though by no means uncritically) the argument that modern liberty was the fruit of progress from feudal to commercial society, and an image of feudalism, set in the context of the four-stage theory, which left little enough room for the original liberties of the Germanic freemen. To Millar in the *Origin of Ranks*, feudalism had resulted from the imposition of an aristocracy of shepherd-kings on the ruins of a system of slave-worked agriculture;[99] to Gibbon in the *Decline and Fall*, primitive German freedom was nothing more than the savage sense of self and personal honour instinctive in nomad herdsmen who neither laboured nor appropriated.[100] Ferguson and Millar, writing in the generation following Thomas Carte's, saw feudalism as a late incident in the evolution of a European tribalism as much Celtic as Germanic. There is a sense, apparent in the context of the present book, in which we can see them as operating within a paradigm, traceable back to Selden, of military and dependent tenures as introduced everywhere by the *Volkerwanderung* of barbaric warbands; Spelman, where he appears in their work, does so as an authority on the evolution towards inheritability of the Lombard, Frankish and

---

[98] Philip S. Foner (ed.), *The Life and Major Writings of Thomas Paine* (Secaucus, N.J.: Citadel Press, 1974), pp. 9–12, 14–16.

[99] W. C. Lehmann, *John Millar of Glasgow* (Cambridge University Press, 1960), pp. 260–1, 266–71, 280–3.

[100] *Decline and Fall of the Roman Empire*, ch. 9.

Norman *feudum*. Once we see this, however, we see no less clearly that in so far as the radical ancient-constitutionalism of the eighteenth century sprang from good old cause and neo-Harringtonian roots, it was derived from exactly the same paradigm. Progressive modernists emphasized the subjection of the medieval proprietor as vassal, in order to maintain that commercial society had evolved decisively away from Gothic barbarism; radicals of nearly every stripe emphasized his independence as freeholder, in order to maintain that commercial society was in danger of degenerating from ancient and native virtue. Radical progressives—who did of course exist—were in the difficulty of having to maintain that the Whig aristocracy was a feudal class, when they wanted to accuse it of misusing a post-feudal system of patronage.

We are then looking at a post-Seldenian and neo-Harringtonian argumentative structure, far removed and not directly derived from the common-law mind and the ancient constitution according to Coke and Davies. The antiquity of the Commons was a detail in the ideology of the Commonwealthmen; the arguments of Brady had become a detail in the evolution of scientific whiggism. All the evidence seems to suggest that the history of the ancient constitution and the feudal law could have been written as a history of debate about property and sovereignty, rather than about common law and immemorial custom. Yet I should still want to argue—as I have argued in ch. I of this retrospect—that Selden was an advanced if authoritative sophisticate in the generation of Coke, and that property theory had some of its many roots in the need to determine the status of custom, representation and law. And in the latter part of the eighteenth century, we encounter what is unmistakably a recrudescence of the prescriptive and imme-morial character of the law and the constitution. There is room for a full-scale study of the ideological significance of Blackstone's *Commentaries on the Laws of England* and of Jeremy Bentham's lifelong campaign to discredit them; and I shall maintain that the case for finding elements drawn from Coke and Hale in Burke's doctrine of prescriptive authority has been made out.

It seems to have been as early as 1782 that Burke used the argument: 'Our constitution is a prescriptive constitution; it is a constitution whose sole authority is that it has existed time out of mind.' He was arguing against parliamentary reformers who contended, alternatively, that the restricted franchise denied Englishmen their natural rights, and that it showed the constitution to have degenerated from its original principles; and in reply to the latter argument more than to the former, Burke affirmed:

> To ask whether a thing which has always been the same stands to its usual principle seems to me to be perfectly absurd; for how do you know the principles but from the construction? and if that remains the same, the principles remain the same.[101]

Burke was exploiting the concept of the immemorial; he was investing the existent with the authority of antiquity, and at the same time denying the concept of an antiquity which could be used to discredit or even evaluate the existent. It was therefore the modern which he was presenting as immemorial, and the effect of his argument was the same as if he had argued that the modern could not be discredited by the ancient on the grounds that the latter was feudal or otherwise obsolete. In the previous year, 1781, Josiah Tucker had argued a modernist and somewhat Scottish case against the same parliamentary reformers, together with the Americans and their English sympathizers—among whom he was inclined to number Burke—and while he was about it had condemned Locke as a republican, a Gothicist, and an apologist for feudalism and slavery.[102] Burke and Tucker were alike defenders of the constitution in its Hanoverian Whig form, but Burke's argument, in looking back to seventeenth-century authorities whom Tucker considered obsolete, contained

---

[101] *The Works of the Rt. Hon. Edmund Burke* (London: Rivington, 1826), vol. x, pp. 92, 98. *Cf. Politics, Language and Time*, pp. 226–8.

[102] 'Josiah Tucker on Burke, Locke, and Price: A Study in the Varieties of Eighteenth-century Conservatism', in *Virtue, Commerce, and History*, especially pp. 160–75.

possibilities denied to Tucker's modernism. When in 1790 he returned to the assault on English radicals, as sympathizers with the revolution in France, the case for prescriptive authority became the case against radical intelligence which supposed that it could ever know social and customary institutions deeply enough to discredit them altogether. The case for the immemorial constitution was reiterated—though, significantly, Burke was less anxious to show that the constitution had always been the same than that Englishmen had always believed that it had; the political culture of the English concerned him even more deeply than their constitutional jurisprudence. He began developing an interpretation of 1688–9 in which the Tory doctrine that the Revolution had been an act of necessity, justified by the obligation to preserve the constitution rather than by any principle which the constitution contained, was married with a Whig doctrine that the constitution was immemorial and therefore not reducible to any set of principles. Invocations of Coke are to be found, as allusions to Hale are to be found elsewhere in Burke's writings; and we cannot doubt that Burke would have endorsed Hale's arguments against Hobbes had he known of them, or that he did not need to know of them in order to develop his own position. There is a good case for holding that we have here an instance of tradition, of the repeated use of a pattern of argument transmitted by the discourse of a culture. Burke knew and assimilated 'the common-law mind' in a way which sets him apart from Hume or Tucker.

But there is more than traditionalism to Burke's *Reflections*, deeply concerned with tradition though they are; and deeply (if ambivalently) as he admired the Whig aristocracy, he knew them to be a modern and even a commercial class.[103] He held that the English ruling order was more stable than the French because it had achieved a closer harmony between landed and

---

[103] Here I should like to associate 'Burke and the Ancient Constitution: A Problem in the History of Ideas' (*Politics, Language and Time*, 1971) with 'The Political Economy of Burke's Analysis of the French Revolution' (*Virtue, Commerce, and History*, 1985).

mobile property, and though he thought the French Revolution to have been in some measure the work of 'burghers' (it is odd that he does not use the French 'bourgeois'), he insisted that it must lead to the destruction of commerce as well as of religion and aristocracy. The boldest move carried out in the *Reflections on the Revolution in France* is the insistence that commerce—contrary to the modernist beliefs of 'our economical politicians' —must rest on and must not destroy the foundations of civilized manners laid by clergy and nobility in the medieval centuries; and the extraordinary emphasis which Burke at times lays upon the importance of chivalry becomes intelligible and even rational when we realize that he is situating the Revolution in the context of the history of manners. His argument could not much be damaged by a feudal reading of the English or the French past, since he removed it from the key of jurisprudence to that of culture. 'Manners,' he once wrote, 'are of more importance than laws'; and with this Montesquieuan aphorism he detached himself from both 'the feudal law' and 'the common-law mind'. His debt to the latter was very great, but at the heart of his doctrine of immemorial prescription *consuetudines* were replaced by *mores*, usage by prepossessions, law by culture. If there is a nostalgia in Burke, it is for a medieval order in which popular manners were under clerical and chivalric direction; and para-doxically, this was to become part of a myth of medieval paternalism developed largely in reaction against attitudes such as he himself expressed in his *Thoughts and Details Concerning Scarcity*. The discovery of poverty[104] was to generate its own historiography: new myths and criticism of myths concerning the English past, with which we move beyond the confines of this book, and into the nineteenth century.

We are still to some extent obliged to take it for granted that Burke's prescriptive anti-rationalism speedily became part of the ideology and rhetoric of the governing classes in the age of the Revolutionary and Napoleonic wars. Historians have dwelt so

[104] Gertrude Himmelfarb, *The Idea of Poverty: England in the Early Industrial Age* (New York: Knopf, 1984).

exclusively on the confrontation between Burke and his critics[105] that the story of his acceptance has, as it were, gone by default;[106] but if we accept the hypothesis that the doctrines for which he is most famous were widely disseminated and adopted, we can further suppose that they helped to form the problematic which confronted the 'Whig party' during its forty years in the political wilderness. Burke was a Whig; the supporters of Pitt came from great Whig families; the conservatism of the age was a refusal to reform the pillars of the Whig political order. But if the Whigs who found themselves in opposition were to return to power on a programme of reform, there must be some re-synthesis of Whig ideology; in particular of the two polar propositions that liberty was ancient and that liberty was modern and progressive. Burke's doctrine, as we have seen, contained modernist implications, latent in common-law thinking since its beginnings, but its image of history was fluid and inapprehensible enough—sufficiently reminiscent of Hale's or Selden's ever-flowing river—to make it very difficult to establish the premises on which reform could ever take place. The Scottish Whig James Mackintosh had early objected that the *Reflections* left the reader with no scientific understanding of why revolutions took place or how they might sometimes be justified. Those scientific Whigs who turned from justifying the Whig order to proposing its reform therefore needed to explain, first, that liberty might be both ancient and modern; second,

---

[105] For this see Marilyn Butler (ed.), *Burke, Paine, Godwin and the Revolution Controversy* (Cambridge University Press, 1984).

[106] There are studies of the reactions against the sympathizers with the French Revolution in Albert Goodwin, *The Friends of Liberty: The English Democratic Movement in the Age of the French Revolution* (Cambridge, Mass.: Harvard University Press, 1979); J. E. Cookson, *The Friends of Peace: Anti-War Liberalism in England, 1793–1815* (Cambridge University Press, 1982); Robert L. Dozier, *For King, Constitution and Country: The English Loyalists and the French Revolution* (Lexington: University Presses of Kentucky, 1983); H. T. Dickinson, *British Radicalism and the French Revolution, 1789–1815* (Oxford: Basil Blackwell, 1985). For a study of the presence of Burke in Wordsworth's later poetry, see James K. Chandler, *Wordsworth's Second Nature: A Study of the Poetry and Politics* (University of Chicago Press, 1984).

that there existed no ancient constitution to which a return could or should be made—as radical arguments shaped before 1789 were continuing to claim; third, that modern reforms did not necessitate a revolutionary breach with the past. Burke had done more to impose these problems on them than to suggest their solutions.

They therefore resumed their debate with feudal, war-band and tribal antiquity. John Millar, whose *Historical View of the English Government* was written some two decades after his *Origin of Ranks* and initially dedicated to Charles James Fox, contended that Norman baronage and knight-service, and also Anglo-Saxon thegnage, made it impossible to believe in any kind of parliamentary ancient constitution. Nevertheless, behind the transition to feudal tenure might be discerned an older allodial system, and while the pre-Conquest witan was doubtless an assembly of magnates, its members possessed and remembered liberties which could be defended. In the post-Conquest centuries this defence took on institutional form and outlived strictly feudal relationships, and by the time of the Stuarts in England it made sense to speak of an ancient constitution— Hume to the contrary notwithstanding—even though its lineaments could not be discovered at an earlier date.[107] Scientific Whiggism was well on the way to integrating old and new. Millar's historical vocabulary was formed in the great decades of the eighteenth-century Scottish Enlightenment, but if—the ideological history of the years 1800–1830 is not yet fully known—we proceed down the roads signposted 'Edinburgh Reviewers' and 'Holland House', we can see Whig historiography acquiring new characteristics. In the latter ambit particularly, John Allen and Francis Palgrave[108] began developing a

[107] John Millar, *An Historical View of the English Government from the Settlement of the Saxons in Britain to the Revolution in 1688*, 4th ed. (London, 1818), vol. 1, pp. 131–4, 171, 185, 200–3, 290–301; vol. III, pp. 156–7, 189–92, 220–7.

[108] John Allen, *Inquiry into the Rise and Growth of the Royal Prerogative in England* (London, 1830); idem, *A Short History of the House of Commons with Reference to Reform* (London, 1831); Sir Francis Palgrave, *The History of England*, vol. I, *Anglo-Saxon Period* (London, 1831); idem, *The Rise and Progress of the English Commonwealth: Anglo-Saxon Period* (London, 1832).

new dialectic between Roman and Germanic components of history. Allen studied the concept of the English monarchy as a corporation sole representing the whole kingdom, and emphasized its origins in Roman law. Palgrave created for the first time something like an English equivalent of the Abbé Du Bos's reading of French history, arguing that early Anglo-Saxon kings were Roman provincial rulers with Roman concepts of *imperium* about them.

But Palgrave in particular also began experimenting with the idea of English land tenures as indicating the presence of the kind of village community which could be detected not only in early Germanic and Celtic law, but in early Roman and perhaps Indian. With J. M. Kemble's *The Saxons in England*, the notion of the German mark-community made its appearance in English historiography: the first major anthropological development since the Scots had elaborated the four-stages theory; and the stage was set[109] for the great nineteenth-century debates about kinship and personality, folkland and bookland, status and contract, which have been revived in our own time by Alan Macfarlane's *The Origins of English Individualism*.[110] There are elements here which look back to Atwood, Selden, Davies and perhaps farther still; but we have passed beyond the point where thinking can be organized around polar concepts inherited from the seventeenth century. Nevertheless, the Victorian debates were about the origins of property, right and representation; the 'science of politics' and the 'science of history' about the processes which might lead to the point where the *liber homo* might appeal to the forms of law, the industrious man to the laws of political economy, and either to the judgment of his peers in parliament or public opinion.[111] The debate about

[109] J. W. Burrow, *Evolution and Society: A Study in Victorian Social Theory* (Cambridge University Press, 1966).

[110] Cambridge University Press, 1979.

[111] The fullest study of the evolution of Victorian political science from its Edinburgh and Holland House beginnings is now Stefan Collini, Donald Winch and J. W. Burrow, *That Noble Science of Politics: A Study in Nineteenth-century Intellectual History* (Cambridge University Press, 1983).

liberty and property had its origins in a debate about English law.

At another door leading from Holland House into the nineteenth century, we find Macaulay, between 1832 and 1859, arguing first[112] that the civil wars had their origin at the point where the crude freedom of medieval arms gave way to the standing army, and the problem of liberty became the problem of controlling the grants and taxes which paid the soldiers—an argument older than Hume, Fletcher and Defoe, or even Harrington, and finding shadowy forewords in the debates of 1628—and arguing secondly[113] that 1688-9 was a preserving revolution because it took its stand on precedent rather than principle: an argument reached by combining several assertions made by Burke. Once again we come face to face with the complexities of the Whig need to show that progress was rooted in antiquity: a need which might not have existed, and could not have been formulated, without the very different complexities of the common-law mind. Holland House leaves us at the dawn of the world inhabited by the Victorian historians and studied by P. B. M. Blaas and J. W. Burrow.[114] The latter's *A Liberal Descent: Victorian Historians and the English Past* leads on with such elegance from themes surveyed in this book and retrospect that it is appropriate to end the latter here.

In his last pages Burrow warns against 'the elegiac quality which tends to attach to the conclusions of historical works, often reflecting not so much anything in the history itself as the fact that the story told about it is reaching its end'. Yet he concludes in a tone recalling Macaulay's New Zealander: 'the great Victorian histories now seem like the triumphal arches of a past empire, their vaunting inscriptions increasingly unintelligible to the modern inhabitants: visited occasionally, it may be,

---

[112] Macaulay, *History of England*, ch. 1.

[113] *Ibid.*, ch. x.

[114] P. B. M. Blaas, *Continuity and Anachronism: Parliamentary and Constitutional Development in Whig Historiography and in the Anti-Whig Reaction between 1890 and 1930* (The Hague: Martinus Nijhoff, 1978); J. W. Burrow, *A Liberal Descent: Victorian Historians and the English Past* (Cambridge University Press, 1981).

as a *pissoir*, a species of visit naturally brief',[115] and all too typical of the latter-day barbarian—the New Zealander with his sketch-book displayed more decorum.[116] I began this book in New Zealand three decades ago, and it is now four since Butterfield published *The Englishman and His History*. It would be easy to say that he celebrated, and both of us began to anatomize, the sources of an English belief that the characteristics of the national politics were continuity, pragmatism and moderation (a belief in fact not much held before Burke's *Reflections*), and to conclude bleakly with a 'That passed away; so may this.' It would at least be an ending less elegiac than epic; but the questions with which epic theatre is supposed to conclude are 'What happened next?' and 'Could it have happened otherwise?' From the vantage-point at which Blaas and Burrow break off, one could speculate on the character of a history of post-Whig historiography; would it be written by and for owls of Minerva, dedicated to the proposition that historiography got better as political consensus decayed? Even this might be to write within the presupposition that the function of English historiography is to articulate the changing state of English national self-consciousness, and this book has been an attempt to distance itself a little from that kind of insularity. Perhaps the distance achieved may be expressed by saying that the book seems to be an essay in a certain species of historical inquiry: into how human beings live within the possibilities of their language systems, and the systems of historical time which their language articulates for them.

[115] Burrow, *A Liberal Descent*, p. 300.

[116] In Macaulay's essay on Ranke (1840), the New Zealander is clearly a Maori. By the time of Anthony Trollope's *The New Zealander* (1855) he has become a pakeha settler, resentfully awaited by his author as a sub-species of American. The work remained unpublished till recently (*Anthony Trollope: The New Zealander*, edited with an introduction by N. John Hall, Oxford: Clarendon Press, 1972). See especially p. 208: 'Not yet at any rate can we bid thee welcome, if thou comest in search of ruins, and desirous of relics of thy Anglo-Saxon progenitors. Neither by thee nor by thy prototype and forerunner of Yankeeland shall it yet be boasted that the remnants of the British constitution afford matter of speculation to the antiquarians either of the East or of the West.' The English dislike of having to share their history with related communities was thus early stated.

Index

Index

Burke, Edmund, viii, 18, 36, 171, 173,
235, 241–3, 249, 276, 321, 337,
359–60, 363, 367, 379–84, 387
Burnet, Bishop, 186
Butterfield, Professor H., vii, viii,
xiv, 240, 264, 265 n. 14, 278,
387
his *The Englishman and His History*,
viii, xi, xiv, 264
his *The Whig Interpretation of
History*, viii
on George III, viii

Caesar, his account of the Germans,
20
Cam, Professor H. M., 240
Camden, William, 56, 92, 96, 149
Capet, Hugh, 83, 98, 101
Carte, Thomas, 349, 368–9, 378
Cartwright, John, 232
Case of Defective Titles, 100
Case of Shirley v. Fagg, 186
Charlemagne, 83
Charles I, 125, 150, 159 n. 2, 194,
233, 308–9, 333, 378
Charles II, 159, 180, 189, 213
Chinese historical scholarship, 5 n. 2
Christianson, Paul, 286
Civil law in English history, 59, 89,
262–3, 280–2, 290, 295, 297,
302
Coke, Sir Edward, 16, 36, 47, 50–1,
63, 120, 154, 159, 182, 191,
201, 228, 240, 250, 263, 265,
268, 277, 281, 286, 301, 302,
305, 334, 337, 341, 372, 379,
381
the classical common-law
historian, 31–2, 38
sees common law as custom, 35;
and as immemorial, 37–8,
233, 274–5
his concept of 'artificial reason'
foreshadows Burke, 35,
173, 242–3
speech in *Calvin's Case*, 35, 274
believes whole constitution to be
immemorial, 37, 39, 338–9
his method of historical argument,
38–41

and parliament, 39–40
in parliament of 1628, 293–4,
296–7
rejects the Conquest, 42–4, 53
accepts apocryphal laws, 43
his account of Magna Carta, 44–5,
289–90
indifference to myth of German
freedom, 56–7, 125–6
on the Anglo-Saxons, 57
attacks Hotman, 65
ignorance of feudal law, 66–7
his credulity, 67–8
compared with Spelman, 94;
Spelman's comment on
him, 104, 240
his doctrine compared to Leveller
anti-Normanism, 125–6
attacked by Hobbes, 162, 163, 166,
167
defended by Hale, 170–1
compared with Hale, 174, 178,
275, 339
Brady criticizes him, 217
recent views of him, 274, 278–80
Coke, Sir John, 293–4, 296
Colepeper, Sir John, 308
Collier, Jeremy, 362
Collingwood, R. G., 256
Comitatus and *comites*, 75, 76, 78, 79,
80, 97–8, 107
Common law in English historical
thought
its general ascendancy, 31, 32,
38–9, 54–5, 68, 266–7
identified with custom by Davies,
32–3, and by Coke, 35
wiser than the individual, 34–6
supposed to be immemorial, 36–8,
41, 272
incompatible with concept of a
legislator, 41
creates an interpretation of English
history, 45, 55, 233, 240–1
helps to form doctrine of an
immemorial parliament,
47–9
distinct from belief in primitive
German freedom, 57–8, 64
common-law ignorance of foreign
law, 58–9, 62–3, 89–90

391

Index

Index

Index

Hoveden, Roger, 106
Hugolinus, 71
Huinzinga, Johan, 7
Humanism, its effects on historical
 thought, 3–6, 259–60
 in the field of law, 9–10, 28
Hume, David, 256, 263, 306, 332,
 334, 375–6, 378, 386
Hunton, Philip, 46, 313–4, 324
Hyde, Edward, first earl of
 Clarendon, 148–9, 150, 217,
 233, 256, 307–8, 331

'Ingulf of Croyland', 43, 106, 207
Inns of Court, 31, 240–1, 279
Ireton, Henry, 320–21
Irish law, 30, 60, 62–3, 99, 266
Italian Relation of England, 85

James VI and I, 17, 32, 35, 45, 54, 62,
 79, 87, 123, 149, 233, 243, 259,
 262, 268, 280, 284–5, 291, 371,
 375
James II, 212, 227, 229, 230, 300, 336,
 350–1, 359
Janus, 36, 269, 275, 287, 373–4
Jason de Mayne, 71
Jefferson, Thomas, 377
John, King, 44, 109, 110, 176, 218,
 222, 225
Johnson, Samuel, 361, 365
Johnston, Nathaniel
 his *Excellency of Monarchical
 Government*, 213, 214, 217
 last years, 227
Judson, Margaret A., 304 n. 86, 325
Jus conquestus, 301, 326–7, 330
Jus gentium, 283, 288–9, 291, 304,
 326, 349–50, 374
Jus gladii, 303, 326

Kahl, Johann, 133, 134
Kames, Lord, 243, 244 n. 1
Kelley, Donald R., 258, 280–1
Kemble, J. M., 245, 385
Kennett, White, 116, 243, 364
Kent and Kentish customs, 30, 99,
 197
Kliger, S. L., 56–7
Knafla, Louis A., 267 nn. 15–16, 269

Knights of the shire
 Spelman's idea of their origin, 111,
 113–14
 Prynne and, 157, 161
 Hobbes and, 165
 Dugdale and, 185–6
 Brady and, 201–5
Kramnick, Isaac F., 369

Laga Edwardi, 42
Lambarde, William, 43, 67, 85, 149,
 165, 183, 199, 259
Lamont, William M., 315–7, 336
 his *Godly Rule, 1603–1660*, 318
Langton, Stephen, 45, 208, 221, 376
Laslett, Peter, ix, xi, 151 n. 1, 187 n. 3,
 346, 353
Laud, William, 54, 195
Law, its importance in the history of
 historiography, vii–viii, 8,
 9–11, 18, 24, 26, 28–9, 62, 251
'Law French', 34, 35
*Leges Edwardi Confessoris, Willielmi,
 Henrici Primi*, 43, 67, 85, 106,
 199–200, 207
Lemaire, A., 20–1
*Letter from a Person of Quality to His
 Friend in the Country*, 342
Levellers, their view of English
 history, 125–7, 137, 160, 232,
 319
Levy, F. J., 259
Libri Feudorum
 in medieval study, 70–1
 Cujas and, 71–7, 84
 Hotman and, 71, 77–9, 84
 Craig and, 80–1, 82–3, 84, 88
 neglected in England, 88–90,
 297–8
 known to Cowell, 91
 becoming known in England, 92
 read by Spelman, 97; his use of
 them, 98–9, 101, 102, 107,
 108, 161
 encourage an over-centralized
 view of feudal society, 215
 and *jus gentium*, 350
Lilburne, John, 46, 126, 232
Limitanei, 79, 134
Littleton, *Tenures*, 65–6, 68, 84,
 101–2

397

Index

Index

Index